BUSINESS
IN FRANCE

D0294527

28108

BUSINESS IN FRANCE

*An introduction to the
economic and social context*

Joseph Szarka

Pitman

Pitman Publishing
128 Long Acre
London WC2E 9AN

A Division of Longman Group UK Limited

First Published in 1992

© Joseph Szarka 1992

British Library Cataloguing in Publication Data
A catalogue record for this book is available
from the British Library.

ISBN 0 273 03630 0

Printed and bound in Great Britain by
Dotesios Ltd, Trowbridge, Wiltshire.

Contents

List of tables	IX
Preface	XI
List of principal French abbreviations used	XV

1 The State and French post-war economic development   **1**

Introduction   1
The boom years: 1945–1973   2
    *General features of the boom. Explanatory frameworks for the
boom years. Economic planning. Short-term economic policies.
Evaluations*
The crisis years: 1974–1986   18
    *Short-term causes of the recession. Structural causes of the
recession. Crisis management under the Right (1974-1981). Crisis
management under the Left (1981-1986). Evaluations*
The recovery: 1986–1991   31
    *The Chirac government (1986-1988). The Rocard government
(1988-1991)*
Conclusions   38

2 Industrial policy and industrial development in France   **42**

Introduction   42
The principles of industrial policy making   44
    Types of industrial policy. Criteria for selective intervention.
Political dimensions of French industrial policy making   49
    *The era of protectionism: 1945-1958. The industrial imperative:
1958-1973. Industrial redeployment: 1974-1981. Modernisation:
1981-1990*
Industrial concentration and the goal of 'critical mass'   56
Nationalisation as a rescue operation   60
Privatisation and the new liberal agenda   64
Small firms and regional industrial development   69
Conclusions   72

3 French business on the world stage   **77**

Introduction   77
Overview of French international competitiveness   79
  The transition to an open economy. French international perform-
  ance. French industrial specialisation. The French State and the
  exports drive. Company behaviour
France's trade balance   89
  The situation in the 1950s. The situation in the 1960s. The situation
  in the 1970s. The situation in the 1980s
French strengths and weaknesses in internationally traded goods   92
  Strengths in traded goods. Weaknesses in traded goods
France's 'invisibles' balance   97
French strengths and weaknesses in services   98
  Strengths in services. Weaknesses in services
France's geographical patterns of trade   101
  France and the EC. Europe beyond the EC. Trade with the USA and
  Japan. Links with developing countries
Conclusions   116

4 Competition policy and market relations   **122**

Introduction   122
The legacy of corporatism   124
Competition law in France   128
  From the 1945 legislation to the Commission Technique des Ententes.
  The 1977 reform and the Commission de la Concurrence. The 1986
  reform and the Conseil de la Concurrence. French State-owned firms
  and EC competition policy
Market relations around the distribution sector   140
  The small retailer lobby and the State. The 1973 loi Royer and its
  consequences. The balance of power between producers and
  distributors
Conclusions   148

5 *Le Patronat*   **152**

Introduction   152
Composition of the *patronat*   153
  What is understood by the patronat?. The patron as inheritor. The
  patron as professional manager. The patron as company founder
Characteristics of the *grand patronat*   159
  The social stability of the grand patronat. The role of the grandes
  écoles. The interpenetration of business and administrative elites
French employers' organisations   166
  Roles and objectives of employers' organisations. The major
  employers' organisations in France. Structures of the CNPF

Conflict and co-operation between employers' organisations
and the State 170
*The post-war compromise (1946–1974). The vagaries of opposition
politics (1974–1983). The ambiguities of consensus (1983–1991)*
Conclusions 176

6 Industrial relations and trade unions **180**

Introduction 180
The institutional framework for employee representation 181
*Conseils de Prud'hommes. Délégués du personnel. Comités
d'entreprise. Sections syndicales d'entreprise. Les lois Auroux.
Overview*
French trade unions 187
*The CGT. FO. The CFTC. The CFDT. The CGC. Union membership.
Union influence*
Industrial relations practices 200
Employee participation. Collective bargaining. Strikes.
Processes of change in French industrial relations 207
*Turbulence in the 1940s and 1950s. The calm and the storm of the
1960s. Economic crisis and labour gains during the 1970s. The
surprises of the 1980s. Toward a new industrial relations model in
the 1990s?*
Conclusions 215

7 French management culture **220**

Introduction 220
National stereotypes revisited 222
Elitism and its consequences 223
Isolated bureaucrats 227
Dependent individualists 230
Honour's logic 236
Conclusions 242

Postword **245**

Index 247

Tables

1.1	Average annual growth rate of GNP in France and selected other countries	3
1.2	Changing patterns of French foreign trade (in %)	9
1.3	GDP growth rates: Plan targets and out-turn: 1952-1975 (in %)	12
2.1	Industrial concentration in France: 1958-1977	57
2.2	Financial performance of French nationalised industrial companies: 1981-1985	62
2.3	Cumulative profits/losses and subsidies received by French nationalised industrial firms	65
2.4	Privatisation in France: 1986-1988	66
3.1	Imports and exports as a percentage of French GDP	79
3.2	CIF–FOB trade balances as percentage of GDP in six major industrial countries in 1984	80
3.3	Cross-national comparison of current account balances: 1967-1987	82
3.4	France's balance of trade: 1979-1989	89
3.5	France's balance of trade: the ten largest surpluses and deficits by sector in 1988	92
3.6	France's recent 'agri-food' surpluses	93
3.7	France's trade and 'invisibles' balances compared	98
3.8	Changes in the structure of French imports and exports by major product groups: 1959-1980	98
3.9	Breakdown of the French 'invisibles' balance: 1981-1988	99
3.10	France's exchanges of invisibles: transport balances	101
3.11	Geographical patterns of trade	102
3.12	Regional exports/imports ratios for traded goods	102
3.13	France's trade balances with EC partners	105
6.1	Membership of major French trade unions: 1912-1990	192
6.2	Results of elections for the *conseils de Prud'hommes*: 1979-1987	196
6.3	Results of elections for *comités d'entreprise*: 1949-1989	197
6.4	Results of the 1985 survey on elections for *délégués du personnel*	198
6.5	Numbers of days lost in France through strike action: 1950-1989	206

Preface

France is marked by strong contrasts. This statement is as true of business life as of any other domain. Change and development have become the watchwords of contemporary France, yet the old and the new frequently co-exist in unexpected combinations.

The glass pyramid erected in the Louvre courtyard (a photograph of which appears on this book's cover) provides a telling image of the contrasts that characterise France. The glass pyramid is a symbol of high-tech modernity, yet it is situated next to a building whose classical proportions epitomise traditional values. The pyramid offers a bold design which at first sight appears to make no attempt to blend in with its surroundings. It illustrates a characteristically French emphasis on creativity, innovation and the right to choose freely.

At the same time, the Louvre pyramid maintains strong elements of continuity with its surroundings. Like the Louvre building itself, the glass pyramid is based on strict principles of geometry. It makes a grandiose statement in its own right, yet serves a prosaic purpose: at one level, the pyramid is merely a window into the basement of the Louvre. At another level, the glass pyramid evokes some of France's most ingrained social structures, in particular elitism and the tendency to centralise authority and power at the apex of a steep hierarchy. This centralising tendency is most marked in the traditional importance of the French state and in the prestige attached to it. It was no coincidence that the Louvre, which is renowned as the home of one of the world's greatest art collections, also housed for a long time the Finance Ministry – which has been the most powerful and prestigious arm of the French State.

Unexpected combinations of the new and the old, of tradition and modernity make it easy to misunderstand French society and French ways of doing business. This book arose from the need for a study of French business which gave a thorough introduction to the subject. Thus detailed presentation and appraisal of the French business world are the main objectives of this book. It sets out to reveal the dynamics of business life in France in their wider dimensions by drawing on economic and social issues.

Nation-centred accounts have their particularities. The French have strong views on their own national identity and development. For the British, France is the archetypal neighbour – familiar yet different. But both the French and the British views of French business have at times become encrusted with half-truths. Closer inspection of reality is a useful exercise.

In the economic arena, the French themselves have frequently bemoaned a lack of French dynamism and entrepreneurship, inadequate industrial specialisations, companies which are dwarfed by foreign competitors and a weak presence on the international stage. Yet the French economy is the fourth largest in the world. The most recent *Fortune* survey (1991) of the largest 500 firms in the world showed that 164 were American, 111 Japanese, 43 British, 30 French and 30 were German. France has strengths in high-tech and engineering industries, such as aerospace, satellites and telecommunications, high-speed trains, computer software, weaponry and nuclear technology. As a member of the 'G7' countries – the group of seven most advanced economies – France has claims to an element of world leadership. Of course, France cannot aspire to the economic might of the USA or Japan, but considered as a medium-sized power, she has been extremely successful in the period since 1945.

From the British side, the French economy is often considered as a haven of protectionism, propped up by extensive State intervention and a general disregard for 'fair' competition. In reality, as a founder member of the EEC and co-signatory to various GATT treaties, France has embraced free trade to a considerable extent. By the end of the 1980s, the French business community was enormously enthusiastic about the European 'Single Market'. Intervention by the French State was less extensive than sometimes supposed and had the long-term objective of reinforcing markets. French interventionism has gradually declined in importance whilst competition policy has been much strengthened.

This is not to deny any truth to other perceptions. Reality usually contains conflicting elements. Undoubtedly, the pace of change has been quicker in some areas than others, some circles of the French business community have been more progressive, others more traditional. Where the old has not fully given way to the new, it is easy to overlook emerging contrasts.

Further, the standards by which we measure are always linked to a time and a place. A frequent assumption is that there is 'one right way' of doing things – the one used here and now – and that methods from other times or places matter less. A different principle is proposed in this work mainly that, so far as the world of business is concerned, at any moment or place there are merely solutions which work and solutions which stop working.

In consequence, this book places a twinned emphasis on local characteristics and on the processes of change. It highlights the particularities of French business by placing them in their context. Comparisons are made with the business world beyond France and attention is paid to the time-frame in question. The object will be to assess the extent to which new characteristics have emerged and to identify both the causes of change and the impediments to reform.

The structure of the book reflects the twinned emphasis on context and change. Each chapter is devoted to a central topic, which is broken down into its thematic components. Each chapter also contains chronological elements which indicate trends and turning-points. The theme-based approach has been utilised to identify specific solutions to business problems and to economic and social development. Chronological elements make it possible to chart development processes.

The time-frame chosen for analysis is the post-war period from 1945 to 1991, which itself is divided into smaller intervals. The frame is sufficiently large both to isolate local characteristics and to watch long waves of change unfurl. The post-war period continues to be the frame of reference for many people today – major decision makers and ordinary citizens alike – for whom it constitutes not dead history but living memory.

The book's structure is intended to facilitate at least two different styles of reading. Readers in search of particular subject matter, defined by theme or by time-period, are invited to 'dip into' the book as suits their purposes. Readers considering a sequential read are offered sustained arguments within each chapter and connecting threads running the length of the book.

The main propositions or connecting threads are that:
(a) the business world makes better sense when viewed as a set of interactions between economic and social development; and
(b) the French have charted the course which works for them, adapting as necessities require and circumstances allow. Attention to the interplay between choice and constraint will draw in key issues related to politics and to technology: in France, exercise of political will has frequently constituted the means to overcome technological impediments or resource shortages.

The book is divided fairly evenly between topics that are broadly economic (Chapters 1 to 3) and those that are broadly social (Chapters 5 to 7). Chapter 4, dealing mainly with competition policy, is a 'fulcrum' chapter linking economic and social themes.

More precisely, Chapter 1 analyses the limits of the State's role in economic development and leads on to a discussion of industrial policy and industrial development in Chapter 2. Chapter 3 considers the internationalisation of French business. Examination of policies and attitudes to competition in Chapter 4 leads on to discussion of the general attitudes, characteristics and composition of the *patronat* or French business community in Chapter 5. Chapter 6 looks at industrial relations and trade unions. The closing chapter looks at some of the cultural traits that characterise French management styles.

Overall, the book tries to convey some of the uniqueness of the French that is familiar to all those who regularly deal with them. It also seeks to give appropriate coverage to the process of convergence currently pulling nations of the industrialised West together.

At the time of completion (Autumn 1991), another period of significant change – with the '1992' programme and the creation of a Western European 'Single Market' – is already unfolding. The 1992 programme is often misunderstood as an ending when in fact it is a new beginning. The realisation has dawned that if a single economy is the goal, it cannot be reached without some new monetary and political mechanisms. At EC level, the process of reaching agreements on such large and sensitive issues is the potentially fraught next stage. Meanwhile, the Eastern European 'Single Market' of the

Comecon countries has collapsed, as has the political machinery that held it together. These processes create diametrically opposed forces: in the West greater convergence and a tendency to internationalism, in the East greater nationalism and greater ethnic diversity.

In consequence, this single nation study is published in a context where the term 'nationalism' is acquiring new overtones and creating new tensions. Every effort has therefore been made to avoid chauvinism. The aim is neither to glorify the French nor to bury them, but to acknowledge that national differences of business cultures and economic strategies exist, that they matter and that they are worth understanding if a greater degree of international harmony and co-operation is the goal.

Inevitably with a study of this scope, there are limitations. A number of people have been kind enough to help me produce a better account and I would like to acknowledge their contribution here. Thanks must go to colleagues who gave freely of their time to read over early drafts, namely John Bramley, Jeff Bridgford, Jeremy Clegg, Peter Holmes, Jolyon Howorth, George Jones, Valentine Korah, Peter Lawrence, Sue Milner, Mike Scriven, Stuart Waby and Vincent Wright. I am indebted to them for the usefulness of their comments. Any remaining errors or shortcomings are the responsibility of the author. Thanks also to Jill O'Brien for patient secretarial assistance, to Bath University Print Unit for transforming the text into camera ready copy and to editorial staff at Pitman Publishing for their part in converting a proposal into a publication. Finally, a word of appreciation to family and close friends for continuing to treat me as a human being - and not as the appendage of a word processor that I became while writing this book!

Reference
Fortune (1991) 'The Fortune global 500', *Fortune*, 124:3 (29 July)

Principal French abbreviations

BFCE	*Banque Française pour le Commerce Extérieur*
CEs	*Comités d'entreprise*
CFDT	*Confédération française démocratique du travail*
CFTC	*Confédération française des travailleurs chrétiens*
CGC	*Confédération générale des cadres*
CGPME	*Confédération générale des petites et moyennes entreprises*
CGT	*Confédération générale du travail*
CNPF	*Conseil national du patronat français*
COFACE	*Compagnie française d'assurance pour le commerce extérieur*
CTE	*Commission Technique des Ententes*
DATAR	*Délégation à l'aménagement du territoire et à l'action régionale*
DGCC	*Direction générale de la concurrence et de la consommation*
EDF	*Electricité de France*
ENA	*Ecole Nationale d'Administration*
FO	*Force ouvrière*
PCF	*Parti communiste français*
RMI	*Revenu minimum d'insertion*
SMIC	*Salaire minimum interprofessionnel de croissance*
SNPMI	*Syndicat national de la petite et moyenne industrie*
TGV	*Train à grande vitesse*

1

The State and French post-war economic development

INTRODUCTION

Since 1945, France has prospered to an extent unimaginable in the first half of the twentieth century. France's economic status is confirmed by membership of the 'G7' countries – the group of seven nations having the most advanced economies. But this level of economic success should not disguise the turbulence and difficulties that France has had to overcome.

The aim of this chapter is to follow through the peaks and troughs of French economic performance between 1945 and 1991. This long-term view will set French business developments in their context and allow an appreciation of what is remarkable about them. The chapter will look at the major changes that have taken place and analyse their causes. To facilitate the analysis, the chapter is divided into three main sections, each devoted to a particular period. The first describes the boom of the post-war years (1945-1973), the second looks at the crisis that followed (1974-1985) and the third sketches the recovery of the late 1980s.

Explanations for French successes and failures vary. A conventional view of the French business world holds that the role of the centralised State in planning, co-ordinating, indeed directing economic growth and development, has been crucial. The French refer to these tendencies as *dirigisme*, a term defined by Cerny (1989, p. 142) as implying that 'key economic orientations and outcomes . . . derive not so much from autonomous market choices as from "state preferences" '. The real weight of the French State is, however, open to question. Although in France the State has variously been congratulated or lambasted for its role in economic affairs, in reality, a wide range of factors have contributed to performance. Accordingly, France's reputation for a *dirigiste* State that was both powerful and effective will be examined and reassessed. The thesis will be that rather than emphasising the top-down policies of a centralised State, a contextualised approach is preferable. In the context of the immediate post-war years, an active partnership between the State and the business world was developed to solve urgent problems of reconstruction and industrial backwardness. Over time, however, the business community has become the senior partner in economic development while the State has grown progressively weaker as its resources and room for manoeuvre has dwindled.

THE BOOM YEARS: 1945-1973

France was devastated by the Second World War and suffered the humiliation of occupation by the German army. Yet in the post-war period the French succeeded in rebuilding their economy at a speed that attracted the admiration of many of their neighbours and rivals. In a key text on the French economy, Fourastié (1979) used the phrase *les trente glorieuses* (the thirty glorious years) to describe the period of boom that took place between 1945 and 1973. But how 'glorious' were those years? And to whom should their success be ascribed?

In the following paragraphs, the general features of the boom years are first considered. We then turn to general explanatory frameworks for the boom years. Explanations for post-war economic development and growth that are valid for most of the industrialised countries include neo-classical explanations, 'Fordism' and internationalisation. The analysis then moves on to explanations of the boom that are more specific to France, particularly the process of economic planning. This leads on to a discussion of the tensions between medium-range planning and short-term macro-economic policies. Lastly, an evaluation is given of the different factors causing the boom.

General features of the boom

The major measurement of economic expansion is the yearly increase in gross domestic product (GDP). Between 1950 and 1973, GDP in France showed yearly increases of around 5 per cent – an impressive achievement (see Table 1.1). Not only was economic growth in France higher than in Britain, the USA or even West Germany in the 1960s, but it also compared very favourably with France's traditionally poor performance during most of the nineteenth and early twentieth centuries.

At the same time as the economy grew, consumer purchasing power rose due to the combined effects of rising real wages and falling real prices. Household incomes rose by around 11 per cent per year between 1949 and 1973 (Kuisel, 1987, p. 20). Essential requirements such as food and clothing became relatively cheaper and demanded a smaller proportion of household budgets. In 1950, food accounted for 43 per cent and clothing accounted for 11 per cent of household spending; by 1973, spending in those areas had dropped to 25 per cent and 8 per cent respectively (Albertini, 1988, p. 232). This increased the amount of discretionary income available to households. A whole range of consumer durables – ranging from Moulinex coffee grinders to Renault cars – came within the means of ever-increasing numbers of ordinary French people. In 1954, 22 per cent of French households had a car, by 1972, the figure rose to 61 per cent. Ownership of televisions for the same years increased even more dramatically from 1 per cent to 76 per cent (Arnaud, 1987, p. 216). This increase in global demand created new mass markets, a mechanism to which we will return.

Table 1.1 Average annual growth rate of GNP in France and selected other countries

	1870– 1913	1913– 1950	1950– 1960	1960– 1970
France	1.6	0.7	5.0	5.8
Great Britain	2.2	1.7	2.8	2.7
USA	4.3	2.9	3.2	4.0
Italy			5.5	
W. Germany	2.9	1.2	7.7	4.8
Japan			9.5	10.0

Source : Albertini, J.-M. (1981) in Parodi, M. *L'Economie et la société française depuis 1945*, Paris: Armand Colin, p.48

At the same time as France experienced substantial *growth* in the economy (understood as increases in the quantity of output), economic *development* (understood as structural change) proceeded apace. Traditionally, France had been a mainly agricultural society but employment in agriculture fell steeply over the post-war years. In 1954, approximately 5 million people still worked on the land; by 1975 the figure had fallen to 2.1 million and it fell again by 1988 to 1.4 million (INSEE, 1990a). In consequence, the proportions of employees in industry and services increased. In 1946, 38 per cent of the working population comprised agriculture workers; 28 per cent worked in industry; and 34 per cent were employed in the service sector. By 1980, the proportions were 8.8 per cent in agriculture, 35.9 per cent in industry and 55·3 per cent in services (Mermet, 1990).

Changing patterns of the sectoral distribution of the workforce were important for a number of reasons. Firstly, the *exode rural* (rural depopulation) led to an increase in the numbers of town-dwellers and in the problems associated with urbanisation. Secondly, farmers and artisans were drawn into salaried employment and workers were displaced from areas of traditionally low productivity (small farms, sewing shops, etc.) to high-productivity activities. These trends contributed to changing professional and social structures and to enhanced economic performance. Thirdly, the social composition of the workforce changed as more women went into employment and as the immigrant population grew, two points to which we will return.

Not only did more people come to work in industry, but the relative weight of industries in relation to each other altered. Older industries such as mining and textiles which emerged from the first industrial revolution came to have relatively fewer workers, while newer industries such as electrical goods, electronics and aeronautics assumed greater importance. For example, in 1913, 42 per cent of industrial workers were employed in textiles and clothing; by 1969, this figure fell to 13 per cent (Kuisel, 1987).

These trends give clues as to why the French economy grew so rapidly but closer analysis is required to understand the reasons for growth and development.

Explanatory frameworks for the boom years

Given the complexity of the rapid economic and social changes of the period, no single explanation is entirely satisfactory. Accordingly, in the paragraphs below, three explanatory frameworks of the boom will be presented:
  (a) the neo-classical explanation;
  (b) 'Fordism'; and
  (c) the internationalisation of the French economy.

The neo-classical explanation

For France, the major statement of the neo-classical explanation is to be found in the works of Carré, Dubois and Malinvaud (1984). Neo-classical economists put the emphasis on production factors; namely labour, capital, and technical progress.

As regards labour, both the quantity and quality of the workforce require consideration. In today's climate of large-scale unemployment, it is easy to overlook the fact that more hands can produce more output. Further, a well-trained, well-educated workforce will be more productive in terms of volume and quality of output. Both of these points need consideration in the context of the post-war years in France.

Turning first to the size of the workforce, there was a labour shortage in France in the 1940s and early 1950s due to the effects of the war. The problem was only gradually resolved. The total French population did increase markedly in the post-war period. In 1946, the population was 40.1 million but rose gradually every year to reach over 52 million in 1973 (INSEE, 1990a). However, the working population stabilised at around 19.5 million between 1946 and 1962. From 1962, it increased gradually to reach 22.2 million in 1975 (INSEE, 1990a). In consequence, population increases appear not to provide a very satisfactory explanation for the earlier waves of economic growth. However, the situation is more complex than first meets the eye.

Firstly, although there was a rapid increase in the birth-rate in the 1950s – the so-called 'baby boom' – its effects did not make themselves felt until much later. There is an inevitable lapse of time between an increase in the population and an increase in the workforce. People born in the late 1940s and 1950s came on to the labour market in the 1960s. Further, measures such as longer schooling and more training delayed their entry. There were also other compressive effects on the size of the workforce, namely earlier effective retirement as well as a changing demography. Between 1950 and 1970, numbers of people aged between 20 and 59 as a proportion of the total population fell from 53.6 per cent to 48.8 per cent (Bauchet, 1986, p. 170). On the positive side, with improvements in the availability and quality of training and education, the quality of the workforce increased, thus offsetting some of the quantitative effects.

However, because of the compressive effects involved, even the stabilisation of the working population required the influx of labour from other sources. Two waves of migration boosted the French workforce. With the ending of French colonialism, large numbers of native French returned to the mainland. The major group were the 300,000 or so *pieds-noirs* (colonial settlers) who returned from Algeria in the early 1960s. There was also an influx of foreign labourers. Traditionally, workers migrating into France had come from the poorer regions of Europe, particularly France's close neighbours Spain, Portugal and Italy. But due to France's colonial heritage, increasing numbers came from the Maghreb countries (Morocco, Algeria and Tunisia) and from West Africa. In 1946, there were over 1.7 million foreigners living in France; by 1975, the total had increased to over 3.4 million. As a percentage of the total population, this represented an increase from 4.4 per cent to 6.8 per cent (INSEE, 1990a). Further, the number of women at work increased: women comprised 35 per cent of the workforce in 1954 but nearly 43 per cent by 1985 (Arnaud, 1987, p. 201).

Also, given the major movements between sectors – from agriculture to industry, from industry to commerce and services – the total picture is one of a high degree of professional mobility. Thus the key element related to labour as an explanatory factor in the growth and development process, is not the *size* of the workforce *per se* but its greater degree of *flexibility*, understood in terms of a willingness to migrate to obtain employment and in terms of increasing levels of qualification.

As regards capital, the post-war years saw a significant increase in investment in capital goods by private and public industries. The State invested heavily in infrastructures (road, rail and air transport, communications, services such as health and education). The construction industry also experienced a boom with a massive expansion of housing fuelled by public and private demand.

This increase in investment is connected with the fairly comfortable position of many French firms. In the 1950s, French companies had relatively few debts since wartime inflation had eroded them. In the 1960s, loans were cheap and abundant, leading to an increase in company indebtedness in the 1960s (Stoffaës, 1989, p. 111). Further, the increase in investment relates to the sense of confidence prevalent in the business community which resulted from the economic stability of the period.

Carré, Dubois and Malinvaud (1984) argue that the major factor in post-war growth was neither the quantity of labour nor the quantity of capital but what they call the 'residual factor', namely technical progress. This is presented under two heads:

(a) the gradual development over time of more efficient production methods;

(b) qualitative effects within both capital and labour factors, with more training and education improving the output of labour and new investment resulting in more efficient capital goods.

In a phrase, the key element emphasised by the neo-classical approach is 'productivity gains'. Technical progress meant that both labour and capital operated at a higher level of productivity, which is, in turn, taken to explain much of the net growth in output and wealth. But at this level of analysis, technical progress is a one-sided explanation for the boom. Complementary elements need to be shaded in.

'Fordism'

Like the neo-classical approach, the 'Fordist' explanation stresses the roles of investment, and of technical and technological progress leading to productivity gains but it builds these elements into a wider-ranging model. The model's key feature is that it relates supply-side improvements to increased consumer demand.

The post-war years saw significant increases in research and development with a large number of technological innovations, leading to many new products and to greater diffusion of old ones. Investments in new machinery, greater automation, reorganisation of working methods and new management techniques all contributed to a new era of mass production and mass distribution. Indeed, as these new techniques were often imported from abroad, especially the USA, Petit (1988, p. 47) suggests that the post-war boom in France was 'first and foremost a realignment with competitors', a kind of catching-up process.

But without mass markets, mass production is impossible. Henry Ford is credited with being among the first to understand that mass production relied on mass markets to sell to. The wealthy few were too small a customer base. Mass markets would necessarily have to include other social strata, including those to which Ford's own factory workers belonged. This, in turn, implied that to convert these strata into consumers, they had to be sufficiently well paid to purchase the new products. In consequence, it was in the interests of producers to reallocate some of the fruits of growth to their workforce. This meant accepting an increase in wages at the cost of depressed short-term retained company earnings; this would contribute to creating mass markets and so ensure long-term expansion and profitability.

Recent commentators have expressed reservations about Ford's own intentions and methods. Foster (1988) argued that Ford's outward altruism disguised considerable cynicism in his exploitation of his workforce. But whatever the judgement on Ford as an individual, higher wages and better living standards for larger sections of the population were fought for and won over the long term.

Whereas 'Fordism' was already well developed in the USA and Britain before the Second World War, it was only after 1945 that it burgeoned in

France. The result was a huge boom in the production and sale of consumer durables such as radios, televisions, fridges and cars.

In common with the neo-classical model, in 'Fordism' 'productivity gains' are the indispensable feature of the 'virtuous spiral' that links increases in output with greater consumer purchasing power. It is these gains which accelerate the adding of value and produce a larger surplus to be divided up between the workforce (higher salaries), the company (new investment) and stake-holders (dividends, interest payments, etc.).

During *les trente glorieuses,* new production methods fuelled productivity gains. The system of 'Fordism' at factory level is intimately linked to the principles of 'scientific management' and the work of F. W. Taylor. The functions of conception and execution were separated. Artisanal design was abandoned and standardised products were developed by industrial designers. Trained 'time and motion' specialists split production tasks into constituent parts to find the 'one best way' of accomplishing them. Factory work was 'deskilled', since the worker at his post was not asked to develop work methods, but was required to perform the same limited actions throughout the working day. The introduction of assembly lines into an increasing number of industries also served to regulate the speed at which workers had to perform. By speeding up the line, operatives were pushed into working faster. But the new methods allowed a reduction in production times and an increase in output. Increased productivity drove prices down, making new types of goods available to ever-increasing layers of the population.

The value of the 'Fordist' model is that productivity is related not only to technical and technological inputs but also to markets. The 'Fordist' system worked because it was able to create and satisfy demand. It balanced the fundamental economic equation. Greater demand meant greater output and more jobs. Full employment and rising wages meant increased demand. This is a simplified schema, but it illustrates the 'virtuous spiral' of the boom years.

The successful functioning of the system is limited by two factors. Without sufficient productivity increases, the system will start to lock up. Also, once markets are saturated, demand dries up. By the end of the 1960s, these potential dangers were becoming realities.

In the context of post-war expansion, the explanatory power of this model is considerable. However, it applies equally to a range of countries and so does not explain divergences in economic performance. Other factors linked more directly to local or national conditions must also be considered.

The internationalisation of the French economy

A major factor in the explanation of growth in the French economy is the gradual opening of her frontiers and the extension of her markets. Traditionally, the French business classes had preferred to lead a sheltered existence, expecting the State to preserve industry's prerogatives by erecting protectionist barriers to reduce foreign competition or indeed, banning imports. Free trade was the exception not the rule in French history.

In the post-war period, a growing consensus argued that protectionism was inefficient for two major reasons. Firstly, being sheltered from foreign competition induced complacency among French producers. The latter were slow in adjusting to new patterns of trade and in improving their competitiveness. Further, protectionism usually leads to 'tariff wars', with rival nations imposing prohibitive customs duties thus closing off their markets to each other. This is to their mutual detriment, since it leads to a poor allocation of resources.

From the 1950s, however, internationalisation of trade has proceeded apace. In France's case, the increase in international trade had two major causes.

Firstly, France, like Britain, gradually relinquished its colonies. The wars in Indo-China (1953-1954) and in Algeria (1954-1962) marked the end of an era of French colonialism. The loss of protected colonial markets meant that French producers had to look for new markets further afield. This factor pushed France toward new international trading arrangements.

The other factor was economic growth in Western European countries. The existence of large, developed markets in close proximity to each other made the growth in intra-European trade a logical and essential step. The desire to prolong the 'virtuous spiral' of economic development experienced throughout Western Europe in the post-war period through closer European trade links was formalised by the Treaty of Rome in 1957. The treaty established the European Economic Community (EEC), with France as one of the six founding members. For France, this move signalled a major break with protectionism. Between 1960 and 1973, imports as a proportion of GDP rose from 10.5 per cent to 15 per cent while exports rose from 1.4 per cent to 14.4 per cent (Nguyên Duy-Tân, 1986, p. 10).

These developments led to a major reorientation of French foreign trade (see Table 1.2). In return for gradually opening her frontiers to European neighbours, France gained access to large, easily accessible and lucrative markets in Europe. The enhancement of trading opportunities with rich neighbours has been a major factor in promoting the growth of the French economy.

In consequence, relatively more of France's output has gone to EC countries, with relatively less going to her former colonies. Though French trade with the Third World declined in relative terms, in absolute terms it has remained significant. Trade links with developing countries have had a lasting impact on France's industrial specialisations and on her balance of trade.

Finally, although the long-term effect of opening her frontiers has undoubtedly benefited France, short-term problems existed too. Large inflows of imports leading to a negative balance of trade have presented perennial problems to French policy makers and business people alike. Despite rear-guard calls for a return to protectionism, the majority response has consistently been to put the emphasis on improving the competitiveness of French products by incremental progress to free trade.

Given the importance of these themes, Chapter 3 is devoted entirely to their development.

Table 1.2   Changing patterns of French foreign trade (in %)

	1950	*1958*	*1966*	*1970*	*1975*
EEC (the six)	20	22	42	44	43
Other non-communist European countries	24	18	21	22	20
Eastern Europe	1	3	4	4	6
Total Europe	45	43	67	70	69
USA	4	7	7	5	5
Other countries	15	13	12	14	15
Zone franc	36	37	14	11	11
Total	100	100	100	100	100

Source: Albertini, J.-M. (1988) *Bilan de l'économie française*, Paris: Editions du Seuil, p.33

We now turn to institutional features of economic management in France which make the French case distinctive.

Economic planning

The existence of economic planning in a market economy is probably the most unusual feature of French economic management in the post-war years. The successful functioning of the system depended on co-operation between governments, the Civil Service and the business community. Though no system was free of internal conflict, it is striking that the planning system managed to function at all, let alone survive over the long term. In principle, planning of the economy exists even today in France, though its heyday is long past. In this section, relationships between the planners and markets will be described and their contribution to the development and growth of the French economy assessed.

The political context which gave birth to the first French plan of 1946 displayed an unusual configuration. At the end of the war, there was a high degree of consensus on major priorities. Economic bottle-necks should be eliminated, production increased and foreign trade augmented. Full employment was the pre-condition for lifting standards of living. The decision to adopt planning was not only a contingency response to optimise the allocation of rare resources but was also in tune with ideological options. Almost all shades of opinion in the political spectrum agreed on the means to achieve those ends, namely a planned economy (Petit, 1984).

The enthusiasm of the Marxist Left is easily explained. It relates to the convergence between the national plan and the Soviet model of a centrally planned economy, a model to which the French Communist party aspired. The acquiescence of right-wing parties is explained by the precedent of a planned economy during the period of right-wing rule under General Pétain during the Second World War. Interestingly, centrists who believed in the tenets of 'modern capitalism' also favoured planning as a way not of destroying but of *reinforcing* the market. These tendencies were further strengthened when, in 1948, it became necessary to administer aid from the Marshall Plan in a rational manner.

In brief, the predilection for planning the economy was one expression of the post-war political will to find a 'third way' between collectivism along the Soviet model and economic liberalism of the American variety. The underlying aspiration was to find a rational method of economic management and industrial modernisation which avoided the uncertainties to which market mechanisms are prone.

This distinctive attitude to State/market relations suggests that the theory and practice of competition had specific characteristics in France as compared to other countries. Changes in French attitudes to competition will be discussed in detail in Chapter 4. At this stage, the most salient characteristic to mention is the widespread distrust among the French in 1946 of the market and capitalism. Memories of the Wall Street crash and the deep recession of the 1930s were relatively fresh. The French wished to avoid a repetition at all costs. In addition, during the German Occupation, French business had either sided actively with the occupier (for example, Louis Renault, whose car plants were nationalised in 1946 as punishment for collaborating) or stayed on the side-lines and so silently acquiesced. In consequence, at the end of the 1940s, the business classes were treated with suspicion. Economic planning was a way of supervising an untrustworthy group. And at that stage, the position of the employers was too weak for them to put up much resistance, however hostile they may have been to planning. In any case, many of them were to find that planning held benefits for them too.

Unlike the Soviet 'Gosplan' model, French economic planning was not coercive, but indicative. As will be seen, this classic distinction wallpapers over a number of ambiguities. Planners aimed to keep a fine balance between State involvement and the autonomous evolution of the market. In principle, the plan gave producers guidelines, not prescriptions. Companies could follow the detailed contents of the plan or not as they chose, but the econometric predictions enshrined in the plan were there to help all.

This distinction was complicated by the fact that the State in the immediate post-war period had significant powers of persuasion at its disposal. This included 'carrots' (for example, financial incentives such as subsidies and 'soft loans') and also 'sticks'. Of these, the most *dirigiste* element was price control (see pp. 128-9 for discussion). Further, the State itself invested in a vast range of activities and so had lucrative contracts in its gift. The negotiation of advantage with the State became an objective of leading French firms. Some became very skilled at the activity, others lost out.

One of the major questions relating to the planning process was whether the planners or the State had the ability to co-ordinate the use of these different levers in a coherent fashion. A review of the major elements of the first six plans will illustrate the range of variables and their degrees of impact.

A general planning office was set up under Jean Monnet in 1946. The ensuing First Plan (1947-1953) aimed to promote the post-war reconstruction effort by favouring heavy industry. Six sectors were targeted – coal, steel, cement, transport, electricity, agricultural machinery. After the chaos of war, the aim was to put the country back on its feet as quickly as possible.

The Second Plan (1954-1957) was more ambitious. It aimed to modernise almost the whole of the economy. Basic industries were no longer the sole priority, yet services did not figure in the plan. The accent was firmly placed on improving French industrial productivity and competitiveness by reducing protectionist barriers and restrictive practices.

By the time of the Third Plan (1958-1961), the technical sophistication of the planning system had markedly increased. Advances in econometry and computerised methods of economic modelling allowed for improved understanding of sectoral interrelationships and for greater predictive accuracy. Growth targets were set for all sectors. State investments in education and other collective amenities were spelt out.

The Fourth Plan (1962-1965) reinforced these latter tendencies by stressing the *ardente obligation* (the burning need) to improve infrastructure, health, cultural provision and research. Regional planning also featured strongly. Indeed, there was a subtle shift in emphasis away from economic and industrial objectives towards social, even political aims.

The Fifth Plan (1966-1970) was extremely ambitious, however. It stressed the need to maintain macro-economic equilibria (a balanced budget, a positive balance of trade, etc.). Industrial policy featured strongly, principally in the form of aid to a limited number of large, fairly high-tech companies assigned the role of achieving success for France in world markets.

In the Sixth Plan (1971-1975) a number of priority areas were identified for State investment. The plan predicted a GDP growth rate of 6 per cent. As events turned out, this was wildly optimistic. The oil crisis left France with 3 per cent growth in GDP in 1974 and a 0.9 per cent fall in 1975 (*Notes bleues*, 1991), pushing the economy into recession. This outcome confirmed the decline of the planners' art.

Over the 25 years or so when planning was credible, the general thrust of the process shifted markedly. Early plans featured measures that were economy-wide. The State, with Marshall Aid, directed significant amounts of essential investment. In time, however, this *dirigiste* strand diminished. Bauchet (1986, pp. 52-3) indicates that the State budget was directly responsible for 50 per cent of all investment in 1947; this figure had dropped to 22 per cent by 1958. The planners realised that the domains in which the State could involve itself had to decrease in order to let the market develop freely.

The State had neither the resources nor the will to intervene across the economy. It targeted its resources primarily in those areas for which the modern welfare state is considered responsible: infrastructure, education, health, social security. These priorities are clearly reflected in the Third and Fourth Plans.

But more ambitious, entrepreneurial goals were not entirely abandoned by the State. Successive governments considered that industrial policies were essential. One of the major ambiguities of the period was the way in which industrial policy overlapped with planning without the two being fully co-ordinated. A central example is the Fifth Plan which promoted 'national champions', namely world-class French industrial firms. Creating national champions involved growth by mergers, a strategy that the State actively supported by favourable legislation and subsidies. Despite appearances, this was not 'old-style' *dirigisme*. In reality, the beneficiaries were industrial conglomerates who had succeeded in bending the ear of the State to their own needs and projects. Because of this type of influence, the planning process has been described as 'a cooperative venture between the managers of big business and the managers of the State' (Cohen, 1969, p. 67).

Planning became a two-way process. The State played a role in the development of private firms but members of the business community were able to influence official policy to their own advantage. In a sense, this outcome is a logical extension of a major, original intention of the planning process which was to promote market capitalism. But it left the planners open to the charge that big business had hijacked the plan. Hall (1982, p. 186) has argued that by the Sixth Plan, the State had lost its independence from social groups and so lost room for policy manoeuvre. These elements illustrate that the picture of France having a powerful *dirigiste* State must be modified.

Given the shifts in content and the ambiguities of execution of the plans, the overall results of the planning process have raised a certain amount of controversy. Hough (1982) marshals over two pages of assessments, which range from pure eulogies to equally bald condemnations. In truth, the evaluation of an indicative planning system within a moderately open market economy is methodologically difficult. Machin (1989) identified three types of possible evaluation:
(a) a comparison between the targets and the outcomes of the plans;
(b) an assessment of the structures and methods of planning; and
(c) an evaluation of the indirect effects of the planning process.

Comparison between the targets and the outcomes of the plans
Turning to the first type of evaluation, Table 1.3 illustrates that outcomes compared very favourably to targets during the boom years.

Table 1.3 GDP growth rates: Plan targets and out-turn: 1952-1975 (in %)

	2nd Plan 1952-7	3rd Plan 1958-61	4th Plan 1962-5	5th Plan 1966-70	6th Plan 1971-5
Target	4.4	4.7	5.5	5.7	5.9
Out-turn	5.4	3.8	5.8	5.9	3.7

Source: Hough, J. R. (1982) *The French Economy,* London: Croom Helm, p.119

The problem with this approach, however, is that it does not establish whether the results were the direct consequence of policies enshrined in the plans or whether the planners made fairly correct forecasts (until the Sixth Plan). Jacques Rueff is reported to have remarked sardonically to General de Gaulle that 'Planners are like the rooster who believes his crowing causes the sun to shine' (Machin, 1989, p. 126).

Tracing effects back to causes is difficult. A comparison between French growth rates and those of its neighbours where there was no planning process is inconclusive. Though in France, the economy grew faster than in Britain, at particular points growth in Italy and West Germany was similar. However, as Machin (1989) pointed out, French growth was more consistent. Whether the consistency can be ascribed to planning is hard to prove, but Estrin and Holmes (1983, p. 85) have argued that planning stabilised the growth process.

Further, by the Fifth Plan, the emphasis was less on growth targets – or the volume of change – than on the direction of change (the concentration and internationalisation of French industry). Detailed discussion of these industrial policy themes appears later in Chapter 2, but it is important to indicate here that the success of the policy makers in identifying and promoting high-growth sectors was patchy. Bourdois (1983) pointed out that planning did little or nothing for fast-growth industries of the post-war period such as cars and domestic appliances. This type of criticism is well founded and useful, but though it points up some of the limitations of planning, it does not provide a global evaluation. The question throughout is whether the French economy would have fared better, or as well, *without* planning. As no incontrovertible *quantitative* data can be gathered to provide an answer, the burden of proof is no more attributable to 'pro-planners' than to 'anti-planners'.

Assessment of the structures and methods of planning
A second type of evaluation consists of an assessment of the structures and methods of planning. Firstly, planning is often associated with interventionist traditions in France. Those traditions are usually linked with Colbert, the creator of a number of State-owned entreprises in the seventeenth century, who gave his name to the practice of *colbertisme*, which was defined by Wise (1989, p. 59) as 'government intervention in large-scale, long-term projects'. In reality, after the first two plans, direct intervention in the economy through the planning process became the exception. Hence Petit (1984) has argued against using historical interpretations drawing on a tradition of *colbertisme* to explain the successes of the planners. In France, periods of intervention had been interspersed with periods of liberalism. In any event, the structure of the planning commissions was not home-grown; it was modelled on the British Development Council.

Most importantly, the planners did not have at their disposal the full panoply of interventionist techniques. The Finance Ministry kept control of short-term policy (see pp. 16-17), of the budget and of the volume and direction of credit allocation. Although France had a large public sector which included nationalised banks and insurance companies, its activities were largely left out of the plans. Likewise, even public sector industrial firms, such as Renault, preserved their independence and stayed largely aloof from the planning process. Such interventions as did occur, for example, price controls and industrial subsidies, usually took place outside of the planning process. In consequence, the fact that France has had a tradition of *colbertisme* has little relevance in explaining and assessing the work of the planners. On the contrary, what is impressive are the limits on co-ordination between various branches of government due to their zealous guarding of autonomy. Despite the rhetoric, planning did not provide an all-embracing, systematic approach to economic and industrial management. The State apparatus was too fragmented and conflict-ridden and individual firms too independent for this to occur.

On the other hand, the planning process did contribute to a climate of renewed confidence after the desperation of the 1930s and early 1940s. The predicted rates of growth were much higher than had historically been the case. Though the first plans were often greeted with scepticism, once early forecasts were met or exceeded, the planning process earned credibility. Hough (1982, p. 119) indicates that even in 1967, over 50 per cent of firms with more than 5,000 employees claimed the plan had a significant effect on investment. At the least, the plans provided guidelines within which companies could, with a growing sense of confidence, develop their own business plans. Indeed, the criticism that was later levelled against the planners by the 1960s was not of over-optimism but of conservatism, of 'playing safe' with their estimates.

The planning process also contributed to the maintenance of a high degree of consensus. The presence of different sections of French society in the various planning commissions allowed the development of *concertation*, namely decision making by mutual agreement. However, this did have its limits. Trade union representation was incomplete. For example, the largest union, the CGT, was excluded between 1954 and 1961 (Gueslin, 1989, p. 67). Further, the major unions criticised the process as serving only business and the State. They were uncomfortable in a situation where the defence of workers' rights and rewards was not the primary object. These factors undermined the long-term credibility of the plan as an expression of thorough-going *concertation*, but planning institutions had nonetheless played a temporary role in defusing social tensions. The fact that the planning process helped restore business confidence and smoothed industrial relations is no small achievement.

Evaluation of the indirect effects of the planning process

The third type of evaluation relates to the indirect effects of the planning process. Machin (1989) points to the creation of a planning network *per se*. Despite the inaccuracies in the planners' projections in the early years, developments in economic science provided the planners with more sophisticated econometric instruments and models. The needs of the planners ensured allocation of funds to improve the national statistics service (INSEE) as well as to set up other research institutions such as CEPREMAP and CREDOC. The very existence of these establishments illustrates one benefit of the planning process. The 'task-force' concept that guided the composition of planning institutions also influenced the development of the Civil Service. Machin (1989) argues that the planning commissions were the model on which DATAR, the regional development board, was based.

Apart from the side-effects of planning on the State, the side-effects on business are worth emphasising. Because planning involved *concertation* between State and business, it reinforced long-standing French tendencies towards *ententes* (collusion and restrictive practices) which reduced the role of competition – a theme to be taken up in Chapter 4.

If the evaluation of the benefits of planning has to be nuanced in relation to their intensity, so too must the time-frame be specified. The halcyon days of planning were the period of relative calm and stability in the 1950s and early 1960s. The social and economic turbulence of the late 1960s and 1970s undermined the planners' art. The events of May 1968, with their violent confrontation between students and workers and the State, demonstrated beyond doubt that the period of *concertation* had passed.

Most damaging of all, the planners had not been able to predict the recession of the 1970s. Increased economic turbulence meant that the task of prediction had grown more hazardous. Inflation was a particular problem. As the forecasts grew increasingly less reliable in the 1970s, the credibility of the indicative planning process was eroded. In fact, a number of wider developments had placed increased strain on the process. The gradual ending of protectionism and the opening-up of the economy to world trade reduced the level of control the French government could exert on the national economy. Being more exposed to world trends made the French economy more difficult to predict and to manage.

These factors made planning an embarrassing affair for French governments as they ran the risk of placing themselves in a 'no-win' situation. To the extent that the plans expressed elements of government policy, they were a statement of intent against which the government's subsequent performance could be measured. However, statements of government intent over the medium term would leave the government stranded if the economic tide turned at an unforeseen moment. Prudence indicated that in turbulent conditions it was better not to make too many promises.

A discrete compromise was reached. Planning survived in principle but went into decline in practice. Officially, the planning process did not end. A Seventh Plan (1976-1980), an aborted Eighth Plan (1981-1985) plus an Interim Plan (1982-1983) led to a Ninth (1984-1988) and a Tenth Plan (1988-1992). But it is debatable whether the plans were taken seriously by the policy makers. Gueslin (1989) argues that President Giscard allowed the planning system to fall into decline. After their electoral victories of 1981, the Socialists revived the planning process, with Michel Rocard as Planning Minister. But economic difficulties and political disagreements meant that early enthusiasm produced few real effects (Holmes and Estrin, 1988). In consequence, Machin's (1989)

contention that French governments since the 1970s have used the planning
commissions for policy preparation rather than policy making is a useful
summary.

Indeed the status of the plan had always been ambiguous. It was indicative,
not prescriptive, yet contained statements of government intent. Further,
although it was intended to provide medium-term guidelines (over a four- to
five-year period), reality would catch up from behind and short-term
considerations would take priority. The plans had repeatedly been in conflict
with the need to implement economic adjustment policies in the short term.
Perhaps the best example of this was the curtailment of the Third Plan in 1961
due to the urgency of the Algerian crisis and the need to bolster the Fifth
Republic under de Gaulle's authority. This type of interference between
objectives was not exceptional. The management of the short-term economic
cycle repeatedly caused the same type of conflict (albeit at varying degrees of
magnitude) between short-term necessities and medium-term intents. In the
last analysis, the planning commissions merely drew up plans. It was the
government that made and implemented policy. In order to look more closely
at the impact of short-term economic management, we next review the turning
points in macro-economic policy during *les trente glorieuses*.

Short-term economic policies

Whereas a common British view holds the 1950s to be a grey and grim time,
French views of the post-war period have often been suffused in the rosy glow
of nostalgia – a temptation to which the phrase *les trente glorieuses* itself lends
witness. The tendency has been to emphasise the economic peaks and
foreshorten the troughs. But though the cyclical periods of recession were far
shorter and less serious than in the 1970s and 1980s, their existence should not
be ignored.

Within the 'long cycle' of *les trente glorieuses,* four shorter cycles can be
discerned: 1948-1953, 1954-1959, 1960-1967, 1968-1973 (Gueslin, 1989). The
general pattern at the start of each of these periods was a spurt of expansion,
with full employment of manpower and resources. Later in each period came
a bout of 'overheating', namely an increase in demand, an increase in imports
and a deterioration in the balance of trade and, moreover, an increase in
inflation. Inflation, running at average minima of 5.3 per cent p.a. between
1949 and 1973, represented a perennial weakness of the French economy
(Gueslin, 1989).

Governments would respond to inflation by a package of deflationary
measures. Thus the *Plan Pinay* of 1952 decreased liquidity in the economy by
launching a State loan, which cut State spending and reinforced protectionism.

The *Plan Rueff* of 1958 was drawn up to prepare France for new economic
circumstances. In the wake of the Treaty of Rome and the opening of the
frontiers to international trade, the competitiveness of French exports had to
be strengthened. The French franc was devalued on world markets by 17.55
per cent. State spending was cut in the fight against inflation (Gueslin, 1989,
p. 39).

⟶ The *Plan de stabilisation* of 1963 (implemented by Valéry Giscard d'Estaing as Finance Minister), imposed price and credit controls and cut State spending.

With each of these plans, once restrictive measures had begun to bite, once inflation was down and the balance of trade improved, the restrictions were slackened. This signalled the start of the next expansionary phase. Hence France, like Britain, managed the post-war economy by a series of stop-go policies. Such short-term economic policies were necessary to smooth out excesses and local difficulties. They succeeded in regulating the economy and in reinforcing the 'Fordist' virtuous spiral but were not the major factor contributing to growth. Such policies do, however, demonstrate the limited ability of the planning process, even in the earlier part of its life, to predict and oversee economic and industrial development over the medium to long term.

Evaluations

A range of explanations covering economic, technological and market-driven factors as well as the political and social dimensions of change have been put forward to explain economic growth and development. Taken together, these different types of explanation point to the underlying momentum beneath the post-war boom. A series of factors come together to push in the same favourable direction. A consensus in favour of progress met with new organisational methods. In brief, both the will and the means to implement change existed.

This combination puts into perspective the importance of the State as catalyst and agent of successful economic adaptation during *les trente glorieuses*. Interpretations which emphasise *dirigisme* as the cause of growth give a partial and finally distorted view.

The will of a new political elite in the immediate post-war period did play a significant role. With France's former leaders discredited after the collapse of the Vichy regime and with the business community demoralised, the situation favoured the blueprint of reform. But political will drew its sources and support from within the populace. It was aided and abetted by popular attitudes, by the consensus on the need to reconstruct the country and improve standards of living. This was the period of *productivisme*, of a willingness to work long hours, when people would scrimp and save for a brighter future.

Other social factors played their part too. The rise of a population of *cadres* (a transition group ranging from white-collar workers to top executives) also had an important role. First identified in 1936 as a social group worthy of the name, the numbers and role of the *cadres* increased during the boom years. Under the German Occupation, the authority and prestige of the *cadres* had not been undermined as was the case with the *patronat* (employers and business owners). Further, whereas the authority of the *patronat* tended to be identified with birth and privilege rather than entrepreneurial skills, the *cadres* represented a meritocratic, scientific approach to management. This gave them a new legitimacy (Petit, 1984).

The outlook of the *cadres* rhymed with that of the planners. Both were oriented towards market solutions rather than to Marxist programmes but were attracted by the rationalist spirit which planning enshrined. Arguably, many *cadres* fulfilled the same function at micro-economic level as that of the State planners at macro-economic level. This concordance of function has led Petit (1988, p. 48) to suggest that the *cadres* were the transmission belt connecting State planners with the real economy.

The notion of *concertation*, of co-operation between different social groups, is much in evidence in this period. Petit's thesis on the middle-management tier of the *cadres* as an essential fulcrum is reinforced by the work of Birnbaum *et al.* (1978) on the French ruling classes. Their study shows that significant proportions of the upper echelons of the Civil Service, State-owned companies and private firms were individuals from the same social and educational background who shared the same values, aspirations and objectives. This social homogeneity, and the interpenetration of political, administrative and managerial elites diminished conflict between the State and the private sector and undoubtedly facilitated both the formulation and implementation of policy. It is important to note that these social factors blur some of the boundaries between public and private sectors. Indeed, the legal and financial dimensions of ownership structures can disguise congruence and continuity of management strategies between public and private sectors. The full development of each of these themes – collusion between the makers and the targets of industrial policy and homogeneity of French elites – will necessitate a chapter devoted to each (see Chapters 2 and 5 respectively).

Put briefly, the argument here is that State interventionism was the visible tip of the iceberg but the 'underwater' arrangements between public and private sector players formed the iceberg's mass and gave it momentum. The real sphere of action of the State as agent of change was thus delimited by the resources at its disposal, by relationships between political, administrative and managerial elites, by the social climate in France and by environmental pressures in the international economy. In the confident and expansionist climate of *les trente glorieuses*, this series of favourable factors disguised the constraints under which the State laboured. In retrospect, explanations emphasising factor inputs, a 'Fordist' style of economic regulation and the effects of greater free trade assume more prominence and credibility than those which ennoble the role of the State or of the planners. By the end of the 1960s, with the social consensus splintering and the international environment becoming more turbulent, the limitations on the State's room for manoeuvre became ever more apparent and more severe.

THE CRISIS YEARS: 1974-1986

After three decades of near uninterrupted growth, the notion of a 'recession' had almost dropped out of the French vocabulary. That the boom years could end was not envisaged, despite signs of growing difficulties by the end of the 1960s. Inflation was again increasing, unemployment was creeping up and social tensions were growing. In May 1968 came a social explosion that marked the end of a long period of relative social and political calm.

Worse was to come in the economic domain. The spectacular oil price-hikes of 1974-1975 and their depressive effects on the national and global economies came as a massive and unwelcome surprise. In 1975, French GDP fell by 0.9 per cent. (*Notes bleues*, 1991). Between the third quarter of 1974 and the third quarter of 1975, industrial output fell by 13.6 per cent (Delors, 1982). Between 1970 and 1975, profit margins dropped from just over 15 per cent to around 10 per cent and investment slumped by 12 per cent between 1973 and 1975 (Brémond, 1985, p. 70). The trade balance in 1974 was at a record deficit of 21.2 billion francs,[1] after being in surplus since 1969. Meanwhile, inflation ran at 13.7 per cent in 1974 and 11.7 per cent in 1975. Unemployment at 848,200 in 1974 was near double the 1969 level. By 1975, it had climbed to 1,081,000; such an unemployment rate of 4.8 per cent was unheard of during the post-war period (INSEE, 1990a). There could be no doubt that the economy in France, as in other developed nations, was in crisis.

A number of the effects of the crisis are still with us. The problems faced and the solutions experimented with have left a deep mark. Further, many of the key political and economic actors continue to figure prominently in French public life. For these reasons, events and conduct in this period will be studied in detail.

In this section, we discuss firstly the surface, short-term causes of the crisis and secondly the deeper, structural factors which increased the severity of the ensuing recession. We then turn to a presentation and evaluation of the economic polices that were intended to manage the crisis. It will be seen that the crisis years prompt further re-examination of the role of the State. By the end of the period, a clearer perception of the limits on the powers of central State led to a more modest appraisal of its role.

Short-term causes of the recession

Spectacular increases in energy prices represent the most obvious, though by no means unique, cause of the recession. In the space of four years, oil prices increased by a multiple of six from $1.70 per barrel of crude in 1970 to $11.25 by 1974. This was the first oil price 'shock'. The second occurred at the end of the decade. The 1978 price of $13 nearly trebled by 1981, peaking at $35 per barrel.

Explanations for the hikes are basically geopolitical. They relate to political developments in the Middle East, particularly the war between Israel and Syria of 1972, the fall of the Shah of Iran in 1979 and the war between Iraq and Iran that started in 1980. The ability of Arab oil producers to exact massive price increases was related to their dominance within the OPEC cartel.

The effects of the oil 'shock' were undoubtedly significant. Energy is necessary for the provision of all goods and services. By the 1960s, Western countries, especially France, had become enormously dependent on cheap oil. According to Rand Smith (1989, p. 180), France imported more oil than any other Western European country. In 1973, oil accounted for 69 per cent of her energy requirement (Arnaud, 1987).

Because energy is required at every stage of production, there was a 'snowball' effect rolling through production systems which acted as a multiplier of the original oil price increase. According to Bouvier (1982, pp. 1579-80), the oil price hike added 3 per cent to annual inflation in France in 1974 but because of this multiplier effect, plus other non-oil inflationary pressures, inflation in France reached 14 per cent. This was comparable with inflation in a number of other countries: 17 per cent in Britain, 19 per cent in Italy, 25 per cent in Japan but 7 per cent in West Germany (Parodi, 1981, p. 63). Moreover, there was the psychological impact. Emotions such as depression and panic were translated into economic behaviours that anticipated further inflation, namely general price rises and large wage claims. These in turn fuelled the inflationary spiral.

Though the shock was sudden, it had a certain logic. During the 1960s, energy prices, along with costs of raw materials from the Third World, had fallen considerably in real terms. This represented a redistribution of wealth from oil-producing and Third World countries to the industrialised nations. Once the opportunity arose in the mid-1970s, producers of energy and raw materials tried to redress the balance. These countries all needed to compete in international markets. Further, they wished to move down the value chain – from extraction activities to manufacturing activities – since this produces greater wealth by increasing the value added.

Asian countries like South Korea, Hong Kong and Taiwan had already industrialised extensively and were becoming increasingly competitive. Western nations came to discover their lack of preparedness to face the new challenge of low-wage countries manufacturing medium-technology products such as televisions, hi-fis and microwave ovens.

Economic problems were compounded by financial and monetary disarray. On 15 August 1971, the USA had halted the convertibility of the dollar into gold. This action put an end to the gold standard and to fixed currency exchange rates inaugurated by the Bretton Woods (New Hampshire, USA) agreement of 1944. The Bretton Woods agreement had helped preserve monetary stability during most of *les trente glorieuses* and facilitated international exchanges by providing a relatively stable trading environment. Its abandonment began an era of floating exchange rates. Prices of goods and services on international markets became dependent on currency fluctuation, so increasing uncertainty and risk factors for sellers and buyers.

A series of counter-productive side-effects ensued. Parodi (1981) points out that efforts to pay bloated oil bills led to significant increases in money supply. In oil-producing countries there was a major increase in monetary reserves which presented problems of recycling. The presence of large reserves seeking investment and purchase opportunities added to the inflationary factors already present. Property speculation was one of their by-products. All this fuelled an inflationary spiral. Yet, due to the recession in industrialised countries, the output of manufactured goods was stagnating. The new economic phenomenon of stagnation combined with inflation came to be called 'stagflation'.

Structural causes of the recession

As the economic crisis increased in length, short-term views stressing oil price hikes came to appear inadequate. Long-range, structural explanations of decline were sought to explain the severity of the recession. These are inevitably more complex than the causal factors already discussed, but for reasons of space, only a short overview is possible here. Nevertheless, a review of the major competing explanations has the benefit of extending horizons.

Marxist analysts put forward the theory of a long-term tendency towards falling levels of profitability. They argued that the cause of the crisis was the over-accumulation of capital in a context where demand was being exhausted. Profitability could only be renewed by a reduction in capital, i.e. company closures, by increased inflation and by credit creation. However, the implication that the long-term fall in profitability is inevitable across the economy is not proven in practice. The profits of companies such as IBM, for example, remained high. The weakness of this analysis is that it underestimates the importance of technological innovation, both in terms of higher productivity emerging from new production processes and in terms of new products creating new markets.

For 'neo-Keynesians', the crisis was due to an excess of supply over demand. The 'excess' has been explained in two ways. Aubert (1982, p. 268) viewed the crisis as one of over-production. Capital accumulation increased faster than output leading to a fall in utilisation of capacity and a decrease in apparent productivity. The consequence was a reduction in investment. When investment did pick up, it sought to restore productivity by reducing the labour content, so perpetuating unemployment.

Conversely, the excess can be considered from the point of view of demand. For some, the root of the problem lay in the faltering of the 'virtuous spiral' of the 'Fordist' system. Demand for consumer durables was stagnating due to two factors. New demographic trends had led to a relative increase in the number of old people and a decrease among the young. In addition, the phenomenon of market saturation appeared to be having an impact. Whereas many new markets had been created in *les trente glorieuses*, by the 1970s, products such as cars, fridges, televisions, etc. competed in replacement or substitution markets, rather than as first-time buys. Sales were correspondingly slower. Against this view one could object that even fairly basic needs – such as housing – have not been fully satisfied in some social groups in Western nations, while vast potential markets exist in other parts of the world.

A variant on this explanation is to tie the problem less to demand *per se* and more to insufficient technical progress leading to a slowing-down of productivity increases. As processes became radically more efficient, later productivity gains were harder to make and smaller in size. However, Bonin (1988, p. 277) warns that the statistics may be misleading. A productivity gain of 4 per cent in 1979 corresponded to a gain of 9 per cent in 1959, because the bench-mark had itself migrated upwards in the intervening period.

Further, Carré, Dubois and Malinvaud (1984, p. 267) point out that the thesis of technical stalemate is weakened by the universality and suddenness of the phenomenon. Presumably, had technical stagnation been the root cause, its effects would have made themselves felt gradually across various industries as they were working at different technological levels. In fact, the crisis manifested itself simultaneously in a wide range of sectors and countries.

Though this argument has much merit, it is worth reflecting also that production methods in many industries had reached a technological plateau. A new surge of productivity in the 1980s due to the micro-chip, computerisation and robotics has since made this clear. The linking of the impact of technological innovation with economic cycles is usually associated with 'long-wave' theory, originally presented by Kondratiev (1935). Kondratiev stressed the role of generic innovations, such as steam or electrical power. (Today we would add nuclear power, information technology and robotics.) Generic innovations lead to a wave of rapid industrialisation followed by a period of stagnation – until the next series of innovations comes along.

In addition, technical progress is tied not only to technology but also to work organisation. By the end of the 1960s, there was growing disenchantment with 'Taylorist' job specifications, with piecemeal tasks and with the dehumanising effects of mass assembly methods. This disenchantment manifested itself in growing absenteeism, high employee turnover, poor work quality, go-slows and union militancy.

These explanations have been incorporated by exponents of the French 'regulation' school into a wide-ranging model (for example, Boyer, 1986; Aglietta, 1987). The distinctive feature of their approach was to emphasise consensus and balance. Indirect salaries, from social security payments, pensions, etc., allowed regulation of consumer spending patterns. Demand was high and output was maintained. But by the 1970s, the system was unable to stop profitability from falling, leading to a crisis. Meanwhile, around 1968, the social consensus had broken down. Hostility to 'Taylorism' has been mentioned. To this can be added other changes in attitudes and values. The *productiviste* spirit of working hard and living for the future had been diluted. Greater stress was placed on leisure time than on the work ethic. The merit of this type of analysis is that it aims to merge social and economic explanations.

Finally, it should be emphasised that controversy exists as to the relative weight to be attached to each type of explanation. The events of the 1970s are still too close for a definitive conclusion.

Crisis management under the Right (1974-1981)

With the benefit of hindsight, it is clear that economic policy making in the mid-1970s was ham-strung. The world environment had changed but governments were hampered by thinking that belonged to *les trente glorieuses*. The recession was seen as a minor, temporary affair which could be managed with the methods of the boom years. Significant employment shedding was not envisaged due to social pressures and expectations.

In France, the corporate sector – not households – paid most of the early oil price increase: the costs were not fully passed on to end-users. With inflation accelerating, employees put forward large wage claims. This maintained demand but led to wage-push inflation, decreased corporate profitability and decreased investment. In summary, the major problems for policy makers were inflation, high energy costs and a trade deficit, all linked to a dependency on oil.

The watchword of the period was to *desserrer la contrainte extérieure*. By this phrase French policy makers understood the need to bring French imports to manageable proportions, after the huge deficits caused by increases in oil prices. Achieving this involved reducing imports and/or increasing exports. Further, imports and exports can vary in volume and/or value. In order to *desserrer la contrainte extérieure*, policy was developed to act on each of the terms of a complex equation.

The major reasons why the cost of imports was so high were the large quantities of oil used multiplied by the high new prices. One strand of policy was to reduce the quantities consumed. All available means were implemented to bring down oil consumption. Speed limits were reduced. Manufacturers were subsidised to produce vehicles that used less fuel. Summer time was introduced early to make more use of natural light and cut back on electricity usage. New regulations on improved insulation were introduced to reduce heating costs. Energy rationing was introduced and quotas fixed on oil imports (Vesperini, 1985, pp. 106-7).

Further, diversification of energy sources was actively sought. As France had very limited fossil fuel resources, President Giscard launched massive investment in nuclear power. The long-term financial and environmental costs of the nuclear electricity programme have still to be calculated. But the short-term economic results of Giscard's energy policy were impressive.

Whereas between 1960 and 1973 both the economy and energy consumption grew at around 5 per cent per year, between 1973 and 1980, energy consumption increased by 1 per cent per year for an economic growth rate of around 3 per cent. In 1973, France produced only 22 per cent of her energy but by 1980, the figure rose to 27 per cent. Commissioning of nuclear reactors is a slow process but gradually the results have worked through the system. Nuclear-based electricity accounted for 1.8 per cent of national energy usage in 1973: it rose to over 6 per cent by 1980 and to 28 per cent by 1986. By 1986 France produced a remarkable 46 per cent of her energy and was exporting electricity to her neighbours. Taken together, energy saving and energy diversification allowed a reduction in oil imports from a 1973 level of 126.6 million tonnes to 110.9 million tonnes by 1980 and to 85.5 million tonnes in 1986 (Arnaud, 1987).

Reducing oil imports by overcoming the problem of energy dependence was one prong of the policy to *desserrer la contrainte extérieure*. Another prong was to increase exports. The major instrument used to this end was State aid in the form of cheap loans to exporters as well as guarantees against inflation. The capital goods sector in particular benefited from these measures. (See pp. 85-6 and pp. 111-15 for further discussion.) As a result, between 1973 and 1980, French exports stabilised at around 10.5 per cent of the total exports of the ten largest OECD countries.

Thus in two major areas, energy and foreign trade, French governments in the 1970s maintained consistent policies. In general, however, French governments in the 1970s, like most others, were disconcerted by the sea-change in the world economy and reacted inconsistently. The key characteristic was a series of stop-go macro-economic policies.

The *Plan Fourcade* of 1974 (named after the Finance Minister of the time) turned the signals to red. It slowed down the economy by interest rate increases, a credit squeeze and by reducing public spending. These measures aimed to reduce inflation. The *Plan* also aimed to redress the trade deficit by addressing the energy issue through energy saving measures and energy import quotas. Employment, however, was safeguarded. Major redundancies required permission from the *Inspection du Travail*, whose allegiance to the Labour Ministry and government ensured that its priorities were social and political rather than economic. Thus the *Inspection du Travail* tended to be reluctant in authorising redundancies, much to the chagrin of employers.

The deflationary measures had their effect in terms of reducing demand. Production fell by 15 per cent between 1974 and 1975 (Gueslin, 1989, p. 55) and investment declined. Consequently, the policy was perceived as aggravating the recession and discontent mounted.

President Giscard d'Estaing and Prime Minister Chirac bowed to public opinion. They turned the lights to green in 1975 with a policy change – the *relance Chirac* – which reflated the economy . To cushion the socio-economic effects of recession, the government increased public spending. There was a rise in 'indirect' wages such as pensions, family allowance, and allowances for short-time working. Employment was boosted by recruiting 15,000 civil servants. The problem of a fall in private investment was addressed by subsidies to housing and by State spending on major industrial projects such as the renewal of France's telephone network and the construction of nuclear power stations. Monetary policy was slackened. Interest rates were cut and the money supply was increased, not least by government recourse to borrowing. This type of demand management is linked to the principles popularised by Keynes. In its 'vulgar' form, Keynesian policy is justified by the belief that recessions can be overcome by government spending. In the immediate post-war period, this approach had been used repeatedly and successfully.

The short-term effects of the *relance Chirac* were fairly beneficial. The GDP rose by 4.2 per cent in 1976 and 3.2 per cent in 1977, a slightly healthier state of affairs than in some of France's neighbours. Fonteneau and Gubian (1986) calculated that 1.2 per cent of each year's growth is attributable to Chirac's policy. Around 160,000 jobs were created in 1975-6, though this was not enough to reverse an overall increase in unemployment. Although exports increased by 10.7 per cent in an international environment in which most industrialised countries had reflated, the trade balance slumped further into the red by another 11 billion francs. Inflation remained high; from its peak of 13.6 per cent in 1974, it barely fell two points to 11.8 in 1974 and was still at 9.6 per cent in 1976 (Pébereau, 1987, p. 293). Thus the results were rather mixed. Indeed, as inflation came to be increasingly considered as the major enemy, this poor performance on inflation reduction sounded the knell for Keynesian reflation. A new policy was required.

In August 1976, Raymond Barre replaced Jacques Chirac as Prime Minister and introduced a package of austerity measures. Barre's major aim was to *rétablir les grands équilibres* – to bring the State budget, the trade balance and the balance of payments into the black. Inflation was to be countered by strict control of the money supply, by a rise in interest rates and by a strong franc.

Barre was in favour of a strong franc for a number of reasons. Firstly, it reduced the value of imports. Oil was paid in dollars, hence a strong franc bought more dollars and bought more oil. By the same token, it made all imports cheaper, so reducing 'imported' inflation. A strong franc was therefore another way to *desserrer la contrainte extérieure*.

Secondly, though a strong franc made French exports more expensive, Barre argued that the net effect was to encourage French companies to be more competitive, to become more specialised and increase their productivity. Sautter (1982) pointed out that the refusal to devalue was a means to encourage firms to resist large wage demands and so defuse wage-push inflation. The policy of a strong and stable franc was reinforced by the creation of the European Monetary System. Between 1979 and 1981 the pivot rates for the franc and the deutschmark remained unchanged, indicating success in stabilising the franc on foreign exchanges.

In terms of State spending, Barre balanced the books fairly consistently yet managed to increase social security spending by an average of 6.6 per cent per year. This social-democratic leaning had to be financed by an increase in taxation. In consequence, the State budget as a proportion of GDP increased from 35.7 per cent in 1976 to 42.5 per cent in 1980. These measures and their effects were to reduce the room for manoeuvre available for the governments of the 1980s.

The liberal element of Barre's approach was evident in a gradual return to market mechanisms. Though Barre imposed a general price freeze in 1976 and a freeze on the tariffs of public utilities (gas, electricity, etc.) in 1977, by 1978 he had abolished nearly all State-imposed price controls.

Barre's policies made progress to turning the economy around. His major aim of restoring *les grands équilibres* was largely achieved. The State budget was still in deficit in 1980, but at a modest level – 1.3 per cent of the GNP as compared to 2.9 per cent in West Germany and 4 per cent in the UK (Gueslin, 1989, p. 56). In 1978, the trade balance was in equilibrium while the balance of current payments was running a surplus. But this good work was undone by the second oil price hike of 1979-1980 which undermined both the trade balance and the fight against inflation.

The perennial objective of modernising the French economy met with some major successes. These included the nuclear programme and improvements in infrastructure. France acquired a new generation of telephone networks and train systems, such as the RER in Paris and the Paris-Lyons link by high speed train, the TGV. There was some improvement in the financial situation of private firms too.

Growth was around the average for industrialised countries but by 1980 inflation was running at 13.6 per cent, which was higher than the OECD average. In fact, during the late 1970s, annual inflation never dropped below 9.1 per cent. Barre's policies had included monetarist elements: monetarists argued that by reducing the money supply, inflation should come down. However the monetarist strand in Barre's policy had not been very restrictive. Money supply grew by 14.3 per cent in 1979 against a target of 10 per cent (Hough, 1982, p. 137). Yet unemployment had also increased. At 6 per cent in 1980, it too was running at higher than the European average. A total of 380,000 jobs were created between 1976 and 1980, but the working population grew more quickly than numbers of jobs available. The result was a net increase in unemployment from 1,081,000 in 1975 to 1,652,900 by the end of 1980 (INSEE, 1990a).

Appraising Barre's policy fairly necessitates recognition of its heterogeneity. Hough (1982, p. 137) has commented that Barre was:

a monetarist in that he sought to control the money supply, a classical economist in his advocacy of free wage bargaining and a Keynesian in his willingness to vary, for example, social security payments and levels of investment of public sector firms.

This combination led to a measure of inconsistency, but it did indicate a supple approach to complex problems (Montbrial, 1984). However, nuances in policy and the real scale of economic problems were both probably lost on the electorate. Redundancies and company closures proved to be more influential in swaying public opinion than successes in restoring *les grand équilibres*.

Crisis management under the Left (1981-1986)

Economic problems played their part in the elections of 1981. When put to the test, the popularity of Giscard and of the Right collapsed. Such was the desire for change that for the first time under the Fifth Republic, a Socialist candidate – François Mitterrand – won the presidential election. In the parliamentary elections which followed, the French Socialist party won an absolute majority and received a mandate to implement their policies. Unsurprisingly, they tried to deliver a different economic package from their predecessors. Unfortunately, Socialist economic policy under Mitterrand was to follow the same stop-go pattern as under Giscard.

The initial Socialist analysis of the crisis assumed that it was a capitalist invention to exploit the less well off. The Socialists argued for a break with capitalism and its representatives – such as the previous government – and so rejected Barre's policies. In any event, it was incumbent on the Socialists both to gain credibility as economic managers and to offer an alternative policy that would succeed where Barre was perceived to have failed. The objectives they set themselves were to end the recession by stimulating output and growth, to reduce unemployment and to curb inflation. The State was to provide the foundations for the new way forward. In 1981, the Socialists still believed that a *dirigiste*, State-led recovery was a viable proposition. Events were to prove them wrong.

The left-wing government implemented a two-fold approach: a short- to medium-range economic policy of reflation to restore demand and a long-term industrial policy to restore competitiveness. To avoid repetition, discussion of Socialist industrial policy, based upon a massive nationalisation programme, will be held over until pp. 54-6 and pp. 59-64 below. Only economic policy will be discussed here.

Under Prime Minister Mauroy, the government reflated the economy in 1981-2. The theoretical basis for reflation was again a 'vulgar' Keynesian analysis. Recession had cut demand, leading to a fall in output. The government assumed that it was sufficient to increase purchasing power to create the demand that would promote output and increase employment.

The Socialists targeted the less well off for increases in purchasing power. This was in line with their ideological beliefs: they considered that they had received a mandate to promote social equity by redistributing wealth. Between 1981 and 1982, old age pensions went up by 62 per cent and family allowances by 50 per cent. Housing allowance went up twice in 1981. The *SMIC* (the statutory minimum wage) went up by 10.6 per cent in 1981-2. This increase also gave a push to the general wage spiral since other workers sought to restore differentials between themselves and the least well paid. The allocation of a fifth week of paid holidays and a reduction in the working week to 39 hours had the effect of increasing the effective wage bill for employers by reducing productivity. These measures increased labour costs by 2 per cent of GDP.

Measures against unemployment included reduction of the retirement age to 60 for men and early retirement at 55 was encouraged. The aim was to free up jobs. Also 140,000 jobs were created in the Civil Service.

Most of these measures required increased government spending. To finance it, the Mauroy government increased taxation of the better off and increased employers' social security contributions. The government also borrowed heavily. The public sector deficit increased from 1.1 per cent of GNP in 1980 to 2.8 per cent in 1982. But the increased debt had a time-bomb effect, for the servicing of the debt has incurred massive costs (see pp.37-8). Government debt as a proportion of GDP increased from around 17 per cent in 1980 to some 21 per cent by 1983 (*Notes bleues*, 1991). On the other hand, monetary policy was fairly restrictive; interest rates remained high and bank loans to the corporate sector were rationed but the State did resort to printing money.

At this point, it is instructive to compare the *relances* of 1975 and of 1981. Although both produced an increase in GNP, there were major underlying differences. Firstly, unlike the *relance Chirac* which aimed to stimulate corporate investment, the *relance Mauroy* sought to stimulate consumption. Capital investment under Chirac was a 'one-off' injection that improved the competitive position of French firms and the French economy. However, the increases in direct and indirect wages under Mauroy were to have long-term, inflationary effects.

Secondly, in 1975 the industrialised nations reflated together but in 1981-2 France was alone in reflating. With inflation on the increase after the second major oil price hike of 1979, the governments of the Western world were generally imposing deflationary economic policies of a 'monetarist' type, involving strict control of money supply, high interest rates and cuts in public spending. Thus with the world recession deepening, France's foreign markets were shrinking. Conversely, the sudden boom in purchasing power in France and the relative openness of her economy made her an attractive target for exports. Because French suppliers were slower to react than foreign competitors and because French companies in a number of consumer product industries are far less competitive than third country producers, the net result was massive consumer spending on imported goods, pushing the trade balance to previously unknown lows. From being in surplus in 1978-9, the trade balance fell to a record deficit of 93.2 billion francs in 1982. For a country that imported most of its energy and had to pay the bill in exports of goods and services, a deficit of such massive proportions was disastrous and unsustainable.

The trade deficit contributed to downward pressure on the franc. Three devaluations ensued: on 4 October 1981, 12 June 1982 and 21 March 1983. However, these were not caused solely by the increase in imports. Firstly, Barre's policy of a strong currency had left the franc overvalued in relation to the mark. The Socialists made the mistake of postponing devaluation and so taking the blame for a weaker franc, rather than devaluing immediately and so shifting the responsibility to the previous administration. Secondly, the arrival in power of a left-wing government – which included four members of the Communist party – produced panic reactions in some conservative quarters who exported their francs to foreign havens. This was linked to a certain amount of speculation against the franc. The combination of supporting the franc and the trade deficit led to a drain on foreign exchanges reserves which fell from $80 billion in 1980 to $34 billion in 1982 (Gueslin, 1989, p. 58). Meanwhile, inflation continued to run high – 11.8 per cent in 1981 – and unemployment topped two million in 1982.

The painful lesson learned in the débâcle was that macro-economic policy in a medium-sized economy such as France could not afford to be out of step with her neighbours and trading partners. Further, the Socialists had underestimated the social-democratic orientation of the previous government in two connected areas. One was the redistribution of wealth to the less favoured by social security transfers; the other the burden placed on firms by increases in *charges sociales* (broadly equivalent to national insurance contributions). Barre had cushioned French society against the recession by passing the costs on to the corporate sector – just as the Socialist government tried to do. But by 1981 room for manoeuvre in these directions was much reduced. The Mauroy government had little alternative but to reverse the trend.

In late 1982, the government did a U-turn on macro-economic policy. A period of 'austerity' began. The main aims of the new policy are reminiscent of Raymond Barre's approach. Finance Minister Jacques Delors aimed to reduce inflation and to restore the *grands équilibres,* particularly the balance of trade and the balance of payments. Achieving this would necessitate modernisation of the economy and a return to profitability of the corporate sector. The concern for the fortunes of firms was a new direction for the Socialists. This was the period of the so-called *découverte de l'entreprise* – the belated discovery that the health of firms is crucial.

To ease inflationary pressures, Delors resorted to one of the most traditional of interventionist policies: the price and wages freeze. Both salaries and prices were frozen between July and October 1982 (Vignon, 1984). This was followed by a reduction in taxation on companies and a freeze on their *charges sociales.* To compensate, the government increased individual contributions and allowed a fall in real terms of social security payments. It increased the burden on income taxpayers by 40 billion francs while public spending cuts totalled 20 billion francs in 1982 and 24 billions in 1983. The aim was to reduce the budgetary deficit as a deflationary measure.

The most striking feature of the new approach was probably the new wage policy of 1983. Breaking with tradition, the Socialist government implemented a gradual end to the index-linking of wages – higher prices would no longer automatically lead to higher wages. Monetary policy was restrictive with ceilings for growth of the money supply set annually, just as it was across the Channel in Mrs Thatcher's Britain.

The major danger of cuts in demand caused by a severe deflation was a fall in output, leading to a fall in employment. To alleviate the situation, the government decided on accompanying measures to sustain employment. These were of two kinds:

(a) social measures (referred to as *le traitement social du chômage*) such as early retirements, reductions in the working week, vocational training for the young; and

(b) job creation schemes, particularly in the Civil Service.

Hall (1987) calculated that these measures created 748,000 jobs between 1981 and 1984. Net employment loss was thereby contained to 436,000 jobs whereas it stood at 1,300,000 jobs in the UK and 1,100,000 in West Germany. Thus Holmes (1987, p. 49) argues that some *relative* success can be adduced to Socialist employment policy to the extent that the rise in unemployment was much less than might have been expected given the fall in growth.

By 1985, improvements in the domestic situation, tied to a healthier world economy, allowed a softening of policy. Income tax was cut in 1985 and 1986. In 1986, corporate tax went down by 5 per cent, a measure which allowed an improvement in company profitability. To compensate, public spending was cut. The Civil Service shrank by 5,000 jobs and subsidies to nationalised companies were reduced. As this policy was very similar to that advocated by the government's opponents, it represented a spoiling action at a time when parliamentary elections were approaching.

By 1986, the Socialist balance sheet looked more healthy. Inflation was down to 2.1 per cent. The growth rate had improved to 2.4 per cent from a low of 0.8 per cent in 1983. The trade deficit fell from 93 billion francs to a small surplus in 1986. The competitiveness of French industry had increased due to a steady year by year fall between 1982 and 1987 of labour unit costs (Albertini, 1988, p. 284). This was due to the joint effects of a drop in real salaries and cuts in employer's contributions to the national insurance system. Short-run competitiveness had also improved by devaluations of the franc. Industrial investment had finally increased (Rand Smith, 1989, p. 193).

Unemployment, however, remained stubbornly high. From a total of 1,652,900 in December 1980, it reached 2,534,400 in December 1985 (INSEE, 1990a). Moreover, unemployment had serious differential effects. Regions in the north and east of France were more seriously affected than Paris or most of the South. The young were hardest hit. In the mid-1980s, 22.9 per cent of available young workers were jobless compared to a global average of 10.6 per cent (INSEE, 1990a). Rates of unemployment for women and foreigners were also higher. Ten years previously these levels of unemployment would have been unthinkable. Had the Socialists been in opposition, they would have decried them. Yet, in 1986, issues such as unemployment and their earlier mismanagement of the economy did not lead to a rout of the Socialists in the parliamentary elections but only to a marginal defeat.

Evaluations

By 1986, it was clear that France had weathered the storm of the crisis years. Most of the economic indicators were positive, bar unemployment. Since 1978, France has suffered a level of unemployment that has been consistently higher than the OECD average (INSEE, 1990b).

However, it has taken two failed bouts of reflation and several changes in government to achieve a widespread acceptance of the need for economic rigour. The first failed reflation under Chirac in 1975-6 had indicated that temporising would not do, but the full conclusions were not widely accepted. Arguably, the second failed reflation of 1981-2 was the *cure de réalisme* that the French needed: it fostered a more realistic view of what French governments could achieve by policy measures alone. The failure of 'voluntarism', of the attempt to pull France up by her bootstraps, was the precondition for the acceptance of the severity of the economic crisis and of the drastic measures required to deal with it. French voters and politicians have come to accept that French policies must be in step with those of their neighbours.

Certainly, the Socialists made austerity a little more palatable by the attention to social equity enshrined in the redistributive aspects of their policy. As Hall (1987, pp. 66-7) shows, although the austerity measures eroded the purchasing power of most social groups, lower-income groups fared relatively better than higher-income groups. This factor may explain why a policy of austerity under the Socialists was less unpopular than under Barre.

But the Socialists have also had to recognise and rectify their early errors. Instead of directing policy towards boosting consumer demand, the need was for supply-side measures that would improve the position of firms. Their policy changes in mid-stream acknowledged this reality. The financial standing of many firms had improved. In 1986, French capitalism was healthier than ten years previously.

In the process, the Socialists restored the prestige of the firm in the eyes of a populace which had a reputation for despising the profit motive. And the Socialists themselves had accepted private and not State enterprise as the motor of the economy.

This was a major turn-around in ideological terms for the French Left. It also signalled the end of a myth built up by governments of both the Left and the Right that the State was powerful enough to resolve national economic adversity. For the French State, the inheritance of the crisis years has been the recognition of a new, more humble role.

THE RECOVERY: 1986-1991

Over the five-year span that runs from 1986 to the end of 1990, France enjoyed the most consistent period of economic expansion experienced since the 1960s. From a growth rate of less than 2 per cent throughout the 1980s (bar 1982), French GDP grew at over 2 per cent from 1986-1990, peaking at 3.7 per cent p.a. in both 1988 and 1989. This section will present the major lines of development of the period and analyse the causes of rapid growth. It will point to the dark clouds that gathered during 1991 and to the challenges that lie ahead. The main argument is that the trend to reduce the State's role has accelerated and probably become irreversible.

The underlying factors explaining the recovery were the combination of a highly favourable environment abroad together with relative social calm and consistently prudent economic policies in France.

By 1986, the French economy was in phase once more with other major economies. Further, they were all moving into a period of expansion. Indeed, the US economy had been expanding since 1983. The ensuing expansion in international trade multiplied opportunities for French exporters.

A second major explanation of growth in the second half of the decade was the collapse of oil prices. In August 1986, the price of a barrel of crude oil was $15, a fall of 45 per cent on its 1985 price. Over-capacity and falling demand due to energy efficiency savings were the twin factors pushing oil prices downward. At the same time, devaluation of the dollar increased the purchasing power of the franc on international markets, bringing the real costs of oil to 1974 levels (Baslé *et al.*, 1989, p. 76). Although the beneficial effects of the price drop did not feed through immediately, the medium-term consequences were to reduce energy costs and improve the profitability of industry.

Other factors also played their role. Falling interest rates encouraged consumption and investment. A recent report by the OECD (1990) indicates that tax cuts which fuelled domestic demand and a slight devaluation near the end of the decade (making French goods cheaper abroad) served to maintain the expansionary momentum.

On the domestic front, dramatic political changes occurred, with government by the Right in 1986-8 and again by the Left after 1988. Yet there was considerable continuity in most aspects of economic policy. Accordingly, such differences as arose will be discussed next, before turning to elements of continuity.

The Chirac government (1986-1988)

In April 1986, as a result of a marginal win for the Right in the parliamentary elections, Jacques Chirac was appointed Prime Minister. By a twist of fate, the oil situation was the reverse of that at the time of his previous appointment as Prime Minister. In 1974, oil prices had soared; in 1986, they collapsed. Although much remained to be done to improve the competitiveness of a number of sectors, inflation was down, employment was rising, albeit slowly, investment had picked up and output was increasing. This upswing provided the ideal environment within which to introduce the package of liberal economic measures Chirac had promised in the parliamentary electoral campaign.

In the ten years of his absence from the post of Prime Minister, Chirac's economic philosophy had greatly altered. The Keynesian outlook that characterised the *relance Chirac* of 1975 had been displaced by a tough liberalism. His role models in economic policy were President Reagan and Mrs Thatcher. From Reagan, Chirac took over 'supply-side' economics and from Thatcher, he took over privatisation and a hardline approach to industrial relations and unions. The overall aim was to improve the operating environment of French business. The major means were deregulation and liberalisation.

In December 1986 one of the first gestures of the government was to abolish price controls which dated back to 1945. The practical effects were limited but the repeal was a symbolic action marking the triumph of market orientated solutions over older French tendencies to *dirigisme* and cartels (for discussion see Chapter 4).

Other liberalising measures followed. Exchange controls, set up in 1968 and tightened in 1981, were gradually abandoned. Cross-border capital movements, one of the major principles of the EC, became possible. From 1988, French nationals could contract loans abroad.

Chirac's supply-side measures involved reducing the costs borne by firms. They began with a reduction of taxation on corporate profits from 50 per cent to 42 per cent. The top bands of income tax were also reduced. In an effort to improve the competitiveness of French industry, he encouraged downward pressure on wages. In the public sector, this led to a bitter strike by railwaymen in the winter of 1986-1987. Ensuing chaos on the railways caused much resentment among the French, both against the strikers but also against the government.

Chirac attempted to make it easier for employers to sack personnel by a repeal in 1987 of the so-called *autorisation administrative de licenciement.* This was a measure enacted during his previous term of office obliging employers to gain permission for significant redundancies from an official body, the *Inspection du Travail.* In principle, increased employment flexibility would make it easier to manage the wages bill and encourage employers to recruit in the early stages of an upswing without fear of being marooned with excess personnel in the event of a rapid ebb in demand. However, this measure made too small a difference to impact significantly on job creation. Unemployment remained high at 10.6 per cent in 1987, with vocational training continuing as the main policy response to mass youth unemployment.

The centre stage of Chirac's policy was occupied by a large privatisation programme. At this point, we give only an overview of privatisation, holding over detailed discussion to pp. 64-9. The justification for privatisation was to 'roll back the State' by allowing, on the one hand, a more efficient management of nationalised firms while, on the other, leaving the State to fulfil only those functions which the private sector could not accomplish as successfully. Privatisation had the additional advantage of substituting State income for State expenditure. Instead of giving subsidies and soft loans to nationalised firms, proceeds from their sale would fill the national coffers. This surplus would enable the government to reduce the public sector deficit or to reduce taxes or both. This, in turn, would increase the government's room for manoeuvre in spending and avoid large, unpopular cuts in the provision of services.

The sale of nationalised companies proved a great success, with millions of French people becoming shareholders for the first time. However, 'black Monday' – the stock market crash of 19 October 1987 – ended the euphoria. Up until that date, many new shareholders believed that stocks and shares only appreciated, leaving the buyers of shares in public firms with a handsome profit. During the crash, share prices tumbled. Though many shareholders held firm and refrained from panic selling, the bubble had burst. The feared economic collapse did not occur, partly through the underlying strengths of the major economies, partly through mild international reflation. However, the French privatisation programme ground to a near halt while the popular electoral appeal that Chirac was hoping to arouse evaporated. In 1988, during the campaign for the Presidency, Mitterrand shrewdly put the nationalisation/ privatisation debate on ice by adopting the slogan 'neither nationalisation nor privatisation' and so cutting the ground from under the feet of his opponent, Chirac.

The Rocard government (1988-1991)

The promise to preserve the *status quo* in economic life appears to have satisfied the electorate. At the least, it did not detract from Mitterrand's popularity. In May 1988, he scored a triumph for himself and for the Socialist party by securing a second term of office, a unique event in the history of the Fifth Republic. Mitterrand now had the opportunity to appoint a Socialist Prime Minister, Michel Rocard, an appointment which was confirmed by new parliamentary elections giving the Left a slight majority. Rocard assembled a politically mixed, though mainly Socialist government.

The fundamentals of economic policy manifested considerable continuity with those of its predecessors. Emphasis was still placed on enhancing the operating environment of French firms in order to increase their competitiveness, increase output and reduce unemployment. But social issues assumed greater prominence, indicating a change in outlook.

There were cuts in income tax, though a new tax, the *impôt sur les grandes fortunes,* has been levied on the ultra-rich. This was termed a 'solidarity' tax as proceeds were destined to finance another new fiscal measure, the *revenu minimum d'insertion* (RMI), a guaranteed basic income for all wageless adults. This measure is aimed to combat the so-called 'new poverty' which emerged in France in the 1980s. Though its Socialist colours are evident, it is a sign of a certain degree of consensus in France that the RMI received extensive support across the political spectrum.

Major challenges remained in the area of employment and industrial relations. Firstly, there were still not enough jobs to go around. Unemployment ran at 10.4 per cent in 1988 in France. Secondly, public sector workers were pushing for substantial salary increases. In October 1988, French nurses staged strikes to protest at pay and conditions. These were followed by conflicts in other public sector organisations, notably the PTT (post and telecommunications) and the RATP (the Paris public transport authority). In contrast to Chirac's aggressive stance to industrial relations, Rocard adopted a 'softly-softly' approach. Agreements were signed fairly quickly. These led in February 1990 to a general reform of civil servant salary scales. Meanwhile in October 1989, strikes at Peugeot marked one of the few major instances of large-scale industrial conflict in the French private sector in the 1980s.

These disputes indicated an undercurrent of discontent in French society. Increases in real wage levels had fallen continuously since the crisis years: from 6.2 per cent between 1970 and 1973, to 4.5 per cent between 1974 and 1978, to 2.2 per cent between 1979 and 1982 and to 1.0 per cent between 1983 and 1987 (Lecointe *et al.*, 1989, p. 144). Purchasing power had fallen in several years in the 1980s and rose by a mere 0.4 per cent in 1987 (*Notes bleues*, 1991). The problem was particularly severe for civil servants whose purchasing power fell almost continuously from 1978, reverting to 1974 levels by 1987 (Coquidé and Makarian, 1988). At the same time, the financial position of firms was buoyant. Salaries and ancillary costs as a proportion of value added declined substantially from their 1980 peaks to fall back to 1970 levels by 1988. Profit levels were at their highest since 1970 (INSEE, 1989). In the mid-1980s, salaried employees and the unemployed had borne the brunt of the recession. The argument for higher wages had some foundation.

The need remained, however, in the private sector to combine an equitable distribution of company earnings with the preservation of international competitiveness. For the government, the need was to keep public spending and the public sector borrowing requirement to manageable limits.

Indeed, bar public spending, the overall economic picture remained relatively rosy in France. Both the Chirac and the Rocard governments could point to a healthy balance sheet. Macro-economic indicators have been generally favourable. Growth in GDP was 2 per cent in 1987 but ran at 3.8 per cent in both 1988 and in 1989 – the best results since 1976 (INSEE, 1990a). Likewise increases in industrial output of 5.4 per cent in 1988 and 4.7 per cent in 1989 established new post-recession peaks. Whereas industrial investment had fallen between 1981 and 1983, the period 1985 to 1989 saw considerable increases, peaking at a year-on-year increase of 12 per cent in 1988. Productivity increased markedly, though not as steeply as in the UK (INSEE, 1989).

Inflation was contained. From 11.7 per cent in 1982, it was cut dramatically to 2.7 per cent in 1987 and settled at near 3 per cent for the following three years. Moreover, the differential between German and French levels of inflation had steadily fallen from a gap of 8.2 per cent in 1980 to a mere 0.6 per cent throughout 1989 and 1990 (*Notes bleues*, 1991). Given France's persistent problems with high inflation over the post-war period as compared to Germany's excellent inflation record, this tiny differential was seen as a major victory in France. Containing price rises in this way makes goods more competitive on foreign markets.

There were net gains in employment too. Over the early 1980s, there were five years of net job losses, but net job gains were 110,000 in 1987, 260,000 in 1988 and 300,000 in 1989. The 1989 figure was the highest level of job gains since the oil crisis of 1973 (*Notes bleues*, 1991). For the first time since 1974, the industrial sector registered a net increase in employment (INSEE, 1990c). In consequence, unemployment fell for the first time since 1973, dropping from its 1987 peak of 10.5 per cent to 10 per cent in 1988, 9.5 per cent in 1989 and 8.9 per cent in 1990.

On the negative side, these were very high unemployment levels for a leading industrial nation in a period of rapid economic expansion. By way of cross-national comparison, for 1989 the average OECD unemployment rate was 6.5 per cent. Of the major developed nations, only Spain at 17.3 per cent and Italy at 12 per cent had higher rates (INSEE, 1990b). Further, despite a major increase in exports, the trade balance was in deficit from 1987 onwards. The balance of trade in manufactured goods was in deficit in 1987 for the first time since 1969 (Baslé *et al.*, 1989, p. 94). These latter developments point to falling international competitiveness and structural weaknesses in French economy, themes which will be developed in Chapters 2 and 3.

There were a number of continuities in government handling of the economy. After the false start of 1981-2, the major aim for economic policy in the 1980s was the reduction in inflation by keeping public spending down and keeping a tight grip on the money supply. As the private sector has been considered the motor of the economy, priority has been given to decreasing the tax burden on it.

When Chirac took over as Prime Minister, the overt stress on these elements of policy making was stronger, but the general thrust of policy remained constant. Since the return of the Left to power in 1988, the budgets of Finance Minister Bérégovoy have been at least, if not more, orthodox than those of his right-wing predecessor Edouard Balladur. Balladur forecast a deficit of 115 billion francs for 1988 (Baslé *et al.*, 1989, p. 100). Yet Bérégovoy ended the year with an actual deficit of 16 billions – though this was mainly due to the 'windfall' of tax receipts increasing as the economy expanded.

As in Barre's day, the aim has been to balance the budget. The State budget (*before* interest payments) ran deficits of 51.5 billion francs in 1986, 27 billions in 1987 and 16 billions in 1988. In 1989 and 1990, the budget was in surplus by 15.7 and 43.3 billion francs respectively. The *total* deficit for 1990 (including interest payments for the year) was 93.4 billion francs. This corresponds to 1.4 per cent of French GDP, roughly half of what it was in 1986 (INSEE, 1991, p. 353).

At face value, this is an impressive performance. In reality, it is creditable but does not tell the whole story. The major problem faced by the French Treasury was the escalation of State debt over the 1980s. As a proportion of GDP, debt rose steadily from 15 per cent in 1978 to 27.6 per cent at the end of 1990 (*Notes bleues*, 1991; INSEE, 1991). The explanations for this phenomenon are:

(a) budget deficits ran at 2 per cent of GDP each year from 1981 to 1988, thereby increasing the public sector borrowing requirement yearly;
(b) in 1990, debts of the nationalised car-maker, Renault, were consolidated into the national debt;
(c) high interest rates compounded the problems of servicing and repaying the debt.

Such is the 'snowball' effect that even the surplus of State income over expenditure in 1989 and 1990 was insufficient to cover interest payments, so adding to the debt (INSEE, 1991).

This leaves current and future French governments on the horns of a dilemma. There are good reasons for reducing State debt *and* reducing fiscal pressure. But in practical terms, this is almost impossible. The need to reduce State debt is clear. Though still manageable at the start of the 1990s, the accumulation of unpaid interest creates a time-bomb ticking away into the next century. But with inflation low and growth in GDP falling to 2.7 per cent in 1990, the 'escape hatches' are blocked. Debt management becomes a function of the relationship between public spending and fiscal policy.

On the other hand, reducing fiscal pressure is arguably necessary. It is necessary because the total tax burden in France has steadily increased from 35 per cent of GDP in 1970 to 44 per cent in 1988. This puts France well above the EC average of 40.6 per cent in 1988 (OECD, 1990). For some time, French business people have complained that, despite reductions of tax levels on profits, their total tax burden (including *charges sociales*) is higher than that of competitors from other EC countries. In the 'Single Market' of 1993, taxation differences will quickly feed through into differences in competitiveness. As regards taxation, the French business community is calling for a 'level playing field'. Likewise the OECD (1990, pp. 66-77) has invited tax reform. Harmonisation of types and levels of tax across the EC represents a difficult ongoing discussion.

Over 1986-1990, some steps towards tax reform were taken. In 1988, tax cuts totalled 40 billion francs, in 1990, 28 billions, of which 16 billions went to firms. The low band of VAT was cut from 7 per cent to 5.5 per cent. The high band of VAT was reduced from 33.3 per cent in 1987 to 22 per cent by 1990 (INSEE, 1991). In 1988, corporation tax was reduced from 45 per cent to 42 per cent. Taxes on reinvested profits were progressively cut from 42 per cent to 37 per cent by 1990 (INSEE, 1989). The local business tax, the *taxe professionnelle*, a type of pay-roll tax, has also been reduced. Because of increased State revenues from rapid economic growth, cuts in public services were avoided. Indeed, some ministries, notably education, received increased budgets. Unfortunately, with the slow-down in growth of 1990 set to continue, painful and unpopular cuts in public spending and in Civil Service employment appear inevitable for 1992 (Seux, 1991). Discussion at government levels of how deep those cuts will go is intensified by the imminence of the 1993 parliamentary elections. The underlying problem is that structural reform of France's complex tax system and social security systems has barely been started. Reform will constitute a difficult, even painful, challenge for the future, particularly if it is to occur in a context of slow economic growth.

This range of developments has reduced the scope for manoeuvre of the French State. Far from looking to influence national economic development by direct intervention, the State has increasingly been confronted by the problem of keeping its own house in order. In the wider economy, with the rehabilitation of the profit motive, with the emphasis on companies as the source of employment and innovation, with management autonomy accepted as a necessary principle, the firm has taken centre stage. The State has come to see itself less as economic actor and more as audience and arbiter.

CONCLUSIONS

By the mid-1980s, *dirigisme* was finally consigned to history. Far from being a powerful monolith, the State's independence of action in the immediate post-war period had often been exaggerated. In reality, its policies were circumscribed by environmental factors while its successes owed at least as much to social and technological development, to its alliance with managerial elites as to government initiatives *per se*. By its entrepreneurial and frequently astute policies, the French state accompanied and accelerated economic development but it was not the catalyst of change. Even in its more successful projects – the TGV, nuclear electricity, the renewal of the telephone network – there was a marked *suiviste* element. The aim was to catch up with competitor nations. Underneath the rhetoric, policy was reactive, rarely proactive.

Once *les trente glorieuses* were over, once the series of factors favourable to economic growth and development became disconnected, the limitations on State action became clearer. In the crisis years of the 1970s and 1980s, the State, whether under right- or left-wing governments, proved equally unable to provide the leadership and support necessary to haul France from recession single-handed. But gradually the realisation dawned that the State could not be expected to do so. Changes in the international environment – the opening of the economy, evolving trade patterns, competitiveness shortfalls, international monetary instability, energy crises – all contributed to the definitive relegation of France to the position of a medium-sized power unable to chart an autonomous course.

Yet though de Gaulle's ideal of an independent France has been dispelled, it has not lost its attraction to the French. In these circumstances, two reactions predominate in France. One is to seek to build a strong France in a strong Europe. The other is to talk of national decline.

However, as Maarek (1988) has argued, talk of decline is misplaced. Relative to the boom years, France clearly suffered major set-backs between 1974 and 1986 but as a member of the 'G7' countries, France is indubitably a leading industrial nation, without mentioning her immense cultural and political heritage.

French firms have had to make substantial adjustments to their operating policies to survive in the extremely competitive world economy, particularly when faced with the threat of Japan and the newly industrialised countries. Increasingly, they have done so without the guiding and shielding arm of the State. Indeed, after a period of enfeeblement and dependence in the late 1940s and 1950s, the French business community has increasingly asserted its independence by open criticism of State interference or by subtle manipulation of policy.

Meanwhile, the State itself grew weaker and has been shown to lack the resources for extensive intervention. The development of the EC has led to increased convergence and an emphasis on common policies. With the 'Single

Market' becoming a reality and with political and monetary union accelerating, there is less and less room for French 'voluntarist' policies of old.

These factors put into perspective recent changes in French government. Edith Cresson replaced Michel Rocard as Prime Minister in May 1991. Her management style is more brusque, her language more colourful but her ministerial team hardly altered nor did government policies in 1991. An EIU report (1991) predicts that:

> the economic policy direction will remain unchanged: preference will go to the model of the neo-liberal social market economy rather than to any full-blooded form of Colbertist intervention.

The forces favouring continuity of policy orientation are likely to prevail. The underlying element of continuity in the role of the State has been to accompany, rather than remodel, the development of the market.

Note
1. By billion (French *milliard*) is understood a thousand million.

References

Aglietta, M. (1987) 'Les outils d'analyse de la grande croissance et de sa crise', *Revue politique et parlementaire*, 931, pp. 41-5

Albertini, J.-M. (1988) *Bilan de l'économie française*, Paris: Editions du Seuil

Arnaud, R. (1987) *Panorama de l'économie française*, Paris: Dunod

Aubert, J. (1982) *L'Environnement économique de l'entreprise*, Paris: Editions d'organisation

Baslé, J. *et al.* (1989) *L'Economie française. Mutations 1975-1990*, Paris: Sirey

Bauchet, P. (1986) *Le Plan dans l'économie française*, Paris: Economica

Birnbaum, P. *et al.* (1978) *La Classe dirigeante française. Dissociation, interpenetration, integration*, Paris: PUF

Bonin, H. (1988) *Histoire économique de la France depuis 1880*, Paris: Masson

Bourdois, J.-H. (1983) 'Trente ans d'essor industriel (1945-1974)', *Les Cahiers français*, 211 (mai-juin), pp. 4-11

Bouvier, J. (1982) 'La crise économique insolite (1974-1979). Divergences des approches' in Braudel, F. & Labrousse, E. (eds.) *Histoire économique et sociale de la France* (Tome IV: 3ème volume), pp. 1577-93, Paris: Hatier

Boyer, R. (1986) *La Théorie de la régulation: une analyse critique*, Paris: La Découverte

Brémond, J. & Brémond, G. (1985) *L'Economie française face aux défis mondiaux*, Paris: Hatier

Carré, J.-J., Dubois, P. & Malinvaud, E. (1984, 3rd ed.) *Abrégé de la croissance française*, Paris: Seuil

Cerny, P.E. (1989) 'From *dirigisme* to deregulation? The case of financial markets' in Godt, P. (ed.) *Policy-Making in France from de Gaulle to Mitterrand*, pp. 142-61, London: Pinter

Cohen, S. S. (1969) *Modern Capitalist Planning: The French Model*, London: Weidenfield & Nicholson

Coquidé, P. & Makarian, C. (1988) 'Salaires: la colère des prolétaires de l'Etat', *Le Point*, 837 (3 octobre), pp. 49-51

Delors, J. (1982) 'France: between reform and counter-reform' in Dahrendorf, R. (ed.) *Europe's Economy in Crisis*, pp. 46-71, London: Weidenfeld & Nicholson

EIU (Economist Intelligence Unit) (1991) *France: Country Report*, no. 2

Estrin, S. & Holmes, P. (1983) *French Planning in Theory and Practice*, London: George Allen and Urwin

Fonteneau, A. & Gubian, A. (1986) 'Comparaison des relances économiques de 1975 et 1981-1982', *Problèmes économiques*, 1,956 (8 janvier), pp. 3-11

Foster, J. B. (1988) 'The fetish of Fordism', *New York Monthly Review*, March, pp. 14-33

Fourastié, J. (1979) *Les Trente Glorieuses: ou la révolution invisible de 1946 à 1975*, Paris: Hachette

Gueslin, A. (1989) *Nouvelle histoire économique de la France contemporaine : 4 – L'Economie ouverte 1948-1990*, Paris : La Découverte

Hall, P. A. (1982) 'Economic planning and the State: the evolution of economic challenge and political response in France' in Zeitlin, M. (ed.) *Political Power and Social Theory*, vol.3 , pp. 175-213, London: JAI Press

Hall, P. A. (1987) 'The evolution of economic policy under Mitterrand' in Ross, G. *et al.* (eds.) *The Mitterrand Experiment*, pp. 54-71, London: Polity Press

Holmes, P. (1987) 'Broken Dreams: economic policy in Mitterrand's France' in Mazey, S. & Newman, M. (eds.) *Mitterrand's France*, pp. 33-55, London: Croom Helm

Holmes, P. & Estrin, S. (1988) 'Planning for modernisation' in Gaffney, J. (ed.) *France and Modernisation,* pp. 110-23, Aldershot: Gower

Hough, J. R. (1982) *The French Economy*, London: Croom Helm

INSEE (1989) *La Croissance retrouvée. Rapport sur les comptes de la nation 1988*, Paris: INSEE

INSEE (1990a) *Annuaire rétrospectif de la France. Séries longues (1948-1988)*, Paris: INSEE

INSEE (1990b) *Vingt ans de comptes nationaux*, Paris: INSEE

INSEE (1990c) *1989: une économie plus forte. Rapport sur les comptes de la nation 1989*, Paris: INSEE

INSEE (1991) *La France à l'épreuve de la turbulence mondiale. Rapport sur les comptes de la nation 1990*, Paris: INSEE

Kondratiev, N. D. (1935) 'The long waves in economic life', *The Review of Economic Statistics*, XVII:6 (November), pp. 105-15

Kuisel, R. F. (1987) 'French Post-War Economic Growth' in Ross, G. *et al.* (eds.) *The Mitterrand Experiment*, pp. 18-31, London: Polity Press

Lecointe, F. *et al.* (1989) 'Salaires, prix et répartition' in Jeanneney, J.-M. (ed.) *L'Economie française depuis 1967*, pp. 137-61, Paris: Seuil

Maarek, G. (1988) 'Le déclin français: mythe et réalités', *Problèmes économiques*, 2.082 (6 juillet), pp. 2-6

Machin, H. (1989) 'Economic planning: policy-making or policy preparation?' in Godt, P. (ed.) *Policy-Making in France from De Gaulle to Mitterrand*, pp. 127-41, London: Pinter

Mermet, G. (1990) *Francoscopie*, Paris: Larousse

Montbrial, T. de (1984) 'Les fondements de la politique économique de Raymond Barre', *Les Cahiers français*, 218 (octobre-décembre), pp. 44-8

Nguyên Duy-Tân, J. (1986) 'Le Commerce extérieur de la France. Environnement international et instruments juridiques', Paris: La Documentation française, *Notes et études documentaires*, no. 4798

Notes bleues (1991) supplément trimestriel, no. 1

OECD (1990) *OECD Economic Studies: France 1989-1990*, Paris: OECD

Parodi, M. (1981) *L'Economie et la société française depuis 1945*, Paris: Armand Colin

Pébereau, M. (1987) *La Politique économique de la France*, Paris: Armand Colin

Petit, P. (1984) 'The origins of French planning: a reappraisal', *Contributions to Political Economy*, 3, pp. 65-84

Petit, P. (1988) 'The Economy and Modernisation: an overview' in Gaffney, J. (ed.) *France and Modernisation*, pp. 44-63, Aldershot: Gower

Rand Smith, W. (1989) ' "We can make Ariane but we can't make washing machines": the State and industrial performance in post-war France' in Howorth, J. & Ross, G. (eds.) *Contemporary France*, vol. 3, pp. 175-202, London: Pinter

Sautter, C. (1982) 'France' in Boltho, A. (ed.) *The European Economy. Growth and Crisis*, pp. 449-71, Oxford: OUP

Seux, D. (1991) 'Budget: les sacrifices de 1992', *Nouvel Economiste*, 804 (12 juin), pp. 10-11

Stoffaës, C. (1989) 'Industrial policy and the State: from industry to enterprise' in Godt, P. (ed.) *Policy-Making in France from de Gaulle to Mitterrand*, pp. 105-26, London: Pinter

Vesperini, J.-P. (1985) *L'Economie de la France de la crise de mai 1968 aux résultats de l'expérience socialiste*, Paris: Economica

Vignon, J. (1984) 'Le Delorisme en économie', *Les Cahiers français*, 218 (octobre-décembre), pp. 60-8

Wise, M. (1989) 'France and European Unity' in Aldrich, R. & Connell, J. (eds.) *France in World Politics*, pp. 35-73, London: Routledge

2
Industrial policy and industrial development in France

INTRODUCTION

Industrial policy is often equated with government intervention. Yet industrial policy is a more complex and subtle affair than simple, direct intervention in particular companies.

This is because, firstly, all macro-economic policies have effects at company level, whether it be fiscal policy, monetary policy, foreign trade policy, energy policy and so forth. Secondly, national (and increasingly EC) legislation in areas as diverse as competition policy, environmental issues, salary agreements and health and safety rulings all condition the operating environment of companies. Thirdly, the availability or non-availability of funds and financial support (investment grants, tax-breaks, subsidised loans, etc.) impact on the corporate sector. Fourthly, public procurement provides the livelihood of many private firms. Fifthly, significant amounts of research are carried out in institutions attached or affiliated to government. Finally, provision of infrastructures (such as roads, railways and telecommunication systems) as well as of education and vocational training usually fall within the remit of the State. For all these reasons, industrial policies – or sometimes just the effects of policy making on industry – form a crucial topic for those concerned with the practical functioning of firms.

Because of the many ways in which public administrations can frame industrial policy, a large number of approaches to industrial policy making are possible, ranging from the deliberate and open to the disguised or inadvertent. Given the multiplicity of ways of framing industrial policy, Bellon and Bandt (1988, pp. 840–1) have argued that:

Tous les Etats ont une ou des politiques industrielles. Parfois, ils le font sans le savoir, comme Monsieur Jourdain faisait de la prose.

Every State formulates one or more industrial policies. Sometimes they do so without realising it, like Monsieur Jourdain speaking prose. (In Moliere's *Le Bourgeois Gentilhomme*).

They exemplify their argument by listing the different modes through which major 'liberal' countries support their industries. In the case of the USA, it is mainly by large-scale public procurement (especially on defence spending) and by spending on research and development. Among the means preferred by Japan are exports promotion through the Ministry of International Trade and Industry, protection of home markets and incentives for rapid technology transfer. Germany is characterised by structured State-industry relations, regional government intervention as well as by financial help to small firms. The tendency in France has been to foster direct State-industry links. This has given France a 'high profile' industrial policy as compared to her neighbours.

This 'high profile' helps explain why France has a reputation as the home of the interventionist State and why the French are defensive about that reputation. The reality is more complex. If the criterion for measuring interventionism is the volume of State aids to industry, EC statistics show that France is close to the European average. The Commission of the European Communities has published two surveys (1989, 1990) on State aids within EC member countries. While the surveys contain caveats on accuracy related to the inherent difficulties of data collection, they are the best sources available.

Over the 1981-6 period, in terms of total outlay, Italy gave most in State aids (first estimated at 27 billion ECU, later revised to 19.6 billions), followed by Germany (19.1 billion ECU), France in third place (16.7 billion ECU) and the UK in fourth (9.4 billion ECU). However, total aids as a percentage of GDP were 2.7 per cent in the case of France, putting her fifth among EC10 countries and at a level marginally below the EC10 average of 3 per cent. Luxemburg and Italy were the highest, at around 6 per cent. Britain (1.8 per cent), the Netherlands (1.5 per cent) and Denmark (1.3 per cent) were the lowest. Over the 1986-8 period, some changes occurred with the highest and the lowest spenders, namely Italy, the UK and Denmark, reducing aid levels.

These statistics indicate that France is in an *intermediate* position in relation to EC neighbours as regards levels of State aids. However in the distribution of aids, France appears to be distinctive. French State aids have been targeted at a narrower range of industries than in most other EC States. Over the period 1981-6, 41 per cent of total aids were highly targeted, but this figure fell to 25 per cent between 1986-8 (Commission of the European Communities, 1990, p. 30).

Accordingly, the thesis in this chapter will be that France's industrial policies are distinctive but more limited in scope than is sometimes assumed. Further, since 1983, 'traditional' interventionism has been in decline. This was due partly to its failures and costs, partly to the increasingly hostile attitude of the French business community to State intervention and partly to increased vigilance from Brussels regarding State aids (see also pp. 137-40).

The next section will deal with the motives and principles of industrial policy. Later sections will discuss its practice in France, firstly by giving an historical overview of the political element in French industrial policies and then going on to a more detailed account of major aspects of industrial policy making and their impact on industrial development. The aims will be to present the content of French industrial policies, to explain major turning-points and to evaluate the impact of industrial policy on the development and performance of French industry.

THE PRINCIPLES OF INDUSTRIAL POLICY MAKING

Types of industrial policy

In his survey of industrial policy making, Grant (1983) listed four schools of thought: the 'pure' market, the social market, selective intervention and Communist approaches. In reality, these schools represent a continuum, with overlaps possible between adjacent schools but, for the sake of exposition, each type will be presented here as a separate case.

The 'pure' market
According to proponents of the 'pure' market, market mechanisms are the most efficient form of resource allocation. For them, policy making will always lead to interventions which deform and impair market mechanisms. In consequence, they argue that industrial policy making is to be strenuously avoided. In this ideal form, the 'pure' market approach is clearly impractical, due to the long list of State policies already given which impact on industry. In practice, this liberal current aims to reduce State involvement to the bare minimum. Thatcherism with its ideology of 'rolling back the frontiers of the State', not only in industry but in health and education provision, was a prime example of this tendency.

The social market
Advocates of a social market can be found in most political groups. They too argue that market mechanisms favour efficient resource allocation but they believe that the weight of the modern State inevitably influences the economy. For this school of thought, the correct response is to accept the inevitability of State influence and formulate coherent policy within the strict confines of institutional and legislative frameworks. Monetary and fiscal policy become the principal policy instruments and are designed with the aim of providing a favourable operating environment for the whole of the corporate sector. In the jargon, these are 'horizontal' policies. They are deemed to be neutral since they impact equally on all firms; market mechanisms are in principle preserved.

However, such policies appear neutral only because geographic considerations are omitted. The population of firms whose environment has been 'equalised' is usually defined in terms of the nation state. Once one looks below or above the level of the State, the picture changes. Viewed from the international level, there are differences in the treatment received by firms of different nations in terms of monetary and fiscal policy. These lead to inequalities and market distortions. For this reason, monetary union and fiscal harmonisation have become important issues in the creation of a genuine Single European Market. Further, at regional levels, a 'neutral' policy may simply enhance the existing opportunities of firms in prosperous areas and exacerbate the current problems of firms in declining regions. Nonetheless, governments of different political persuasions in many countries have accepted this approach as the best compromise.

Selective intervention

Selective intervention involves organised co-operation between State and industry. Particular sectors, indeed firms, are singled out for special treatment. Clearly, the principle of 'neutrality' is laid to one side. The distortion of market forces is usually justified by arguments related either to overriding national needs or to enhanced economic rationality. This approach has been implemented frequently but not exclusively by left-wing governments. In the process of selective intervention, particular sectors or firms are promoted, their resources are augmented and their market position bolstered. In the jargon, this involves the implementation of 'vertical' or targeted policies. Yet even where such policies succeed in reinforcing the stature of their targets, there is always a down-side, namely, the targeting of the few is to the exclusion of the many. Moreover, the selection procedure itself is delicate. Identifying the beneficiaries of State aid is hazardous, as will be seen below.

Communist approaches

Communist approaches constitute the fourth 'school'. In the 'Gosplan' model pertaining in the ex-Soviet Union and Eastern Europe during most of the post-war period, decisions on the allocation of resources were made by State bodies. The major difference between the centrally planned economy and selective intervention is the scale of intervention. In addition, the former is coercive whereas the latter is usually co-operative. Both stress the exercise of rational choice by the State over the role of market forces. In practice, poor information flows, blinkered ministerial and factory bureaucracies, inadequate distribution methods and inattention to genuine needs created a massively inefficient system in Eastern Europe that lay in ruins by the end of the 1980s.

In the case of France, industrial policy has frequently been considered as *'l'expression de la rationalité collective'* (Morvan, 1983), yet this does not imply any particular ideological affiliation. Political leaders across the political spectrum from de Gaulle to Mitterrand have pointed to structural weaknesses in the French economy and to deficiencies in the operation of market forces.

The solution generally proposed has been *volontarisme*. In French industrial policy discussion, the term *volontarisme* refers to top-down initiatives taken by the State to correct perceived market failures. Partnership between the State and public or private firms has been considered the means to push French industry forward on the world stage. This belief in the State as a rational arbitrator underpinned the planning process (analysed on pp. 9-16). During most of the post-war period, this belief manifested itself in a predilection for selective intervention in industry. However, intervention was not limited to national plans. Indeed, most of the instances of direct State intervention in industry have occurred outside of the framework of the plan.

Criteria for selective intervention

Stoleru (1969) cites five criteria typically used to justify intervention, namely:
  (a) the 'indispensable' nature of the sector or firm;
  (b) its size;
  (c) its potential;
  (d) its prestige;
  (e) its military importance.
All of these are apparently worthy criteria. In reality, they present problems of implementation.

A case can be prepared for almost any industry or firm as being 'indispensable'. By the very fact of their existence, firms provide employment and create wealth. On the other hand, it is impossible to achieve a consensus on industries or firms that are dispensable. Government can rarely afford to impede any form of wealth and job creation. Industries such as tobacco and arms are cases in point. Yet if all existing firms are somehow essential, then the criterion of indispensability fails to discriminate between those firms worthy of State involvement and those which are unworthy.

The size of an industry or company often indicates its importance within a national economy. The car industry is an example. Regardless of political complexion, governments have rarely stood on the side-lines when a major national car company has run into difficulties. This has been equally true in Britain (with BMC/BL/Austin-Rover), in the USA (Chrysler) and in France (Renault).

Yet this criterion has its own problems of implementation. Firstly, there is the question of the unit of measurement. Should size be considered in terms of turnover, profitability, value added, exports earnings or employment? Where each unit of measurement points to the same conclusion, there is no difficulty. But in the 1970s and 1980s, some major employers with massive turnovers also made large losses (e.g. in cars, steel, textiles). Hence the units of measurement can point to conflicting conclusions. This creates controversy and ambiguity over strategy formulation. Secondly, there is the problem of ongoing structural change. The major industries (by size) of the nineteenth century are not the same as those of today. Coal, steel and textiles have declined in relative importance. Electronics, information technology and bio-technology represent growth sectors. A significant problem for industrial policy makers is to decide whether to reverse, halt, palliate or accelerate structural change of this kind.

A major trend in industrial policy has been the attempt to 'pick winners'. By assessing the potential for growth of various sectors and firms, policy makers hope to select today the fittest and the best firms of tomorrow. But as with any type of prediction, this is a risky affair. Developments in science and technology can provide valuable pointers, but deciding precisely which of a range of firms is best placed to fully exploit the new opportunities is much harder. The exercise assumes that the State has the expertise to 'pick winners'. However, it may have no more – and in some cases may have less – expertise than that of the financial sector. The information available to both may be equally imperfect, either because the firms in question have not made their financial and market position clear or simply because forecasting the future is always a hazardous activity. In consequence, public funds may go not to the firms which are best placed in technical and marketing terms but to the ones having the best understanding of and connections with the State apparatus.

Methodological difficulties are compounded because the criterion of potential is often confused with the criterion of prestige. Terms such as 'precision engineering' (as undertaken by Rolls-Royce, Jaguar, etc.) and 'high-technology' exercise a strong fascination. The terms themselves are often close to value judgements. Prestige is also frequently linked to expressions of national pride. These 'sub-texts' may be justifiable when openly presented. Investment in prestige may be desired as an end in itself. But it should not be dressed up as economic rationality. A major example of prestige taking precedence over economic rationality was Concorde.

The final criterion is the military importance of particular sectors or firms. There are probably fewer difficulties in implementing this criterion but for reasons of military and electoral strategy, democratic governments are disinclined to publicise State aid to the arms industry. In the USA, the term industrial policy is rarely used by politicians. However, the size of US spending on military research and development influences the prosperity of a large cross-section of American industry. In the ex-Soviet Union, excessive spending on the military has retarded the development of the economy as a whole. That military spending takes its toll on an economy is clear too from the counter-examples of Germany and Japan. As the principal losers of the Second World War, they were subsequently debarred from significant military expenditure. The compulsory reorientation of their economic options away from military towards civil purposes partly explains their post-war economic success. Yet it should be acknowledged also that defence spending has pushed out the frontiers of science and technology. This is clearly not because *all* major discoveries have come from the arms race. However, major new technologies of the twentieth century – electronics, information technology and the nuclear industry – were all initially exploited and developed for their military potential.

In its handling of these criteria, industrial policy making in France has been fairly representative of its genre. As will be seen, reasons for particular policy decisions often resulted from a fudge. Criteria of importance, size, potential, prestige and military impact have been permutated in the apparent belief that no one criterion can withstand close inspection but that some combination will carry conviction. The notion of preserving 'national champions' has frequently brought together the different criteria in one 'compelling' synthesis. Thus a firm like Sacilor (steel) could be considered indispensable because of its place in the economy, the size of its exports and its role as a major employer despite making massive losses for many years.

An alternative approach to the targeting of firms has been to work backwards from the problems of implementation and consider first what is possible in practical terms. Having made an inventory of their capability for intervention, of the instruments at their disposal, policy makers select those firms with whom the State can establish a visibly successful working relationship. Some firms may be too small, others too independent and so can be ruled out. Something akin to this process has occurred in France. The French State seems to have sought partners which appeal to it firstly on functional grounds and only secondly in terms of the criteria outlined above. In a sense, this prejudices the issues. But it also puts a stop to the infinite regression whereby almost any firm might be presented as a candidate for intervention.

This brings us to the key issue. Knowing *how* the French State chose to intervene selectively only gives a partial insight into the process of industrial policy formulation. The main question is *why* it intervened. An important factor in the process was that until the 1980s a wide political consensus considered that industrial development could not be consigned to the vagaries of market forces. Bandt (1987, p. 49) indicates that the major hypothesis underpinning French industrial policy was the existence of fundamental structural weaknesses in French industry. There was a deep-seated belief that French industry could not succeed on its own. Partnership with the State would be its salvation. The State had a duty to promote development.

These propositions may be questioned. They may relate more to value judgements and excessive expectations on the part of the French. But the fact remains that by the second half of the twentieth century, the State had become too inextricably meshed with French industry to free itself easily. At times of crisis and industrial collapse the help of the State was repeatedly solicited. It became common for employers and unions alike to put pressure on the State to bail out collapsing companies. But the State also saw itself as an entrepreneur having the means to launch major new projects, a tradition that goes back to Colbert in the seventeenth century. By limiting its intervention to defined industries, it could hope to preserve economic stability and impart momentum to other sectors by 'knock-on' effects. At the same time, this approach preserved a capitalist, free-market system. Anything else was considered by a majority of voters and politicians as impractical or ideologically unacceptable. Only from the mid-1980s did this predilection for intervention diminish markedly in scale.

The remainder of this chapter follows a two-fold approach. The next section gives a chronological overview of the development of industrial policy. This will allow clarification of the *political* dimensions of industrial policy. In later sections, a thematic approach is adopted to pick up *economic* interrelationships.

POLITICAL DIMENSIONS OF FRENCH INDUSTRIAL POLICY MAKING

State intervention in industry has often been the translation into practice of an ideology of national independence. As such, it represents a central element of continuity in post-war industrial policy making. Examples include increased investment in France's nuclear industry subsequent to de Gaulle's decision to take France out of NATO and to accelerate development of the French *force de frappe* (nuclear strike capability). In the 1960s, de Gaulle promoted the French computer industry because the American government refused the sale of information technology for use in the nuclear programme. Giscard favoured massive investment in nuclear-based electricity because of French dependence on oil from the Middle East. The major aim of nationalisation under Mitterrand has again been the reinforcement of 'national champions'.

But if continuities can be discerned so too can turning-points. Changes in policy resulted from changes in government and in circumstance. Distinguishing turning-points involves a division into historical periods linked to political changes. Following Baleste (1986), four major periods of industrial policy can be distinguished between 1945 and 1990.

The era of protectionism: 1945-1958

The duration of the Fourth Republic (1946-1958) has come to represent a transitional period. During those years, political life was marked by instability and the search for new directions.

The need to reconstruct after the war encouraged intervention in industry. The section on economic planning in Chapter 1 indicated that in the 1940s the institutional means to achieve efficient intervention was the planning process. Initially, basic industries were targeted for State aid, namely coal, steel, cement, transport, electricity and agricultural machinery. Major companies in those sectors benefited from State loans and grants. In 1947, the State financed half of industrial investment (Morvan, 1983). The State also rationed available bank finance; only major companies were eligible.

These interventions resulted in distortions in the finance market which became evident once the State withdrew from the sector in the 1950s (Messerlin, 1987). The financial sector found itself unable to cope with the needs of industry during 1950-5. However, by the second half of the decade, financial institutions were able to adapt.

During this period, import quotas and high tariff barriers prevented foreign goods entering French markets to any large extent. These State-led measures were preferred by industry as a means of protecting their markets, but they also had perverse effects. Far from strengthening French industry, they weakened it. Competitive pressures were weak because of the limited impact of foreign entrants. Among French firms, there was a tendency towards collusive behaviour, themes that will be discussed in detail in Chapter 4. Closed markets also tended to limit the horizons of French companies to France and to French colonies. Colonial markets tended to be less demanding than European or American markets. For these reasons, French firms often produced lower quality and less competitive goods than those of industrialised neighbours. All this was to change.

The industrial imperative: 1958-1973

The setting-up of the Fifth Republic in 1958 greatly enhanced political stability in France. General de Gaulle was its architect and first President. During the 10 years and four months of his presidency he left his mark on every aspect of French policy making. When de Gaulle resigned in 1969, his former Prime Minister, Georges Pompidou, succeeded him as President and continued with the major elements of his predecessor's industrial policies.

X A transition to greater free trade was effected in 1957 by the creation of the European Economic Community. France also participated in GATT talks to facilitate greater international trade. A period of real if slow adjustment had begun.

Industrial policy in the period was increasingly designed to improve the overall competitiveness of French industry. Measures of both a 'vertical' and 'environmental' nature were introduced. Fiscal policy was redesigned to give more incentives to corporate investments and to exports. Company contributions to national insurance were lightened. The State maintained wage controls until 1968.

'Vertical' measures included sectoral plans. The *Convention sidérurgie* for steel in 1966 and the *Convention construction navale* for ship building in 1967, were instances of the will to safeguard and promote major employment industries. The State gave considerable assistance to a limited number of long-established firms. A policy of encouraging concentration was adopted. This far-reaching aspect of French industrial policy making of the period will receive detailed treatment on pp. 56-9.

X Gaullist ambitions for national independence and prestige gave impetus to the so-called *grands projets*. These were long-term initiatives in high-tech growth sectors. Their end results included Concorde (supersonic plane), Airbus (passenger aircraft), Ariane (satellite launcher) and the TGV (high-speed train). State aid also went to the information technology industry (via the *Plan Calcul* in 1966) and the nuclear industry. Major research centres such as the Atomic Energy Commission (CEA), the National Centre for Space Studies (CNES) and the National Centre for Scientific Research (CNRS) were established or augmented. The underlying aim was to modernise French technology (Davie, 1987).

Industrial policy in this period, like the Roman god Janus, had two faces. One face looked to the past in its attention to traditional sectors and the other looked to the future in its promotion of new technologies. At one level, these characteristics presented a certain even-handedness in policy making which made sense in the buoyant economic climate of the time. However, they were to be the source of incoherence in the 1970s, once industrial problems became severe.

Industrial redeployment: 1974-1981

After Pompidou's death, Valéry Giscard d'Estaing became President in 1974. The new occupant of the Elysée Palace made significant changes to policy for two reasons. Giscard, though a right-wing politician, wished to distinguish himself from his predecessors. Secondly, economic crisis demanded urgent action. Falling corporate profitability due to soaring oil and raw material prices in the 1970s and decreased competitiveness in a context of increased challenges from developing countries necessitated modifications of industrial policy. From the Gaullist emphasis on military independence, Giscard was forced to find solutions to energy dependence in particular (see also pp. 23-4 above) and economic dependence in general.

An analysis frequently put forward in the period was the notion of France occupying an intermediate position in an international division of labour. It was thought that changing industrial structures and technological development were producing a three-tier world economy. At one extreme were labour-intensive producers, usually situated in the Third World, selling raw materials and basic goods. At the other extreme were the technological leaders, principally the USA, Japan and Germany, specialising in high value added, capital-intensive processes. France was considered to be midway between the two poles. In a rapidly changing environment, she risked losing ever more ground to the leaders and becoming more technologically dependent on them. Meanwhile fast developers such as Korea, Hong Kong, Singapore and Taiwan threatened to overtake. The conclusion drawn was that France needed to increase specialisation in high-technology industry. But her relative size and wealth precluded an across-the-board strategy. Under Giscard, French industrial policy put the emphasis on a *politique des créneaux*: this was a 'niche' strategy promoting the development of a limited number of 'winners' in high-priority sub-sectors.

The industries to benefit from this policy were the nuclear energy industry, the defence industry (including aeronautics and electronics), telecommunications and rail. Large State subsidies were bestowed on a small number of companies in those sectors. Reporting on the unpublished Hannoun investigation, Labarde (1979) indicated that in 1976 six firms received 50 per cent of total subsidies to industry. They were the CGE (telecommunications), Empain-Schneider (installations for nuclear energy), Thomson-CSF (military electronics), CII-Honeywell-Bull (computers), SNIAS and Dassault (both military aviation).

There was a certain logic to this style of industrial policy. In each case, firms were in close partnership with the State. The State had developed interlocks with producers by links at almost every stage of the production cycle, running through from research and development, to design, manufacture and sale.

In telecommunications, the *Direction générale des telecommunications* (now France-Télécom), operating within the French Ministry for Post and Telecommunications (PTT), acted like a private enterprise. In the 1970s to 1980s, it was responsible for overseeing R&D, laying down equipment specifications, purchasing telecommunication systems and operating them. These ranged from telephone exchanges to satellites.

Likewise in the Defence Ministry, the *Délégation générale à l'armement* (DGA), being responsible for procurement, undertook not only the supervision of industrial contracts but was also at the 'sharp end' of strategic decision making on defence.

Similar structures were developed for the nuclear industry. The space industry is centred around the CNES, which works for both civil and military applications. Satellite systems are essential both for the armed forces and the PTT, hence the French State financed two-thirds of the development costs of Ariane, the satellite launching system. In each of these cases, the administrative apparatus shaped the organisation and development of the industries with whom it dealt.

State-industry interlocks were reinforced by personnel movements between administrative bodies and private companies – so-called *pantouflage*. For example, Dechery (1986) noted that two former DGA chiefs – André Martre and Hugues de l'Estoile – took top positions in French defence companies. The first headed up Aérospatiale, the second become the 'number 2' at Dassault. (The theme of *pantouflage* will be developed further on p. 165.)

In return for their services to the State, 'partner' firms received subsidies, with research often being financed by public funds. The French State also provided them with reliable, 'cost-plus' and therefore profitable markets.

But public procurement contracts were not limited to France. Products such as nuclear power stations, telephone exchanges, fighter planes, etc. were also marketed to foreign governments by producer firms with State help. Such export sales require government authorisation and government to government contacts at the highest levels. They can touch a delicate nerve. Subsequent to French sales of nuclear technology to Iraq in the late 1970s, Israel bombed an Iraqi nuclear power station. Further, deals are usually clinched only where the seller can mobilise large, long-term loans at attractive interest rates. Here too the involvement of national states is the norm. French governments backed their industrialists by providing export guarantees and underwriting financial arrangements. After the oil price hikes of the mid-1970s, the exports drive was spearheaded by this State-industry partnership. Government sponsored sales of construction projects and arms helped pay the oil bill (see pp. 85-7 and p. 115).

Thus the State-industry partnership led to successes in particular niches. Beneficiary firms increased their markets and contributed to a healthier balance of trade. But with the French State as the first and largest purchaser, the market of these firms was guaranteed. Arguably, the international competitiveness of beneficiary firms declined due to their cosseted position. Nor did all targeted sectors develop equally. Information technology was poorly served with a lack of continuity in ownership and counter-productive State interference (Zarader, 1983). Giscard's rhetoric of fostering a more liberal economic system in which the State played a more limited role can therefore be questioned (Green, 1985).

With 'knock-on' benefits being limited, the objection arose that industrial policy encouraged the creation of an *industrie à deux vitesses* (a two-speed industry). A fast lane was reserved for a limited number of State assisted companies while the others, particularly small- and medium-sized firms, plodded along in the slow lane (Mazier, 1983; Savy & Valeyre, 1982).

The aim of national independence led to short-sightedness. For example, the development of the SECAM television transmission system shot the French consumer electronics industry in the foot. In the short term, a national standard that was incompatible with the widely used PAL system protected French industry but in the long term it increased its costs, depressed its competitiveness and merely postponed the day of reckoning with highly efficient Japanese producers (Levavic, 1986).

Major industries such as steel, mechanical engineering and textiles experienced major decline (Dahmani, 1983; Dacier *et al.*, 1985). France, like her neighbours, experienced substantial deindustrialisation in the late 1970s. Factory closures and massive redundancies were the order of the day. Regions such as the Nord-Pas de Calais and Lorraine, whose industrialisation dates from the first industrial revolution, were severely and disproportionately hit. Their industrial base was concentrated in those 'traditional' sectors which had become least competitive: textiles, coal and steel. If a high rate of bankruptcy and closure was the most extreme result of the recession, the phenomenon of reduced profit margins also applied to the vast majority of firms. Indeed, during the late 1970s, the State imposed higher *charges sociales* on firms (national insurance contributions). The corporate sector bore a greater part of the costs of the oil shock than households, so further undermining their weakened financial position. Policy of the period did little to resolve the wider industrial crisis.

Modernisation: 1981-1990

The Socialists in opposition had frequently criticised the medium- range policy adopted under Giscard as being too limited in scope to overhaul French industrial structures. They also criticised industrial policy under de Gaulle, Pompidou and Giscard for its lack of continuity, its inefficient usage of State subsidies and public procurement and its insufficient investment in research. According to this argument, industrial policy was responsible for technology gaps filled by dependence on the USA. Clearly, such criticism had political motivation. In fact, the industrial policies of the Right from 1958-1981 had been consistent in aiming to emancipate France from technological and economic dependence.

On arrival in office in 1981, the Socialist government drew up a long-term programme of industrial modernisation to overcome the perceived defects of previous administrations. Their industrial policy subdivides into three broad strategies, with privatisation under the Chirac government constituting a further element.

Their first strategy was intervention on a massive scale, involving a wave of nationalisations in 1981-2. A whole political rhetoric was attached to the nationalisation programme. Nationalisation was seen as a way of breaking with the failure and injustices of capitalism. The commitment to nationalise was contained in the *Programme Commun* of 1972, drawn up jointly by the Socialist and Communist parties. The broad left alliance promised to bring under public ownership a number of industries that were considered to be 'essential' to national prosperity. The candidates for nationalisation were the firms which had benefited from a long-standing partnership with the State. Subsidies and public procurement contracts meant that the prosperity of firms such as the CGE, Thomson-Brandt and Dassault flowed directly from the State. For the Socialists, this justified nationalisation, which became a way of 'socialising' the investments of the State. In principle, nationalisation would also lead to more efficient management and a more socially just distribution of the wealth created by nationalised firms. However, when in 1981 a left-wing government had the opportunity to nationalise, the economic climate had drastically altered since the heady days of the *Programme Commun*, which predated the recession. The real motivation for nationalisation became economic necessity while the results of the operation proved unexpected. Detailed consideration of the economic and financial aspects of nationalisation will be developed in the section on nationalisation as a rescue operation later in this chapter.

When nationalisation was discovered not to be a panacea, a second industrial strategy, based on sectoral plans, was implemented between 1982-5. In this phase, the government set about overhauling industrial structures. This involved redefining the *métiers* (specialisations) of the nationalised companies and redrawing the boundaries between them.

The justification for the operation was to construct coherent *filières*. The theory of *filières* met with considerable approval in Socialist circles, perhaps not least because it contradicted Giscard's policy. Whereas Giscard had put the emphasis on *créneaux*, on a limited niche strategy, *filières* were conceived as production systems running the entire length of an industry or sector. For example, the French electronics industry had concentrated on assembly processes but the *filière* was incomplete, since it was lacking in the manufacture of chips and components. The aim was to fill in the gaps. This would ensure national self-sufficiency – a Gaullist theme which by the 1980s was so widespread and familiar as to have lost party-political connotations. During his period as Industry Minister, Chevènement attempted to implement this policy (Holton, 1986).

In practice, *filière* theory turned out to be another variant on the theme of industrial concentration by vertical integration. Modernisation involved detaching subsidiaries from State-owned parent companies and attaching them to a different nationalised company, in order to achieve a more efficient 'fit'.

This restructuring programme benefited from industrial logic, but paid little attention to market competition. After nationalisation, the management of CGE, the telecommunications giant, succeeded in achieving a long-standing goal which had eluded them as a private sector firm, namely the acquisition of a monopoly position in France (Cohen and Bauer, 1985, pp. 200–3). Once privatised in 1986, they retained their monopoly. The steel giants Sacilor and Usinor also merged to form a single company. A tradition of promoting two 'national champions' per major sector was abandoned. In principle, this policy had maintained some element of competition between rivals. With the constitution of quasi-monopolies as a matter of State policy, even this degree of competition disappeared. The official justification was that the French market could only sustain one giant per sector and the competitiveness of that giant would be tested in any international competition for contracts.

Sectoral plans aiming to benefit private firms were also drawn up. The *Plan Machine-outil* failed to halt the decline of the machine-tool industry (Cohen and Bauer, 1985). However the *Plan Textile* proved a more innovative and useful measure. Firms were offered reductions in their *charge sociales* in exchange for commitments to maintain or increase staffing (Dubois, 1988). The interesting feature of this measure was its combination of an environmental or 'horizontal' approach within a single sector. Sectoral intervention had not yet disappeared, but was adopting a new complexion. French industrial policy was moving away from direct intervention on a selective basis, to a broad-based 'environmental' approach.

In 1986, with a change of government came a change of industrial policy. The stress was placed on an environmental approach and on privatisation. The right-wing government of Jacques Chirac set out to privatise 65 State-owned companies. The economic and financial details and the broader consequences will be discussed in the section on privatisation and the new liberal agenda later in this chapter. The aim here is to indicate the extent to which industrial policy decisions sprang from political preferences. After the Socialist nationalisations of 1981-2 and the success of Conservative privatisations in Britain, for Chirac, privatisation was as much a political as an economic programme. Traditionally, the Right has put greater emphasis on market mechanisms than the Left, thus the liberal policies of Chirac are entirely in character. But privatisation was also a bold way of distinguishing the Right from the Left during election campaigns. The cost and problems of nationalisation had made it unpopular. Privatisation was envisaged as a popular strategy. Whatever the political rhetoric around *capitalisme populaire*, buying and selling shares in the privatised companies was lucrative. This, together with cutting taxes from the proceeds of sales, promised to enhance Chirac's electoral appeal in the 1988 presidential elections.

In fact, Mitterrand was re-elected. But on their return to government in 1988, the Socialists under Prime Minister Rocard made no attempt to renationalise. Interventionist policies declined further in importance. The ambitions of the State have been curtailed by three factors: previous failures, financial constraints and EC rulings. EC competition policy has progressively become more constraining. State aids to industry have come under increasing scrutiny by Brussels as giving unfair advantage and distorting competition. (These themes are developed on pp. 137-40.) In consequence, Rocard, like Chirac, has placed the emphasis squarely on the environment in which firms operate. Environmental policies thus constitute the third major industrial strategy of the socialists in the 1980s.

The major instruments at the State's disposal have been reductions in corporate taxation and in *charges sociales* (for details, see p. 38 above). These reductions, in the context of a more favourable world economic environment, contributed to industrial recovery. Investment rose by 5 per cent in 1986 and 1987 and by 13 per cent in 1988. Industrial production, which had stagnated between 1980 and 1986, increased by 5.4 per cent in 1988 and 4.7 per cent in 1989 (*Notes bleues*, 1991). The decade of the 1980s finished with a welcome bout of expansion. Environmental policies have served to accompany the expansion. However, with the worsening of the economic climate at the start of the 1990s, new challenges lie ahead.

In summary, French industrial policy has changed markedly in character. It has moved away from 'vertical' policies and selective intervention towards 'environmental' policies. Not only is this a distinctive reorientation of industrial policy, but it has occurred through greater cross-party consensus on the needs of industry and on industrial development than ever before. By the end of the 1980s, it seemed that industry was no longer a political football.

Having given an overview of the impact of political choices on French industrial policy, we turn next to detailed consideration of the interrelationship between industrial policy and industrial development.

INDUSTRIAL CONCENTRATION AND THE GOAL OF 'CRITICAL MASS'

In the 1960s and 1970s, the creation and promotion of large firms had a central position in French industrial policy. With the announcement in the Fifth Plan of 1966 of the intention to create two industrial giants per major sector, it became official policy to encourage and aid industrial concentration by company mergers.

The process of industrial concentration involves firms growing larger in order to maximise production efficiency and capture greater market share. Large companies are capable of achieving greater economies of scale and greater economies of scope. Both of these concepts require commentary.

Greater size can confer economies of *scale* since an increase in the size of production plants and/or production runs reduces unit costs and increases profitability. Economies of scale can be achieved by *horizontal* concentration (i.e. by increasing productive capacity in broadly the same processes) or by *vertical* concentration (i.e. by investing in activities which are upstream or downstream of a firm's original activity). In general, economies of scale relate to production processes within an industry. In some sectors – such as chemicals, telecommunications, information technology – satisfactory levels of profitability are closely tied to achieving 'critical mass', by which is understood a high market share and a high volume of output.

Economies of *scope* arise from size-related factors that go beyond production processes and exist in areas such as finance, distribution, research and development, computerisation and other central services. Examples include the fact that the large firm finds it easier to raise finance than the small firm and generally can do so at lower rates of interest. The large firm can develop sophisticated sales and distribution systems to cover its wide range of products which a limited product range could not support. Similarly, advantages can be gained in R&D etc.

The French State was bent on creating industrial giants because, in the 1960s, French industry was perceived to be lacking 'critical mass'. There were elements of truth in this interpretation. Even the largest French firms were considerably smaller than European or especially American rivals. Stoffaës (1989, p. 110) points out that in 1966 not a single French company figured among the top 15 firms in the world in sectors such as steel, chemicals, pharmaceuticals, paper making, textiles, the food industry or electrical engineering. The policy of the period was thus directed towards creating firms of international stature which would be capable of defending home markets and competing successfully abroad.

In many industries, a gradual concentration process can be traced back to pre-war or even nineteenth century beginnings. But during the 1960s and 1970s, the process accelerated markedly (see Table 2.1). The largest 500 French firms almost doubled in economic importance between 1958 and 1977.

Table 2.1 Industrial concentration in France: 1958-1977 (Equity of France's 500 largest firms as a percentage of equity of total French industry)

Year	Top 500 (in %)	Year	Top 500 (in %)
1958	31.4	1969	38.5
1959	34.9	1970	46.0
1960	31.1	1971	40.8
1961	33.6	1972	54.2
1962	35.0	1973	57.4
1963	32.2	1974	57.9
1964	29.8	1975	57.0
1967	36.2	1976	59.0
1968	37.5	1977	61.0

Source: Gilly, J. and Morin, F. (1981), 'Les groupes industriels en France: concentration du système productif depuis 1945', Paris: La Documentation française, *Notes et études documentaires*, nos. 4605-6, p.27

Government legislation encouraged the concentration process. Stoffaës (1989, p. 111) pointed out that a 1965 bill allowed firms to take inflation into account when re-evaluating assets. They could set aside greater amounts for depreciation and reduce corporation tax. The accruing tax advantages were a major motivation for mergers.

The concentration process resulted in the creation of a number of major firms. Ugine-Kuhlmann (metals) was the result of a merger in 1966, as was Thomson-Brandt (electronics). In the aeronautics sector, 1967 saw the merger of Dassault and Breguet. In 1968, the steel firms Sidelor and Wendel merged.

By the 1970s, a smaller number of companies were involved in the concentration process. The major firms were becoming even larger. In 1972, Pechiney-Ugine-Kuhlmann (later called PUK, then Pechiney) was formed as was Saint-Gobain-Pont à Mousson. (The first produced non-ferrous metals and chemicals; the second glass, building materials, mechanical engineering products.) In 1974, Berliet merged with Saviem (trucks), Agache-Willot took over Boussac Frères (textiles), Peugeot merged with Citroën and the combine later went on to purchase Chrysler-Europe. With fewer firms being involved, the process had entered a phase of 'super concentration'.

The result of the process has been that levels of concentration now vary markedly between industrial sectors. Concentration (as measured by the combined 1987 turnover of the leading four companies per sector) is high in coal, gas, electricity, water, steel, aeronautics, cars, arms, information technology, artificial and synthetic fibres and rubber but is low in most other sectors (INSEE, 1990). By the early 1980s, world-class French companies had appeared in a number of sectors. These include Elf-Aquitaine (oil), Renault and Peugeot (cars), Michelin (tyres), Usinor and Sacilor (steel), Pechiney (aluminium), Bouygues (construction), CGE (electrical equipment) and Saint-Gobain (glass and insulating materials). Thus 'critical mass' was achieved in the production of many intermediate and capital goods but small- and medium-sized enterprises (SMEs) have continued to predominate in a number of consumer goods sectors.

Concentration was not, however, an unmitigated success. The merger policy produced structural distortions. The process of creating two 'national champions' (e.g. Renault and Peugeot, Usinor and Sacilor) per sector led to a sharing of markets which distorted competition. Such inconsistencies between the concentration policy and competition policy will be developed on p. 133.

The emphasis on large size was to the detriment of SMEs and fostered tendencies towards a 'dual' economy. Large numbers of medium-sized companies were taken over by large firms. This reduced the stock of innovative, independent firms. Large firms often had unfair advantages: a number received State aid while most SMEs did not. Moreover, during the crisis years of the 1970s, SMEs fared relatively better than large firms in terms of market share, capital accumulation and employment (Amar, 1987; Devilliers, 1987). These developments have led to a revaluation of the role of small firms (see pp. 69-72).

'Critical mass' proved a beguiling notion. Greater size does not automatically lead to greater efficiency. Indeed, examples exist of the opposite tendency. A merger was sometimes seen as the easy solution for two firms displaying lack-lustre performance, when the underlying problem was a lack of viability of either.

In the period of falling demand subsequent to the oil crisis of the mid-1970s, over-capacity became a major problem. The problem had been exacerbated by the concentration process with its emphasis on *gigantisme*, on adding to capacity. A typical example was the construction of the giant steel works at Fos, near Marseilles. Being based on quite unrealistic market forecasts, no real provision was made for closure of old plants in the north and east of France. In the rapidly changing environment of the late 1970s, giant French corporations in steel, chemicals and cars were slow in perceiving threats and did little to claw back dwindling market share, particularly from foreign rivals. By the time such industrial 'dinosaurs' reacted, the time for preventive medicine had passed and major surgery was required. Entire plant closures and mass redundancies were the order of the day.

Too often the concentration process had turned French firms into disparate consortia. After a merger or take-over, separate fiefdoms, with borders corresponding to the old firms, continued to exist. In-fighting prevented the full exploitation of economies of scale. The quest for economies of scope had encouraged excessive diversification. The 'digestion' of new acquisitions proved a drain on limited managerial resources. For example, Saint-Gobain, whose products were traditionally in glass, bought into the computer industry by acquiring the French arm of Olivetti. There was no complementarity between the different businesses of the firm.

The concentration mania of the 1970s eventually led to waves of rationalising and restructuring. With a few exceptions, such as BSN, firms went back to their original *métiers* – to the specialisations, technologies and markets they knew best and in which lay their major competitive advantages. This policy (known as *recentrage*) involved selling off new acquisitions that did not fit their profile. Thus Saint-Gobain wrote off the take-over of French Olivetti as ill-judged and divested in 1982.

The policy of *recentrage* was usually a constrained choice. During the recession of the late 1970s, most firms experienced falling levels of profitability. By the turn of the decade, the situation bordered on the catastrophic. Such 'stars' of the merger process as Rhône-Poulenc, Peugeot-Citroën, PUK, Usinor, Sacilor and Thomson all made major losses in 1981. Dechery (1986, p. 205) indicates that with financial costs soaring to 28 per cent in 1981 and returns falling, French corporations experienced their worst financial squeeze for 15 years. The financial haemorrhage was near lethal. Drastic solutions were required, as will be seen in the next section.

Industrial policy had done little to solve the problems, but its emphasis on large size had worsened at least some of them. Due to the problems of the 1970s, the 'big is beautiful' philosophy was questioned while interventionist industrial policy started to lose credibility.

NATIONALISATION AS A RESCUE OPERATION

The arrival of the Socialists in office in 1981 precipitated major developments
in industrial policy, notably by nationalisation. Political and social justifications for nationalisation were advanced by the coalition government of
Socialists and Communists (see p. 54). But underlying economic and industrial
needs transformed nationalisation into a rescue operation.

The recession had created massive problems. Usinor, Sacilor and
Rhône-Poulenc were close to bankruptcy. In 1981, there were widespread
fears that some 'national champions' would either go under, causing mass
redundancies, or be taken over by foreign buyers.

French steel was in a catastrophic state. The situation of the steel companies
Sacilor and Usinor was unique since, under the Barre government, they had
been bailed out of bankruptcy by huge State loans. The size of the loans made
the State the major shareholder in everything but name. Official nationalisation
in 1981 regularised the anomaly.

In 1981-2 a total of seven industrial companies, two major financial
institutions (Paribas and Suez) and 36 small banks went into State ownership.
The list of nationalised industrial companies reads like a roll-call of the firms
involved in the concentration movements of the 1960s and 1970s. They were
Usinor, Sacilor (both steel), PUK (special steels and non-ferrous metals),
Saint-Gobain (glass, construction materials), Thomson and the CGE (electronics and telecommunications). All bar the CGE and Saint-Gobain were in a dire
financial situation. The State also obtained a majority interest in Dassault
(military aviation), Matra (electronics, weaponry), Bull (information technology) and a minority interest in Roussel-Uclaf (pharmaceuticals).

Given that a significant public sector existed from the nationalisations of
1936 (the deposit banks, Air France, part of the SNCF) and 1945 (Renault,
insurance companies), the total size of the public sector in 1982 was immense.
It accounted for 16 per cent of GDP, 25 per cent of employment, 22.5 per cent
of total value added and around 31 per cent of investments. Before 1982, the
public sector accounted for 12 per cent of French exports; after 1982, that
figure rose to 31 per cent. The public sector was responsible for 30 per cent
of total French industrial output, but its concentration in a limited number of
sectors meant that 75 per cent of artificial textiles and arms and over 80 per
cent of steel and aviation production were in the public sector. In addition,
90 per cent of bank deposits and insurance policies were dealt with by
nationalised institutions. Of the three major insurance groups, the State owned
80 per cent of the capital of the AGF and over 90 per cent of the UAP and GAN.
However, a preponderance in banking and insurance predated the Socialists.
Before 1981, 75 per cent of deposits were in publicly-owned banks. In
banking, the Socialists tightened the long-standing bonds of ownership
between the State and the banks, but did not proceed to structural reforms or
other major changes in the sector.

Industry received most of the government's attention and support. In a sense, nationalisation was the logical conclusion to a long period of close partnership between the State and the *nationalisées* (the newly nationalised firms). Moreover, it would allow a rationalisation of the State-industry partnership. As Eck (1988, p. 97) points out, the State as provider of credit had been unable to restructure its partner firms: nationalisation was intended to give to the State the powers of leverage required.

Rand Smith (1990, p. 81) observed that the *nationalisées* had several characteristics in common: economic importance due to large size, prior dependence on the State for markets and subsidies and a major exports role. Given these features, it was considered imperative for France that their position be consolidated. In this espousal of the theme of the 'national champion', there was undoubtedly continuity between the policy of the Socialists and that of previous governments. The ambition of recapturing market share within France from foreign firms and of expanding abroad has Gaullist undertones of the search for national independence.

The broad aim of nationalisation was thus to forge a French *fer de lance* (spearhead) that would cut through international competition. The more precise objectives were to modernise industry, create jobs and promote foreign trade. It was also hoped that a new model for industrial relations would be created within the State sector.

The underlying assumption made by the government was, as ever, that the prosperity of firms was directly related to State intervention. It was also believed that nationalisation would allow the firms to be turned around quickly. Discussion of the mechanisms and outcome of nationalisation will show that both assumptions were erroneous.

The mechanisms of nationalisation were cumbersome and expensive. The State's purchase of the *nationalisées* proved expensive for two reasons. Firstly, despite the argument put forward by Michel Rocard and Jacques Delors favouring 51 per cent ownership, the group within the Socialist party which favoured 100 per cent purchase carried the conviction of President Mitterrand. Secondly, the price paid to purchasers frequently represented an overvaluation of enfeebled companies, suffering to varying degrees from poor management, underinvestment, old equipment and uncompetitive products. Dechery (1986, p. 163) indicated that the State paid 45 billion francs, with the bankrupt steel sector eating up most public funds. The political objective of appeasing shareholders meant that taxpayers probably paid over the odds.

The results of nationalisation were poor in the short term but reasonably good in the medium term. As Table 2.2 shows, most of the nationalised companies were in the red between 1981-3. But some private sector firms experienced similar problems. For example, in 1983 Peugeot made losses of 2.59 billion francs while Michelin lost 2.18 billions (Cambessédès, 1986, p. 104).

Closer inspection of financial performance shows considerable variations between sectors and firms. Saint-Gobain and the CGE consistently made profits. Spectacular losses were attributable to a small number of firms. The steel companies (Sacilor, Usinor) and Renault together lost over 77 billion francs between 1981-5, over four times the losses of all other public sector firms put together. A recovery was to come very slowly, but the Socialist government had underestimated the depth of the recession of the early 1980s and the gravity of the problems besetting firms in both public and private sectors.

Table 2.2 Financial performance of French nationalised industrial companies: 1981-1985 (in millions of francs)

Firms	1981	1982	1983	1984	1985
Sacilor	-2 897	-3 737	-5 610	-8 100	-5 250
Usinor	-4 240	-4 604	-5 456	-7 600	-3 470
CDF-Chimie	-1 213	-834	-2 654	-865	-1 530
EMC	-312	-946	-160	0	–
Rhône-Poulenc	-340	-844	+98	+1 989	+2 310
Pechiney	-2 510	-4 600	-463	+546	+730
Saint-Gobain	+578	+369	+724	+500	+730
Thomson	-170	-2 208	-1 251	-50	+130
CGE	+586	+638	+662	+650	+760
Bull	-449	-1 351	-625	-500	–
Renault	-675	-1 281	-1 576	-12 555	-10 920

Sources: 1981-1984 Rouilleault, H. (1986) 'Groupes publics et politique industrielle', *Problèmes économiques*, 1963 (26 février), p.8. (Originally published in *Economie et prévision* (1985), 4.)
1985:   Cambessédès, O. (1986) *Faits et Chiffres*, Paris: Les Editions SGB

Managements were given a brief to make the nationalised firms profitable. The key to profitability was a restructuring process. The immediate effect of restructuring was to aggravate losses since plant closures and redundancy payments have an immediate negative impact on the balance sheet. But in the medium term, restructuring allowed a more rational division of labour between the *nationalisées* and a return to profitability.

Increased specialisation and efficiency gains were achieved by a redistribution of subsidiaries between parent companies. Thomson specialised in radar, electronic components and household electronics, shedding telecommunications to the CGE. Pechiney's special steels division went to Usinor. The chemicals industry was cut up three ways. Elf-Aquitaine regrouped activities based on derivatives of oil, chloride and fluoride. CDF-Chimie concentrated on plastics, paint and fertiliser while Rhône-Poulenc specialised in downstream elements such as pharmaceuticals (Eck, 1988, p. 96). The process also meant that certain firms succeeded in shedding loss-making activities, immediately improving their balance sheet. Less fortunate firms on the receiving end of loss-making activities, such as CDF-Chimie, became burdened by structural handicaps.

Investment received a high priority. The Socialists considered that industries such as steel, chemicals, electronics and information technology had suffered from a lack of investment in productive capacity and in research. The State mobilised considerable amounts of capital to correct these perceived market failures. Between 1982 and 1986, the newly nationalised firms received over 64 billion francs in government aid (Durupty, 1988).

The real problem was the distribution of aid. Three firms – Usinor, Sacilor and Renault – turned into black holes for public monies, accounting for over 50 per cent of total subsidies (Durupty, 1988). All three had carried over large handicaps from the 1970s – over-capacity, obsolete equipment, overmanning and product lines that were poorly suited to markets. Their continued disastrous performance unbalanced the rest of Socialist industrial policy, sucking funds away from 'sunrise' industries such as electronics.

The employment record of the nationalisation programme is likewise uneven. The aim of safeguarding industrial employment was abandoned. Between 1981 and 1985, 54,113 jobs were lost in public sector industrial firms. If we take 1981 as the base line, this represented a fall in public sector industrial employment of 5.4 per cent, but this was a much smaller figure than the 12.4 per cent reduction in employment in private industrial firms in the same period (Durupty, 1988). Although mass redundancies destroyed the idea of employment in a nationalised company as a job for life, overall employment in the nationalised sector still appears to have enjoyed some protection.

Labour shedding tailed off in the mid-1980s, reducing redundancy payouts. The restructuring process bore fruits as one after the other nationalised companies returned to profitability. In 1986, all bar Pechiney, Usinor-Sacilor and Renault, were in the black: they too made a profit by 1988 (Jannic, 1991). In 1987, the State-owned industrial sector as a whole (including both 'old' and 'new' nationalised firms) turned in a profit of 7.2 billion francs. It was the first time during the 1980s that this had occurred. Cumulative losses in 1982-6 amounted to 73.7 billion francs; cumulative profits in 1987-90 were 82.8 millions (*Notes bleues*, 1991).

The Socialists had discovered that company profitability was essential. In the process, their whole approach to industrial policy and economic management had changed. Zinsou (1985, p. 61) has neatly summarised the about-turn:

On est passé ainsi de l'idée de rupture avec le capitalisme à l'idée sensiblement différente de rupture avec les carences du capitalisme.

Thus the government went from the idea of breaking with capitalism to the palpably different idea of breaking with the failures of capitalism.

Nationalisation turned into a very different operation to the one envisaged by ideologues of the Left in the early 1970s. As Cohen (1986, p. 15) has tellingly said, the Socialist nationalisation programme became *'une bonne leçon de capitalisme'* (a good lesson in capitalism). In the process, Socialist ministers also became good capitalists.

Nationalisation became an expedient to legitimatise the massive transfer of public monies necessary for the restructuring and modernisation of several layers of France's industry. Despite surface changes in motivation, a pattern of State aid to a small group of companies remained a consistent feature of French industrial policy. The major achievements of nationalisation were that none of the firms involved went to the wall, none were taken over by foreign capital and all (eventually) turned in profits. But with profitability as the major criterion, nationalised firms came to behave almost exactly like private firms, eroding the justification for keeping them in State ownership.

Nationalisation was a rescue operation that worked, but at significant cost to the taxpayer and, in time, to the Socialist government. Industrial policy based on large subsidies to ailing giant firms became unpopular among the business community and the electorate.

PRIVATISATION AND THE NEW LIBERAL AGENDA

The unpopularity of the Socialist government led to a marginal victory by the Right in the 1986 parliamentary elections. Jacques Chirac was nominated as Prime Minister and put into practice liberal policies among which privatisation enjoyed pride of place.

Liberals have long held that the subsidies received by public companies undermine normal market mechanisms and distort competition. Liberals also argue that private companies are more efficient, more competitive and more profitable than public ones. Chirac considered that French nationalised firms were tied up in administrative red tape and subject to interference from the State as owner. In principle, French publicly owned companies had to obtain permission from the State for investments, take-overs, closures and major lay-offs. They were unable to raise finance on capital markets but were obliged to go to the State as sole shareholder. The *président directeur-général* (chairman and chief executive) of public sector firms was nominated by the President of the Republic. The real extent of State influence is debatable, however. French State-owned firms enjoyed considerable managerial au-tonomy and drew market and financial benefits from their alliance with the State. Nevertheless, Chirac presented privatisation as a way to improve performance. A programme of privatisation had been implemented in countries as diverse as Germany, Spain, Italy, Japan , the USA and, of course, the UK. Chirac proposed to do the same in France.

But improved performance of State-owned firms was not the only objective. The value of the shares of firms nationalised in 1981 had quadrupled by 1986. The sale of their shares would increase the size and role of the rather small French *bourse* (stock market). The sale would also fill Treasury coffers, enabling the government to opt for some combination of reduced taxation, reduced public sector borrowing or increased subsidies to remaining nation-alised firms.

The practice of privatisation proved highly pragmatic. The implicit claim that privatisation would turn loss-making companies round was not put to the test. The first two corporations to be privatised – Saint-Gobain and Paribas –

were in fact among the most profitable and attractive of State-owned companies. Their flotation could hardly fail.

Cynics in France talk of a tendency to *nationaliser les pertes, privatiser les profits* (nationalise losses, privatise profits). The figures in Table 2.3 indicate that there is truth in this assertion. Only profitable firms from the second half of the table were sold off. The table indicates, however, that the profitable companies were also the ones which received the least State aid. Public monies were not siphoned off to any large extent to private shareholders as a result of the privatisation process. On the contrary, the increase in the market value after nationalisation of firms such as Saint-Gobain and the CGE made their privatisation a profitable transaction for the State.

Table 2.3 Cumulative profits/losses and subsidies received by French nationalised industrial firms (in billions of francs)

Firms	Results 1981-1985	Subsidies 1982-1986
Sacilor	-25.30	16.3
Usinor	-25.00	16.1
Renault	-27.40	12.0
CDF-Chimie	-6.50	3.0
Pechiney	-3.90	3.6
Bull	-2.80	3.7
CGCT	-2.30	2.0
Thomson	-1.90	3.6
EMC	-0.60	0.5
SNECMA	-0.02	1.1
Matra	+0.40	0.7
Aérospatiale	+0.80	0.2
Dassault	+1.90	–
Saint-Gobain	+2.50	–
CGE	+2.60	0.6
Rhône-Poulenc	+3.00	0.7

Source: Durupty, M. (1988) 'Les privatisations en France', Paris: La Documentation française, *Notes et études documentaires*, no. 4857, p.20

In all, the 1986 privatisation bill gave a list of 65 firms to be sold off. There were though constitutional limits on privatisation. Since 1946, French constitutions have specifically excluded the sale of public services and monopolies. Public utilities could not be put on sale, as has been the case in Britain. (The sale of TF1, the largest French State-owned television channel, was something of a borderline case and so raised considerable controversy.)

Initially, privatisation met with success. The first privatisations were vastly oversubscribed. In part, this was due to the intrinsic worth of the companies themselves. Also, in the case of the first privatisations, the share price was set sufficiently low to allow a substantial bonus to purchasers on resale. This caused controversy as the Finance Minister, Edouard Balladur, set the selling price (though with advice from a Privatisation Commission). With most of the later privatisations, however, margin for a quick profit reduced because of the uproar around earlier 'giveaway' sales and because successful flotation no longer depended on it. Table 2.4, which gives share prices in francs at four points, sets the controversy over selling prices into context.

Table 2.4 Privatisation in France: 1986-1988

Firms	Date privat- ised	Size of sale in bill- ions	Number of new share hold- ers	Init- ial price of share	Price on 1st day of trade 1987	Price end Mar 1987	Price mid- Mar 1988
Saint Gobain	24.11.86	6.3	1.5	310	369	415	414
Paribas	19.01.87	6.1	3.8	405	480	320	300
Sogenal	09.03.87	0.6	0.85	125	225	94	104
BTP	06.04.87	0.1	1	130	176	138	128
BIMP	21.04.87	0.1	0.52	140	170	188	194
CCF	27.04.87	1.7	1.5	107	125	107	114
CGE	11.05.87	8.0	2.3	290	323	215	229
Havas	25.05.87	1.1	0.5	500	540	409	515
Société générale	15.06.87	9.1	2.3	407	432	299	299
TF1	29.06.87	1.2	0.42	165	178	170	185
Suez	05.10.87	6.5	1.6	317	261	279	240
Matra	20.01.88	0.4	0.3	110	123	–	136

Source :　Bizaguet, A. (1988) *Le secteur public et les privatisations,* Paris: PUF, p. 93

The only pattern that emerges is that share prices on the first day of trading were always higher than the initial quotation. In subsequent periods, however, share prices fluctuated considerably. Some fell, such as the banks *Sogenal* and *Société générale.* Movements in share prices were not simply a function of the privatisation process but were linked to the sector, specialisations and performance of the firms themselves and to changes in the economic climate. Viewed in the medium to long term, investing in shares in privatised French companies has offered comparable benefits and risks to shareholding in other private firms. The thesis of a 'giveaway' clearance is largely unjustified.

Turning to wider outcomes, in the year between September 1986 and August 1987, a larger slice of privatisation was completed in France than in Britain during the previous five years. Privatisation netted some 120 billion francs for the French Treasury. The 1987 Finance Bill indicated that 30 per cent of sales revenue was diverted back into grants to remaining State-owned firms, the other 70 per cent going to repayment of public borrowing. In net terms this amounted to 51.5 billion francs, against a debt standing at 1240 billions in January 1987 and a year-on-year increase in public debt of 109 billions.

When privatisation was halted in February 1988, over a third of the programme had been completed. The number of shareholders had massively increased from approximately 1.5 million in 1980 to some 6 million by the end of 1987. The *bourse de Paris* was over 20 per cent larger than in 1980, though still small in comparison to stock exchanges in other major world capitals.

Privatisation was stopped partly because of the impending presidential elections but an even more serious problem arose which nearly scuppered the privatisation programme. This was the stock market crash of 19 October 1987. The crash changed attitudes among the French populace to privatisation. In a SOFRES survey undertaken early in 1987, 58 per cent of respondents cited a quick profit as the major motivation for purchases of shares in privatised companies. A CREP survey of the same period shows that only 20 per cent of respondents thought that such purchases involved any risk. The October crash changed perceptions on both counts. Though most new shareholders did not succumb to panic selling, the popularity of privatisation was massively dented.

Other criticisms of the programme can be made. The management of privatised firms were cushioned against external buffets by government controls. The majority shareholding was entrusted in each case to a *noyau dur* (a 'hard core') of firms. Members of the 'hard core' were hand-picked by Finance Minister Balladur. The aims of having a 'hard core' were to achieve stability and ensure the companies would not pass into foreign ownership. Sales to foreigners were limited to a maximum of 20 per cent of each firm. The preponderance of large company holdings and the nomination of main board members by the Finance Minister had the effect of minimising the influence of small shareholders and undermining the proposition that privatisation resulted in a more democratic form of capitalism. The limited number of firms inside the *noyaux durs* and their representation by personalities known to be close to the government attracted significant criticism. Durupty (1988, p. 127) refers to 'an excessive degree of personalisation in French capitalism'. Bauer (1988) has argued that, regardless of expressed ideologies, these controls illustrate characteristically French limitations on free-market liberalism. Privatisation had other side-effects; savings accounts in banks were depleted while some companies postponed rights issues.

For all these reasons, the privatisation programme ran out of steam by early 1988. In his presidential campaign, Mitterrand advocated a policy of *ni nationalisation ni privatisation* (neither nationalisation nor privatisation) – the so-called *ni-ni* policy. Given the climate of the time, this element of his electoral stance was received relatively favourably. At any event, he easily beat Chirac in both the first and second rounds of the 1988 presidential elections.

As a statement of medium-term industrial policy, the *ni-ni* policy rapidly became unworkable (Bentégeat, 1990; Manière, 1990; Sicot, 1989). In the run-up to 1993, companies could not stand still. A public sector firm, like any other, needs to generate finance for investments and acquisitions. Where retained earnings and State resources are not sufficient – as has proved to be the case – recourse to the finance markets is the logical solution. Even before privatisation under Chirac, nationalised firms had resorted to issues of various

bonds and *certificats d'investissement* which gave a return on investment but
no ownership or voting rights.

The freezing of the boundary between public and private sectors was never
a realistic option. All firms need to seize market opportunities as they arise.
The acquisition of majority holdings in the private airlines UTA and Air Inter
by State-owned Air France in 1990 constituted an example of creeping
nationalisation.

The activities of Pechiney, the aluminium company, illustrate even more
complex manoeuvres. Pechiney's purchase of American Can was a *de facto*
French nationalisation of a US firm. Pechiney then created a new subsidiary
called Pechiney Internationale to which the assets of American Can and of
other reputable operating divisions were assigned. Pechiney sold off 25 per
cent of the new subsidiary on the stock market. This amounted to a partial
privatisation. Likewise, the commercial partnership signed by Renault and
Volvo involved a form of partial privatisation, with Volvo taking a 20 per cent
stake in Renault while Renault took 10 per cent of Volvo. These complicated
financial schemes illustrate that a policy of '*ni nationalisation ni privatisation*' was not really respected over the 1988-1991 period. The policy had
simply ignored what Wright (1990, p. 198) called the 'traditional instability' of
the boundary between public and private sectors in France.

Appearances finally caught up with reality. A decree of 5 April 1991
legalised privatisation of up to 49 per cent of State-owned firms outside of the
insurance sector, where a maximum of 25 per cent had been permitted. This
half-way house saved face, as Mitterrand could argue that the '*ni-ni*' policy
was about full-scale privatisation, while appeasing pragmatists, such as Prime
Minister Rocard who had been pressing for 51 per cent nationalisation since
1981 (Moatti, 1991). The policy of partial privatisation has survived the arrival
of Prime Minister Edith Cresson, an outspoken advocate of strong industrial
policy. In August 1991, it was planned to sell off 20 per cent of *Crédit local
de France* on the stock market for about 1.5 billion francs (Marshall, 1991).
Further sales are likely.

Partial privatisation has the advantage of generating cash either for the
company (in the case of a new rights issue) or for the State (where the State
sells part of its stake). In allowing private firms to enter the capital of public
companies, new international alliances can be formed. This is crucial
in the context of increasing levels of integration in European and world
markets.

Cynics may also argue that partial privatisation is a political spoiling
manoeuvre, for the Right is again promising 100 per cent privatisation should
it win at the 1993 parliamentary elections. However, after strong expansion
in 1988-9, the 1990 downturn has led to falling output and profits. The market
situation of a number of State-owned firms is again uninviting. Comparing
1990 with 1989 performances (Renard, 1991), Renault's profits fell by 87 per
cent and those of Usinor-Sacilor (steel) and Rhône-Poulenc (chemicals) fell by
around 50 per cent. Bull (information technology) went back into the red in
1989 and made huge losses of 6.79 billion francs in 1990. Thomson

(electronics) went into the red in 1990. Once again it appears that the government will be siphoning public funds to keep them afloat.

The poor performance of these firms raises yet more doubts about the value of recent French industrial policy. The real test for future privatisation or for any other industrial policy is to find a solution for strategically important but loss-making computer and electronics firms.

SMALL FIRMS AND REGIONAL INDUSTRIAL DEVELOPMENT

The major trait of the concentration-nationalisation-privatisation cycle has been the small number of firms involved. This factor indicates the limits within which French industrial policy has evolved. Those limits will be revealed more clearly by a review of French industrial geography and the role of small firms.

Early industrial development in France occurred in a limited number of regions. Up until approximately the 1960s, France's industrial geography could be summarised quickly and neatly by the *ligne Le Havre-Marseille*. This imaginary line bisects France on a diagonal running from the north-west to the south-east. Above the line lay France's industrialised regions, including Marseilles, Lyons and Paris, below the line lay the agricultural rest.

Industrial development was extremely vigorous in a limited number of regions due to the presence of natural resources or to the geographical advantages of their locations. The first industrial revolution was in mechanical engineering (in Ile de France, Rhône-Alpes, Nord-Pas de Calais, Alsace), textiles-clothing (Nord, Rhône-Alpes, Alsace) and iron and steel making (Nord, Alsace-Lorraine), using local coal as the energy source. With the exception of the clothing sector, big firms became the norm.

In the twentieth century, growth of electrical and electronic engineering occurred in the Île de France, Rhône-Alpes, central France and the Loire valley. Car, lorry and train construction have been concentrated in Île de France, Rhône-Alpes, Nord-Pas de Calais and Franche-Comté. The aviation industry is split between the Île de France and Midi-Pyrénées. Levels of regional specialisation and concentration have thus been high.

In a changing industrial landscape, a number of post-war trends stand out. With increased competition from newly developing nations from the 1970s and upheavals in industrial structures, many 'traditional' industries went first into relative, then absolute decline. The regions and towns in which they were based (Alsace-Lorraine, Nord-Pas de Calais, Roubaix, St-Etienne) suffered severely as a consequence of company closures and mass redundancies. The 'big is beautiful' ideology was questioned and partially rejected.

In addition, France has suffered a perennial problem of over-centralisation around Paris, not only in the political and administrative domains but also in economic and industrial structures. Concerns over the consequent creation of a *désert français* in the provinces were eloquently expressed by Gravier as early as 1947. Concerns about distortions in national development led to a powerful movement aimed at the *aménagement du territoire* – the rebalancing of regional structures. This movement comprised a series of State initiatives dating from the 1960s onwards aimed at upgrading the provinces at every level from the cultural to the economic.

Ironically, as regards industrial development, the process of an *aménagement du territoire* was itself largely a centralised affair. Its implementation was entrusted in 1964 to the *Délégation à l'aménagement du territoire et à l'action régionale* (DATAR). Until the recession of 1974, DATAR's brief was to help resolve the problem of industrial polarisation by encouraging large firms from France's industrial heartlands to set up subsidiaries in the provinces. State subsidies were available to willing firms. Between 1960 and 1967, approximately 700 establishments left the Île de France, leading to a drop in industrial employment there. Their destinations were 'underdeveloped' regions such as Brittany and Normandy. Turpin (1983a, p. 17) indicates that by 1975, greater homogenisation of regional industrial structures had occurred, partially erasing the *ligne Le Havre-Marseille.*

However, the reliance on large, 'foot-loose' firms proved unsatisfactory. Firstly, only those activities which involved low transport costs and low levels of worker skills were realistic candidates for decentralisation. Secondly, those firms who could set up subsidiary plants away from their base tended to retain their former sourcing patterns. Typically, suppliers and sub-contractors did not move to the new location, imposing a ceiling on industrial growth in the 'underdeveloped' province. Thirdly, large firms took in labour but tended to stifle local entrepreneurship. Most importantly, these tendencies slowed down the development of the small firm sector in those regions. Thus hoped-for multiplier effects were limited to in-firm job creation and salary spending. Moreover, given the lack of an industrial heritage and skills in those provinces, the jobs created required few qualifications and could not therefore command high salaries. All in all, 'foot-loose' firms did less to stimulate regional economies than hoped.

The promotion of decentralisation encountered other obstacles and dangers. Some firms resisted pressure to relocate. They stressed the logic of their own markets over the preferences of the State. Among those able and willing to relocate, official policy ran the risk of encouraging firms to move not to the provinces but abroad. After all, if a major attraction of the provinces was cheap labour, 'off-shore' production could be cheaper still. Finally, the impetus to promoting 'foot-loose' development collapsed during the recession years of the 1970s. Car manufacturers and mechanical engineering companies, which previously were able to consider relocating, were hit hard by the crisis. In a context of falling demand, they found themselves with excess capacity. The large companies who previously created employment were constrained into shedding jobs. The solution had itself become a problem.

In consequence, the role of DATAR changed radically. Deindustrialisation as a result of recession meant that regions with a long tradition of industrial development (such as northern and eastern France) were in far greater distress than 'underdeveloped' ones (Turpin, 1983b). From promoting factory development on green sites, DATAR was entrusted with creating new types of jobs in the industrial heartlands. DATAR was assigned the role of attracting foreign investment (Attali, 1985). The State designated 15 *pôles de reconversion*: these were priority areas for industrial renewal in devastated sectors such as ship-building, coal-mining and steel in the Nord and Lorraine.

The two billion francs of State aid which was poured into those regions went towards anaesthetising the misery but could not eliminate deep-rooted problems. In areas where large companies had long dominated the local economy, entrepreneurship was stifled and limited due to the reasons discussed above in relation to 'foot-loose' industries. With the closure of major factories and the absence of a lively small firm community, the revival of the local economy turned into a long, sometimes impossible, haul.

But while large industrial firms were forced to cut back severely as a result of the recession, small firms fared relatively better (Amar, 1987; Devilliers, 1987). Rural and recently industrialised regions coped better in the crisis years than old industrial regions (Aydalot, 1984). As a result, in the 1980s, the traditional view of industrialisation in France has been extensively revised. The accent has increasingly come to be placed on small rather than on large firms. Economic development has been more rapid in the south than in the north. The *ligne Le Havre-Marseille* is no longer a rigid division.

Because the development of the new industrial geography is a contemporary, ongoing phenomenon, only provisional explanations can be offered. Reference has already been made to the impact of recession on large firms with obsolete equipment and surplus capacity. In addition, there has been a trend in many markets away from standardisation towards more tailoring of products. As a result, the long product runs which contributed significantly to large firm economies of scale are less frequently realisable. Shorter product runs tend to favour small establishments. Small firms can be extremely flexible, adapting rapidly to market change and innovating to suit new needs. At their best, smaller unit size facilitates cost minimisation and allows for smoother relations between employees and management.

The downside is that in an imperfect world, not all small firms can combine these advantages. But all small firms *are* very vulnerable, especially in today's turbulent environment. With the loss of a major customer, a cash flow crisis, a managerial error of judgement or simply a personal problem experienced by the owner, a small firm may go under overnight.

In addition to big versus small firm issues, geographical and social issues have contributed to the new trends. Aydalot (1986) has reported the thesis of an 'urban-rural shift'. This results from a combination of 'push' and 'pull' factors. The social, economic and environmental consequences of overcrowding of cities have pushed entrepreneurs and new firms into less developed regions. With the development of better transport and communications, infrastructure advantages previously accruing to conurbations no longer apply to the same extent. Further, with today's greater emphasis on the quality of life, the countryside is seen as a more attractive place to live than the city. This is particularly marked with the 'sun-belt' phenomenon – for example, migration in the USA to California or in France to Provence.

The outcome of these trends amounts to something other than a reversal of ideologies. Replacing 'big is beautiful' with 'small is beautiful' can be a sterile exercise. A better balance is required. Two directions are possible. The first is in terms of giving closer attention to *optimum* company size. The second is in terms of developing mutually beneficial relationships between small, medium and large firms by co-operative practices and network arrangements.

The change in attitudes to small firms and new patterns of regional development have produced a new industrial landscape. Ironically, while some of the negative phases of the development – the creation of industrial dinosaurs – can be ascribed to official industrial policy, its positive aspects have occurred *independently* of government action. This is one of the contributory factors to a dwindling of interest in interventionist industrial policy. Recent government enthusiasm for the small-firm sector has attempted to compensate for previous oversights. France's new Prime Minister, Edith Cresson, has taken up the small-firm cause with new tax reductions (Mercier and Coulange, 1991) but policy in favour of small firms remains underdeveloped.

CONCLUSIONS

French industrial policy in the post-war period has had its successes and failures, but both have illustrated its limits.

Explanations for French failures can be advanced using criteria put forward by the OECD (1988). In sectors requiring support, the OECD report stressed that:

(a) eligibility criteria should be precisely defined;
(b) a clear distinction be made between economic objectives and social aims;
(c) collaboration be sought between social partners from the start;
(d) policy be consistent but flexible; and
(e) measures be implemented that revitalise the sector or firm.

In France, however, these conditions were rarely respected. Criteria for eligibility for State support were usually dictated by urgency and decided on an *ad hoc* basis. The 1981-2 nationalisations are a prime example. A clear distinction was rarely made between economic and social objectives. The need to safeguard employment was often paramount, with less attention to the viability of firms or operating divisions. Only fairly late in the day were measures considered that would revitalise the sector or firm. In its policy on textiles, the State never took the initiative to insist on revitalising measures. In steel, it was only in the mid-1980s and after a long haul that restructuring began to provide dividends. Traditionally, the justification for State intervention has been its provision of rational, long-term direction. In practice, this has only been the case with the *grands projets* (such as telecommunications and nuclear energy). Short-term views have been the norm elsewhere.

In addition, the OECD (1988) argued that in developing sectors State intervention should not distort or hinder competition and that access to new technological developments be as wide as possible. Industrial policy making in France has given little consideration to these elements.

In sectors where French successes can be adduced, the distinguishing policy trait is of a *politique des firmes*, or favouritism towards a 'happy few' firms at the expense of the many. However, restricting access in this way has allowed a concentration of scarce resources. The State-industry partnership produced spectacular results in select fields. Such *grands projets* as the TGV, Airbus, Ariane, the renewal of French telecommunications or indeed the French contribution to the Channel Tunnel illustrate that the partnership can work.

Where industrial policy has been a success a number of highly specialised conditions have been met. Mazier (1983) has summarised them as follows: close co-operation between the State and industrial firms at every stage, the existence of major research centres, continuity in the provision of subsidies and in the supervision of their usage, a *filière* strategy and a major public procurement programme. Moreover, criteria for success in the *grands projets* were generally technological prestige rather than profitability. Taken as a whole, the list offers a convincing recipe for a particular sort of success. Indeed, the major criticism is that, where these conditions are fulfilled, it is hard to see how a firm could fail.

Even with policy successes, the price paid by the State and by the taxpayer has often been high. Calculations of financial cost tell only part of the story. The 'happy few' firms have used industrial policy as a means of exercising influence over the State, of imposing private interest on public will (Bauer and Cohen, 1981, 1985). Industrial structures were modified, alternative options for development were closed down, regional and small firm issues became an afterthought.

French industrial development has been decidedly uneven. Major developments were frequently restricted to State-directed, often classified, sectors such as the nuclear industry, weaponry, aviation and avionics, telecommunications and high-speed trains. Here industrial policy has been marked with positive achievements. However, it has been almost totally ineffective in consumer industries, whether they be textiles, television sets or personal computers. Two complementary explanations for this situation exist, one relating to technology transfer, the other to marketing skills.

Stoffaës (1989, p. 122) has indicated that a higher proportion of research is financed by the French State than among her neighbours but that access to innovation by firms is more limited. Technological transfer is greater in the Japanese consumer electronics industries and the American information technology industries.

In France, despite vociferous enthusiasm since the 1960s for American-style marketing, the emphasis has consistently been on the supply-side of the equation. French technology policy has put *engineering* prowess first. Consumer marketing skills were developed entirely outside of industrial policy.

The need to amend these trends became clear in the 1980s. With successes and failures finely balanced, the dramatic but expensive business of selective intervention lost popularity, giving way to an 'environmental' approach that seeks to cover the total population of firms. Primarily this involves taxation policy, but increasingly stress is being placed on education, training and research, the latter having become the new 'home' of industrial policy.

Finally, the process of European integration and the strengthening of competition policy within the EC – themes which will be treated in the next two chapters – have also reduced the scope and the will for intervention at a national level. Whether the shift to an 'environmental' approach at the end of the 1980s signals the end of selective intervention is not, however, a foregone conclusion. Strong industrial policy still has its advocates in France, including Prime Minister Cresson. Future efforts may be directed towards developing a European industrial policy in order to fend off American and Japanese challenges.

But the lessons from the limitations of previous French industrial policies are clear. For industrial policy to have a useful future, it must demonstrate an ability to service large viable markets, sustain a high degree of technology transfer and translate into gains for a substantial number of firms in terms of profitability and employment.

References

Amar, M. (1987) 'Dans l'industrie, les PME résistent mieux que les grandes entreprises', *Economie et statistique*, 197, pp. 3-11

Attali, B. (1985) 'Reindustrialising France through urban and regional development' in Zukin, S. (ed.) *Industrial Policy: Business and Politics in the United States and France*, pp. 179-84, London: Praeger

Aydalot, P. (1984) 'The reversal of spatial trends in French industry since 1974' in Lambooy, J.G. (ed.) *New Spatial Dynamics and Economic Crisis*, pp. 41-62, Tampere: Finnpublishers

Aydalot, P. (1986) 'The location of new firm creation: the French case' in Keeble, D. & Wever, E. (eds.), *New Firms and Regional Development in Europe*, pp. 105-23, London: Croom Helm

Baleste, M. (1986) *L'Économie française*, Paris: Masson

Bandt, J. de (1987) 'French Industrial Policies: Successes and Failures' in Beije, P.R. *et al.* (eds.) *A Competitive Future for Europe? Towards a New European Industrial Policy*, pp. 433-61, London: Croom Helm.

Bauer, M. (1988) 'The politics of State-directed privatisation', *Western European Politics*, 11:4, pp.49-60

Bauer, M. & Cohen, E. (1981) *Qui gouverne les groupes industriels?*, Paris: Editions du Seuil

Bellon, B. & Bandt, J. de (1988) 'La politique industrielle' in Arena, R. *et al.* (eds.) *Traité d'économie industrielle*, pp. 840-57, Paris: Economica

Bentégeat, H. (1990) 'Le ni-ni est mort, tuons-le!', *L'Expansion* (25 janvier-7 février), pp. 30-7

Bizaguet, A. (1988) *Le Secteur public et les privatisations*, Paris: PUF

Cambessédès, O. (ed.) (1986) *Faits et Chiffres*, Paris: Les Editions SGB

Cohen, E. (1986) 'Nationalisations: une bonne leçon de capitalisme', *Problèmes économiques*, 1.972 (30 avril), pp. 13-18

Cohen, E. & Bauer, M. (1985) *Les grandes manoeuvres industrielles*, Paris: Belfond

Commission of the European Communities (1989) *First Survey on State Aids in the European Community*, Luxemburg: Office for Official Publications of the EC

Commission of the European Communities (1990) *Second Survey on State Aids in the European Community in the manufacturing and certain other sectors*, Luxemburg: Office for Official Publications of the EC

Dacier, P. *et al.* (1985) *Les Dossiers noirs de l'industrie française*, Paris: Fayard

Dahmani, A. (1983) 'La sidérurgie: le poids de l'assistance permanente' in Bellon, B. & Chevalier, J.-M. (eds.), *L'Industrie en France*, pp. 121-54, Paris: Flammarion

Davie, A. (1987) *Les Politiques industrielles*, Paris: Hatier

Dechery, B. *et al.* (1986) *Competing for prosperity. Business strategies and industrial policies in modern France*, London: Policy Studies Institute

Devilliers, M. (1987) 'Performances et comportements comparés des petites et grandes entreprises depuis le second choc pétrolier', *Problèmes économiques*, 2031 (1 juillet), pp. 6-11

Dubois, P. (1988) 'L'industrie de l'habillement, l'innovation face à la crise', Paris: La Documentation française, *Notes et Etudes Documentaires*, no. 4852

Durupty, M. (1988) 'Les privatisations en France', Paris: La Documentation française, *Notes et études documentaires*, no. 4857

Eck, J.-F. (1988) *Histoire de l'économie française depuis 1945*, Paris: Armand Colin.

Gilly, J. & Morin, F. (1981) 'Les groupes industriels en France: concentration du système productif depuis 1945', Paris: La Documentation française, *Notes et études Documentaires*, nos. 4605-6

Grant, W. (1983) *The Political Economy of Industrial Policy*, London: Butterworth

Green, D. (1985) 'Industrial policy and policy-making, 1974-1982' in Machin, H. & Wright, V. (eds.) *Economic Policy and Policy Making under the Mitterrand Presidency 1981-84*, pp. 139-58, London: Frances Pinter

Holton, R. (1986) 'Industrial politics in France: nationalisation under Mitterrand', *West European Politics*, 9:1 (January), 67-79

INSEE (1990) *Tableaux de l'économie française*, Paris: INSEE

Jannic, H. (1991) 'Comment doper l'industrie française', *L'Expansion* (2-15 mai), pp. 54-60

Labarde, P. (1979) 'Les aides de l'Etat à l'industrie deviendront plus sélectives', *Le Monde* (23-24 septembre), p. 13

Levavic, R. (1986) 'Government policies towards the consumer electronics industry and their effect: a comparison of Britain and France' in Hall, G. (ed.) *European Industrial Policy*, pp. 227-44, London: Croom Helm

Manière, P. (1990) 'La fin du "ni-ni"', *Le Nouvel Economiste*, 730 (26 janvier), pp. 22-7

Marshall, A. (1991) 'Paris signals policy shift on asset sales', *The Independent*, 8 September, p. 8

Mazier, J. (1983) 'Les limites de la stratégie de redéploiement', *Les Cahiers français*, 212 (juillet-septembre), pp. 14-19

Mercier, A.-M. & Coulange, J.-P. (1991) 'PME: la potion fiscale d'Edith Cresson', *Le Nouvel Economiste*, 812 (30 septembre), pp. 16-17

Messerlin, P. (1987) 'France: the ambitious state' in Duchêne, F. & Shepherd, G. (eds.), *Managing Industrial Change in Western Europe*, pp. 76-110, London: Frances Pinter

Moatti, G. (1991) 'Les nationalisées sans frontières', *L'Expansion* (18 avril - 1 mai), p. 32

Morvan, Y. (1983) 'La politique industrielle française depuis la Libération: quarante années d'interventions et d'ambiguités', *Revue d'Économie Industrielle*, 23 (1er trimestre), pp. 19-35

Notes bleues (1991) supplément trimestriel, no. 1

OECD (1988) 'Les effets des politiques industrielles', *Problèmes économiques*, 2.081 (29 juin), pp. 12-17.

Rand Smith, W. (1990) 'Nationalisations for what? Capitalist power and public enterprise in Mitterrand's France', *Politics and Society* (March), pp. 75-99

Renard, F. (1991) 'La petite grippe des entreprises françaises', *Le Monde* (17 mai), p. 34

Rouilleault, H. (1986) 'Groupes publics et politique industrielle', *Problèmes économiques*, 1963 (26 février), pp. 5-14

Savy, M. & Valeyre, A. (1982) 'Bipolarisation industrielle et développement régional', *Revue d'Economie Industrielle*, 19, (1er trimestre), pp. 105-9

Sicot, D. (1989) 'Le "ni-ni" est-il viable?', *Science et Vie Economie*, 56 (décembre), pp. 34-8

Stoffaës, C. (1989) 'Industrial policy and the State: from industry to enterprise' in Godt, P. (ed.) *Policy-Making in France from de Gaulle to Mitterrand*, pp. 105-26, London: Pinter

Stoleru, L. (1969) *L'Impératif industriel*, Paris: Seuil

Turpin, E. (1983a) 'Le tissu industriel régional entre 1954 et 1975', *Les Cahiers français*, 211 (mai-juin), pp. 12-17

Turpin, E. (1983b) 'Les régions face à la crise (1975 - 1979)', *Les Cahiers français*, 211 (mai-juin), pp. 28-30

Wright, V. (1990) 'The nationalisation and privatisation of French public enterprises 1981-1988: radical ambitions, diluted programmes and limited impact', *Staatswissenschaften und Staatspraxis*, 2, pp. 176-201

Zarader, R. (1983) 'L'informatique: une stratégie contrainte pour une industrie stratégique' in Bellon, B. & Chevalier, J.-M. (eds.) *L'Industrie en France*, pp. 219-49, Paris: Flammarion

Zinsou, L. (1985) *Le Fer de lance*, Paris: Olivier Orban

3

French business on the world stage

INTRODUCTION

With the development of a genuine world economy in the twentieth century, it is no longer possible to view business in a purely national perspective. In consequence, the real test of the competitiveness of French firms is their performance in EC and world markets.

Performance in international markets is closely linked to the trading strategies each nation adopts towards its partners. Most importantly, no modern State can avoid making choices between either protectionist or free-trade policies. Where natural barriers to free trade are low, a nation State can choose the degree of openness of its economy, but it can never choose not to choose. Today all States have a *de facto* policy towards trade and currency movements.

France has had a reputation for protectionism. There is no doubt that it was justified in the nineteenth and most of the twentieth centuries. In 1955, customs tariffs on industrialised goods were 11 per cent in Holland and Belgium, 12.5 per cent in Germany and 18.5 per cent in France. In terms of trade in all goods, the difference between protectionist France and quasi-free trade Germany was even more stark. In the 1950s, some 60 per cent of French customs duties were higher than 15 per cent; only 2 per cent of German duties were at that level (Bonin, 1988, p. 168). Sheahan (1963, pp. 233-4) noted that almost every international meeting on trade liberalisation in the 1950s contained special criticism of French import restrictions. Protectionism was reinforced by the non-convertibility of the franc during the Fourth Republic (1944-1958). These measures were designed to preserve national independence, one of the major and consistent themes in French political and economic life.

The French are currently sensitive to the image problem that they have inherited from their history of protectionism. Sicot (1990) offers a representative view. He argues that France's poor reputation on free trade is no longer deserved. He accepts that in recent years France has intermittently put on displays of crude and ineffective protectionism but contrasts them to the subtle but efficient forms of discrimination against foreign products exercised by competitor states. The underlying contention in this argument is that market behaviour is to be measured in relative, not absolute, terms. Absolute degrees of either free trade or protectionism are hard to find. What matters is how comparable the behaviour of various interacting players is to each other.

The problem with the relative approach is to find a common measure. With the issue of free trade, the problem is acute. Controversies rage. In GATT talks on free trade, the USA and the EC have frequently failed to agree on standards acceptable to both. Nations are prone to consider that their own standards are universal. The British tend to view France as a persistently protectionist State. This view has to be correlated to a greater orientation towards free trade in Britain due to a different history. As compared to Japan, however, France has a far more open economy.

Without pretending to settle the controversies, this chapter will first present measures (see pp. 79-81) by which nations can be compared on the question of openness to trade. The major argument will be that, compared to her previous performance, France has discarded most, though not all, of her protectionist armoury. In world terms, this means that France falls somewhat short of the standards of leading champions of free trade but is far removed from the protectionist enclave she used to be. On free trade, as in so many areas, France today occupies an intermediate position.

The key point is that France has changed greatly. French support for free trade, particularly within Europe, has increased markedly. With the signing of the Treaty of Rome in 1957, France enjoyed the distinction of being among the founding countries of the European Economic Community, an indication of a major shift toward free-trade policies. Opening the French economy to Europe and to greater market pressures was a large step in the gradual abandonment of economic *dirigisme* which was charted in Chapters 1 and 2. It was essential as a stimulus to increased economic growth and to the development of world-class French firms.

The increased importance to France of a European dimension accompanied the loss of her Empire. France's colonies embraced islands in the Pacific Ocean and parts of Indo-China, but lay mainly in Northern and Western Africa. These dominions gave France an international presence. It was believed that they conferred prestige, and international leadership has been a key theme in French public life. In addition, the colonies provided a closed trading zone for French business.

Loss of Empire led to a dwindling of colonial markets. A major adjustment process within French patterns of international trade was precipitated during the 1950s and 1960s. Further adjustments have been required since the 1970s, due to the enhanced importance of Middle Eastern economies after the oil price shocks and due to increased competition from Japan and from newly industrialising nations such as Korea, Singapore, Hong Kong and Taiwan.

Over a relatively short period, French business has been subject to something akin to a revolution. Changes have occurred quickly and encountered varying degrees of success. Applied wholesale, the protectionist myths are invalid. But when the French economy is considered sector by sector, pockets of protectionism can be found alongside the enthusiastic embrace of competition in an international economy. French policies and the attitudes of the French business community have changed, but in a fragmented, heterogeneous fashion.

Assessment of French business on the world stage is thus a complex task. It is essential to identify the specialisations and behaviour of French business, its comparative advantages and disadvantages in *sectoral* terms. It also involves appraisal of French business in *geographical* terms, namely the examination of the ability of French firms to conserve home markets and to seek out opportunities abroad. This chapter first reviews overall international competitiveness, moves on to sectoral strengths and weaknesses in both goods and services and then discusses relations with France's major international trading partners.

OVERVIEW OF FRENCH INTERNATIONAL COMPETITIVENESS

The transition to an open economy

The essential development in French foreign trade since the 1950s has been the progressive opening-up of the economy. Both imports and exports have increased dramatically, as Table 3.1 indicates.

Table 3.1 Imports and exports as a percentage of French GDP

	1960	1965	1970	1973	1978	1981	1982	1983	1984
Imports	10.5	10.6	13.6	15.0	17.3	21.3	21.5	20.6	21.4
Exports	1.4	10.3	12.7	14.4	16.6	18.4	17.6	18.2	19.4

Source: Nguyên Duy-Tân, J. (1986) 'Le commerce extérieur de la France. Environnement international et instruments juridiques', Paris: La Documentation française, *Notes et études documentaires*, no. 4798, p. 10

Large-scale international trade has come to play a fundamental role in the French economy.

Further, as Table 3.2 illustrates, the degree of openness of the French economy is comparable to European neighbours such as Germany or Italy, while it is considerably more open than that of the USA or Japan. It is true that free trade relates not just to policy but is also a function of natural boundaries and internal economic area. The USA benefits from significant domestic resources, large markets and many world-beating firms. Japan consists of a series of islands and has a unique culture. Nevertheless, the comparison illustrates that the myth of 'fortress France' does not hold.

The increase in international trade is explained mainly by two developments. One was the gradual dismantlement of much of France's protectionist armoury as a consequence of the Treaty of Rome (1957) which created the European Economic Community. The other was France's participation in successive negotiation rounds of the General Agreement on Trade and Tariffs (GATT) which, through trade barrier reductions, have promoted incremental increases in world free trade since 1947.

Table 3.2 CIF-FOB trade balances as percentage of GDP in six major industrial countries in 1984 (except USA which is FOB-FOB) [1]

	FRG	*Italy*	*UK*	*USA*	*Japan*	*France*
Imports	24.7	23.6	23.9	9.1	11.1	21.4
Exports	27.0	20.6	21.5	5.9	13.7	19.4

Source: Nguyên Duy-Tân, J. (1986) 'Le commerce extérieur de la France. Environnement international et instruments juridiques', Paris: La Documentation française, *Notes et études documentaires*, no. 4798, p. 11

France's gradual abandonment of protectionism is explained by the greater benefits of free trade. In principle, free trade promotes the most efficient allocation of resources by removing artificial trade barriers around the world, so allowing producers to specialise in those areas where they have greater comparative advantages. This increases competitiveness, ensures cheaper and better goods and services as well as greater choice. The danger is that imbalances result in a particular country because imports outstrip exports. In the short term, trade imbalances are almost inevitable. However, longer-term deficits can have serious economic and social consequences. Where a national industry is undercut and eliminated by foreign products (for example, as happened in Britain with Japanese motor-cycles and zips), an industrial base is lost and unemployment results.

The results are even more serious when structural trade imbalances are financed by borrowing. In parts of the Third World and Latin America, a major debt crisis arose in the 1980s due to debtor nations being unable to generate enough foreign exchange earnings to even service their debt, let alone repay it. Conversely, international tensions and problems of recycling have arisen where nations (for example, Germany, Japan, or Arab oil-producing nations in the 1970s) consistently achieve surpluses.

Such dangers are inherent in a free-trade system and explain the aversion of some States, including France at various historical periods, to opening their frontiers to trade. At the start of the 1980s, during a period of economic difficulty and massive deficits with trading partners, the proposition to return to protectionism was mooted within the ruling French Socialist party but rapidly dropped. This decision confirmed that France had been definitively won over to free trade.

France simply cannot do without the energy, raw materials, intermediate and capital goods she imports. To pay the imports bill, exports are essential. In French, this necessity is termed *la contrainte extérieure*, sometimes referred to in English simply as the 'external constraint' (Estrin and Holmes, 1985). The open system places an onus on French firms to be efficient exporters and offers them opportunities to profit from markets around the world. France's survival as a major nation depends on their performance.

French international performance

Contrary to the despondent analyses that frequently appear in the French press, France's international business performance in the post-war period has been tolerably good to impressive. But this blanket evaluation has been made only to indicate the large view and will be variously qualified in the discussion to follow. Closer inspection reveals a range of successes and shortcomings which have to be related to time-period, type of product and trading zone. These will be progressively developed in the chapter. At this stage, a number of criteria are introduced to evaluate French international performance.

The key economic indicator of a country's international performance is its current account balance. Though a nation's current account is much less straightforward than an individual's current account with a bank, the underlying principle is comparable, namely, the current account records the relationship between income and outgoings. Its major components are the trade balance and the services or 'invisibles' balance. (Once short-term and long-term capital movements are included, together with various adjustments for currency fluctuations and errors, the sum total is referred to as a country's balance of payments.)

The trade balance relates to the exchange of physical goods. The 'invisibles' balance relates mainly to the exchange of intangible services. Balances are calculated by subtracting imports from exports. If exports are higher than imports, the balance is said to be in surplus. If imports are higher than exports, the balance is said to be in deficit. Of course, a surplus is generally healthier and more desirable than a deficit, though deficits can be sustained provided either that the country's currency reserves can cover the deficit or that it obtains coverage by borrowing.

Keeping the current account in equilibrium (with exports matching imports) is a fairly easy task in a protectionist system, but much less so in an open economy. Over the long term, the French economy has succeeded in moving in the right direction. However, France's current account traversed a long period in the red, mainly due to oil price hikes and the recession.

The figures in Table 3.3 illustrate these points and also allow comparison with other major economies. France has been unable to register the surpluses that have become the norm in Germany or Japan. However, France is not the only country to have run into problems with current account. The USA ran massive deficits during the late 1980s. By the end of the decade, Britain too was in the red.

A second performance indicator is foreign penetration of domestic markets. Imports have taken a growing share of French domestic markets for industrial goods. In 1970, 18 per cent of demand in French markets for industrial goods went to imports; by 1987, the figure rose to 32 per cent (Milewski, 1989, p. 44).

However, given France's protectionist past, this development can be considered in a favourable light as it indicates greater openness to free trade.

Table 3.3 Cross-national comparison of current account balances: 1967-1987 (in billions of current dollars)

	France	FRG	USA	Japan	UK
1967	0.2	2.5	2.6	-0.2	-1.1
1968	-0.9	3.0	0.6	1.0	-1.2
1969	-1.5	1.9	0.4	2.1	1.2
1970	0.1	1.0	2.3	2.0	1.9
1971	0.5	1.0	-1.4	5.8	2.7
1972	0.3	1.2	-5.8	6.6	0.5
1973	1.5	5.0	7.1	-0.1	-2.6
1974	-3.9	10.6	2.0	-4.7	-7.9
1975	2.7	4.3	18.1	-0.7	-3.5
1976	-3.4	3.7	4.2	3.7	-1.6
1977	-0.4	4.0	-14.5	10.9	-0.2
1978	7.0	8.9	-15.4	16.5	1.9
1979	5.2	-5.4	-1.0	-8.7	-1.3
1980	-4.2	-13.8	1.9	-10.7	7.1
1981	-4.7	-3.6	6.9	4.8	13.5
1982	-12.1	5.1	-8.7	6.9	7.8
1983	-4.7	5.3	-46.2	20.8	5.7
1984	-0.8	9.7	-107.1	35.0	2.7
1985	-0.3	16.8	-115.1	49.2	4.2
1986	2.9	38.5	-138.8	85.9	-1.4
1987	-4.6	44.6	-154.0	86.7	-4.4

Source: Jeanneney, J.-M. (ed.) (1989), *L'Economie française depuis 1967,* Paris: Seuil, p. 413

Thirdly, France has experienced falls in her global market shares (Holcblat and Tavernier, 1989). This is partly due to her geographical specialisations. France has a strong presence in the Middle East and Africa. That presence was a positive stimulant during the 1970s and early 1980s when the economies of those regions were buoyant. However, with oil price slumps and debt problems in the 1980s, they have been much less dynamic. In the latter period, the Pacific Basin has been the area to expand most rapidly, but this is an area in which France is underrepresented. Falls in world market shares also relate to French difficulties in competing in the open markets of industrialised countries as compared to the Middle East and Africa where State-to-State negotiations induce a very different business environment. These themes will be developed below. Arguably, it is in OECD markets that the true competitiveness of French firms is tested.

Fourthly, apart from national accounts (such as the balance of trade), company accounts also provide evaluative criteria of international competitiveness. Delattre (1986) showed that French industries and firms which appear in a positive light in terms of their exports volume do not all fare equally well when measured in terms of corporate profitability, debt and growth in output. The French professional electronics industry, aviation, cars and especially steel suffer from a heavy burden of debt. Yet all figure prominently as net exporters. Only a few sub-sectors of 'agri-food' and pharmaceuticals succeed in combining high exports, high profitability and growth with low indebtedness.

In brief, even though any specific evaluation has to be qualified in terms of time-period and firm, this range of measurements indicates that the international competitiveness of French business has been mixed.

Next we present broad explanations for performance under three complementary heads, firstly in terms of industrial specialisations, secondly in terms of the role of the State and thirdly in terms of firm behaviour.

French industrial specialisation

From Ricardo to Porter (1990), the notion of comparative advantage has been used to describe the place of nations in the system of international trade. Comparative advantages can arise from factor inputs (raw materials, labour, capital), technological expertise and local demand. In the theory, a country is understood to have a comparative advantage if its particular products are cheaper and/or more attractive than those of competitor nations. Once comparative advantages in specific sectors have been established, it is in a nation's interest to specialise in those sectors where it is most competitive and import goods from other sectors where it is less competitive. Degrees of specialisation are thus frequently taken as a structural explanation for levels of national competitiveness.

In the literature on French competitiveness, this approach has repeatedly been invoked. Analysts who believe that national specialisations continue to be an important reality usually cite as proof the trade surpluses of Germany and Japan, who are interpreted as specialists, in contradistinction to the trade deficits of France or Britain, who have lower levels of specialisation. However, in recent years, there has been considerable disagreement over France's levels of specialisation and their effects. There follows a review of the different schools of thought.

Analysts such as Sachwald (1990) and Abadie (1989) consider that France does have significant specialisations – but the wrong ones, largely because of the limited demand for them. The most critical case of this kind is put forward by Adda and Smouts (1989, pp. 177-83). They argue that France has specialised in sectors linked to national independence: the nuclear industry, arms, aeronautics and professional electronics. In most cases, the strengths are in military hardware whose markets are limited. French nuclear technology has largely been unsaleable. Only in aeronautics does France benefit from worthwhile civil markets, but these fluctuate greatly. While France has been putting too much effort into military hardware, where technological transfer is limited, she has fallen back in high-growth, high-tech sectors such as information technology, which thrive through extensive technological transfers.

As Le Houcq and Strauss (1988) argue, France's lack-lustre performance in high-tech has become a serious national problem. The consequence of inappropriate specialisation has been increased French technological dependence on other industrialised countries. Of equal concern to the French is that France's geographical and product specialisations both showed a relatively high degree of dynamism in the 1970s, but both showed low growth in the 1980s. Thus a number of analysts are expressing alarm at the seriousness of France's current situation.

A different case is put forward by those who consider that France is inadequately specialised. France's level of specialisation has variously been described as 'intermediate' (Milewski, 1989), 'fragile' (Turpin, 1989), or 'insufficient' (Abadie, 1989). In a fairly typical example of this approach, Mazier (1983) contended that France is underspecialised in relation to her competitors because, in 1980, the top five export sectors accounted for 54 per cent of the balance of trade surplus in Japan, 24 per cent in the USA, 22 per cent in West Germany but only 11.5 per cent in France. Similarly, Orléan (1986) compared Germany, Japan, France, Italy and the UK and emphasised the sector-wide strengths of Germany and Japan. The former is strong in chemical industries, mechanical engineering, machine-tools and cars; the latter in cars, mechanical engineering and consumer electronics. On the other hand, he contended that France, like Italy, had only two examples each of strengths throughout a sector. These were metal-working and transport for the former; metal-working and mechanical engineering for the latter. To this could be added a number of specific but isolated strengths in other sectors.

Milewski (1989, pp. 56-66) has given a good explanation of why this school of thought considers underspecialisation to be problematic. Strength right across a sector increases upstream/downstream synergies within a country. It also promotes leadership which allows firms to be pricemakers in international markets. On the other hand, individual firms in national sectors lacking overall coherence find themselves isolated and forced into being pricetakers. Milewski concludes that France's problems with international competitiveness and trade deficits are caused primarily by the lack of self-reinforcing *filières*, that is by inadequate industrial structures. For this school of thought, the solution lies in acting upon industrial structures. Usually this means calling for State intervention, a theme taken up below.

However, there is controversy over the *need* for national specialisation. For example, Holcblat and Husson (1990, p. 108) point out that 50 per cent of intra-European trade is in the same products. As examples in the later part of this chapter will show, France trades as a 'generalist'. Most EC countries do likewise. The German case is the exception, not the rule. Commentators such as Abd-El-Rahman and Charpin (1989) and Banque Indosuez (1990) show that in the European context variations in the business environment between nations have diminished. Trading patterns, in those circumstances, result not from national determinants but from the strategies and performance of individual companies.

Further, the existence of highly developed intra-sectoral exchanges in

Europe calls into question the validity of the theory that has come down from Ricardo. In the theory, regular exchanges of similar products should not happen if factor inputs created efficiency differentiations. Consequently, some commentators such as Michalet (1984) simply reject the theory as outdated. They argue that in the global economy the nation State as a unit of analysis and the notion of national comparative advantages have little meaning. Stress is placed instead on multinational companies which accumulate advantages drawn from regional factor inputs by an optimal localisation of facilities in different parts of the globe.

These latter approaches share in common an emphasis on the transnational dimension and on company behaviour as the basic variables in the competitiveness equation. For them, the stress should be placed not on national policy frameworks but on company behaviour in the international arena, themes to be picked up in the section on company behaviour later in this chapter.

The French State and the exports drive

In a far-sighted analysis, Arnaud-Ameller (1970) diagnosed the principal problem of the French approach to foreign exchanges as a lack of dynamism demonstrated in a tendency to export surplus stocks rather than to seek out foreign markets as a priority in themselves. Export activities in the 1960s were limited to too few companies: about 5,000 large firms out of a total population of 140,000 in 1966. Arnaud-Ameller predicted that France's surplus on the trade balance of manufactured goods would disappear and proposed that efforts – requiring incentives from the State – be made to reposition French exports in higher technology, 'grey matter' products rather than in average quality and/or high manual labour goods. Arnaud-Ameller's forecasts of trade deficits were realised. The call for more State intervention was answered, but with mixed results.

To accelerate the integration of French firms into the global marketplace, the French State chose to intervene. Already in the 1960s the State had encouraged mergers: the aim was to create 'national champions' who were capable of competing in international markets (see pp. 56-9). State involvement in the exports drive increased in the 1970s. A number of justifications have been advanced for this:

(a) urgency due to the oil crisis (see pp. 19-20 and 23-4);
(b) increased risks incurred by firms in foreign markets due to higher levels of economic and political instability;
(c) commercial risks due to higher costs of prospecting, currency exchange fluctuations and dangers of non-payment;
(d) lengthier time-frames increased the uncertainties related to production (e.g. the likelihood of greater price variations of production inputs) and longer distances caused problems for delivery, replacements and after-sales services;
(e) differences in the availability and costs of loans to buyers due to higher French inflation and interest rates.

To neutralise at least some of these dangers, the French State set up a number of services. Exporting information services were provided by the *Centre français du commerce extérieur* (French Foreign Trade Centre). Soft loans were often provided, mainly via the *Banque française du commerce extérieur* (BFCE). Insurance against economic and commercial risks has been provided by the *Compagnie française d'assurance pour le commerce extérieur* (COFACE).

To take the case of a major export contract, typically negotiations between the French State and a client State led to a *protocole financier gouvernemental*, a contract which frequently provided subsidised Treasury loans and COFACE guarantees to the French exporter. French export subsidies have been high. They totalled 14.1 billion francs in 1987 – equivalent to almost half of the trade deficit for that year (Milewski, 1989, p. 110).

These measures greatly contributed to the success of the post-oil shock exports drive, with the trade balance approaching equilibrium by 1979. They also led to a number of perverse effects. Firstly, most of the benefit from these measures was enjoyed by a limited number of firms, usually in large-scale construction projects. There was logic in this as the *grands projets* lent themselves to inputs from multinationals, of which there are only a select few in France. Delattre (1983, p. 22) indicates that French export strengths largely coincided with a limited number of such 'national champions', for example, Saint-Gobain, the CGE, etc. On the nationalisation of a number of those firms in 1981-2 (see pp. 59-64), the revelation of their poor financial position proved a shock but as Estrin and Holmes (1985, p. 59) pointed out, these firms had become 'pensioners of the State' whose export positions had been cushioned by the French State. In short, State help had provided 'feather-bedding', with many costs borne by the French taxpayer (Garcia, 1977, p. 57). In the process, public subsidies to large firms producing intermediate goods diverted resources away from other sectors of the economy. These included small firms in general as well as consumer industries and information technology in particular. Yet the latter are the areas in which France has largest trade gaps.

Secondly, because of the availability of cheap loans, the inherent competitiveness of the French exporter becomes less important. Without State subsidies (as soft loans or tied aid), it is unlikely that French companies could have obtained the *grands contrat* with developing countries whose importance will be set out on pp. 111-15. Also, subsidies to exporters make trade less 'free', to the extent that market forces are distorted. However, the French were not unique in this; they often merely emulated the practice of competitor nations.

Thirdly, the true value to France of these schemes is unclear. The writers of the Sixth Plan (1971-1975) questioned the value for France of a policy that involved paying the oil bill in foreign debt (see Milewski, 1989, p. 39). The criticisms of Adda and Smouts (1989, pp. 189-92) are even more pointed. They see French trade policy as a sleight of hand which refinances France's trade deficit with industrialised countries by borrowing money on international markets and lending it to near-bankrupt developing countries so that they may buy French goods. French loans to high-risk debtor nations guaranteed by the

State amount to some 225 billion francs (Alimi, 1991). Receipts have fallen from a peak surplus of 109.6 billion francs to 82.6 billions by 1988. Thus State policy is veering away from *grands contrats* with developing countries towards increased sales to industrial countries (DREE, 1989, pp. 121-31). Further, the stress is less on State involvement and more on corporate performance.

Company behaviour

With State involvement found wanting, the spotlight returns to the competitive behaviour of firms themselves. Here it is customary to consider competitive behaviour in terms of price competition and non-price competition.

Though in general, firms themselves set their prices, for reasons to be explained, they are not able to control every aspect of price formation. In reality, price competitiveness in international markets has three major components: production costs, profit margins and exchange rate influences.

Production costs can be subdivided in terms of costs of raw materials, labour-related costs, capital costs and taxes. France is unevenly endowed in natural resources. Though rich in agriculture, France is poor in raw materials. French firms purchase most primary commodities on international markets at rates which vary with global demand and with the level of the franc. The individual firm has no control over these price developments.

In the area of labour-related costs, firms again have only limited control. As regards salaries, though firms have sought to keep wages down, in world terms, France is a high-wage country. Unit labour costs are much higher in France than in developing or industrialising countries or in Southern Europe. But they are lower than in the USA, Germany or Holland.

As Holcblat and Husson (1990, pp. 98-9) point out, these figures need to be taken in the context of productivity: statistical information relating wages to productivity is fragmentary, but such figures as are available suggest France fared relatively well in relation to major OECD nations. The problems seem to lie elsewhere.

A frequent complaint of French employers relates to high taxes and high *charges sociales* (employers' national insurance contributions). When taxes and *charges sociales* are added together, French firms carry a heavier burden than firms in the USA, Japan or other European countries (Holcblat and Husson, 1990, p. 101). These costs reduce French competitiveness. Recent governments have reduced the burden (see p. 37) but French firms are calling on the State to do more, particularly in the area of *charges sociales*.

In export markets, exchange rate movements also impact on price competitiveness. Depreciations of a national currency make exports cheaper while a strong currency makes exports more expensive. Devaluations of the franc in 1982 and 1983 helped improve the price competitiveness of French firms.

Further, export profit margins and exchange rate movements tend to be linked. Appreciation of the national currency can force exporters to decrease their profit margins while devaluation can offer the opportunity to enhance profits. Thus in 1981-1983, French export prices increased more rapidly than domestic prices, indicating a tendency to value export profitability more highly than market share (OECD, 1984). Export prices continued to rise between 1985 and 1988, probably in relation to a need to compensate for the start of the decade when world demand was low. In addition, by the late 1980s, many French firms were working near the limits of their production capacity, hence managers may well have reasoned that if they could sell almost as much as they could make, then they could afford to keep prices high (Abd-El-Rahman, 1990).

However, prices form only one explanation for competitiveness. Price competitiveness is most important for standard products. In real life, firms differentiate their products by adding greater value not only in terms of product build (intrinsic quality, design, reliability) but also in terms of a range of factors such as innovativeness, technological content and service before and after sales. The overall competitiveness of a firm will result from all of these factors, including price. This makes it difficult to distinguish between the effects of price and non-price factors. To the extent that generalisation is possible, Debonneuil and Delattre (1987) have argued that, in France's case, price competitiveness alone does not explain losses in French shares of international trade.

A very useful complementary approach to the understanding of trade imbalances is to relate them to investment patterns. Artus and Bleuze (1990) attribute the French trade gap to inadequate investment. They indicate that between 1984 and 1988, investment outside the financial sector increased by 29 per cent in Germany, 37 per cent in the USA and 67 per cent in Japan but by only 22 per cent in France. In consequence, French industrial capital fell behind in terms of quality (due to age factors) and quantity. After the world economy took off in the mid-1980s, French firms found themselves working at near full capacity (capacity utilisation rates were 79.3 per cent in 1987, 85.5 per cent in 1989). In this analysis, French business simply could not keep up with demand because of insufficient investment.

The simple solution would be more investment. The problems with the solution are, firstly, in finding the resources. At the end of the 1980s, companies were penalised by high interest rates. Secondly, with France having fallen behind in the manufacture of capital goods, particularly machine-tools, the French firms that do expand capacity by buying new machinery frequently resort to imported products. Sachwald (1990, p. 134) attributes the 1988 trade deficit mainly to this factor. The effect is negative in the short term but should lead to longer-term competitiveness.

To summarise, over the long term, the response of French business to the challenge of increased international competition has been mixed, but has included its share of successes. However, trends since the 1980s have given cause for anxiety in France. In order to give detailed treatment to those trends, France's trade balance, services balance and major trading partners will be successively discussed.

FRANCE'S TRADE BALANCE

A country's trade balance indicates the relationship between imports and exports of 'visible' goods, namely primary commodities and manufactures.

Given that the economic wealth of Western nations has largely been based on industrialisation, the ability of a country to produce and market industrial goods is a prime indicator of economic success. During the 1980s, it was sometimes assumed that services and a 'tertiary' economy could replace manufacturing industry as the main source of wealth creation, but this view has largely been dropped. The two sectors are in fact complementary; both are essential. Hence each will be discussed in this chapter.

As Table 3.4 shows, France's trade balance since the 1970s has been almost consistently in deficit. The long-term view over the post-war period shows that this is not unusual but is linked to the development of trade cycles. These will be analysed decade by decade.

Table 3.4 France's balance of trade: 1979-1989

Year	Imports (FOB) (in billions of francs)	Exports (FOB)	Balance	Exports/imports ratio as % [2]
1979	437.1	426.7	- 10.4	97.6
1980	547.6	489.8	- 57.8	89.4
1981	626.7	575.8	- 50.9	91.9
1982	725.4	632.2	- 93.2	87.1
1983	771.6	722.7	- 48.9	93.7
1984	874.8	850.1	- 24.7	97.2
1985	936.7	906.0	- 30.7	96.7
1986	863.2	863.7	+ 0.5	100.1
1987	921.0	889.6	- 31.4	96.6
1988	1030.0	997.0	- 33.0	97.0
1989	1186.9	1143.2	- 43.7	96.3

Sources: Arnaud, R. (1989) *La France en chiffres. Forces et faiblesses de l'économie française,* Paris: Hatier, p. 68 and Ministère de l'Economie (1990) 'Le commerce extérieur de la France en 1989', *Problèmes économiques,* 2,195 (17 octobre), p. 9

The situation in the 1950s

The balance of trade was in chronic deficit in the early 1950s. The major explanatory factors for this were:
- the costs of post-war reconstruction and of rearmament in the Korean war and in France's colonial conflicts;
- high levels of domestic inflation increased the prices of French products and reduced competitiveness on foreign markets;
- import penetration of French markets increased due to rising demand.

These developments were corrected in the late 1950s by:
• an austerity policy in 1957-8 which reduced demand;
• massive devaluation of the franc in 1958 – first by 20 per cent then by 17.5 per cent (Garcia, 1977).
These policies helped restore price competitiveness to French exports: 1959 was a boom year.

The situation in the 1960s

In the 1960s, the trade balance fell back into deficit. This was due to a combination of:
• increased penetration of French markets by other European producers subsequent to the creation of the EEC (the phasing-out of tariff barriers between 1958 and 1968 within the 'common market' deprived French producers of a traditional source of protection of domestic markets);
• decolonisation ended recourse to protected foreign markets.
These processes had begun in the 1950s, but the effects hit French industry hard in the 1960s. Completion of the adjustment process and recovery of competitiveness took until the end of the decade.

The situation in the 1970s

Just as the previous decade had started on a strong note so in the early 1970s the French trade balance was broadly in equilibrium. Again, global developments undermined progress. The major problems were:
• a quadrupling of oil prices in 1973-4;
• strengthening of the dollar against the franc.
With oil being denominated in dollars, the compounded effect of oil price hikes and dollar appreciation was a massive rise in the value of French imports, plunging the trade balance into deficit.

Short-term efforts to turn off the flow of oil and reduce the trade imbalance inevitably achieved limited results due to France's chronic dependence on Middle Eastern oil as an energy source. In the medium to long term, positive results were achieved by investing in nuclear energy, by applying tight monetary and budgetary policies (see pp. 23-6 and 29) and by a State-led exports drive in developing countries (see pp. 111-15). By 1979, there was a close match between levels of imports and exports.

The situation in the 1980s

Once again the decade started with a slump in the balance of traded goods. The causes were:
• the second oil price hike of 1979-1980;
• reflation by the Socialist government which fuelled demand and sucked in imports.
The spectacular and massive trade deficit of 93.2 billion francs in 1982 sent

shock waves through the economy and necessitated a quick about-turn from reflation to a macro-economic policy of austerity.

The results in the medium term were surprisingly good: a gradual reduction in the trade gap leading to a small surplus by 1986. The main explanatory factors were:

- three devaluations of the franc, improving the price competitiveness of French goods;
- the austerity policy cut domestic demand and contained the increase in import penetration;
- strong international recovery from the recession allowing expansion in export markets;
- reductions in the imported energy bill due to cuts in oil prices in 1986 and to devaluation of the dollar.

Yet since 1987, the trade balance has been in persistent and increasing deficit. The decline is all the more worrying for French industrialists and policy makers because the business cycle was at its peak towards the end of the decade and energy prices remained low. Despite these stimuli, an upturn in the trade balance did not materialise at the turn of the decade, as had occurred in previous ten-year cycles. The trade deficit was merely contained: it stood at 50.1 billion francs in 1990 as against 43.7 billions in 1989 (Ministère de l'Economie, 1991).

This was perhaps as good a result as could be expected given the turbulence in 1990 that arose due to a number of factors:

- the world economy was moving into recession;
- the Gulf crisis meant an embargo on trade with Iraq and Kuwait and hampered exports to other Middle Eastern countries;
- many debts from previous exports to Iraq remained outstanding.

Developments in the Middle East are of great consequence to France due to traditional diplomatic links and to trade links, particularly the dependency on Middle East oil (see pp. 18-19 and 115 for discussion).

The situation and outlook in 1991 were slightly better, given the relatively limited effects of the Gulf War itself, but broadly comparable in other respects. France cannot expect a boost from the international economy. She relies on major contracts with Middle Eastern countries to finance oil purchases but may benefit less from the rebuilding of Kuwait than the UK and the USA. Oil prices will probably rise in the medium term. As regards Europe, the French business community is enthusiastic about the completion of the Single Market, officially scheduled for 1 January 1993 (see pp. 107-8). Overall, however, France's trade balance looks set to deteriorate further. For all these reasons, the international competitiveness of French industry is currently being analysed in France with increasing concern.

To locate specific strengths and weaknesses, we next turn to a sector by sector analysis of French performance in internationally traded goods.

FRENCH STRENGTHS AND WEAKNESSES IN
INTERNATIONALLY TRADED GOODS

Over the last 30 years, France's industrial strengths and weaknesses have altered considerably.

Though already a major food producer in the 1950s, France has come to specialise more intensively in foodstuffs. In the fifties and sixties, France's other specialisations were basic industries (electricity, glass, upstream steel products) and traditional consumer industries such as textiles-clothing, leather and publishing.

By the 1970s, the traditional consumer industries were in decline but the car sector had grown rapidly in importance (Guibert, 1975). Meanwhile, France's long-standing weakness in the production of capital goods had diminished but so too had many of her advantages in basic industries (Camus *et al.*, 1981).

Since the recession of the mid-seventies, French industry has made efforts to reposition in high-growth, high-technological sectors. Some measure of success was achieved but, as Mazier (1983) argued, the 'niche' strategy that

Table 3.5 France's balance of trade: the ten largest surpluses and deficits by sector in 1988 (in billions of francs)

Surpluses		
1.	Cereals	+28.9
2.	Wines and spirits	+26.2
3.	Cars, cycles and spare parts	+23.8
4.	Perfume	+12.0
5.	Milk and dairy products	+10.5
6.	Drinks, alcohol and tobacco	+9.8
7.	Aviation	+8.2
8.	Non-tropical oleaginous products	+7.7
9.	Steel	+7.2
10.	Pharmaceuticals	+6.5
Deficits		
1.	Energy	-66.7
2.	Professional electronics	-23.1
3.	Textiles-clothing	-17.3
4.	Paper and cardboard	-14.3
5.	Non-ferrous metals	-14.3
6.	Consumer electronics	-12.3
7.	Chemical products	-11.6
8.	Coffee, cocoa, tropical fruits	-8.5
9.	Preserves	-8.0
10.	Leather and shoes	-7.2

Source: Arnaud, R. (1989) *La France en chiffres. Forces et faiblesses de l'economie française*, Paris: Hatier, p. 69

was adopted did not produce or confirm superiority across the whole of any industry as was the case with German chemicals, American information technology or Japanese consumer electronics. In consequence, an inventory of France's major surpluses and deficits reveals a disparate mix of strengths and weaknesses (see Table 3.5).

The rest of this section analyses the detail of the major elements found in Table 3.5.

Strengths in traded goods

Agriculture and food processing

France has become the leading food producer in the EC. As Table 3.6 illustrates, France receives substantial earnings from exporting food products.

Table 3.6 France's recent 'agri-food' surpluses (in billions of francs)

	1984	1986	1988	1989
Exports	141.5	143.1	168.4	189.2
Imports	116.1	116.5	128.2	141.0
Balance	25.4	26.6	39.2	48.2
Imports/exports ratio as %	121.8	122.8	130.3	134.1

Source: Ministère de l'Economie (1990) 'Le commerce extérieur de la France en 1989', *Problèmes économiques*, 2,195 (17 octobre), p. 13

In terms of specific products, cereals and alcohol are France's top earners; dairy products are also significant (see Table 3.5). French wines achieve huge foreign sales, even in Japan (Ministère de l'Economie, 1990). Though a net exporter of foods, France inevitably runs deficits on items such as tropical fruits and coffee. More surprising are deficits in processed meat products and a worsening balance on biscuits!

Underneath the successes told by the statistics are more disquieting features. Agriculture is a net exporter but receives major subsidies from the EC, a point to which we return in the section on France and the EC later in this chapter. The French food-processing industry is underdeveloped. Approximately two-thirds of France's agricultural surplus is in unprocessed products; only one-third is in processed-food and drink (Arnaud, 1989, p. 88). Since value added is greater in the processed food sector than in agricultural commodities, the French economy is failing to exploit fully its natural resources. Due to these structural factors, France re-imports processed food from the European neighbours to whom it exports the 'raw material'. This is a surprising situation for a nation that prides itself on its gastronomy.

The limited nature of France's successes in agriculture and food processing emerges from international comparisons. Arnaud (1989, p. 128) cites a survey indicating that of the 110 largest food-processing firms in the world, 46 are American, 19 are Japanese, 18 British and only 7 are French. Though firms such as Moët-Hennessy-Vuitton and Perrier enjoy an international reputation, they specialise only in limited market segments (mainly spirits and mineral water respectively). In BSN, France has its only international food-processing company comparable in product range and market size to giants such as Anglo-Dutch Unilever or Swiss Nestlé.

The contrast between France's strength in agriculture and relative weakness in food processing illustrates the uneven ability of French industry to exploit fully its potential comparative advantages.

The car industry

Peugeot, which is still a family-controlled firm, and State-owned Renault are the major French car manufacturers. Production of cars and spare parts provides France with a major trade surplus. This surplus is an indication of the strength of France's indigenous car industry.

However, dark clouds have been gathering on the horizon. France's share of the world market has steadily fallen. In 1979, France's output accounted for 17 per cent of the world market; by 1988, her share fell to 12.4 per cent (DREE, 1989). Given that growth within the world market has partly been in newly industrialised countries, this development is not necessarily an absolute sign of weakness in French companies. Nevertheless, it remains true that the French have not been able to make inroads into the largest single car market in the world – the USA – whereas the Japanese have.

The French car industry has the benefit of a strong, home market base. In 1988, French car manufacturers accounted for 63 per cent of car sales in France. The long-term trend, however, is to falling domestic market share. The French State, spurred on by the French car trade lobby, has traditionally limited Japanese imports to France. Jacques Calvet, head of Peugeot, has been vocal in his opposition to Japanese manufacturers setting up within the EC. He fears that they will take greater market shares in Europe from domestic producers, just as they did in the USA. However, Calvet has been overruled. New EC agreements foresee an opening-up of European car markets. The Japanese car industry is set to increase its penetration of French markets. The international competitiveness of French manufacturers will be further tested.

Civil aviation

Airbus has been one of the success stories of aviation in recent years. The 37.9 per cent stake of the State-owned firm Aérospatiale in the Airbus consortium assures France a healthy balance of trade in the aeronautics sector. The problem is that Airbus is a single product line whose sales fluctuate considerably from year to year. This makes French aviation a strong but erratic earner of foreign currency. Nonetheless, aviation successes illustrate strong French presence in a high-tech sector.

Steel

After years of massive losses and enforced restructuring, Usinor-Sacilor, France's huge steel combine, moved into profitability in 1987. In output terms,

Usinor-Sacilor is the second largest steel producer in the world (after Nippon Steel). Performance on exports markets has been impressive, with the firm including Mercedes-Benz among its customers. Overseas sales have been reinforced by a policy of acquisitions abroad.

The major problem of the company is the enormous scale of its debts. As a nationalised company, Usinor-Sacilor owes 17 billion francs to its shareholder the State (Clavaud, 1990). Much of this has gone in new investment. But State subsidies are subject to increasingly vigilant scrutiny from the European Commission: they are a source of distortions in international competition.

Usinor-Sacilor's return to profitability in late 1988 coincided with a period of international economic expansion. During the current down-turn, its financial position is less secure since firms in or supplying to the construction sector are among the hardest hit by the recession. Relatively small falls in demand have been accompanied by large falls in profitability. In 1990, European production fell by 3.9 per cent relative to 1989, while world production fell by 2 per cent. On the French balance of trade, the surplus for steel fell from 6.1 billion francs to 2.7 billions (Fédération française de l'acier, 1991). Profits in Usinor-Sacilor fell by 54 per cent from their 1989 peak of 7.6 to 3.5 billion francs in 1990 (Renard, 1991). The long-term outlook for French steel remains unsettled.

Arms

France has been the world's third largest exporter of arms after the USA and the USSR. Over 90 per cent of production is from State-owned firms.

The surplus from arms makes a major contribution towards the trade balance. In 1983, the arms industry had the largest surplus of all sectors: 33.1 billion francs worth of exports while arms imports were negligible (Dussauge, 1985, p. 167). In 1987, sales of arms produced a surplus of 26.4 billion francs while non-military industrial goods registered a deficit of 36.7 billions (Milewski, 1989, p. 37).

After the oil crisis of the mid-seventies, arms sales were massively promoted by the State as a means of correcting trade imbalances. Whereas in 1970, the French arms industry exported 19 per cent of its output, by 1978 that figure had doubled and it remained stable at around 40 per cent during the 1980s (Dussauge, 1985, p. 14). Major customers were in the Middle East, including Iraq, Syria and Egypt. Put crudely, weapons were bartered against oil.

A French policy of arms sales to the Middle East undoubtedly contributed to an excessive military build-up in the area. However, the USA and the USSR, who are the world's largest sources of arms sales, were also heavily responsible for the build-up. This concentration of weaponry played a role in the Iraq-Iran war and Iraq's invasion of Kuwait in 1990.

Following the defeat of Iraq in 1991, the international mood is to prevent the filling of another powder-keg in the Middle East, implying reductions in arms sales to the area. This, together with the so-called 'peace dividend' accruing from the ending of the Cold War, is set to reduce arms production in France. Further, the superiority of American arms technology, as demonstrated in the Gulf War, will also inhibit exports of French weaponry. For these reasons, France's large foreign earnings from arms sales may dwindle in the 1990s. However, in 1990, weaponry sales remained France's largest surplus in manufactures (Ministère de l'Economie, 1991).

Luxury goods

In the field of luxury goods, France enjoys a highly favourable public image internationally. Taken together, they produced a balance of trade surplus of some 50 billion francs in 1988 (DREE, 1989, p. 58).

Luxury goods, however, constitute a rather mixed collection of products – they include wines, spirits, perfumes and high fashion goods – rather than a coherent industrial sector. In marketing terms, some coherence exists to the extent that similar groups of customers purchase these products. Questions can be raised though in relation to the relative size of this customer base. Can France afford to specialise extensively in goods for the upper income brackets? Profits may be high but volume is limited.

In summary, surpluses on the French balance of trade are drawn from a mixture of industrial sectors, having localised strengths, but relatively few synergies and commonalities. Elements of a central pattern exist as regards the role of the State, as it has protected French agriculture and nationalised a number of key exporting companies – Usinor-Sacilor, Pechiney, Renault, Aérospatiale, Air France, Dassault, Thomson-CSF. Up to a point, this suggests a core of French specialisations in the nexus formed by mechanical engineering-transportation-arms.

But this is a partial view. Up-market luxury goods are a totally different business. Finally, reasons of space have excluded mention of individual firms from other sectors who have been highly successful in international markets.

Weaknesses in traded goods

Information technology

In this key development sector of our age, French industry is seriously weak. In other high-technology areas (such as the pharmaceutical industry and electrical engineering), French imports and exports are in near equilibrium, but in information technology, the trade deficit is enormous. The deficit in 1988 was 15 billion francs, with a cumulative deficit for the decade of some 60 billions (Dubois and Levy, 1989).

Despite the international success of French software firms such as Cap-Gemini-Sogeti, no solution is in sight to make good the deficits. The history of the French computer industry is uninspiring, being marked by a series of unsuccessful State interventions punctuated by American take-overs of French firms, culminating in nationalisation in 1981. In hardware manufacture, the major French survivor is State-owned Bull, which recorded massive losses in the early 1980s and again at the end of the decade. In 1990, losses amounted to 6.79 billion francs (Renard, 1991). The French government proposes to bail it out again.

In brief, the French computer industry remains uncompetitive in relation to American front-runners and subsists on State hand-outs.

Consumer goods

In sectors such as consumer electronics, textiles, clothing and other household goods, the balance of trade is in deep deficit. French firms have failed to make a significant impact in export markets. Indeed, import penetration has steadily risen. In textiles and clothing, this has occurred despite efforts to maintain protectionist barriers against developing nations by the Multi-Fibre Arrangement.

Consumer electronics has been a long-standing weakness. The nationalised giant, Thomson, with interests running from consumer electronics to arms, maintained satisfactory profitability in the mid- and late-1980s, but in 1990 was again in the red. A major loss of 2.47 billion francs was recorded (Renard, 1991).

In summary, French manufacturing industry has significant weaknesses in market-driven, consumer sectors. Consumer marketing has traditionally been the Achilles heel of French business. Great strides have undoubtedly been taken since the 1960s in improving marketing expertise, yet major lags persist.

As discussed earlier, the State has played a role in building up French strengths in sectors where sales negotiations occur on an industry-to-industry or State-to-State basis. In consumer mass markets, the State has repeatedly shown itself unable to exercise a long-term beneficial influence.

The causes are structural. State deals are a totally different business to mass markets. In order to correct trade imbalances, intervention in consumer sectors is not a viable solution. French industry must develop inherent competitiveness.

FRANCE'S 'INVISIBLES' BALANCE

France is the second largest exporter of services in the world – behind the USA but ahead of the UK (DREE, 1989, p. 61). In recent years, France's balance of international exchanges of services has consistently been in surplus. Despite the lower level of internationalisation of the service sector, earnings from 'invisibles' have made a major contribution towards counter-balancing trade deficits and overcoming the 'external constraint'. Table 3.7 gives recent statistics.

However, the *volume* of exchanges in services is much lower than in 'visible' trade. Table 3.8 puts the size of the services balance into historical perspective.

The extent to which the services surplus has served to compensate a trade deficit is all the more remarkable given the disproportions in size between

Table 3.7 France's trade and 'invisibles' balances compared

	1984	1985	1986	1987	1988
Trade balance	-39.6	-48.5	-16.9	-55.3	-54.3
Invisibles balance	+32.3	+45.4	+37.1	+28.6	+29.7
Current account balance	-7.3	-3.1	+20.2	-26.7	-24.6

Source: Arnaud, R. (1989) *La France en chiffres. Forces et faiblesses de l'economie française,* Paris: Hatier, p. 68

trade and services. In each year in the 1980s, the value of trade was about twice that of services. David appears to be propping up Goliath. It is notable that exports of services have exceeded or been comparable to imports of energy, an area which has given policy makers and industrialists grave concern. If her current account is to return to good health, France may need to give the same attention to services.

Table 3.8 Changes in the structure of French imports and exports by major product groups: 1959-1980

	Exports (%)			Imports (%)		
	1959	1973	1980	1959	1973	1980
Agriculture and food processing	11.7	16.6	13.7	33.5	15.8	10.8
Energy	3.6	2.1	3.6	19.3	11.7	24.5
Manufacturing industry	66.0	64.9	66.5	39.1	62.6	55.4
Services	18.7	16.4	16.2	8.1	9.9	9.3
Total	100.0	100.0	100.0	100.0	100.0	100.0

Source: Brémond, J. & Brémond, G. (1985) *L'Économie française face aux défis mondiaux,* Paris: Hatier, p. 148

FRENCH STRENGTHS AND WEAKNESSES IN SERVICES

The term 'services' covers a wide and disparate array of activities. It includes commercial services such as sales of insurance, financial products and patents. Other services comprise tourism and leisure, transport and telecommunications. In the French balance of payments, the rubric 'services' also includes so-called *services liés aux échanges de technologie*. These are technology transfers, which are usually linked to *grands contrats* ('major contracts'). Civil engineering projects undertaken in the Middle East and Third World to improve infrastructure are typical examples of *grands contrats*. In practice, these projects are undertaken by industrial companies, but the activities are recorded as 'services'. Hence the terms of reference can be confusing, if not anomalous, but the sums involved are far from trivial as Table 3.9 illustrates.

Table 3.9 Breakdown of the French 'invisibles' balance: 1981-1988 (in billions of francs)

	1981	1982	1983	1984	1986	1987	1988
Commercial services	-8.7	-11.7	-7.7	-12.2		-3.8	+0.6
Services linked to technology transfers	+21.9	+29.6	+31.0	+30.4	+22.6	+22.8	+19.3
Revenues	+2.6	-2.2	-11.4	-19.4			
Tourism	+8.1	+12.1	+22.4	+29.1	+22.2	+20.3	+24.7
Government services	+7.1	+4.0	+1.0	-2.1			
Various	+1.3	-0.4	-1.2	-1.0	+1.1	-1.0	-5.1
Total	+32.3	+31.4	+32.1	+24.7	+45.9	+38.2	+39.5

Sources: Nguyên Duy-Tân, J. (1986) 'Le commerce extérieur de la France. Environnement international et instruments juridiques', Paris: La Documentation française, *Notes et études documentaires,* no. 4798, p. 19 and DREE (1989) *Où en est la compétitivité française?* Paris: La Documentation française, p. 63

We next examine the sectoral strengths and weaknesses that lie behind these figures.

Strengths in services

Tourism
Tourism has become the major net earner of foreign currency in the service sector. France is the fourth largest tourist market in the world, behind Spain, Italy and the USA. Levels of net earnings have fluctuated in relation to a number of factors:

- Currency exchange developments. At its peak in 1985, tourism earned 30 billion francs. The peak related to the strength of the dollar and the inflow of American tourists. Subsequent to the fall in the dollar, French receipts from tourism fell back in 1986 but increased again towards the end of the decade.
- Short-term variations in numbers of incoming tourists. Examples include the fall in 1987, partly as a result of the 1986 terrorist bombings in Paris and the large increase in 1989, due to the celebrations of the bicentennial of the French Revolution.
- French patterns of holiday-making. Every year, the numbers of French people taking their holidays outside of France increase, reducing the potential surplus from tourism.

Longer-term trends need also to be assessed in the light of increasing competition from other countries, notably Spain and Portugal. France has not been marketing herself as forcefully as competitors and it has done relatively less to diversify the types of holiday offered, to improve and extend accommodation and leisure facilities (DREE, 1989).

Tourism receipts at home have however provided a platform for the development of major hotel chains such as Accor, which has 773 hotels in 58 countries. After the USA, France is the second largest provider of services in the international hotel sector (Arnaud, 1989).

Technological transfers

France has successfully developed expertise in large-scale projects which, in the French balance of payments, are referred to as *grands travaux* (major construction projects) and *coopération technique* (technical co-operation). Taken together, these activities have in recent years produced large surpluses on the current account. They have been particularly important in trade with the developing countries (see pp. 111-15).

Telecommunications

France Télécom, the State-owned operator of French telecommunication networks, enjoys satisfactory current performance but has unclear future prospects. By its very nature, international phone usage tends to equilibrium, with callers between countries alternating in the logging and payment of calls. In the provision of equipment, France registered a surplus of 2.77 billion francs in 1987. However, international competition between suppliers is increasing as are pressures for deregulation (DREE, 1989).

Weaknesses in services

Services to exporters

In this amalgam sector, which includes services such as transport and insurance, France has lagged behind. Exporters tend to sell their goods 'free on board' (FOB) (i.e. excluding delivery and insurance): this applied to 50 per cent of French exports in 1984 and 54 per cent in 1986. On the other hand, importers tend to buy CIF (cost, insurance, freight): this applied to 55 per cent of imports in 1984 and 60 per cent in 1986 (DREE, 1989, p. 63). This situation has led to imbalances in opportunities for French suppliers and in the national accounts.

Insurance

In terms of market size of all insurance services, France lies fifth behind the USA, Japan, Germany and the UK. However, foreign companies take 25 per cent of the French market. The reinsurance sub-sector is underdeveloped in France and is a major drain on the current account: it registered deficits of 0.6 billion francs in 1985, 1.1 billion in 1986 and 2.6 billion in 1987. French insurance firms are said to suffer from size disadvantages (foreign competitors are larger), a poor distribution network and high taxes (Achard, 1988; DREE, 1989).

Transport

As Table 3.10 indicates, France runs a surplus in air and rail travel but runs deficits in all other modes of transport. In rail and air, the French State, with ownership of the SNCF and Air France, enjoys dominant market positions. However, in other areas of transport where a free market operates, French companies have found it harder to compete.

Table 3.10 France's exchanges of invisibles: transport balances (in billions of francs)

	1985	1986	1987
Air	5.1	3.1	2.8
Rail	1.4	1.3	1.1
Sea	- 3.0	- 2.5	- 1.8
Road	- 1.6	- 1.9	- 1.9
River	- 0.2	- 0.2	- 0.2

Source: DREE (1989) *Où en est la compétitivité française?* Paris: La Documentation française, p. 65

Patents

France has a persistent yearly deficit in patents (2.4 billion francs in 1983). The sums involved are relatively small but this situation reflects badly on French ability to innovate and assume technological leadership. To a great extent, French industry relies on imported ideas in research and development. Importing 'grey matter' in the form of patents inevitably creates production and marketing lags. The danger of long-term technological dependency exists, causing anxiety in France.

Having looked at the product areas whose exchanges in international markets have most impact on France's economic well-being, we now turn to a discussion of France's major trading partners.

FRANCE'S GEOGRAPHICAL PATTERNS OF TRADE

France's international trade patterns have changed radically over the post-war period as Table 3.11 shows.

Contained within each row of figures is a different 'story', unfolding in time. At this stage, only the largest changes are highlighted, namely the massive decline in trade with the developing countries of Africa – the site of much of France's lost empire – and the equally massive increase with industrialised countries, especially within the EC.

On the whole, increased trade with industrialised countries has been a favourable development. Its implications require discussion of two factors which pull in different directions. The first is the question of the ability to pay. France has traditionally enjoyed large trade volumes with developing countries whose solvency can be erratic due to the major internal problems many of them face. To offset these problems, a relative increase in trade with richer, more solvent buyers in OECD countries is an advantage.

Table 3.11 Geographical patterns of trade (in %)

	1949	1958	1969	1973	1979	1987	1989
Imports							
EC	26.3	32.0	55.6	54.6	50.1	61.0	60.0
Rest of OECD	28.7	21.2	19.4	20.1	20.5	20.0	20.7
Eastern Europe	2.0	3.3	3.4	3.1	3.4	3.2	2.8
Middle East	7.9	9.6	6.0	8.4	14.0	2.9	2.9
Africa	24.8	25.4	9.5	6.1	4.9	4.9	4.4
Others	10.3	8.5	6.1	7.7	7.1	8.0	9.2
	100.0	100.0	100.0	100.0	100.0	100.0	100.0
Exports							
EC	33.4	34.7	52.9	55.6	53.1	60.4	61.2
Rest of OECD	13.8	16.9	19.9	19.8	19.4	18.8	17.9
Eastern Europe	4.9	3.7	4.6	4.0	4.5	2.6	2.5
Middle East	0.8	1.6	2.0	2.6	5.2	3.1	3.0
Africa	38.2	34.0	12.1	9.1	9.3	6.4	6.0
Others	8.9	9.1	8.5	8.9	8.5	8.7	9.4
	100.0	100.0	100.0	100.0	100.0	100.0	100.0

Sources: Camus, B. *et al.* (1981) *La Crise du système productif,* Paris: INSEE, p. 171 and Ministère
de l'Economie (1990) 'Le commerce extérieur de la France en 1989' *Problèmes économiques,* 2,195
(17 octobre), p.15

On the other hand, France has tended to obtain surpluses (at least in
accountancy terms) from trade with developing countries while she has
usually run a trade deficit *vis-à-vis* OECD countries. Table 3.12 illustrates
where and when deficits or surpluses were obtained and gives information on
regional exports/imports ratios for traded goods.

Table 3.12 Regional exports/imports ratios for traded goods (in %) (excluding arms)

	1949	1958	1969	1973	1979	1987	1989
EC	104	101	82	97	96	90	92
Rest of OECD	40	74	89	96	86	85	78
Eastern Europe	200	105	119	123	119	73	80
Middle East	9	16	29	29	34	96	95
Algeria	133	217	77	158	169		
Rest of 'Empire'	125	86	127	138	176		
Africa						119	123
Others	70	98	121	111	107	114	111
Average all areas	82	93	86	96	91	91	91

Sources: Camus, B. *et al.* (1981) *La Crise du système productif,* Paris: INSEE p. 176 and Ministère
de l'Economie (1990) 'Le commerce extérieur de la France en 1989', *Problèmes économiques,*
2,195 (17 octobre), p. 16

Table 3.12 points up shortfalls in competitiveness in relation to other
industrialised countries. It indicates that the surplus with developing countries

played an important role towards compensating for deficits with developed countries. With relatively less trade going to developing countries and more taking place with OECD countries, the short-term effect on the trade balance appears to have been negative.

But it is not a black and white picture. Close inspection of Table 3.12 reveals a cyclical trend, with France traversing periods of weakness but eventually catching a second breath. Trade with EC countries was in equilibrium in 1958 but, with the ending of internal customs barriers in the Common Market, France was running major deficits by 1969. Trade with EC partners returned to near equilibrium in the 1970s, but sizable deficits recurred in the 1980s. A similar story emerges from data on French trade with the rest of the OECD. Historically, shortfalls in competitiveness have been overcome. The question is whether French business can do it again in the 1990s.

In summary, assessing the regional distribution of French trade requires balancing a number of variables. The volume of exchanges (whether in relative or absolute terms) with a particular zone is only one, though certainly important, variable. The customer's solvency and his methods of payment represent another crucial factor. The possibility (or the necessity) of balancing imports with exports – or indeed ensuring a surplus – is yet another. Finally, the dynamism of a particular region is important too. For the export trader, it is essential to know whether markets are growing, static or declining and to act accordingly. These factors will be taken up in the zone by zone analyses that follow.

France and the EC

With over 60 per cent of French foreign trade going to other EC countries, discussion of France's particular strategies within the EC is essential.

A consistent aim in the construction of the European Community has been to improve the competitiveness of European economies in relation to non-EC competition. This has involved reinforcing market mechanisms within the EC but it has also meant rejecting national isolationism as non-viable in the long term. Already in the 1940s the Frenchman, Jean Monnet, one of the founding fathers of the EEC, saw the need to transform Europe from a patchwork of protectionist States to an open and integrated economy. In France, this implied a need to leave behind the *dirigiste* tradition of a centralised State intervening extensively in the economy. France has effected a gradual but successful transition to a largely open, market economy. The first and largest step towards this was France's initiative in the creation of the EEC.

The signing of the Treaty of Rome in 1957 by the original six (France, Germany, Italy, Belgium, the Netherlands and Luxemburg) instituted a free-trade zone in which, in principle, goods, services, workers and capital would cross internal borders without hindrance. Achieving integration has proved to be a long haul. Only the briefest of outlines will be attempted here.

Market integration in the EC necessitated firstly the elimination of internal tariff barriers and the setting-up of a common rate of customs duties on trade with non-members. Customs union was completed in 1968. Its aims were to promote free trade within the EC, to encourage greater competition and so exercise downward pressure on costs and prices.

Integration also required the creation of institutions with the authority to make policies and with the instruments with which to implement them. Institutions included the European Commission, European Parliament and European Court of Justice. Instruments included the Regional Development Fund, a Social Fund, subsidies for the development of infrastructure and research and, the largest fund of all, the Common Agricultural Policy (CAP).

France as a founding member has had a certain amount of success in achieving national objectives within EC frameworks. As Moreau Defarges (1984, p. 29) put it *'la France a toujours rêvé d'une Europe à la française'* (France has always dreamt of a French-style Europe). Traditionally, French strategy has involved pursuing independence from perceived external domination, notably from the USA. This book has indicated that independence was often pursued through protectionism against the outside world and, on the domestic front, through an industrial policy that supports a select number of enterprises by research subsidies and public procurement. France's strategy within the EC has often been to seek translations of these national policies to European level.

France's key role in the development of the CAP is a good case in point. Despite a long tradition as an agricultural country, France before the formation of the EC was a small and inefficient agricultural producer. French production costs were relatively high and productivity in the 1950s was a third below that of Germany, Switzerland or Austria. French produce tended to be consumed in France; little was exported (Tardy, 1981, p. 440). But over the life of the EC, France's specialisations in agriculture have increased markedly. Production of cereals has increased massively and France exports a large surplus (see Table 3.5 on p. 92).

Success in this sector is partly, but not wholly, the result of increased indigenous efficiency. A comparison between France's trade in food products with EC countries and with non-EC countries is revealing. In 1977, French 'agri-food' exports to EC countries were 44 per cent higher than imports. But with non-EC countries the situation was reversed: 'agri-food' imports were 46 per cent higher than exports (Tardy, 1981, p. 451). Part of the explanation relates to types of produce traded. France inevitably runs deficits in coffee, exotic fruit, etc. But the major element of the explanation is connected to the effects of the CAP. The CAP provides subsidies, agreed prices and guaranteed sales to EC farmers. In consequence, prices of agricultural produce in the EC are frequently higher than those of equivalent goods on world markets. Wheat prices in the EC compared to world prices were 95 per cent higher in 1968 and 53 per cent higher in 1986. For sugar, corresponding figures were 255 per cent and 200 per cent; for butter, 404 per cent and 175 per cent (Gubian *et al.*, 1989). France, as the EC's major agricultural producer, has benefited greatly from this opportunity to sell produce at prices above world levels to a large and stable market. France's large balance of trade surplus in food produce has therefore to be understood in the context of highly advantageous CAP subsidies.

The CAP is widely regarded outside the EC as a form of protectionism, since it bolsters European production and puts quotas and taxes on imported produce. French spokesmen have regularly defended the case for the CAP, arguing that EC agricultural subsidies are simply more visible but no greater than those existing elsewhere (Wise, 1989). Indeed, the EC and the USA have regularly been at loggerheads over what constitutes trade barriers to agriculture. Meanwhile, France seems to have successfully pursued traditional national policies of interventionism and protectionism by transposing them to the European level.

Though French agriculture has fared well within the EC, French firms in the industrial sector have on balance had greater difficulties in rising to the challenge. Increased volumes of trade with EC Member States have meant that France has a less geographically diversified client base and is more dependent on EC partners. France's trade balances with EC partners stack up unevenly, as Table 3.13 shows.

Table 3.13 France's trade balances with EC partners (in billions of francs)

	CIF-FOB balances			Exports/imports ratio (%)		
	1984	*1986*	*1988*	*1984*	*1986*	*1988*
FRG	-27.8	-39.3	-50.3	81	77	76
Holland	-16.4	-10.3	-1.8	70	80	97
Belg/Lux	-4.5	-9.0	-9.6	94	89	90
Italy	-0.6	-6.3	-5.1	99	94	96
UK	-9.0	14.9	17.4	88	126	123
Spain	-4.5	-3.2	7.4	85	91	117
Denmark	0.2	0.4	-1.0	103	106	89
Ireland	-1.9	-3.2	-4.8	67	54	44
Greece	2.7	2.7	3.3	163	170	180
Portugal	-0.1	-1.1	1.6	99	86	115
TOTAL EC (12)	-61.9	-54.4	-42.9	86	90	93

Source: Ministère de l'Economie (1989) 'Le Commerce extérieur de la France en 1988', *Problèmes économiques*, 2,143 (4 octobre), p. 12

The major feature of France's intra-EC trade is the deficit with Germany, which is particularly large and growing. A trade deficit with Germany is not altogether surprising. Germany is the major supplier to every Western European country, with the exception of Ireland. However, France has been achieving surpluses with Spain, Portugal, Greece and the UK.

Further European market integration is the object of the '1993' initiatives launched by the Single European Act of 1986. The essential mechanism for market integration, as set out in the influential Cecchini Report (1988), is the removal of non-tariff obstacles to trade within the EC. Non-tariff obstacles include barriers due to differences in technical norms, administrative formalities linked to exports/imports procedures, disparities in national taxation systems and nationalistic preferences in the attribution of public procurement contracts. Removal of these obstacles should produce a 'supply-side shock' leading to greater competition, downward pressures on costs and prices, and a stimulation of demand within the EC. The results are intended to be an increase in economic growth and a decrease in unemployment due to a better allocation of resources. In the 1990s, a 'self-sustaining virtuous circle' should reflate flagging Western European economies and improve European competitiveness in relation to third party rivals, particularly from the USA and Japan, and reduce trade deficits with them.

Japan and the USA are alike in having home markets which are sufficiently large to sustain product development and form the base from which to launch major export drives. Lacking a home base of the same size, France, like other European countries, has found the struggle uneven. One of the prime motivations for the consolidation of the EC is to put European nations on an equal footing with the US and Japan in terms of size and stability of home markets, capacity for technological and marketing leadership and co-ordinated international trade policies.

The unknown factors in the process include the extent to which new institutional arrangements will produce a bigger economic 'cake' after 1993 and whether the 'cake' can be shared out in a relatively equitable fashion between all EC Member States. The danger is that the 1993 initiatives will induce a zero-sum game in which the economic 'cake' grows no larger but some nations, sectors and firms benefit disproportionately at the expense of others. To tilt the balance towards favourable outcomes, the acceleration in exchanges of goods and services is being accompanied by initiatives in the areas of social, fiscal and monetary policies. Yet the problems of achieving European co-ordination in these areas are great. Progress has been slow and uncertain.

Even in economic terms, it is essential that the EC becomes more than a 'common market'. A market only allows for *distribution* of goods. Integrated European *production* systems are required to capitalise fully on European strengths and increase the efficiency and world competitiveness of the European economy. However, the extent to which genuine European production systems have arisen or will exist is a vexed issue (Bernis, 1990). Two major approaches exist. One is to look at developments due to mergers and take-overs occurring in Europe. The other is to consider progress made in terms of European co-operation.

In recent years, mergers and acquisitions have accelerated in pace. Many have involved French firms. Gordon (1990, p. 72) noted that in 1988, France was the fourth largest international investor after Japan, the USA and the UK. Between 1986 and 1988, CGE-Alcatel took control of ITT, Rhône-Poulenc bought Union Carbide fertilisers, Bull took over Honeywell Information Systems and Saint-Gobain bought Oberland, a glass company with whom it had synergies and Pernod Ricard acquired Irish Distillers (Abbou, 1988; Mamou *et al.*, 1988; Banque Indosuez, 1990). Just as in the 1970s (see pp. 56-9), the aim has been to achieve 'critical mass' in order to compete on equal terms with German, American and Japanese giants.

A number of co-operative ventures leading to a genuine European dimension have involved French participation. They include Airbus (involving French Aérospatiale, German MBB, British Aerospace and Spanish Casa), the Channel Tunnel as well as agreements between Renault and Volkswagen. Other examples of co-operation include the space programme (Ariane and Hermès) and the European Fighter Aircraft. European Community initiatives to encourage European co-operative research and development include ESPRIT and RACE (information and communications technology), BRIDGE and ECLAIR (bio-technology), BRITE (manufacturing industry) and EUREKA (advanced technology), which was initiated by President Mitterrand in 1985.

Although the results are currently limited to a number of cases, co-ordination of European production systems is a promising way forward. Champions of European industrial policy, such as Geroski and Jacquemin, (1985) have called for European initiatives to achieve greater production integration. A French-led push for a European industrial policy would be quite in character. To what extent such a push can be successful in the post-1992 European economy is currently not clear. But it may offer French business increased opportunities to enter into world-beating alliances with partners from EC countries.

The French business community has been extremely enthusiastic about the '1993' programme. Surveys of managers in both large and small firms point to levels of enthusiasm for '1993' that are far higher in France than elsewhere (Barsoux and Lawrence, 1991).

This raises the question of why the French should be more enthusiastic. A number of explanatory factors stand out. Firstly, the French business community looks on 1993, the year the Single Market 'officially' opens, as a *rendezvous avec l'Histoire;* as confirmation of France's historical integration into Europe. Many business people are keen to cast off finally the protection-ism that historically constituted French policy, the poor reputation it gave France abroad and the inadequate market adaptation that went with it at home. From being a 'no-go' area, the French believe that their country will be the new cross-roads of Europe, linking Germany to the UK via the Channel Tunnel and uniting South and North Europe by various TGV links.

Secondly, the 'Single Market' presents an opportunity to reinforce French competitiveness by greater internationalisation. The aim is to build a strong France in a strong Europe.

Thirdly, the French business community sees the Single Market programme as a means of reinforcing pressure on the French State to undertake a number of reforms for which it has consistently lobbied. These include reform of the tax and social security systems. The French business community considers itself to be more highly taxed than any other national group in the EC, despite tax reductions (see also p. 37). European Community moves to tax harmoni-sation, on VAT for example, are welcomed by French business because this would involve reductions to European levels, boosting demand and improving French price competitiveness. Meanwhile the Cresson government has promised more tax concessions: tax on all profits is to be reduced to 34 per cent from 1992 (Mercier and Coulange, 1991).

Fourthly, bar the few beneficiaries of State aid, company owners have increasingly disapproved of government intervention in business by subsidies or nationalisation, which they consider expensive and ineffective. With EC competition policy growing firmer and vigilance in Brussels towards market distortions caused by State interventions increasing (see pp. 137-40), French opponents of interventionism have found new allies. In political circles, these arguments have not fallen on deaf ears. Both the Chirac and Rocard governments have avoided interventionism (see pp. 32-7) while a report from the *Sénat* (the upper house of the French parliament) called for reform of taxation, the public sector and methods of public procurement (François-Poncet and Barbier, 1988).

In brief, the popularity of '1993' in France is related both to the long-term struggle of major sections of the French business community to shake off what it considers to be the dead hand of the State and to the continued search for larger markets abroad.

Europe beyond the EC

It is a pity that the word 'Europe' has increasingly been used to refer to the EC. In reality, Europe is even more diverse than the culturally rich but disparate entity known as the EC. Two other major trading blocs also exist, the EFTA countries and the former 'Eastern bloc'.

France trades extensively with the EFTA countries and runs fairly substantial deficits with Norway and Sweden – 13.1 and 5.3 billion francs respectively in 1989 (Ministère de l'Economie, 1990). These are largely explained by the need to import specific products, notably wood pulp.

In 1989, Switzerland provided France with her second largest trade surplus of 16.4 billion francs (after the UK – 18.4 billions). Geographical proximity, cultural ties and Switzerland's service economy combine to explain this trading success.

The former 'Eastern bloc' countries constitute a special case. French relations with them need to be understood in the very particular context of post-war Eastern Europe where Marxist ideology dictated the centralisation of all major economic decision making and the creation of 'planned' economies. At the height of the 'Cold War', contact with the West, including economic exchanges, was avoided where possible. In the planned economies, even in periods of *détente*, imports and exports were strictly controlled. Instead of multilateral trade, various forms of counter-trade (e.g. barter, counter-purchase, buy-back, switch-trading, etc.) have been preferred. These procedures achieved the twin aims of avoiding payment with rare currency reserves and of maintaining equilibrium in international exchanges. In the process, the scope for Western entrepreneurship was much reduced.

During the early 1970s, exchanges between East and West accelerated as Eastern Europe rushed for growth by purchases of Western goods and technologies. By the early 1980s, however, relations were again under strain. In part, the causes were economic – poor competitiveness of Eastern goods, balance of payments difficulties and the debt crisis experienced by Eastern bloc countries, especially Poland. Political problems also intruded – coolness on the part of the West due to the Soviet Union's war in Afghanistan, to Jaruzelski's declaration of martial law in Poland and, belatedly, to Ceausescu's monstrous regime in Rumania. Between 1980 and 1987, East–West trade fell from 85.3 to 79.1 billion current dollars. Since 1988, however, trade flows have improved again (Andries, 1990).

French trade relations with the East followed the ebb and flow of these larger political developments. In the 1970s, France exported considerable volumes of machine-tools, but with cut-backs in the 1980s, sales of capital goods were reduced. Sales of French food products have continued to be important. Major French imports are fossil fuels from the USSR, chemical products and consumer goods from the other Eastern European countries. In broad volume terms, exchanges with the USSR accounted in the 1980s for two-thirds of trade with the East. The remaining third was mainly with Poland, former East Germany and Rumania. The rush for growth in the East in the 1970s provided France with trade surpluses.

Conversely, the austerity policies that followed Eastern Europe's worsening debt situation led to French deficits in the 1980s. This situation caused some concern in France (Nguyên Duy-Tân, 1986). However, by the end of the 1980s, France's imports from Eastern Europe were falling (3.2 billion francs in 1987; 2.8 in 1989) and the trade gap had closed to a small deficit of 0.3 billion francs in 1989 (Ministère de l'Economie, 1990).

The sudden collapse of the Communist governments in Eastern Europe in 1989 caught French industrialists largely off guard. Having written off Eastern European exports markets for so long, French marketing networks, local knowledge and general motivation were limited. Similar comments apply to Britain. In consequence, the pickings in terms of major new opportunities have gone to Germany. To give but one measure, of the 327 joint ventures existing in 1989 between EC countries and the USSR, France was responsible for 32, the UK for 54 and Germany for 139 (Andries, 1990).

French efforts have also been handicapped by an unfortunate association made in Eastern Europe between the former *dirigiste* style of economic management in France and the Marxist centralised economy. Wishing to throw off the latter, Eastern European policy makers are chary of the former (Boyer, 1990). However, this constitutes another instance of old perceptions of France fossilising into irrelevance. These trends may represent lost opportunities both for France and Eastern European countries as the French industrial policy model of the 1970s may still have its uses. The transition to genuine market economies in the East cannot occur overnight. The transition from *dirigisme* to an open, market economy took France approximately 20 years. In the East, the road to economic reform may yet require an industrial policy comparable to French initiatives. On the Western side, there is need for greater financial and industrial co-operation with the East. In this respect, French business has been slow off the mark.

Trade with the USA and Japan

France does, of course, have business links with all OECD countries but for reasons of space only the two largest nations not yet mentioned can be discussed here: the United States and Japan.

Three main factors have impacted on French links with the USA: American technological and economic leadership, American protectionism, and currency fluctuations.

In France, as in other European nations, American multinational companies are a long-established phenomenon. The converse is less true as regards French firms in the USA. French firms have attempted to penetrate US markets both by acquisitions and new plant construction, but with varying degrees of success. In the 1970s, Renault bought AMC, the fourth largest American car producer, but failed to make significant in-roads into the US market and was forced to divest. In the 1980s, falls in the value of the dollar encouraged French firms to invest in the USA, for example Pechiney's take-over of American Can. But the size disequilibrium between firms originating in the largest economy in the world and the medium-sized one that is France inevitably persists. Moreover, American technological leadership in key sectors such as information technology maintains the gap.

Because of the size and wealth of its markets, the USA is immensely attractive to foreign firms but it is a less open economy than that of France or Britain. As a percentage of GDP, US imports and exports represent around 10 per cent; in European countries, the levels are more than twice as high (see Table 3.2 on p. 80). Part of the explanation lies in America's immense natural and human resources, giving her the ability to satisfy until recently almost all the needs of her markets. But US administrations have also exercised a tendency to erect barriers to the outside world where it has suited the powerful American business lobbies. Such barriers have inevitably hampered French trade.

Conversely, when in the mid-1980s, expansion in the US economy sucked in imports, France benefited. In 1985, France enjoyed a trade surplus with the USA of 2.1 billion francs (Ministère de l'Economie, 1989). But by the end of the decade, with the US economy stagnating, the French trade balance with the USA plunged back into the red, running deficits of 5.9 billion francs in 1986, 10.9 in 1988 and 21.3 in 1989 (Ministère de l'Economie, 1989, 1990). In 1989, the USA accounted for France's third largest trade deficit.

After Germany, Japan accounts for France's second largest trade deficit, amounting to 29.2 billion francs in 1989. Yet in 1973 France's exchanges of industrial products with Japan had been in near equilibrium. During the 1970s, Japanese goods penetrated world markets extensively, while Japanese home markets remained closed. By 1979, France ran a 5.4 billion franc deficit, increasing to 10.1 billion in 1981 and to 27.5 billion in 1988 (Ministère de l'Economie, 1989).

Deficits are concentrated in a limited number of product areas: cars, consumer electronics and professional electronics. Japan's strengths to date have been less in outright technological leads, as with the USA, than in the ability to identify consumer market trends and exploit them by high-volume, low-priced goods. Japanese success in France is unsurprising. As indicated in the section on weaknesses in traded goods, consumer mass markets are precisely where French firms are weak.

Although there will be no 'quick fix' for these difficulties, neither can it be assumed that European producers are inherently and permanently inferior. The point made during discussion of the 1993 initiatives in the section on France and the EC bears repetition here. The completion of the 'Single Market' is directed at improving European competitiveness *vis-à-vis* rivals from the Pacific Basin and is probably the only remedy for correcting the imbalances experienced by France and other European nations.

Links with developing countries

France's links with developing countries are distinctive in many ways, unique in some. In terms of trade relations with developing countries, France runs deficits in raw materials and energy supplies, as well as in textiles, clothing and leather goods. In most other sectors France enjoys a surplus. France has major surpluses in steel, glass, construction materials and construction projects, capital goods, cars and transport and pharmaceuticals. A major strand of French trade policy has been to compensate for deficits with the industrialised world by surpluses with developing countries.

Behind the trade figures lie complex political issues. France has put considerable effort into promoting a reputation for fair play in its diplomatic relations with developing countries. During the Fifth Republic, every French president has espoused the rhetoric of solidarity with the Third World (Cadenat, 1983, pp. 22-4). To what extent have pious intents been translated into actions? Chipman (1989) observed that France's primary motivation in her relations with the developing world has been the search for prestige. Smouts (1989, p. 234) went further in claiming that 'France displays the greatest gap between ambitious, candid and generous rhetoric, and a conservative practice weighed down by history'.

A colonial past still has a major impact on French trade with developing countries. Most of France's dealings with the Third World continue to be limited to African countries which were formerly part of her empire. This is particularly clear in the case of French aid. Ex-colonies in the Maghreb and south of the Sahara received 96 per cent of French aid in 1962, 85 per cent in 1980 (Cadenat, 1983, p. 43).

The other developing area in which France maintains a major interest is the Middle East. France has historically been influential in the area (notably in the Lebanon), but it is the importance of oil to the French economy which has amplified French involvement.

On the other hand, France has very few dealings with other developing nations. This holds good for the newly industrialising nations of the Pacific (with the exception of Hong Kong). It is true also of most of Latin America – with the exception of the oil producing States, Venezuela and Mexico, with whom France developed relations similar to those with Middle East oil producers (*see below*). In the 1980s, Latin America accounted for around 2 per cent of France's international trade (Ministère de l'Economie, 1990).

Thus in the received French view, the Third World is divided into two halves, one half being the French-speaking former colonies in North and sub-Saharan Africa with parts of the Arab world, the other half being the rest. This narrow view has been imprinted on to trading patterns. In consequence, the present analysis will concentrate on Africa and the Middle East, but the very different economic and political circumstances that prevail in each region will require separate discussion.

France and Africa: from colonialism to the *zone franc*

French exports to her Empire peaked in 1952, with 42 per cent of total exports going to her colonies (Bonin, 1988, p. 164). These markets yielded relatively good profits, since they were protected from foreign competition and lower world prices. But between 1954 and 1962, France lost her Empire. In that period, independence was granted to a large number of colonies, including Morocco, Tunisia, Cameroon, Mali, Madagascar, Ivory Coast, Chad, Central African Republic, Congo, Gabon, and Algeria.

Decolonisation, together with the removal of trade barriers within the EC, led to a large-scale reorientation of trade. Whereas in 1961, 61 per cent of imports into one-time French colonies came from France, by 1970 that figure had dropped to 50 per cent. This trend was even more pronounced in the case of Algeria, which in 1958 purchased 17 per cent of all French exports but only 3 per cent by 1969 (Camus *et al.*, 1981, p. 176).

The same factors also led to a spectacular worsening of France's international trade position. From a massive surplus in the balance of trade, France went into a small deficit: the exports/imports ratio fell from 204 per cent in 1959 to 98 per cent in 1969 (Camus *et al.*, 1981, p. 172). Without protectionist barriers, French firms found it hard to compete. The high prices and low quality that frequently characterised goods sold to the colonies could not be sold on other markets. Protectionism within a colonial empire had diluted the competitiveness of French producers.

Relations between former African colonies and France have continued to be important. Although Franco-African exchanges declined, exchanges between Africa and the EC increased. France played an important role in negotiations leading to the several Yaoundé and Lomé conventions which link 60 African, Caribbean and Pacific countries to the EC.

The most significant part of France's economic legacy to sub-Saharan Africa is an area of monetary union based on the French franc, called the *zone franc*. This is a unique institution today.

Most of the *zone franc* is in West and Central Africa. There are 14 states in the zone: Benin, Burkina Faso, Ivory Coast, Mali, Niger, Senegal, Togo, Cameroon, Central African Republic, Chad, Congo, Gabon, Equatorial Guinea and the Republic of the Comoro Islands. These States are grouped around two separate central banks which issue so-called CFA francs. France formally guarantees the convertibility of CFA francs against the French franc at a fixed exchange rate of 0.02 CFA francs to the French franc.

The major advantages for participating African nations result from the creation of an open trading zone in conditions of currency convertibility and monetary stability. These features contrast with the lack of large international financial centres in Africa, the inconvertibility of most African currencies and the macro-economic instability characterising the region. Stable exchange rates helped protect *zone franc* countries from outside shocks and helped hold down inflation; domestic investment has also been high (Chipman, 1989). Monetary integration within the *zone franc* may, in time, lead to fuller economic integration on the EC model (Adedeji, 1991) or indeed, greater integration with the EC itself (Chipman, 1989, pp. 214-16).

Controversy surrounds the disadvantages to African nations. Firstly, monetary union involves some loss of sovereignty. It has been claimed that the strictures of monetary union put a strait-jacket on the formulation of economic policy making in *zone franc* member States. However, from the close analysis put forward by the Guillaumonts (1988) it emerges that both economic policy and performance have varied within *zone franc* States, suggesting that such strictures as exist are relative.

Secondly, CFA francs have no international status independent of the French franc. Further, devaluation of the latter affects the trading position of *zone franc* States. The major devaluation of the French franc in 1969 produced shock waves that prompted a restructuring of monetary arrangements in the zone three years later. The restructuring provided for greater African autonomy. It allowed greater cushioning of the impact of devaluations of the French franc on the zone. It also reduced French influence over CFA franc issuing banks. This latter measure dampened some of the criticism against France of continuing to exercise colonial-style interference in monetary policies of sovereign States (Villeroy de Galhau, 1990). France preserved a right of veto on modifications of the statutes and of major decisions taken by the *zone franc* central banks (Chipman, 1989) but the right seems to have fallen into abeyance. The relative autonomy of the zone is illustrated by the build-up of excess credit in the late 1980s and African demands for annulments of debts. Economic crisis in Africa has undermined the stability of *zone franc* banks (Hazera, 1990).

The advantages of the system to France were, firstly, an increase in nominal reserves. Part of *zone franc* reserves are held in French francs by the French Treasury and could be mobilised in defence of the French franc. But since the 1972 reforms, this no longer occurs to any significant extent.

Further, there have been advantages for French business. The *zone franc* by its nature allows free movement of capital and repatriation of profits at a fixed exchange rate (Adda and Smouts, 1989, p. 70). This eliminates many of the uncertainties that exist in other parts of the Third World for firms seeking to do business.

Finally, according to the national accounts, France still enjoys trade surpluses with Africa. These totalled 8.9 billion francs in 1987 and 12.5 in 1989 (Ministère de l'Economie, 1990). In principle, these surpluses go towards compensating deficits run up with industrialised countries. Commentators such as Martin (1989) consider that these factors add up to neo-colonialism.

The real value of export surpluses has been questioned, however. Adda and Smouts (1989, pp. 79-91) put forward two arguments to show that these surpluses exist only on paper. Firstly, all trade within the *zone franc* is, by definition, conducted in basically the same unit of currency. Setting off a *zone franc* surplus against, say, a *deutschmark* deficit is not entirely convincing. Secondly, total foreign aid to Africa (of which France provides approximately one-third) is equivalent to some 85 per cent of the value of African imports. In consequence, French aid – particularly when it is tied aid – can be said to subsidise French exports.

Two further factors play a role in the complex distribution of relative advantage. The first is that both aid and monetary union serve to stabilise the prices of the raw materials (notably minerals) from Africa which France and the West in general need.

Secondly, French economic relations with Africa have been largely limited to financial and commercial agreements. There has been little French investment in Africa in industrial capacity and France buys relatively few manufactures from developing nations. Adda and Smouts (1989, p. 194-6) pointed out that, over the period 1970-1984, whereas most industrialised countries invested as much as they lent to developing nations, French investments amounted to a third of French loans. In addition, France imports fewer industrial goods from developing nations than other major countries: manufactured goods from developing nations as a proportion of total imported manufactures in 1986 was 6.8 per cent for France, 8.8 per cent for Germany, 9.3 per cent for the UK, 14.1 per cent for Japan and 28.4 per cent for the USA.

Such policies are likely to maintain African nations in a state of underdevelopment, ever dependent on primary commodities whose values fluctuate with the vagaries of the weather and of Western demand. These factors, together with the lack of an industrial base to create wealth, make repayment of loans problematic. Economic conditions, together with famine caused by climatic disasters, the AIDS epidemic, social conflicts and parlous political arrangements, make the future for much of Africa bleak indeed. While it would be pointless to make any one nation the scapegoat for a series of disastrous circumstances, France is nonetheless in a position to strike a more generous balance between types and volumes of products exchanged with African States and the financial arrangements (aid or loans versus investment) that accompany them.

France and the Middle East

After the enormous oil price hikes of the early 1970s, efforts were made at the highest levels of the French State to launch a major exports drive to the Middle East in order to generate earnings to pay for oil. In 1974-5, Prime Minister Chirac headed delegations to sign trade treaties with countries in the region. Between 1970 and 1975, exports to Syria increased by 300 per cent, to Saudi Arabia by 600 per cent, to Libya by 700 per cent and to Iraq by 900 per cent (Cadenat, 1983, pp. 108-9).

The 1970s and early 1980s were the heyday of a policy of *grands contrats* – large-scale projects such as the construction of underground systems (in Teheran and Cairo), infrastructural development such as building road and rail routes, sewage and water treatment plants, together with car factories and even nuclear installations in Iraq (Cadenat, 1983). To these must be added arms sales. According to Adda and Smouts (1989, p. 183), four-fifths of France's arms exports went to the Arab world.

The *grands contrats* became a crucial feature of French exporting activity. In 1973, total surpluses from what in the jargon are called *coopération technique* and *grands travaux* stood at 2.6 billion francs; they rose to 14 billions in 1978 and to 27 billions in 1983 (INSEE, 1984). In 1983, contracts for *coopération technique* and *grands travaux* in the Middle East accounted for a surplus of 12 billion francs. To indicate proportions, this was equivalent to some 45 per cent of the total current account deficit for that year.

Overall, France succeeded in the objective of closing the trade gap with the Middle East. Adda and Smouts (1989, p. 188) calculated that trade deficits on energy amounted to 847 billion francs over 1974-1982 while the *grands contrats* bought in 768 billions – covering 90 per cent of the deficit. The combination of receipts from *grands contrats* with reductions in expenditure from falling oil prices resulted in the deficit with OPEC countries falling from a peak of 66 billion francs in 1980 to a deficit of just 5 billions in 1987.

However, falling revenues for oil producers and insolvency problems for Third World countries have recently been offering fewer opportunities for new *grands contrats*. It remains to be seen to what extent French firms will be able to draw advantage from the rebuilding of Kuwait and Iraq but early indications suggest that the USA and perhaps Britain will get the lion's share. Future French arms sales to the region will be limited both by the wish to avoid a repeat of the arms build-up and due to the prowess demonstrated by American technology in the Gulf War. This raises questions about how France would pay for an oil price hike in the future.

In brief, recent developments are undermining France's policy of compensating for deficits with the industrialised world by surpluses with developing countries. With this solution largely exhausted for the future, new challenges lie ahead for French business and economy.

CONCLUSIONS

The challenge facing French business is to accelerate its adaptation to a world economic order. There is a need for greater geographical and sectoral diversification.

Geographical diversification is required because France's main markets are in stable or slow-growing regions. The concentration on the EC is understandable, even necessary, but should not set up artificial limits. Markets in Africa and the Middle East, France's major non-European export destinations, have been tailing off. On the other hand, French firms are barely present in today's dynamic markets of the Pacific Basin or indeed, in Eastern Europe, whose markets look set for expansion near the turn of the century.

'In terms of sectoral diversification, France is underrepresented in current and foreseeable growth sectors (such as information technology and bio-technology) and has weaknesses in consumer sectors.

In the rapid post-war transformation from a closed, protected economy to a fairly open economy, the State played a leading role. But the degree to which the French State will have real influence over future stages of the adjustment process is likely to be low. In terms of both geographical and sectoral adjustment, room for manoeuvre in public policy has been much reduced. This is due to developments in world markets. Whereas geographic reorientation could be achieved by policy initiatives in the 1970s and early 1980s due to the availability of opportunities for State-to-State business, in the international environment of the 1990s, such opportunities have been much reduced. The State export-drive apparatus – BFCE loans, COFACE guarantees, etc. – is more suited to State-to-State deals in restricted markets than the firm-to-firm deals appropriate in the regional markets currently showing growth. Thus the protective and supportive arm of the State has gradually been withdrawn, leaving the 'invisible hand' of the market.

The initiative for exports and overseas investments now lies with French firms themselves. Yet criticisms of the shortcomings of French firms have remained surprisingly constant over time, namely failing to adjust to the needs of foreign markets, relying on opportunistic selling rather than on sustained marketing and a lack of permanent distribution networks and after-sales facilities (Arnaud-Ameller, 1970; Garcia, 1977, pp. 43-6; Cadenat, 1983, pp. 98-99; Donnellier, 1990).

Too often the assumption was that the export drive only concerned large firms. However, studies have shown that though exports of individual small- and medium-sized firms are relatively small, collectively they can sustain significant export volumes (Dubarry and Cardot, 1981; Roncin, 1982). Moreover, a recent study by Jemain (1990) of French firms who are leaders in their sector shows that SMEs are well represented. If France is to enhance international strengths and reinforce and diversify industrial and commercial structures, then the exporting behaviour and performance of SMEs becomes an important issue. Particularly in the 'Single Market' conditions of post-1992 Europe, small firms will have a big part to play.

Yet past successes should not be underestimated. The extent to which France has integrated into a world economy constitutes a major and successful revolution. France is no longer the archetype of the protectionist State.

However, various forms of 'neo-protectionism' persist. Within the EC, they include continued advocacy of the CAP, subsidies to State-owned firms (see also pp. 137-40) and various non-tariff barriers. Top French civil servants can still consider that their aim is to '*défendre la maison France*', namely to protect France PLC (Royo, 1990). Nationalist sentiments have not disappeared in France but then, they have not vanished elsewhere either.

In addition, the French tend to view international trade agreements in terms of 'reciprocity' (Bauer and Bertin-Mourot, 1985; François-Poncet and Barbier, 1988). Reciprocity involves an 'eye for an eye' approach which ignores structural differences between economies, particularly between the developed and developing worlds. It is sometimes a short-term view leading to the creation of trade barriers. A current of Euro-protectionism still exists in some French quarters, namely support for free trade in the EC but with high barriers to the outside world. These tactics still constitute obstacles to free trade in a 'pure' sense. However, it can be objected that very few nations are purists and that the French economy is more open than, for example, that of Japan or the USA.

But regardless of the nuances over the degree of openness of various national economies, in many business domains the national framework has already been transcended. The challenge now facing French firms is to achieve greater integration within a European and world economic order that is something other than a collection of national economies.

Notes
1. Attentive readers may detect variations in the reporting of figures. These are due to irregularities in the compiling of the relevant statistics by the official authorities.

   In the case of trade figures, the most obvious differences arise due to the alternative of accounting either for the value of the goods themselves (in the jargon, FOB – free on board; in French, FAB – *franco à bord)* or for the goods plus insurance and transport (CIF – cost insurance, freight; *CAF – coût, assurance, fret*).

   In the case of France, room for even greater statistical variance exists due to the presence of two authorities for the compilation of figures. French customs collates trade figures; the *Banque de France* draws up the French balance of payments, which of course includes trade figures also. The *Banque de France* treats French overseas dominions and territories (the *DOM-TOM)* as part of France. French customs figures refer only to metropolitan France and treat the *DOM-TOM* as part of the rest of the world. There are other small differences between the two institutions in the classification of some product types.

   A major inconsistency of both reporting agencies relates to sales of military equipment. Statistics on sales by product types may or may not include military hardware – the choice made is usually specified. However, tables on geographical destinations of exports do not include sales of military hardware for reasons of confidentiality.

Even key statistics can vary, since they are periodically revised in the light of more accurate information as it becomes available. Other difficulties include changes in rubrics and in the content of what is reported. Thus for reasons inherent in the work methods of the statistics gathering agencies, small discrepancies in data collected from different sources arise.

2. The exports/imports ratio, called in French the *taux de couverture*, is frequently used by French statistical authorities as an index of performance. In principle, a figure of 100 per cent indicates that exports and imports are in exact equilibrium. A figure above 100 per cent indicates that exports are greater than imports, a sign of strong performance. A figure below 100 per cent indicates that imports are greater than exports, a sign of weak performance.

But equilibrium at 100 per cent only holds good where both imports and exports are expressed as FOB figures. Often, exports of goods are expressed as FOB figures and imports as CIF figures. In these cases, equilibrium in the value of the goods themselves is reached when exports are around 93-97 per cent of imports.

References

Abadie, P. M. (1989) 'L'adaptation du secteur industriel aux nouvelles exigences de la modernisation et de la concurrence', *Problèmes économiques*, 2,141 (20 septembre), pp. 3-7

Abbou, E. (1988) 'L'évolution récente du mouvement de concentration des entreprises: bilan et perspectives', *Problèmes économiques*, 2,100 (23 novembre), pp. 1-10

Abd-El-Rahman, K. (1990) 'Stratégies des firmes et résultats du commerce extérieur français', *Economie prospective internationale* (2ème trimestre), pp. 95-110

Abd-El-Rahman, K. & Charpin, J.-M. (1989) 'Le commerce industriel de la France avec ses partenaires européens', *Economie et statistique*, 217-18 (janvier-février), pp. 63-9

Achard, P. (1988) 'Le marché unique de 1992: perspectives pour les banques, les assurances et le système financier français', *Problèmes économiques*, 2,077 (1 juin), pp. 13-15

Adda, J. & Smouts, M.-C. (1989) *La France face au Sud. Le miroir brisé*, Paris: Editions Karthala

Adedeji, A. (1991) 'The European integration process; lessons for Africa', *The Courier ACP - EEC*, 125 (January-February), pp. 50-3

Alimi, J. (1991) 'Exportation: gloire au contribuable', *L'Expansion* (20 juin-3 juillet), pp. 48-54

Andries, M. (ed.) (1990) *The Future of Relations between the EEC and Eastern Europe*, Brussels: Club de Bruxelles

Arnaud, R. (1989) *La France en chiffres. Forces et faiblesses de l'économie française*, Paris: Hatier

Arnaud-Ameller, P. (1970) *La France à l'épreuve de la concurrence internationale*, Paris: Armand Colin

Artus, P. & Bleuze, E. (1990) 'Déficit du commerce industriel de la France et capacités de production: un examen sectoriel', *Economie et statistique*, 228 (janvier), pp. 19-28

Banque Indosuez (1990) 'Les échanges commerciaux européens', *Problèmes économiques*, 2,202 (1 décembre), pp. 8-15

Barsoux, J.-L. & Lawrence, P. (1991) 'Countries, cultures and constraints' in Calori, R. & Lawrence, P. (eds.) *The Business of Europe. Managing Change*, pp. 198-217, London: Sage

Bauer, M. & Bertin-Mourot, B (1985) 'Grands patrons. Oui, mais au libéralisme', *Nouvel Economiste*, 482 (22 mars), pp. 60-5

Bernis, G. de (1990) 'L'Europe et l'industrie', *Problèmes économiques*, 2,185 (25 juillet), pp. 1-6

Bonin, H. (1988) *Histoire économique de la France depuis 1880*, Paris: Masson.

Boyer, A. (1990) 'Gestion à la française: que pouvons-nous apporter à l'Europe de l'Est?', *Revue française de gestion* (juin-juillet-août), pp. 108-12

Brémond, J. & Brémond, G. (1985) *L'Économie française face aux défis mondiaux*, Paris: Hatier

Cadenat, P. (1983) 'La France et le Tiers Monde', Paris: La Documentation française, *Notes et études documentaires*, nos. 4701-2

Camus, B. *et al.* (1981) *La Crise du système productif*, Paris: INSEE

Cecchini, P. *et al.* (1988) *1992: The European Challenge. The Benefits of a Single Market*, London: Wildwood House

Chipman, J. (1989) *French Power in Africa*, Oxford: Basil Blackwell

Clavaud, R. (1990) 'Usinor-Sacilor, champion du monde', *L'Expansion* (11-24 janvier), pp. 76-83

Debonneuil, M. & Delattre, M. (1987) 'La competitivité-prix n'explique pas les pertes tendancielles de parts de marché', *Economie et statistique*, 203 (octobre), pp. 5-14

Delattre, M. (1983) 'Points forts et points faibles du commerce extérieur industriel', *Economie et statistique*, 157, pp. 15-30

Delattre, M. (1986) 'L'évolution des branches industrielles de 1979 à1984: continuités et ruptures', *Problèmes économiques*, 1,978 (11 juin), pp. 2-12

Donnellier, J.-C. (1990) 'L'image des produits français de grande consommation à l'étranger', *Problèmes économiques*, 2,163 (21 février), pp. 12-19

DREE (Direction des relations économiques extérieures) (1989) *Où en est la compétitivité française?*, Paris: La Documentation française

Dubarry, J. & Cardot, Z. (1981) 'Les PMI et l'exportation', *Chroniques du SEDEIS*, 7 (avril), pp. 229-33

Dubois, G. & Levy, P. (1989) 'La dernière chance de l'informatique française', *Nouvel Economiste*, 690 (14 avril), pp. 24-30

Dussauge, P. (1985) *L'Industrie française de l'armement*, Paris: Economica

Estrin, S. & Holmes, P. (1985) 'International trade and the external constraint' in Morris, P. & Williams, S. (eds.) *France in the World*, pp. 51-68, Portsmouth: Association for the Study of Modern and Contemporary France

Fédération française de l'acier (1991) 'L'industrie sidérurgique en 1990: premiers chiffres', *Problèmes économiques*, 2,218 (27 mars), pp. 29-31

François-Poncet, J. & Barbier, B. (1988) *Une Stratégie pour la France: l'Europe*, Paris: Economica

Garcia, A. (1977) 'Les instruments de la politique française du commerce extérieur', Paris: La Documentation française, *Notes et études documentaires*, nos. 4404-5

Geroski, P. A. & Jacquemin, A. (1985) 'Corporate competitiveness in Europe', *Economic Policy*, 1 (November), pp. 171-218

Gordon, C. (1990) 'The business culture in France' in Randlesome, C. *et al.*, *Business cultures in Europe*, pp. 58-106, London: Heinemann

Gubian, A. *et al.* (1989) 'L'intégration européenne' in Jeanneney, J. (ed.) *L'Economie française depuis 1967*, pp. 87-106, Paris: Seuil

Guibert, B. (1975) 'La mutation de l'industrie', *Economie et statistique*, 68 (juin), 23-37

Guillaumont, P. & Guillaumont, S. (eds.) (1988) *Stratégies de développement comparées: zone franc et hors zone franc*, Paris: Editions d'organisation

Hazera, J.-C. (1990) 'Afrique: les gagneurs et les autres', *Nouvel Economiste*, 773 (7 décembre), pp. 76-9

Holcblat, N. & Husson, M. (1990) *L'Industrie française*, Paris: La Découverte

Holcblat, N. & Tavernier, J.-L. (1989) 'Entre 1979 et 1986, la France a perdu des parts de marché', *Economie et statistique*, 217-218 (janvier-février), pp. 37-49

INSEE (various years) *Annuaire Statistique de la France*, Paris: INSEE

Jemain, A. (1990) 'Grands groupes et PMEs: les entreprises françaises premières mondiales de leur secteur', *Problèmes économiques*, 2,198 (7 novembre), pp. 9-14

Le Houcq, T. & Strauss, J.-P. (1988) 'Les industries françaises de haute technologie: des difficultés pour rester dans la course', *Problèmes économiques*, 2082 (6 juillet), pp. 8-11

Mamou, Y. *et al.* (1988) 'Vague de rachats et de fusions en France', *Problèmes économiques*, 2,075 (18 mai), pp. 12-19

Martin, G. (1989) 'France and Africa' in Aldrich, R. & Connell, J. (eds.) *France in World Politics*, pp. 101-25, London: Routledge

Mazier (1983) 'Les limites de la stratégie de redéploiement', *Les Cahiers français*, 212 (juillet-septembre), pp. 14-19

Mercier, A.-M. & Coulange, J.-P. (1991) 'PME: la potion fiscale d'Edith Cresson', *Nouvel Economiste*, 812 (30 septembre), pp. 16-17

Michalet, C.A. (ed.) (1984) *L'Intégration de l'économie française dans l'économie mondiale*, Paris: Economica

Milewski, F. (1989) *Le Commerce extérieur de la France*, Paris: La Découverte

Ministère de l'Economie (1989) 'Le Commerce extérieur de la France en 1988', *Problèmes économiques*, 2,143 (4 octobre), pp. 6-14

Ministère de l'Economie (1990) 'Le commerce extérieur de la France en 1989', *Problèmes économiques*, 2,195 (17 octobre), pp. 8-17

Ministère de l'Economie (1991) 'Le commerce extérieur de la France en 1990', *Problèmes économiques*, 2,234 (17 juillet), pp. 1-7

Moreau Defarges, P. (1984) 'L'Europe à re-formuler. La communauté au lendemain de la clarification d'Athènes', *Politique étrangère*, 49, pp. 21-37

Nguyên Duy-Tân, J. (1986) 'Le commerce extérieur de la France. Environnement international et instruments juridiques', Paris: La Documentation française, *Notes et études documentaires*, no. 4798

OECD (1984) *OECD Economic Surveys: France*, Paris: OECD

Orléan, A. (1986) 'L'insertion dans les échanges internationaux: comparaison de cinq pays développés', *Economie et statistique* (janvier), pp. 25-39

Porter, M. E. (1990) *The Competitive Advantage of Nations*, London: Macmillan

Renard, F. (1991) 'La petite grippe des entreprises françaises', *Le Monde* (17 mai), p. 34

Roncin, A. (1982) 'L'engagement des PMI dans l'exportation', *Economie et statistique*, 148 (octobre), pp. 39-51

Royo, M. (1990) 'Le patronat à l'heure de Bruxelles', *Nouvel Economiste*, 774 (14 décembre), pp. 50-3

Sachwald, F. (1990) 'La compétitivité européenne: nations et entreprises' in Montbrial, T. de (ed.) *Rapport annuel mondial sur le système économique et les stratégies,* pp. 111-200, Paris: Dunod

Sheahan, J. (1963) *Promotion and Control of Industry in Postwar France,* Cambridge,

Mass.: Harvard UP

Sicot, D. (1990) 'Bienvenue aux produits étrangers!', *Science et vie economie*, 66 (novembre), pp. 20-7

Smouts, M.-C. (1989) 'The Fifth Republic and the Third World' in Godt, P. (ed.) *Policy Making in France: From de Gaulle to Mitterrand*, pp. 235-44, London: Pinter

Tardy, G. (1981) 'La France dans l'Europe' in Pagé, J.-P. (ed.) *Profil économique de la France au seuil des années 80*, pp. 435-73, Paris: La Documentation française

Turpin, E. (1989) 'Le commerce extérieur français: une spécialisation encore fragile', *Economie et statistique*, 217-18 (janvier-février), pp. 51-60

Villeroy de Galhau, F. (1990) 'La coopération entre la France et les Etats de la zone franc', *Problèmes économiques*, 2169 (4 avril), pp. 20-3

Wise, M. (1989) 'France and European Unity' in Aldrich, R. & Connell, J. (eds.) *France in World Politics*, pp. 35-73, London: Routledge

4

Competition policy and market relations

INTRODUCTION

A consistent theme in the transformation of French business has been the shift from State direction to market regulation. Previous chapters have shown that State intervention in the economy and industry declined, and protectionist barriers round home markets were progressively dismantled. The ensuing influx of foreign goods have made French producers more vulnerable, and the need to cover essential imports means that French products must be marketed abroad. These factors, together with the recessions of the 1970s and early 1980s leading to closures and unemployment, drove home the necessity to increase the competitiveness of the French economy.

The attempt to improve competitiveness through a sharpening of policies and attitudes towards competition will be the central issue in this chapter. Before turning to France as a specific case, however, it is worth reviewing why competition and competition policy are considered desirable.

A market functions successfully when it matches supply to demand. Competition plays a central role in this process. It involves complex, sequential interactions between buyers and sellers. In theory, by their patterns of purchase, buyers (the market) trigger two main mechanisms.

Firstly, markets are said to promote the optimum allocation of resources. Where an appropriate number of sellers exists, buyers exercise a choice over the products and services they acquire and purchase according to their preferences. Enterprises which respond to market preferences accrue resources whereas enterprises which fail to satisfy the market do not, and eventually disappear. One of the assumptions here is that market participants know best. Although this can be a questionable assumption, no better alternative is usually available.

Secondly, markets promote productive efficiency. Those enterprises which offer goods and services that conform to market expectations usually operate at different levels of efficiency. Levels of performance translate, among other things, into differences in selling price. For a given quality and level of availability, buyers will purchase at the lowest price. In consequence, firms selling at higher price are generally constrained into improved productivity, leading to cuts in their costs and selling prices. At a later stage, such increments in productive efficiency, often as the result of innovation, are rewarded by the market in the form of increased turnover, profitability, market share, etc.

These mechanisms can be brought into sharper focus by reference to monopolies. The monopoly enterprise which is both able and willing to exploit its advantages to the most cynical extreme can sell the products it prefers to produce (rather than what buyers prefer), it can set its prices as high as it chooses and has no incentive to restrict its costs or otherwise seek to make the best use of its resources. Further, because resources are being diverted from products and productive processes that buyers would prefer had they a choice, resources are said to be 'misallocated'.

These are simplified schema but they serve to emphasise key issues[1]. A gulf separates the example of the monopoly from the theory of perfect competition. In between the two lie various degrees of market failure or success.

Unscrupulous firms can undermine market mechanisms by collusion. Examples of collusion include agreements to set common prices, to restrict output or to share markets. In such cases, profits are higher than under normal market conditions. This is to the detriment of buyers. It also wastes resources, because colluding firms have undermined competitive pressures to achieve the best possible performance.

Situations can also arise where firms evict competitors from markets by superior performance. In achieving success they may do no wrong. But regardless of the process, the result is the same as in the case of collusion namely, the distortion or elimination of competition in the market.

In most countries, the formulation of competition policy and competition law has been the response to these problems. The main objectives have usually been to ensure and promote allocative and productive efficiency through the free play of market forces.

Depending on nation and time-period, other considerations have also been involved. Competition policy may seek to protect some types of competitors from the actions of others (usually small enterprises against larger enterprises). In the USA, industrial concentration resulted in the creation of huge firms or 'trusts' in the nineteenth century. Political objections were raised to the exercise of power having no democratic, constitutional basis. In the US tradition of 'antitrust' legislation, questions of economic efficiency have sometimes taken second place to a primary aim of preventing the excessive concentration of economic power.

As Gardner (1990, p. 27) indicated, a number of other public interest criteria can intervene in the formulation of competition policy. These include considerations related to consumer benefits, health and safety, environmental protection, as well as employment and exports promotion.

In terms of its effects on market participants, competition policy takes two main forms. One is to regulate *conduct* (business practices of various kinds), the other is to regulate *structure* (the number and nature of companies in a market).

Not all competition policies include these various elements. A competition policy is often a pragmatic, *ad hoc* response to local conditions. It is therefore revealing of the attitudes of the policy maker and of the circumstances pertaining at a particular time and place. Further, political and social considerations frequently intrude into economic decisions. To function successfully, competition needs a consensus in its favour.

The French are popularly supposed to have an aversion to competition. Brault (1987, p. 5) stated:

On dit volontiers que les Français n'aiment pas la concurrence. Cette idée reçue est peut-être aujourd'hui dépassée.

People readily say that the French do not like competition. This received idea has perhaps run its course now.

This chapter will analyse what lies behind both halves of this statement.

The next section argues that a French bias against competition did exist and that its roots are to be found in corporatist traditions which the State upheld at decisive historical moments. However, attitudes and values in France have changed dramatically over time to produce a consensus today which is favourable to competition, considering it to be a stimulant to economic and social progress. By an analysis of the evolution of competition law between 1945 and the present day, the section on competition law in France demonstrates how obligations to compete have been sharpened. The section on market relations around the distribution sector takes a case-study approach in analysing the French distribution sector, but in presenting the characteristics of the latter it also considers market relations between producers, distributors and consumers. This will give a wider view of the chapter's issues, since competition is often understood simply as a 'horizontal' relationship between rivals producing much the same products. The case study of 'vertical' relations between suppliers and buyers will show the wider problems of reconciling conflicts of legitimate interests.

The chapter argues that although blind spots can be discerned in French competition policy (notably in the treatment of public sector undertakings), the cliché of a continuing aversion to competition is belied by a willingness, indeed enthusiasm, to compete at local, national and international levels which has permeated most of the French business environment to a previously unknown degree.

THE LEGACY OF CORPORATISM

Over the centuries, corporatism has taken a number of forms in France. Barel (1990) offered six definitions to cover the various types of corporatism and the different historical periods in which they occurred. In this discussion, only the two most relevant variants will be discussed.

The first form is social organisation by trade, occupation or profession into 'corporations'. Because membership is open only to members of an occupation, 'corporations' have frequently developed restrictive practices which prevent other social groups from undertaking their specialisations.

Such professional practices continue to exist in France today. Infamous and frequently quoted examples are the *notaires* (notary public), taxi-drivers and pharmacists. Each of these professions has a monopoly on its activities, is entitled to limit the numbers entering the profession (the so-called *numerus clausus*) and sets common prices under State supervision. They can also enjoy other privileges.

The *numerus clausus* is particularly astonishing in the case of taxis. Gurviez (1988) claimed that in 1959 there were 14,000 taxis in Paris and that 20 years later there were still 14,000 taxis in Paris!

In the case of the *notaires*, fees on the transfer of property are calculated as a percentage of price irrespective of the complexity of the transaction. The result has been to inflate the cost of property sales in France.

Finally, pharmacists in France have an official monopoly over sales not only of medicines, but of paramedical goods such as bandages, dressings, vitamin tablets, etc. and also enjoy a *de facto* near-monopoly on sales of cosmetic cleansers and related beauty products. In consequence, consumers end up paying considerably higher prices for mundane household products.

In each of the above cases, competition has largely been eliminated by a professional grouping (though not without opposition, see p. 145). The will and the ability to eliminate competition demonstrated by these three examples are not limited to occupational groups in France, but they do illustrate typical sources for the stereotype of a French aversion to competition.

Yet in two famous historical instances, the French State set out to ban corporations and employee associations altogether, namely Turgot's Edict of 1776 and the Chapelier Act of 1791. These measures destroyed the power of the major corporations. In reality, though extreme cases such as the examples cited still exist, they are the exception today and should not be taken as typical. As Closets (1982) indicated 'adjacent' professions are often regulated in inconsistent ways. Doctors do not enjoy the privileges of pharmacists nor lawyers those of the *notaires*. Market pressures have become the norm in most professions.

The corporatist legacy, however, only starts with the practices of specific professions. A second and wider form also existed. The desire to partition markets, allocate output and set prices on a consensual, rather than on a competitive basis, has run deeper and wider. Repeated instances of it existed in the attitudes of French business communities. It also left a mark on State policy making. At this deeper level, corporatism refers to a collective set of strategies, implemented by professional groups and *firms* within a particular sector, at times in concert with the State, to achieve a regulation of market relations to suit their joint objectives. The obligatory reference point for this type of corporatism in France is constituted by the events of the 1930s and the early 1940s. Without discussion of these, market relations and competition policy in post-war France would be virtually incomprehensible.

The events of the 1930s discredited the market economy for many French people. Though the effects of the Wall Street crash took longer to translate into economic depression in France than in the USA, UK or Germany, by the mid-1930s company bankruptcies and chronic unemployment raged in France too. The collapse in demand reinforced a tendency to 'jungle' capitalism, namely heightened exploitation of the workforce and cut-throat competition between suppliers.

The following quotation summarises the massive disenchantment of the period with the market economy and evokes the attempt to find a happier alternative:

A côté des entreprises qui réussirent de façon inespérée et réalisèrent de magnifiques bénéfices, combien d'autres furent acculées à la faillite et à la ruine. 'Saine épuration', disait-on alors. (...) A travers toute cette époque, l'exploitation de l'homme par l'homme atteignit sans doute des degrés jamais encore atteints. (...) La concurrence est en effet un stimulant certain, mais une effroyable gaspilleuse d'énergie, laquelle, tous comptes faits, coûte beaucoup plus cher à la collectivité que les frais nécessités par l'entretien d'une économie ordonnée. (Lengelé, 1942, pp. 35-7)

Alongside firms who succeeded unexpectedly well and made splendid profits, how many others were reduced to bankruptcy and ruin. 'A healthy shake-out' was the comment at the time. (...) Throughout the period, the exploitation of man by man undoubtedly reached depths never experienced before. (...) Competition is a definite stimulus, but also an appalling squanderer of energy, which, all things considered, is considerably more costly for the community than the price of maintaining an ordered economy.

Despite the Marxist echoes, Lengelé was no red revolutionary. In fact, he belonged to that section of the French business classes which rapidly adopted the ideas of French-style national socialism. The economic views of the French far-right included a dislike of market regulation and an aversion to competition. The practical solutions implemented were, firstly, the consolidation of cartels in order to distribute orders and maintain prices. (French industry was already extensively cartelised before the Second World War.) Secondly, many people on the Right came to embrace planning to produce an *'économie ordonnée'*. For them, planning was to be undertaken on a corporatist basis, principally by industry representatives. This perspective contrasts with the aims of the Marxist Left, which also favoured planning, but that directed by the State.

Under the German Occupation of France, the right-wing Vichy regime (1940-44) set about implementing corporatist solutions in a systematic manner. Under Vichy, by a law enacted on 16 August 1940, industry was placed under the control of a central bureaucracy. A so-called *comité d'organisation* was placed at the head of each industrial and commercial sector.

In theory, the corporatist model embraced both employers' federations and employee unions, thus eliminating class struggle. In practice, the *comités d'organisation* were run by business men and civil servants in collaboration with occupying forces, so alienating the rank and file.

The *comités d'organisation* exercised extensive powers (albeit under German supervision) such as the right to levy contributions, draw up regulations, requisition or close factories and plan production. All firms in the sector were obliged to join the central committee and to implement its decisions. In effect, this produced State-organised cartels, with prices set centrally. Further, Kuisel (1981, p. 142) noted that the 'committees' were frequently the continuation of existing cartels and trade organisations.

The allocation of raw materials between sectors was carried out by a central agency entitled the *Office central de répartition des produits industriels*. The assurance of both allocative efficiency and productive efficiency, which in the liberal economy is left to the market, had been taken on by the State. Competition had no place in the Vichy model.

As Kuisel (1981) indicated, one of the problems with Vichy policies lay in the confusion between corporatist and statist modes. In theory, there are major differences between a corporatist system and a State-managed economy. In the former, sector representatives wield predominant influence, in principle, in a decentralised, consensual and entrepreneurial mode. In the latter system, the State has the upper hand, making and implementing decisions through a centralised, bureaucratic hierarchy. Under Vichy, the system had a corporatist veneer but functioned in a preponderantly *dirigiste* mode.

In the immediate post-war period in France, elements of statist and corporatist practices and attitudes survived. The State continued to exercise 'rational' control of the economy by the planning process (see pp. 9-16) and, as the next section will indicate, by price controls. The business community was permeated by corporatist thinking.

In 1947, Georges Villiers, then President of the *Conseil National du Patronat Français* (the peak-level employers' federation) made the following rallying call:

Nous essaierons de faire comprendre aux patrons de bonne volonté que tout retour à un libéralisme excessif est impossible et que c'est à eux de s'imposer, dans le cadre de la profession, les disciplines nécessaires. (quoted by Lefranc, 1976, p. 142)

We will try to convince good-willed business men that any return to the excesses of liberalism is impossible and that it is up to them to exercise appropriate discipline within their particular sectors.

The corporatist legacy is evident here in the rejection of market forces in favour of regulation by interested parties.

In a context where liberalism was still discredited, corporatist 'discipline' quickly led to cartels. Goetz-Girey (1954, p. 30) noted that the *comités d'organisation* of the Vichy era were transformed first into business agencies and then some of their functions were taken over by employers' organisations. The process reinforced such collusive practices as dividing markets up between cartel members and setting joint prices.

Such then was the nature and strength of the corporatist legacy. Given this context, post-war competition law was necessary in order to restore a genuine market economy.

COMPETITION LAW IN FRANCE

Against the full range of possible measures, French competition policy in its 1945 version was selective and limited. It has been built up considerably since, albeit in piecemeal fashion. The evolution of French competition policy will be traced in this section and compared to developments in competition policy in the UK, the USA and the EC.

From the 1945 legislation to the Commission Technique des Ententes

The coalition government of 1945 took immediate measures to reintroduce a market economy in France. To overturn the heritage of corporatism and Vichy, new laws were required to promote competition.

The legislators were starting almost from scratch. The only existing legislative measure of any relevance to competition was the short and vague article 419 of the 1810 *Code pénal*, prohibiting speculation and collusion to achieve exorbitant profits. However, jurisprudence in relation to article 419 went markedly against modern conceptions of good competitive practice. In 1912, the Court of Aix judged article 419 to be inapplicable to firms *'qui s'entendent et se réunissent uniquement pour l'organisation rationnelle de leur production'* (who convene and come to an understanding solely in order to organise their output in a rational manner). The 1921 ruling of France's highest court, the *Cour de Cassation*, went in the same direction (Brault, 1987, p. 22). This permissive approach to collusion contributed to the cartelisation of the French economy (Caron, 1988).

New competition law was enacted on 30 June 1945 by two *ordonnances* (government decrees). The major element was the prohibition of actions liable to *entraver le plein exercice de la concurrence* (hinder full play of market forces).

The *ordonnances* prohibited a number of anti-competitive practices, including the formation of *ententes* (cartels). They outlawed compulsory price setting by suppliers (notably the setting of minimum prices) and selling at a loss. Competition was largely conceived in terms of relationships between producers of similar products. Thus 'horizontal' *ententes* (i.e. cartels between producers of equivalent goods) were subsequently policed more severely than 'vertical' restraints (between firms at successive stages of production or distribution).

At the same time, the government gave itself extensive control over prices. Thus the *Direction générale des prix* (General Price Authority), under the supervision of the Finance Minister, had powers to set price ceilings, to freeze prices or even reduce prices with respect to any sector or firm. The Blum government imposed price cuts of 5 per cent in January 1947 and a further 5 per cent the following month. Generally, however, flexibility was maintained by discussions between professional organisations and civil servants (Sheahan, 1963, pp. 33-7).

Why did the French government follow this route? In the immediate post-war years, France suffered from a shortage economy. Demand exceeded supply. Nor could production shortfalls be quickly rectified. Major barriers to new entry included the inadequacies of the financial system and the dislocation of the distribution system, both due to the war. The existence of cartels also discouraged entry. Finally, foreign firms were prevented from entering French markets by protectionism. To strengthen its hand in the fight against inflation and against black marketeers exploiting the shortage economy, the government felt obliged to impose price controls.

Clearly, this approach to competition policy is open to criticisms. A number apply to price controls. An emergency measure became a long-term institution; price controls were finally abolished only in 1986. However, they undermine market mechanisms. At its inception, competition policy was stamped with the hallmark of economic *dirigisme*. This is a paradoxical state of affairs since *dirigisme* and the freeing of market forces logically contradict each other.

Although price controls sometimes hurt, according to Jenny and Weber (1986) they were tolerated by the business community precisely because they reduced competition. During *les trente glorieuses*, firms saw price control as involving less danger than severe price competition. At the same time, they were comfortable in the knowledge that markets were growing. They could increase sales without having to capture market share from competitors. Whatever the effect of controls on profit margins at particular moments, business expanded over the medium term. Thus price control reinforced latent corporatist tendencies and preserved the *status quo*.

Over time, price controls did lose some of their importance, but in periods of economic crisis and high inflation they were reimposed with severity. However, the repeated recourse to price controls conditioned approaches to price formation in sectors and at times when the French State did *not* directly intervene in price formation. *Ententes* on price were often a direct, almost logical, extension of government intervention (Donnedieu de Vabres in Brault, 1987, p. 153). State controls on prices conditioned firms into assuming that, since parallel pricing was frequently imposed by the State, concerted practices in the domain of pricing were ethically admissible or indeed of practical necessity even when price controls were dropped.

The second major oversight arose over monopolies and mergers, an area in which the legislation made no provisions. Hence, it did not oversee *structural* change in the economy. This policy orientation was understandable in the 1940s in a country of intermediate size whose firm population counted a myriad of small enterprises but few industrial giants. The situation in France was thus quite unlike that of the USA where major corporations were created in the nineteenth century leading to antitrust legislation as early as 1890 with the Sherman Act. However, this extremely partial view of the coverage of competition policy was to imprint itself on French competition law for some three decades.

Thirdly, though collusive behaviour was made unacceptable, article 59 of the 1945 *ordonnance* gave ready-made exemptions for firms involved in *ententes*, thereby diluting its usefulness.

The first exemption covered concerted practices resulting from government decrees and acts. This was logical in a system where prices could be set by the State. However, the problems deepen when one considers that cartels could be State-led. The steel industry provides perhaps the most striking example of such a State-led cartel. All iron and steel producers were obliged to join an industry federation known as the *Chambre syndicale de la sidérurgie* where decisions on matters such as allocation of orders were taken by majority vote; the decisions then went to the Industry Minister for ratification (Goetz-Girey, 1954). In such instances, State actions reinforced corporatist tendencies.

The second exemption related to *ententes* which contributed to *'le progrès économique'*. Where concerted practices led to some form of *'progrès économique'*, they were described as *bonnes ententes* (legitimate cartels) in contra-distinction to *mauvaises ententes* (illegitimate cartels) which were considered as having no beneficial side-effects. Interestingly, this distinction can already be found in Lengelé's treatise (1942, pp. 186-91). It also finds its way into the 1957 Treaty of Rome. Further, whether it be far-right propaganda in 1942, a French government bill in 1945, or the European Community charter, the same reasoning, almost the same phraseology, recurs. Acceptable justifications include increased specialisation, improved production or distribution, or indeed technical or industrial progress in some wide sense as a result of a *bonne entente*. Whether these justifications constitute good grounds is not the issue here. The key point is that in the French legislation, no burden of proof was placed on firms to *quantify* economic progress in economic terms. When brought to book, firms acting in concert used article 59 as a simple escape clause, claiming that theirs was a *bonne entente*.

Finally, no separate regulatory authority was set up to enforce the legislation. The lack of a watch-dog in the late 1940s limited the deterrent effect of the decrees. Parties to concerted practices could safely assume that chances of detection were slight and so had little motivation to take the legislation seriously.

Over time, loopholes in the legislation have been filled in and it has been policed more adequately. A major step was taken in 1953. A decree of 9 August set up a competition authority, the *Commission Technique des Ententes* (CTE). This represented progress as it indicated the existence of political will to enforce the legislation.

However, the effectiveness of the competition authority proved limited. The CTE was a consultative body with no independent powers. Only the Minister of Finance could ask the CTE to investigate complaints or anomalies in market functioning. He rarely did so (Carabiber, 1967, p. 64). The investigations and proceedings of the CTE were undoubtedly long and involved. Once the CTE had deliberated, it had no power to enforce its verdict. It simply reported to the Finance Minister who had the option of referring the case for prosecution, negotiating directly with the authors of the *entente*, or dropping proceedings. Frequently, the Minister of Finance would simply ask colluding parties to desist. Even where action was taken, proceedings were shrouded in confidentiality. In consequence, firms did not have a clear view of the content and enforcement of competition law; both the punitive and the deterrent effects of the legislation were minimal (Brault, 1987, pp. 46-50). In a phrase, the CTE was a watch-dog without teeth.

Yet in the 1950s, *ententes* were flagrant and rife. Jenny and Weber (1976, pp. 64-73) reported on the highly developed systems used by firms to run *ententes*. Colluding companies frequently drew up written contracts stipulating the agreements and conditions that membership of a cartel entailed. Since cartel members had been known to ignore the collectively agreed terms of the *entente* when it suited their individual interests, such contracts stipulated the nature of eventual sanctions and the means to be used to enforce them.

Many *ententes* were flagrantly anti-competitive. Examples include a cartel whose members aligned their prices on the firm having the highest production costs or the *entente* which simply agreed to a permanent freezing of the *status quo* in terms of respective market shares (Carabiber, 1967, p. 68). Incriminated firms were capable of putting forward highly sophisticated arguments to justify collusion. The list includes the defence of employment, the protection of home markets against foreign invasion, improved competitiveness, greater specialisation, higher investments. They were also capable of blatant cynicism. In its 1966 report (quoted Jenny and Weber, 1976, p. 120), the CTE laments the *'mauvaise foi'* (bad faith) of firms whose typical defence was firstly to deny the existence of an *entente*, yet once its existence is proved, then claim that the *entente* contributed to economic progress!

The scale of the problem and the lack of effectiveness of the French solution are revealed by the fact that after the formation of the Common Market thousands of *ententes* were notified to the European Commission in order to qualify for exemptions to anti-collusion legislation allowed by Article 85, Section 3 of the Treaty of Rome (Glais and Laurent, 1983, p. 24). Finally, Bellon (1980, p. 20) lists a number of long-standing cartels including a cartel between CGE and PUK in the electrical cables market dating from 1931 and a cartel between BSN and Saint Gobain in glass markets lasting until 1969. In brief, the burden of anti-competitive attitudes from the early 1940s weighed heavily in the 1950s and 1960s.

Gradually however, EC competition law had a strong influence on French law. Of major relevance are Articles 85 and 86 of the Treaty of Rome. Article 85 prohibiting cartels, collusion and concerted practices in general corresponded closely to existing French legislation, but eventually reinforced prosecution of vertical *ententes*. On the other hand, the content of Article 86, prohibiting abuse of a dominant position, found its way into the French legislation in 1963 and represents a new strand of competition policy. Abuse of a dominant position included monopoly behaviour and the elimination of competitors.

This increase in the jurisdiction of the CTE had few practical effects, however. Between, 1963 and 1975, the CTE adjudicated less than a dozen times (Jenny and Weber, 1976, p. 114). A 'softly-softly' approach was taken to enforcement, with persuasion being preferred to punishment. Even in its central activity, the control of cartels, the CTE achieved little. In its 1970 report, the CTE complained that firms still blithely ignored legislation against *ententes* (quoted Jenny and Weber, 1976, pp. 134-5). In doing so, the CTE underlined its own impotence.

A substantial part of the CTE's problems stemmed from the conflict between industrial policy and competition policy in the period. In the 1960s, industrial policy favoured mergers in order to create corporate giants capable of competing on the world stage. But as Jenny and Weber (1976, pp. 85-7, 252-4) have pointed out, an industrial policy favouring concentration not only ruled out an antitrust component to competition policy, it also made *ententes* acceptable in that, in the 1960s, cartels often prepared the way for mergers. In a sense, changes in ownership structures would merely consecrate previous parallelism of business strategies. Thus the CTE's lack of jurisdiction to intervene in matters relating to industrial structures restricted its room for manoeuvre in relation to the collusive behaviour of France's largest and most important firms. It was hampered even in its primary and limited objective, the pursuit of cartels.

The 1977 reform and the Commission de la Concurrence

Reform of competition policy was acknowledged as necessary and occurred during a period of international economic turbulence. The oil crisis had revealed structural weaknesses in the French economy (see pp. 21-2). It was essential to reinforce the competitiveness of French firms.

The liberal Prime Minister, Raymond Barre, favoured a strengthening of market forces. Logically, this would have included price deregulation and the repeal of the 1945 legislation. However, after the oil price hikes, it was essential to avoid a further surge in inflation. Barre adopted the half-way house of reinforcing competition law without abolishing price controls.

Reforms were introduced by a law enacted on 19 July 1977. A new regulatory agency was set up, the *Commission de la Concurrence* (the Competition Commission). Thenceforth, not only the government and the Minister of Finance but a number of other bodies – local authorities, professional organisations, unions and consumer associations – had a legal right of recourse to it. Punishments for offences were detailed and, in the case of a prosecution, decisions were to be disseminated, so reinforcing the deterrent effect of the law. Indeed, the early rulings of the *Commission de la Concurrence* were relatively severe (Glais, 1988, p. 827).

For the first time, the regulatory agency was accorded a role in the area of mergers. By Article 6 of the 1977 law, reference could be made to the *Commission de la Concurrence* if a merger was *'de nature à porter atteinte à une concurrence satisfaisante sur le marché'* (of a kind likely to hinder satisfactory competition in the market). This role extension was a major, albeit belated, innovation. Antitrust legislation in the USA dates from 1890, in the UK, from 1948 and renewed subsequently, particularly with the Monopolies and Mergers Act of 1965.

The inclusion of these dispositions in the 1977 legislation signalled a questioning of the assumptions of industrial policy of the 1960s which had actively encouraged large-scale mergers. It was implicitly recognised that big was not necessarily efficient, that large company size could distort competition, so damaging the interests of small firms and consumers.

These positive developments in terms of principles must be acknowledged, but their practical impact was limited. In the area of industrial concentration, the *Commission de la Concurrence* was to play only a small practical role. There were several reasons for this.

Firstly, the recession of the late seventies dampened the merger mania of the late 1960s and early 1970s, reducing the scope for judicial inquiries.

Secondly, the *Commission de la Concurrence* could only give a view in the three months *subsequent* to a merger. However, as Glais (1988, pp. 830-1) argued, antitrust policy is more effective when the authorities have the power to intervene *before* the merger takes place. Such powers had indeed been conferred on German regulatory agencies in 1973 and on US ones in 1976 by the Hart-Scott-Rodino Antitrust Improvement Act (Werner, 1980). Despite these precedents, the French were taking a softer line in 1977.

Thirdly, in the legislation the phrase *concurrence satisfaisante* (satisfactory competition) is vague and open to subjective interpretation. The aim may have been to provide the Finance Minister with latitude for discretion, but in the interests of clarity, it would have been preferable to provide clear guidelines on when mergers required investigation.

The final limitation is the most important since it applies to *Commission de la Concurrence* rulings not only on mergers but on all anti-competitive practices. The *Commission de la Concurrence* was not invested with independent authority to enforce its rulings. It merely advised the Minister of Finance. The latter was empowered to inflict fines (5 per cent of a firm's turnover or 5 million francs for non-firms) or to refer the case to the courts where appropriate. But the Minister was not bound by the rulings of the *Commission de la Concurrence* and could drop proceedings if he so chose. This happened in a number of cases, producing two kinds of consequence. Firstly, as Glais and Laurent (1983, p. 28) pointed out, it weakened the judiciary by its '*élimination du juge au profit du ministre*' (replacement of judges by ministers). Although in France, the political theory of a separation of powers between government, parliament and the judiciary maintains its currency, competition law is one area which illustrates that practice can be quite different to theory. Secondly, the Minister's handling of particular cases left an impression of arbitrary behaviour and reduced the deterrent effect of competition law (Jenny, 1990, p. 74).

Its lack of powers made the *Commission de la Concurrence* a soft target and it suffered serious attack. It was fairly active between 1978-80, but gradually became less prominent. In 1980 it was consulted 27 times, 11 times in 1982 but only 5 times in 1984. In addition, the length of time between the transmission of the Commission's views and a Ministerial decision grew steadily longer (Brault, 1987).

This fading in its role is linked to the recourse to a price freeze in 1982 by the Socialist government in its fight against the raging inflation of the period. Given that French competition law has been linked closely to price behaviour, a return to a stringent application of price controls inevitably hampered the *Commission de la Concurrence*. Further, in their early years of office the Socialists had little time for market mechanisms and competition policy. However, their *découverte de l'entreprise* (literally, the discovery of the firm) during 1983-4 signalled a new concern with the marketplace, leading to a partial reform of competition law in December 1985. However, analysis of the 1985 legislation is omitted here since political events quickly overtook it.

The 1986 reform and the Conseil de la Concurrence

By the mid-1980s, the climate was right for a major reform of competition law. Discussions among jurists had revealed the inadequacies of previous legislation. Public opinion was favourable to reform, as shown by widespread support for the publicity campaigns mounted in favour of deregulation of petrol prices by the Leclerc group (see p. 145). A survey carried out by Glais, Hardouin and Jolivet (1987, p. 120) indicated substantial opposition in the business sector to the maintenance of price controls. The price control system was considered to be something of a Bastille: though there were few 'captive' prices, it represented a symbol of unacceptable State interference. The major French employers federation had also been lobbying for reform (Conseil National du Patronat Français, 1987).

Given this ground swell of opinion, proposals for extensive deregulation formed an important part of the right-wing platform in the 1986 parliamentary elections. After the victory of the Right, one of the first policy initiatives of the new government under Prime Minister Chirac was to enact an *ordonnance* on competition of relatively radical content and far-reaching consequences.

The decree of 1 December 1986 aimed to contribute to the modernising of the economy by a reinforcement of market mechanisms. Its major innovation was to abolish almost all of the remaining price controls contained in the 1945 *ordonnance*. This was a minor revolution. Up to 1986, State controls still applied on prices in cinemas, cafés, garages and hairdressing salons (Mousseron and Selinsky, 1988, p. 49). In the area of price controls, it had taken fully 40 years to make a clean break with *dirigisme*.

The abolition of price controls in 1986 implied a need to strengthen the enforcement of competition law in order to avoid a rise in inflation. The *Commission de la Concurrence* was replaced by the *Conseil de la Concurrence* (Competition Council). Despite appearances, this was no cosmetic exercise. For the first time, the watch-dog had teeth. It was invested with independent powers to curb anti-competitive practices and to punish guilty parties. In addition, the *Direction générale des prix* was transformed into the *Direction générale de la concurrence et de la consommation* (Directorate-General for Competition and Consumer Affairs). The DGCC was given the task of investigating suspected infringements of competition law and bringing cases before the *Conseil de la Concurrence* where necessary, a task which it has accomplished increasingly vigorously.

For the first time, firms could complain directly to the regulatory agency and report anti-competitive practices. Earlier systems had reserved the prerogative for judicial inquiry on anti-competitive practices mainly to Finance Ministers. This had been a perversity of French *dirigisme* since excluding the recourse of market participants to the regulatory agency could only weaken the effectiveness of competition policy. It is surprising that it took so long to give firms the opportunity to 'blow the whistle' and thereby amplify the deterrent effect of the legislation. Since 1986, most complaints have indeed come from firms (Jenny, 1990). This is to be expected since firms are among the first to suffer from the anti-competitive practices of others and have the most at stake.

The wording of the new legislation also represents an advance in the direction of greater clarity. Previous Acts and statutes had been marred by vague terminology such as the 1945 reference to the *plein exercice de la concurrence* (the full play of market forces) or the 1977 reference to *concurrence satisfaisante* (satisfactory competition). The 1986 text (article 7) prohibits such actions which *ont pour objet ou peuvent avoir pour effet d'empêcher, de restreindre ou de fausser le jeu de la concurrence sur le marché* (have as their object, or may produce the effect, of preventing, restricting or distorting market competition). This improvement in clarity has facilitated enforcement.

Jenny (1990) showed that the jurisprudence of the *Conseil de la Concurrence* in the repression of anti-competitive practices now places the emphasis on *process*, rather than on *performance*. Whereas previously, it had been necessary to demonstrate that practices under investigation had effectively undermined market forces (the performance criterion), the *Conseil de la Concurrence* now seeks to determine whether company behaviour goes against the grain of competitive processes. The *Conseil de la Concurrence* considers that due regard for the competitive process requires the following factors:

(1) independent decision taking by firms in a market;

(2) ignorance of competitor strategy; and

(3) abstaining from the creation of artificial barriers to entry into a market.

Departures from this process signal infringement of the law. The advantages of the process approach are that it is relatively more straightforward and quicker to apply than the performance approach.

The 1986 *ordonnance* instituted a number of other changes. It reduced the size of the loopholes in the 1945 statute on *ententes*. While exceptions related to State intervention hold, exemptions related to increases in 'economic progress' have been considerably tightened. Firms must now provide proof that their *entente* has positive effects *and* distribute an equitable share of proceeds to users. They must also demonstrate that their *entente* does not eliminate competition to a 'substantial' degree. Though reform arrived late in the day, the approach is stricter.

The 1986 text represents a turning-point in French competition policy. The signs are that the new legislation has sharpened up competition and so had a salutary effect on the competitiveness and long-term prospects of French companies.

However, the 1986 *ordonnance* does not represent a total break with the past. Even in the are a of price control, remains of the old *dirigiste* system still exist. The Minister of Finance retains emergency powers to control prices. This may be considered merely a measure of prudence and a last recourse. However, State intervention in prices is still practised in a number of areas which were covered not by the 1945 *ordonnances* but by later legislation. These include utilities (gas, electricity, water) and infrastructures (rail and air fares, motorway tolls, pharmaceutical products and health services), as well as insurance. Most, but not all, of the latter are in the public sector.

In addition, the *Conseil de la Concurrence* still plays only a minor role in the important area of merger control. This area was the subject of considerable controversy during the framing of the 1986 legislation and led to a compromise. Opponents of merger control considered it archaic and inappropriate, hence it was not strengthened. Its implementation was maintained in its old form. The Finance Minister retains sole prerogative for putting cases before the *Conseil de la Concurrence*. He is not bound by the views of the latter and has personally retained powers for enforcement of the legislation.

The scope of merger control was defined and delimited. The Minister can only intervene if very large firms are involved in a merger. The 1986 *ordonnance* specifies that one of two relatively high thresholds have to be passed before action can be taken: either combined company sales must exceed 25 per cent of the relevant national market or combined pre-tax turnover must exceed 7 billion francs with at least two of the individual companies concerned each turning over at least 2 billion francs. One of the effects of this approach is that government retains the right to debar take-overs of major French firms by foreign capital: it has an indirectly protectionist element. Companies referred to the *Conseil de la concurrence* in 1988 included Henkel-Colgate, Rowntree-Macintosh and 3M-Spontex, but purely French mergers have also been investigated. Overall, relatively few references related to mergers have been made to the *Conseil de la concurrence* since its creation (Glais, 1990). In 1990, of 639 mergers in France, 50 were investigated by the DGCC and 7 cases were brought before the *Conseil de la concurrence* (Le Bourdonnec, 1991).

In general, however, enforcement of competition legislation has been vigorous. Over the period between 1986 to 1989, the yearly number of investigations into restrictive practices conducted by the DGCC increased nearly three-fold from 6,240 to 17,389 (DGCC, 1991). The *Conseil de la concurrence* has been far more active than its predecessor. It imposed fines to the value of 22.5 million francs in 1988 and 358 millions in 1989. It deliberated on 82 cases in 1989 and 123 in 1990 (INSEE, 1990, 1991).

Though on specific points of practice French competition law has maintained its distinctiveness, the reinforcement of competition policy stemming from the 1986 reforms gives the lie to the received idea that the French authorities still lack the will or the means to take competition seriously. But a blind spot persists. The private sector is extensively subject to competition, yet, as the next section will demonstrate, anomalies exist in the State sector.

French State-owned firms and EC competition policy

European Community competition policy covers too wide a range of factors to be fully covered here. Hence the focus here is on current developments in European competition policy regarding State-owned firms in competitive sectors of the economy [2].

Ideally, market conditions for public and private sector firms should be identical. But the actions of State-run monopolies and the distribution of State aid to firms in competitive sectors of the economy distort market competition within a number of countries, including France. The 1986 French legislation did not settle these anomalies of competition law relating to State-owned enterprises.

Moreover, this is not simply a national issue, which French policy makers can settle as they see fit. In 'open' international markets, and particularly within the burgeoning single European economy, the existence of such distortions to competition cannot be a matter of indifference to trading partners. In a recent case, Prime Minister Cresson, who was still at the start of her term of office, proposed to increase subsidies to the State-owned electronics giant, Thomson but was overruled by the European Commission (Castle, 1991). Subsidies of this type distort home markets and raise barriers to foreign competitors. They constitute a form of 'neo-protectionism', a problem that was raised at the end of the last chapter and will be developed further here.

Market distortions initiated by national states have aroused considerable criticism. Much of that criticism is grounded in the competition law of the EC. Article 90 of the Treaty of Rome specifies that State monopolies are subject to the same principles on trade and competition as are private enterprises. Article 92 prohibits State aids which 'distort or threaten to distort competition', but allows for a number of exceptions including aid of a social character and regional aid.

Readers of these articles may find them vague or inconsistent, but as Papaconstantinou (1988, pp. 202-20) argued, the drafters of the rules wished to leave EC Member States room for manoeuvre but permit tighter definitions for a later stage of the EC's life. Thus Medhurst (1990, p. 115) finds that though the Treaty of Rome does not define State aid, in the case history of the European Court of Justice, such aid certainly includes subsidies.

Further, Articles 93 and 94 place on the European Commission the duty of keeping both old and new aids 'under constant review' and give the

Commission powers of enforcement, including the power to demand repayment of unacceptable subsidies. Repayments have indeed been enforced. In 1987, there were 22 such cases, 10 against Belgium, 5 against France, 4 against Germany, 2 against Holland and 1 against Britain (Jacobs and Stewart-Clark, 1990, p. 96). Article 37 also requires EC Member States to 'progressively adjust any State monopolies of a commercial character' to end discrimination in production or marketing. In brief, the Treaty of Rome does not underwrite the maintenance of the *status quo* as regards State monopolies and aids but provides a framework calling for evolutionary change.

Yet though the terms of the Treaty of Rome are fairly tough, the realities of implementation have been softer. Because the EC did not attempt systematic surveys of State aids in member States until the late 1980s, the data on which to form judgements was largely lacking. Once surveys were completed, the scale of the problem became clear. The extent of State aids prevalent in the EC is simply incompatible with Article 92 of the Treaty of Rome. Two EC surveys (Commission of the European Communities, 1989, 1990) have concluded that the volume and proliferation of State aids had a negative impact on competition and on the completion of the internal market. If the spirit of the treaty is to be respected, tougher enforcement of its articles on competition is required. This of course assumes the existence of the necessary political will and power at EC level.

Certainly the duty of 'constant review' is being taken seriously by Sir Leon Brittan in his role as EC Competition Commissioner. Not only are new aid packages subjected to increasing scrutiny with regard to their effects on competition, but older schemes are also being reassessed. Sir Leon has stated that 'market circumstances change, and subsidies which were merited at the outset may now be damaging to the Single Market' (in Jacobs and Stewart-Clark, 1990, p. 12).

Subsidies, however, are only part of the issue. The severity of problems increase when other forms of preferential treatment are brought into the reckoning. State monopolies can combine with State aids and extensive public procurement programmes. The major sectors in which this applies are rail and air transport, telecommunications and energy.

Although national railway companies have not been targeted for investigation by the European Commission, during the 1980s both air transport and telecommunications were. As a result, some deregulation has occurred in each sector. Of particular interest is a 1988 European Commission directive based on Article 90 relating to liberalisation of the market in telecommunications terminals equipment (which turns over some 10 billion ECU per year in the EC). Though the directive was challenged, the European Court of Justice upheld its validity. As Filori *et al.* (1989) pointed out, these events indicate that the Commission has grown bolder in its application of Article 90. They also show that European legislation on State monopolies has teeth.

In 1991, attention was focused on the energy sector. Sir Leon Brittan commented that the precedent of using Article 90 that was set in telecommunications may be a 'sensible' option in the energy sector (Walker, 1991).

Energy is a key sector not only because the energy industry has a crucial role as a supplier of 'goods' to consumers, but also as a supplier to the rest of the economy. Energy costs transfer through into the prices of other goods and services, particularly those of industry. Hence energy costs impact on the competitiveness of downstream producers. The crucial point is that distortions of market mechanisms resulting from monopolies and subsidies in the upstream energy sector are amplified as they pass through the production system.

Distortions to competition in energy markets have long been recognised by the European Commission. In 1979, the Commission noted price differentials within the EC of some 30 per cent for petrol, 50 per cent for domestic fuels and even more for gas and electricity. The causes identified were tax differences, variations in methods of financing, widely differing price controls and variations in industrial structures and productivity (Economic and Social Committee of the EC, 1981). But little was done about these distortions.

The French State has come under fire for market distortions caused by firms in public ownership. But the causes of distortion warrant close inspection. As regards the levels of State aids in France, surveys conducted by the Commission of the European Communities (1989, 1990) indicated that, relative to European neighbours, they were near the average (see p. 43 for data). Given this intermediate position on aids, it would be inappropriate to single France out as a particular culprit.

However, a number of distortions to competition are compounded in particular sectors, notably in the provision of electricity. The State monopoly *Electricité de France* (EDF) is Europe's largest producer of nuclear-based electricity. EDF has received major State grants and loans towards R&D and towards the construction of nuclear power stations. EDF is a net exporter of electricity and claims to be a low-cost producer.

The firm's critics decry the lack of 'transparency' in company accounts. The true levels of operational costs in the nuclear industry are:

(a) notoriously hard to evaluate; and

(b) rarely disclosed.

But as Carson (1991) noted, it is difficult to reconcile EDF's cheap electricity tariffs with debts to the State of 240 billion French francs and an operating loss of some 2.5 billions per year. With privatisation and de-integration pushing British electricity production into an economic 'experiment' (Vickers and Yarrow, 1991), it would indeed be surprising if, in the near future, criticisms of EDF's subsidised monopoly practices were not redoubled.

An illustration of the dangers to competition caused by energy subsidies was provided in the Pechiney case. In 1989, Pechiney, a French State-owned company having a near-monopoly of aluminium production in France, announced its intention to set up a new smelter near Dunkirk. The French government was backing Pechiney with a package of measures including aid and a contract for cheap electricity. Energy represents a major part of metal manufacture costs. Low electricity prices would clearly give Pechiney a competitive edge in international markets. The EC threatened an inquiry. The deal between Pechiney and the French State was quickly altered. The aid package was reduced and electricity prices increased.

France is not alone, however, in giving energy subsidies. For example, Germany subsidises domestic coal production by a levy on electricity, the *kohlpfennig*. Further, German power stations are obliged to buy coal produced in Germany. Preferential treatment to the energy sector is accorded in other countries too.

Given the difficult political circumstances, the European Commission was slow to act but finally decided to launch EC-wide proceedings into market distortions in the energy sector. On 21 March 1991, the Commission took infraction proceedings against 9 EC states (Germany, Belgium and Luxemburg have been exonerated), accusing them of preserving monopolies in the import and export of electricity. Similar accusations are levelled against Belgium, France and Denmark regarding gas (*Target 1992*, 1991a). In addition, the European Commission has forced governments across the community to transmit detailed balance sheets and profit and loss accounts of State-owned manufacturing firms to the Commission; the aim is to improve control over State aid to industry (Hill, 1991).

It is too early to judge the outcome of these proceedings. Talk of breaking up national monopolies altogether seems inappropriate. *Electricité de France* and *Gaz de France* are unlikely to be dismantled. But given that Sir Leon Brittan has gone on record recommending that EC Member States should protect no more than 20 per cent of electricity production on grounds of security of supply (*Target 1992*, 1991b), EDF may yet be obliged to conduct its business differently.

If EC competition law were applied fully, the final element in France's conversion to competition, namely the subjection of State monopolies to market disciplines, would be accomplished. That application, however, assumes that an EC-wide consensus will be reached. But as regards policy towards the public sector, towards public procurement and State aids, France is not the only country holding up the completion of the 'Single Market'.

MARKET RELATIONS AROUND THE DISTRIBUTION SECTOR

The discussion about market relations and competition policy has so far turned mainly on general objectives of economic efficiency and their implementation through legal means. In this final section, competition in and around the distribution sector is used to provide a case study of the changing characteristics of French market relations.

Market relations in the distribution system are of major interest as distribution represents the interface between producers and consumers. The issues are wide-ranging and cut across a range of sectors. Moreover, this is an area in which the aims of competition policy are most open to debate.

Glais (1990, p. 270) has argued that the policy objective should be to protect competition, rather than protect competitors. This is an attractive formulation, but applies mainly to horizontal relations between rivals. What should happen within vertical, buyer-seller relations? Should policy protect the retailer against the producer, or the producer against the retailer, or neither? Should the accent be placed on protecting consumers or not? Further, is consumer protection limited to economic interests and health and safety aspects or do wider welfare issues matter too?

In this complex area, French policy decisions and legislation have had to keep up with changing social attitudes and business practices. Study of the distribution sector will reveal the delicate balancing act involved in attempts made by the State to reconcile, at any one moment in time, conflicts of interest between producers, small shopkeepers, large distributors and consumers. Analysis will show shifts in the balance of advantage as market participants switch strategies in reaction to legal reforms and to developments upstream or downstream. The nub of the argument will be that major changes in market strategies render inappropriate any static stereotype regarding supposed French aversion to competition. On the contrary, competition, particularly in distribution, is often fierce.

The small retailer lobby and the State

The French distribution sector has been characterised by its degree of fragmentation, with large numbers of small shops practising high levels of mark-up. Yet the small retailer lobby succeeded in enlisting the help of the State against large store rivals on two major occasions, once under Pierre Poujade in the 1950s and again under Gérard Nicoud two decades later. Both movements had in common vociferous and violent types of protest tactics that ended in government capitulation. Superficially, it would seem that intimidation of the State led to increased intervention and the preservation of anti-competitive, indeed backward, practice. Closer inspection reveals a more complex picture. Though both movements scored apparent victories, in reality they achieved only short-term concessions, with market forces soon reasserting their dominance.

In 1953, Poujade, the owner of a small stationery shop, protested against economic grievances by starting a tax strike. So successful a lobbyist was he that by 1955 he was organising mass rallies bringing together hundreds of thousands of similarly disaffected and angry shopkeepers, artisans and small farmers. In the 1956 parliamentary elections, Poujade and his supporters (including Jean-Marie Le Pen, now leader of the *Front National*) won 52 parliamentary seats; this despite the fact that the movement had no political programme, merely a common store of reactionary tendencies (Anderson, 1974). By its onslaught, the movement intimidated the government and extracted tax concessions.

Yet the storm quickly blew over. With the return to politics of General de Gaulle in 1958 and the massive electoral swing in his favour, the Gaullists made short work of evicting all of Poujade's followers from their parliamentary seats.

Political defeat made economic rectification easier. Whereas in the 1950s small shopkeepers had attempted to restrict manufacturers from selling to the newly created supermarket chains which were undercutting them, the 1960 Fontanet *circulaire* (an administrative order) made illegal the refusal of sales to large retailers. New tax reforms favoured larger rather than smaller shops.

These policy changes tipped the balance back to the 'modern' wing of the distribution sector, namely the supermarket chains whose large sales volumes allowed them to charge low prices. Many small retailers found it impossible to survive while retail chains experienced boom. Between 1966 and 1971, the stock of small shops fell by 20,000 while 1,887 supermarkets and 143 hypermarkets were opened (Berger, 1981). Over the years between 1970 and 1973, supermarkets and hypermarkets increased their market share by over 7 per cent, their fastest rate of increase up until then, or since (Regimbeau, 1987, p. 5). Poujade's movement had merely postponed the unleashing of market forces in the distribution sector.

But the creation of a more competitive environment in distribution aroused a second cycle of opposition. In 1969, under the leadership of Gérard Nicoud, small shopkeepers and artisans rallied en masse and again demonstrated that violent protest pays. By 1972, with memories of the tumultuous May 1968 demonstrations still fresh and with parliamentary elections imminent, the right-wing government was forced to make legislative concessions to an interest group that counted among its 'natural' electorate.

Political decisions which map economic policy onto sectional interests are not unique to France. But the manner in which virulent demonstrations influence political decisions and market relations is distinctive. Instances include the 1984 lorry drivers blockade of roads throughout France (Segrestin, 1985) while the spate of violent protests by French farmers (against British lamb, Spanish strawberries, etc.) is a near-obligatory reference point. The frequency of such incidents make it tempting to see here a characteristically French trait.

The 1973 loi Royer and its consequences

Legislative concessions to shopkeepers were contained in the 1973 *loi d'orientation du commerce et de l'artisanat*, usually referred to simply as the *loi Royer* (named after its sponsoring Minister).

The *loi Royer* had a considerable impact on the distribution sector and has not been repealed. Its underlying aim was to redress the balance between small and large retailers in favour of the former. Small shopkeepers were perceived as suffering unfair competition from large supermarket chains. Many supermarket chains were not only themselves large but were grouping together to form *centrales d'achat* (buyers' consortia). These factors had increased the power of leverage of the chains over suppliers and allowed the chains to negotiate hefty price reductions. Small retailers, however, found it more difficult to do the same. They had to buy at higher cost and sell at higher prices, so becoming less competitive in relation to supermarket chains.

To protect the small shop, the 1973 Act prohibited any unjustified price reductions by producers. But the 1973 legislation also included a range of measures to improve market relations such as a prohibition of *publicité mensongère* (misleading advertising) and consumer organisations were given the right to defend consumer interests before courts of law. These measures gave greater visibility to the application of consumer protection legislation and gave greater coverage to competition law.

The most significant parts of the *loi Royer* were clauses specifically designed to shield small shopkeepers by restricting the expansion of supermarket chains. Official authorisation was required to open stores having a large floor-area, with progressive ceilings set in relation to store size and geographical location. Shopkeepers were allocated by right a significant number of representatives on the local vetting committees which decided whether large stores would be granted permission to open or not. This gave small retailers a right of veto over projects which might threaten their own businesses. Corporatism was far from dead in France.

Predictably, the vetting committees stifled large store openings. Berger (1981, p. 96) records that supermarket openings were 30 per cent lower in 1974 than the previous year. Further, the vetting committees did not use their discretionary powers to produce a better balance between large and small stores. This could have been achieved by refusing permission in centres where large stores were already concentrated and by granting permission where they were underrepresented. On the contrary, analysis of geographical variations in authorisation rates between 1974 and 1980 has shown that committees in rural *départements* which had high densities of small shops but few supermarkets refused permission more often than in urban areas where supermarkets were already more plentiful (Keeler, 1985; Perron, 1991). As Brault pointed out (1987, pp. 131-2), planning limits on numbers of supermarkets in any area gave small shopkeepers (and indeed existing supermarkets) a *rente de situation* which limited incentives to increase competitiveness.

Consumer polls in the late 1960s showed 75 per cent of respondents in favour of an increase in supermarket numbers and only 16 per cent against. Thus consumer preferences and interests appear to have been ignored.

At this stage of the analysis, the *loi Royer* seems a clear case of protecting competitors, rather than competition. Questions therefore arise over whether, over the long term, the *loi Royer* was wrong in principle or in practice.

Turning first to wider principles, a comparison with the UK is useful. The British food retail sector is currently highly concentrated. Small, independent retailers account for around 9 per cent of food sales in Britain (Sicot and Vatimbella, 1990, p. 153). Britain therefore provides an interesting point of contrast with France, where small retailers accounted for 33 per cent of food sales in 1989 (DGCC, 1991).

Burke, Genn-Bash and Haines (1988, pp. 180-6) point out that one of the major issues in the decline of small retailers in the UK has been the extent to which discounts extracted by the major supermarket multiples, through their massive buying power, has forced producers to cross-subsidise their sales by obliging small retailers to pay relatively more. This factor, which goes unseen by consumers comparing prices, made it even harder for the independents to survive the onslaught of the multiples.

Yet the demise of small local stores entails differential consequences. Disadvantaged groups, such as pensioners, the disabled and car-less mothers, suffer disproportionately because out of town hypermarkets cater for car owners. Protection of the small store can entail a decrease in market competition but lead to an increase in consumer welfare in a larger sense. The problem for policy making is that the consequences of the former are easier to quantify than those of the latter. Approached from the angle of general welfare, the principles underpinning the *loi Royer* have a certain relevance, but the conflict between different social groups and their objectives inevitably raises controversy.

Turning to practice, the 1973 Act produced a number of negative short-term effects. In the longer term, its effects have arguably been neutral or mildly beneficial. In the 1970s, not only did the Act slow down large-store openings but successful openings were implemented at high cost. Acceptable sites became more expensive. Sicot and Vatimbella (1990, pp. 18-23) detail the financial 'sweeteners' – such as contributions to urban renewal schemes, conference centres, etc. – offered by large distributors to woo 'reluctant' local community leaders into accepting stores that consumers wanted anyway. Indeed when 'sweeteners' dissolved into old-fashioned bribes, political scandals broke out. This is the least reputable aspect of the consequences of the *loi Royer.*

On the positive side, the legislator's aim of ensuring balance between small and large stores has been achieved. Incremental increases over the long term in the market share of large stores meant that by 1989 the multiples and the small retail sector each had 50 per cent of the market (DGCC, 1991). But the spread of the *grandes surfaces* (hypermarkets and large-area supermarkets) was slowed down in the mid-1970s by the *loi Royer*, giving small retailers time to catch their breath.

But the respite was temporary. Major changes occurred in food retailing where the number of independent shops declined from 316,000 in 1960, to 260,000 in 1975, to 134,796 in 1984. Employment in the sector fell from 105,000 in 1973 to 82,000 in 1982, a drop of 22 per cent. The market share of small shops in food sales fell from 81 per cent in 1962 to 33 per cent in 1989 while that of large stores increased from 1 per cent to 65 per cent (Regimbeau, 1987; Sicot and Vatimbella, 1990; DGCC, 1991). Thus the competitive pressures unleashed by the *grandes surfaces* swept thousands of small food shops away. The picture is further complicated by the spread of *supérettes* (mini-supermarkets). These usually had a sales floor-area just below the thresholds indicated in the *loi Royer* and so were exempt from its provisions, but this formula again took business away from the traditional small retailer.

Macro-economic trends contributed to these developments. In the crisis years of the late 1970s and the 1980s, the fight against inflation became the number one priority. As large stores specialised in price-cutting, official authorisations for openings increased dramatically. There were on average 164 authorisations per year between 1975 and 1986, but an average of 458 in 1987 and 1988 (Sicot and Vatimbella, 1990, p. 21). However, the composition of the large-store population also changed: the bulge occurred in DIY, furniture and gardening centres, with relatively fewer supermarket applications.

The small retailers that survived often redesigned their business. Broadly speaking, they have adopted two types of new strategies. One was to offer a more specialised range of goods or services, of a higher quality than the more prosaic supermarkets. The other was to form associations and co-operate, principally by making joint buying agreements, operating under a specific *enseigne* (trade name) but retaining independent ownership. Forming themselves into purchasing consortia allowed small retailers to negotiate with suppliers on a more equal footing. These consortia negotiate favourable bulk-purchase rates comparable to those obtained by rival supermarket chains. In effect, small retailers duplicated the advantages of the large chains by copying their strategy. The major associations are Intermarché and Leclerc.

The second is particularly important for two reasons. Firstly, the Leclerc group is the largest trader in France. Secondly, though all stores trading under the Leclerc trade name are owned by individuals, the inventor of the formula, Edouard Leclerc, still leads the group in a particularly aggressive manner and is an outspoken advocate of the free market.

His combative energies have been directed towards reducing prices in general and eliminating restrictive practices in particular. He has been successful in both. Surveys among French consumers show that the Leclerc group is considered to offer the lowest prices (Sicot and Vatimbella, 1990, pp. 83-5). Moreover, Leclerc's high standing among French consumers results from his attacks on restrictive practices that artificially inflate prices. Edouard Leclerc has attacked government price controls on petrol, both in publicity campaigns and by cutting prices at the petrol pump. He has been active in opposing the French equivalent of the net book agreement. He has also sought to wrest sales of para-pharmaceutical products from chemists, who have enjoyed a corporatist monopoly (see p. 125).

Edouard Leclerc's values and activities are fiercely competitive. He is the complete reversal of a Poujade or a Nicoud. Rather than engaging a rear-guard combat to hijack government into protecting the *status quo* in retailing, his group has actively sought modernisation by a marketing strategy that allies the business objectives of his group with assuring consumer satisfaction. That the Leclerc group is market leader in the French distribution sector is proof both of the success of the strategy and of the revolution in attitudes to competition in France. The competitive momentum is not imposed from outside the sector but comes from within. In food retailing, France now has one of the most competitive distribution sectors in Europe and the one with the lowest profit margins (Regimbeau, 1987).

The balance of power between producers and distributors

However, if a new equilibrium has been struck between the needs of distributors and consumers by the greater intensity of competitive pressures, the price has partly been paid by producers.

Negotiations between producers and distributors inevitably contain an element of tension. In France in the 1980s, however, tension turned into conflict as distributors cut prices not only by reducing their own margins but by constraining suppliers into selling at lower prices. The size and influence of the multiples is such that the threat of dropping a manufacturer's lines from the shelves is often enough to 'persuade' the latter into acceptable lower returns (in preference to none at all). Sicot and Vatimbella (1990, p. 104) noted that Leclerc has twice the turnover of BSN, the largest French food group, and that by boycotting Gervais-Danone for declining an invitation to reduce prices, Leclerc brought Gervais-Danone to its knees in a matter of months.

The range of convoluted strategies used by distributors to exact reductions, discounts and rebates from producers is too large to survey here. But the central part of their strategy requires mention. It revolves around the *centrales d'achat*. As Mousseron (1986, pp. 45-50) indicated, the *centrales d'achat* started as genuine purchasing agencies working for the supermarket chains but their role gradually evolved away from buying towards reference listing (*référencement*). The *centrales d'achat* simply added products to the list of goods handled in return for negotiated advantage. Further, the consortia added more members, becoming *super-centrales*. Producers found that they had first to persuade the *centrales d'achat* to recommend their products (the process of *référencement*) then actually sell them to individual members of the consortium. By this stage, the term *centrales d'achat* had become a confusing misnomer. The two-stage process complicated the producer's task and made it more costly for him.

The problems were compounded by the abusive behaviour of certain *centrales d'achat* which would simply consolidate the global turnover of participating firms to extract price reductions from suppliers – but without agreeing to match price reductions with commitments on future purchase quantities (Mousseron and Selinsky, 1988, pp. 128-9). A further complaint from producers was that the discounts they gave to distributors were frequently not passed on to consumers (Sicot and Vatimbella, 1990, p. 115). Given that some *centrales d'achat* brought together for purchasing purposes a number of chains which were otherwise quite independent in terms of ownership and trading operations, it is perhaps not surprising to note that more cases of collusion from the distribution sector were brought before the *Commission de la Concurrence* than from any other sector (Glais, 1984, p. 424).

The difficulties this state of affairs presented to producers were recognised in the 1986 reform of French competition law. The new legislation took over from German law the prohibition of abuse of a position of relative dominance. It gives legal right of redress to companies that consider that they have been exploited by trading partners. The wording covers a range of eventualities but embraces the situation where small- or medium-sized suppliers are confronted by a large buyers' consortium seeking to extract advantage by excessive discounts or other unfair terms and conditions. This offers a measure of producer protection.

In principle, it is no longer necessary to demonstrate market domination on the part of the large firm (a complex and fraught procedure), if it can be demonstrated that the larger firm has abused a commercial partner who had no alternative but to trade with it. In practice, the scope of the amendment has been obscure. The amendment has been invoked in a case currently before the *Conseil de la Concurrence* against the supermarket chain Cora, who forced its suppliers to finance its take-over of the SES chain of supermarkets. The outcome of the case should clarify the scope and meaning of the legislation (Le Bourdonnec, 1991).

Distributors have other ways of harnessing their suppliers' finances. Gordon (1990, p. 75) notes that hypermarkets rotate their stock every 24 days on average, but take 60 days to pay suppliers. This gives 36 days in which to invest receipts. Sicot and Vatimbella (1990) indicated that in 1988, half of Carrefour's profits came from this type of investment. These financial dealings help explain how French *grandes surfaces* operate on profit margins on sales of around 1 per cent. France simply has the longest payment terms in Europe: the average *real* time for payment (across all sectors) is 90 days (Le Bourdonnec and Peyrani, 1991).

Meanwhile suppliers have proportionately larger amounts tied up in unpaid goods. When a chain goes bankrupt, as happened with Codec in 1990 and Montlaur in 1991, the consequences are a financial nightmare for their suppliers. Yet even in normal circumstances, long payment terms create cash flow problems for suppliers, especially for small firms. The Cresson government has looked into reducing the normal payment period to 30 days in order to improve the lot of small business, but so far without taking any action.

These developments illustrate that a turn-around has occurred in market relations between producers and distributors. In the shortage economy of the immediate post-war years, producers called the shots and distributors were happy if they received supplies. Once the retail trade was dominated by the multiples, many producers found themselves in a dependent position. Conversely, from a position of relative weakness, not to say reactionary leanings, the retail trade has achieved a position of dominance, indeed leadership.

In the process, consumer preferences have assumed greater prominence. Retailers have sought to give consumers satisfaction by improving their competitiveness through policies of aggressive price-cutting and by giving better service and improved quality.

The alliance of consumers and distributors has involved some deterioration in the position of producers. A different balance may be desirable. There has been some interest in partnership arrangements between producers and chains, along the lines that Marks and Spencers have with their suppliers, but this would be a fresh development in France (*LSA*, 1991).

In summary, competition policy has been repeatedly adjusted to adapt to changes in the balance of power. Earlier adjustments contained elements of special treatment and heavy-handed intervention. In recent years, however, the aim has been to maintain the interests of consumers, distributors and producers in equilibrium by the provision of checks and counter-checks to be deployed by market participants themselves, rather than by State interference. This is particularly important in a fast-moving sector, where market participants rarely stand still.

Bertrand (1991) noted that after spreading terror among producers for six years, the *supercentrales d'achat* are breaking up into their constituent elements. The chains appear to be looking for a European dimension as separate entities. During the 1990s, this may indicate a new chapter in market relations in a sector in which competitive pressures are likely to increase even more.

CONCLUSIONS

As the next chapter will illustrate further, elements of heterogeneity exist within the French business community. The corporatist legacy has not been entirely erased. Nevertheless in many sectors competition is now viewed as a positive and constructive force for change.

The new awareness of the business community was fostered by a competition policy that grew gradually clearer and firmer. The economic analyses used to frame competition law have undoubtedly improved in terms of their sophistication (Glais, 1990). The need to balance the conflicting interests of producers, distributors and consumers became better understood. The regulatory authorities became more independent of government and their powers have been enlarged.

In the process, the role of the State has been modified. The realisation that interventionism distorts or destroys markets has gradually gained influence. Donnedieu de Vabres indicated that the aim of reforming competition law in the 1980s was to create:

une situation où l'Etat ne sera plus le 'gérant' de l'économie mais le 'garant' de la liberté de celle-ci. (quoted Mousseron and Selinsky, 1988, p. 227)

a situation where the State will no longer manage the economy but guarantee economic freedom.

Rather than managing market relations itself, the State's role is now considered to lie in the provision of conditions under which free market competition can flourish. Much progress has been made in that direction, though glaring anomalies do still exist, principally within the French nationalised sector but also within a few surviving corporatist bastions.

What then is the outlook for the future? If competitive reflexes have sharpened, will they dull with time? The 1986 reform of competition law has led to a more lasting change than the more timid 1977 adjustments. Price liberalisation in the late 1980s took root in a way it did not in the late 1970s.

In 1978, Prime Minister Barre failed to repeal the 1945 *ordonnances* on price control; the error was not repeated in 1986. Further, price liberalisation in 1978 fell foul of massive inflation (11.8 per cent in 1979, 13-14 per cent in 1980-81). Although much of this was 'imported' in the form of escalating oil prices, it reduced the government's room for manoeuvre; interventionism became the order of the day both under Barre and the succeeding Socialist Mauroy government. In 1986, however, the return to free prices occurred in a setting where both oil prices and general inflation were falling. With inflation remaining low over the following five years and with a shift away from interventionist policies under the Chirac and Rocard governments, liberal competition policy met with consensus and took root.

Further reforms are desirable however. In a recent study, the OECD (1990) called for a reinforcement of market mechanisms in a number of areas including insurance, banking and legal services and also for further deregulation in air transport and inward investment. With 1993 fast approaching, the likelihood is that France will reaffirm her support of the goals of European integration - involving free competition in open markets - and persevere in reforms consistent with those goals. Nowhere is this more necessary than in the State sector.

Notes

1. For extended discussions of the economic issues related to competition policy and competition law, see Burke, Genn-Bash and Haines (1988); Gardner (1990), pp. 3-24 or Glais (1990).

2. For fuller discussion of EC competition law see Gardner (1990); Glais (1987); Korah (1975); Papaconstantinou (1988).

References

Anderson, M. (1974) *Conservative Politics in France*, London: George Allen and Unwin

Barel, Y. (1990) 'Territoires et corporatismes', *Economie et humanisme*, 314 (septembre-octobre), pp. 60-70

Bellon, B. (1980) 'Origines et conditions des restructurations en France' in ADEFI (eds.) *Les Restructurations industrielles en France*, pp. 11-28, Paris: Economica

Berger, S. (1981) 'Regime and interest representation: the French traditional middle classes' in Berger, S. (ed.) *Organizing interests in Western Europe. Pluralism, Corporatism and the Transformation of Politics*, pp. 83-101, Cambridge: CUP

Bertrand, P. (1991) 'Puissance d'achat à redéfinir', *LSA*, 1265 (11 juillet), pp. 16-17

Brault, D. (1987) *L'Etat et l'esprit de concurrence en France*, Paris: Economica

Burke, T., Genn-Bash, A. & Haines, B. (1988) *Competition in Theory and Practice*, London: Croom Helm

Carabiber, C. (1967) *Trusts, cartels et ententes. Législation et jurisprudence des principaux pays de la CEE*, Paris: Librairie générale de droit et de jurisprudence

Caron, F. (1988) 'Ententes et stratégies d'achat dans la France du XIXe siècle', *Revue française de gestion* (septembre-octobre), pp. 127-33

Carson, I. (1991) 'Who's subsidising watt?', *Eurobusiness*, 3:5 (April), pp. 22-5

Castle, T. (1991) 'Thomson aid confusion on Cresson climbdown', *The European* (21-23 June), p. 17

Closets, F. de (1982) *Toujours plus!*, Paris: Grasset

Commission of the European Communities (1989) *First Survey on State Aids in the European Community*, Luxemburg: Office for Official Publications of the EC

Commission of the European Communities (1990) *Second Survey on State Aids in the European Community in the Manufacturing and certain other Sectors*, Luxemburg: Office for Official Publications of the EC

Conseil National du Patronat Français (1987) *L'Entreprise et le nouveau droit de la concurrence*, Paris: Editions Techniques Professionnelles

DGCC (*Direction générale de la concurrence et de la consommation*) (1991) 'Rapport au parlement sur les pratiques tarifaires entre les entreprises en France', *Bulletin Officiel, Concurrence, Consommation et Répression des fraudes*, 51:1 (12 janvier)

Economic and Social Committee of the EC (1981) *Community competition policy*, Brussels: Economic and Social Committee, Press, Information and Publications Division

Filori, J.-C. *et al.* (1989) *The European Single Market. A New Business Environment*, Brussels: Club de Bruxelles

Gardner, N. (1990) *A Guide to United Kingdom and European Community Competition Policy*, Basingstoke: Macmillan

Glais, M. (1984) 'Six ans de répression des ententes illicites et des abus de position dominante: un bilan de l'activité de la Commission de la Concurrence', *Revue trimestrielle de droit commercial et de droit économique*, 3 (juillet-septembre), pp. 419-46

Glais, M. (1987) 'Les fondements micro-économiques de la jurisprudence concurrentielle (française et européenne)', *Revue économique*, 1 (janvier), pp. 75-115

Glais, M. (1988) 'La politique de la concurrence: l'exemple français', in Arena R. *et al.* (eds.) *Traité d'économie industrielle*, pp. 820-39, Paris: Economica

Glais, M. (1990) 'Les apports théoriques récents en économie industrielle et la nouvelle gestion de la politique de la concurrence', *Revue d'économie industrielle*, 51 (1er trimestre), pp. 255-75

Glais, M., Hardouin, M. & Jolivet, E. (1987) *Analyse des politiques de contrôle des prix dans certains secteurs, sous l'angle de la concurrence et des échanges intra-communautaires*, Luxemburg: Office for the Official Publications of the European Communities

Glais, M. & Laurent, P. (1983) *Traité d'économie et de droit de la concurrence*, Paris: Presses Universitaires de France

Goetz-Girey, R. (1954) 'Monopoly and competition in France' in Chamberlin, E. H. (ed.), *Monopoly and Competition and their Regulation*, pp. 21-42, London: Macmillan

Gordon, C. (1990) 'The business culture in France' in Randlesome, C. *et al.*, *Business Cultures in Europe*, pp. 58-106, London: Heinemann

Gurviez, J.-J. (1988) 'Les fortins du corporatisme', *L'Expansion* (21 octobre - 3 novembre), pp. 96-9

Hill, A. (1991) 'Brussels tightens control of State aid to industry', *Financial Times* (25 June), p. 10

INSEE (1990) *1989: une économie plus forte. Rapport sur les comptes de la nation 1989*, Paris: INSEE

INSEE (1991) *La France à l'épreuve de la turbulence mondiale. Rapport sur les comptes de la nation 1990*, Paris: INSEE

Jacobs, D. M. & Stewart-Clark, J. (1990) *Competititon Law in the European Community*, London: Kogan Page

Jenny, F. (1990) 'Concurrence: la nouvelle règle du jeu', *Revue française de gestion* (novembre-décembre), pp. 73-8

Jenny, F. & Weber, A.-P. (1976) *L'Entreprise et les politiques de concurrence. Ententes, cartels, monopoles dans les économies occidentales,* Paris: Editions d'Organisation

Jenny, F. & Weber, A.-P. (1986) 'Politique des prix et corporatisme', *Economie et humanisme,* 287 (janvier-février), pp. 25-31

Keeler, J. T. S. (1985) 'Corporatist decentralisation and commercial modernisation in France: the Royer law's impact on shopkeepers, supermarkets and the State' in Cerny, P. G. & Schain, M. A. (eds.) *Socialism, the State and Public Policy in France,* pp. 264-91, London: Frances Pinter

Korah, V. (1975) *Competition Law of Britain and the Common Market,* London: Elek

Kuisel, R. F. (1981) *Capitalism and the State in Modern France,* Cambridge: CUP

Le Bourdonnec, Y. (1991) 'Concurrence: ce qui reste à faire', *Nouvel Economiste,* 809 (30 août), pp. 24-5

Le Bourdonnec, Y. & Peyrani, B. (1991) 'Commerce-industrie: la rivalité jusqu'où?', *Nouvel Economiste,* 805 (19 juillet), pp. 24-9

Lefranc, G. (1976) *Les Organisations patronales en France,* Paris: Payot

Lengelé, R. (1942) *La Mission économique et sociale du patronat français,* Paris: Bernard Grasset

LSA (1991) 'Le partenariat industrie-distribution: utopie ou réalité?', *LSA,* 1248 (14 mars), pp. 43-63

Medhurst, D. (1990) *A Brief and Practical Guide to EC Law,* Oxford: Blackwell

Mousseron, J. (1986) *Producteurs, distributeurs: quelle concurrence?,* Paris: Librairies techniques

Mousseron, J. M. & Selinsky, V. (1988) *Le Droit français nouveau de la concurrence,* Paris: Librairie de la Cour de Cassation

OECD (1990) *OECD Economic Studies: France 1989-1990,* Paris: OECD

Papaconstantinou, H. (1988) *Free Trade and Competition in the EEC. Law, Policy and Practice,* London: Routledge

Perron, R. (1991) 'Les commerçants dans la modernisation de la distribution', *Revue française de sociologie,* XXXII: 2 (avril-mai), pp. 179-207

Regimbeau, J. (1987) 'Loi d'orientation du commerce et de l'artisan' (titre III, chapitre II), *Conseil économique et social* (30 janvier), pp. 4-24

Segrestin, D. (1985) *Le Phénomène corporatiste. Essai sur l'avenir des sytèmes professionnels fermés en France,* Paris: Fayard

Sheahan, J. (1963) *Promotion and Control of Industry in Postwar France,* Cambridge, Mass.: Harvard UP

Sicot, D. & Vatimbella, A. (1990) *La Distribution,* Paris: Syros

Target 1992 (1991a) 'Down with gas and electricity monopolies', *Target 1992,* 5 (May), p. 2

Target 1992 (1991b) 'Competition in electricity and gas markets', *Target 1992,* 6 (June), p. 1

Vickers, J. & Yarrow, G. (1991) 'The British electricity experiment', *Economic Policy,* 12 (April), pp. 188-232

Walker, L. (1991) 'Energy is late to the game', *The European* (17 May), p. 18

Werner, J. (1980) 'Le droit antitrust américain', *Revue suisse du droit international de la concurrence,* 10 (septembre), pp. 57-76

5
Le Patronat

INTRODUCTION

The themes of economic renewal, industrial restructuring, the internationalisation of the French economy and the increase in competitive pressures treated earlier in this book all point to important changes in the attitudes and behaviour of French management. Accordingly, a closer examination of the evolution of French managers as a social group will be the object of this chapter.

In the early 1950s, the American David Landes wrote a scathing account of the inadequacies of French business. He observed that most French firms were small, family-owned and run as extensions of a bourgeois household, with the term *maison* being used interchangeably for home, family or business. In his view, French owner/managers were conservative, chary of competition, respectful of vested interests and reluctant to take growth opportunities, because of a lack of daring and innovation. They turned out too many product lines and so were inefficient but held customers in low regard and ignored the meaning of marketing. With even large firms being dominated by family dynasties dating from the nineteenth century, Landes (1951, p. 350) concluded that French management had an 'inhibitive influence on economic development'.

This is a harsh judgement, but one which serves as a bench-mark to measure the extent to which French management has changed. Most of its components no longer apply; a few perhaps do.

This chapter will analyse the social origins of French managers and the career patterns that take them to the top. The issue to be treated will be the extent to which recruitment methods in France allow the selection of those individuals who are best able to manage. Later sections deal with French employers' organisations. They study how employers act as a collective agency and discuss how far employers' organisations have furthered the causes of business, particularly in their relationships with the State. Through an analysis of French *patrons* both individually and collectively, the chapter will argue that Landes' view of the French business community as backward has become an unacceptable generalisation. The *patronat* today is a hybrid entity: among its constituents lie a number of great strengths although questions arise over the persistence of certain traditional features.

COMPOSITION OF THE *PATRONAT*

What is understood by the patronat?

The terms *patron* and *patronat* are habitually used by the French in discussions of their business classes. Hence it is essential to define what the terms mean and to whom they actually refer.

Turning first to definitions, the word *patron* is far from neutral. Although in English, *patron* can be translated either as 'employer' or 'boss', in French it has a whole series of wider connotations. Weber (1988) provided a revealing commentary on the meaning of the word. It has two Latin sources: *pater* and *patronus* – father and patron saint. Associated connotations are the company owner as *paterfamilias* (the father as head of the family) and as *patron de droit divin* (boss by divine right).

The chief executive as *paterfamilias* points up a trait traditionally associated with French management, namely paternalism. On a positive note, the paternalist manager sought to ensure the welfare of his workforce. However, he was unwilling to accept any dilution of his authority. In acting as a traditional father – a *bon père de famille* - the temptation was to treat the workforce as his 'children'. He patronised his workers by assuming that their childlike irresponsibility made them dependent on a father figure (himself) and debarred them from participation in decision-making processes.

The investiture of personal authority in the figure of the *patron* attempted to draw legitimacy not only from traditional family structures but also from the ideology of the *ancien régime*. Before the 1789 revolution put an end to the old regime, royalty ruled by divine right. According to the theory of monarchy, Providence had willed the king to reign, hence no questioning of his authority was permitted. In analogous fashion, the boss who exercised sole authority within a company because he had founded it and/or owned its capital considered himself as ruling by divine right – hence the (ironical) phrase *patron de droit divin*.

This personalistic and absolute view of authority largely ruled out compromise and power sharing. Such views have complicated negotiations with employees. Unions were long considered as illegitimate by employers and even when accepted as partners in dialogue were treated with suspicion. These industrial relations themes will be developed in Chapter 6. The same views also led to a centralisation and concentration of authority at the company's apex – its chairman – so downgrading the role of middle management by circumscribing its opportunities for taking initiatives and decisions. These latter themes of management culture will be developed in Chapter 7.

The core of the problem has been an identification between the firm and its owner, between the right to manage and ownership (Bauer, 1990). Indeed, this view has spread into the business literature in France which habitually deals with *patrons*, rarely with managers. Although this approach contains an element of bias (from which it must be acknowledged this chapter is not entirely free), it reflects a particular sociological context. In France, the family business with an identifiable owner/manager has traditionally been predominant and, as will be seen, remains so.

Indeed in French, ownership, legal rights and responsibilities are all covered by the term *patrimoine*. This term again has roots in the Latin word *pater*. Further, *patrimoine* refers not only to current ownership but also to a heritage. Inherited wealth implies a dynastic element which connects directly to themes of family descent, the legitimacy of the father's authority and indirectly to the rationale of divine right and the role of monarchy. In brief, *patron* is a loaded term containing a whole series of cultural norms and values.

Turning to the question of who is being referred to, it is common practice in French to talk about an entity called the *patronat*. It is as if *patrons* were considered to belong to a distinctive social group. This conception contains an element of truth, but is not altogether valid. The *patronat* can be subdivided in a number of ways of which the most important is by the distinction between a *grand patronat* and a *petit patronat*. The *petit patronat* is understood to be a fairly large group comprised of owner/managers of small- to medium-sized companies. The *grand patronat* is a highly select group of the heads of France's major companies.

In consequence, very different estimates of the size of the *patronat* are possible. Saglio (1977) proposed two. If the criterion were that firms have at least six employees, the number of *patrons* would be approximately 200,000. Clearly this would include both the *grand* and the *petit patronat*. However, this is a questionable amalgam. The owner of a small firm having less than ten employees has next to nothing in common with the chief executive of a multinational conglomerate. If only medium- and large-sized firms were considered (i.e. firms with 50 or more employees) the population of *patrons* would be around 30,000. This would constitute a more comparable, though far from homogeneous group.

Hence some French observers prefer an even more limited definition of the *grand patronat* in order to differentiate it from the *petit patronat*. An example is Bauer and Bertin-Mourot (1987) who discussed only the chief executive officers (CEOs) of France's 200 largest firms. Although 200 is an arbitrary figure, it is frequently used as a reference point in French discussions. Here the emphasis is firmly on the most powerful members of the *grand patronat*.

Clearly, changes in criteria produce different estimates. On the basis of its 1982 survey, INSEE (1987, p. 35) calculated that there were 133,000 *patrons* having ten or more employees, of which 22,000 were women. But whatever the criteria, *patrons* are in a small minority when compared to a total working population in France of over 23 million in the 1980s.

This is not a numbers game, however, the unit of analysis does matter. Depending on whether one takes a narrow or a broad view of the composition of the *patronat*, the features of the population change. Brizay (1975, pp. 285-6) indicated that whereas 60 per cent of the *total* population of *patrons* came from 'humble' origins, 67 per cent of the top echelons of big business came from the upper classes. Taking a broad perspective produces a population of *patrons* that is not only larger but also one in which social mobility plays a large role. In a perspective which concentrates on the most powerful employer group, the *grand patronat*, the characteristics of the population are stability and a low level of social mobility. This raises questions about the nature of career patterns in French management and the selection processes that accompany them. These will be discussed in the section on characteristics of the *grand patronat* later in this chapter.

Next, we take a different approach to the identification of the *patronat* by examining the modes by which individuals become *patrons*. This approach yields three sub-groups, namely company founders, heirs and professional managers. Each will be treated separately. Because of their historical predominance, the case of the heirs and company dynasties will be considered first.

The patron as inheritor

Family business is a central feature of French capitalism. It is unsurprising that inheritance should figure so prominently.

An archetype of the family dynasty is that of the de Wendel family, who were steel barons in the nineteenth and earlier twentieth century. Clairvois (1988) provided a telling biography of François de Wendel who was head of the Wendel empire between 1903 and 1949. François de Wendel was the ninth heir to the Wendel empire and a true *patron de droit divin*. Because this dynastic element resembled royal practice, he was nicknamed François II (Francis the Second). He was termed a *maître des forges* (ironmaster), a term redolent of the paternalism that was a characteristic of this type of *patron*.

Not only was François de Wendel's authority unchallenged within his personal empire but his influence extended far beyond. He was a *député* (member of parliament) and sat on the main board of the *Banque de France*, the French central bank. He combined economic and political power with influence on the State apparatus.

Undoubtedly, the category to which the de Wendels belonged has declined in influence. The de Wendel empire gradually crumbled and disappeared in name in the merger mania of the 1960s. Its remains, going under the name of Sacilor, have been nationalised. Similar tales can be told about a number of major French business families.

But major family firms have not disappeared completely. The scions of world-famous firms such as Rothschild and Michelin still take an active role in the firms they own. Other dynasties exist, such as in L'Oréal and Peugeot, where family owners appoint professional managers but prefer to remain behind the scenes themselves. In addition, new dynasties are appearing in France's largest companies. They include Dassault (aviation), Bouygues (construction), Leven (Perrier water), Trigano (Club Méditerranée), Salamon, Rossignol (both sports equipment manufacturers) and Bich (Bic pens and razors).

Not only is family ownership the norm in small- and medium-sized firms, it continues to play a major role in the French economy. Morin (1988) discovered that of the 200 largest privately-owned French enterprises in 1987, no fewer than 71 (57 per cent of the sample) had as majority shareholders a single individual or family. In 54 of those, the major shareholder also ran the business. Some annual variation in figures is inevitable – the 1987 figure of 71 fell to 62 in 1988 and rose to 68 in 1989 (Morin, 1989, 1990). But the overall picture clearly shows that in France family capitalism is alive and well. The negative feature of family dynasties is that they limit appointment by merit alone.

The patron as professional manager

Professional managers now play a central role in most firms but as a group they represent a relatively recent social phenomenon.

Their importance in economic life was first noted in the United States by Berle and Means (1932) who put forward the thesis of a 'managerial revolution'. By this they understood a separation of ownership from the functions of management in major corporations. As corporations grew larger, they needed more financial resources and turned to increased numbers of shareholders. The multiplication of shareholders meant that no single person – such as a François de Wendel – could own the corporation or exercise personal control. This development emancipated professional management who became empowered to chart the course of the firms which employed them. Though professional managers clearly have responsibilities to share-holders and society at large, their emancipation ended the era of the 'divine right' of owner/managers. As a result, legitimacy in management functions no longer devolved from family, inheritance and/or property rights but from personal merit, from professional skills and experience and from exercising leadership in the field.

The professionalisation of management had important social consequences. Whereas in the nineteenth century, management positions were almost solely reserved for members of capital-owning families, the 'managerial revolution' opened the doors to management suites to a larger cross-section of society. In the USA, the replacement of dynastic structures by a meritocracy led to a greater democratisation of economic life. In the case of France, similar processes have occurred, but far more slowly. The 'managerial revolution' took place much later than in the USA and has remained less developed.

Lévy-Leboyer (1980) explained the lateness of the revolution by the slow growth of mass consumer markets in France. Mass markets were retarded by four factors. Firstly, France is a much smaller country than the USA, whose large population favoured the early growth of mass markets. Secondly, the depression of the 1930s and the deflationary economic policies of the period severely depressed mass demand in France at a moment when it had the potential to grow. Thirdly, major French companies maintained their industrial specialisations in intermediate goods (such as steel, glass, construction materials) rather than diversifying into mass consumer markets. This orientation was due to the outlook of their managers. Having been trained in the major engineering schools, their primary interest was technological achievements. They tended to consider the servicing of mass markets as lacking in prestige. Indeed, the conceptions and practice of marketing did not develop in France until as late as the 1960s. Fourthly, the trend towards the creation of large corporations was impeded by the small size of the French stock exchange. The formation of a dispersed shareholding class – which was essential for the separation of power from ownership which characterises the 'managerial revolution' – took longer.

With ownership remaining in family hands, the phenomenon of the large, multinational corporation has been less widespread in France; indeed, its development was retarded until the 1960s, when the State intervened to hasten the process. Chapter 2 discussed the development of an industrial policy which, having favoured concentration by mergers, lead to nationalisation and then privatisation of a number of France's major firms. The architects of France's industrial policy did not set out to extend the 'managerial revolution', but perhaps the most progressive aspect of the concentration-nationalisation-privatisation cycle was to wrest a number of France's largest firms from family capitalism, expose them to market norms and consolidate the professionalisation of management.

The processes are incomplete, however. On the one hand, family capitalism remains important. On the other, questions arise over maintained State-ownership. Around a dozen of France's largest industrial corporations are still owned by the State. Previous chapters have indicated that State subsidies have resulted in market distortions and preserved uncompetitive businesses. Further, the extent to which managers of nationalised enterprises are unencumbered by interference from their shareholder – the French State – and have a free hand to manage, is a controversial theme. Case studies of the behaviour of nationalised firms have shown that both conflict with the State and dependence on the State occurred in the past (Anastassopoulos, 1981). Since 1983, when profitability became the major criterion of performance even in the public sector, the independence of CEOs in State-owned firms has grown. Thus Mangolte (1986, p. 97) argued that the latter are comparable to firms having a dispersed group of shareholders.

These factors make the assessment of the extent of the 'managerial revolution' problematic. Certainly, the numbers of professional managers in France have increased dramatically. Bourdois (1983) indicated that between 1954 and 1975, numbers of *cadres supérieurs* increased by over a million and those of *cadres moyens* by over 1.6 million: broadly speaking, these groups correspond to British supervisory and managerial grades. Undoubtedly, the development of the professional category of *cadres* has renewed management practices in France. The problem for those interested in the development of French management strategies is that French studies of *cadres* are generally of a sociological nature rather then business orientated: they analyse social classes rather than professional behaviour. This perhaps stems from the fact that '*cadre*' corresponds to a rank in French, whereas 'manager' corresponds to a function in English. In any event, the current limitations of the literature impede close inspection of the professional contribution of *cadres*.

Further, in the strict sense of the term, the 'managerial revolution' involves *top* managers - and not owners - having the final word on business strategy. But to judge who really decides entails practical difficulties and may involve a subjective element. For example, it is credible that Jacques Calvet, the CEO of Peugeot, has always acted independently of the Peugeot family and will continue to do so but neither half of the proposition can readily be proved.

Despite the problems, some broad quantitative indications of the extent of the 'managerial revolution' can be gleaned from work done by Morin (1988). Out of the 200 largest privately-owned companies in France, only 17 had a widely dispersed group of share-holders in 1987 and so are run entirely by professional management. In these firms, we find the 'managerial revolution' in its purest state. In another 17 firms, professionals had been given a free hand to manage by the families that have a majority stake in the firm.

In relation to these figures, two further caveats are in order. Firstly, though institutional investments in company shares (i.e. insurance companies, pension funds) run at a lower level in France than in Britain, they are growing in size. In the process, more 'family' firms are likely to be owned by the institutions, which will probably give more scope for autonomous professional management. Secondly, not only can business inheritors gain professional credentials but professional managers often acquire ownership of the firms they run. In the 1980s, there was considerable momentum for employees to acquire shares in the companies where they work and this was particularly true for managers. Management buy-outs became an important phenomena. With professional managers becoming owners and with owners acquiring professional skills, the boundaries between owners and professionals are porous indeed.

Notwithstanding the wider complexities, it remains the case that in France relatively few firms are run by managers who do not own them, even among those large firms where one might have expected the contrary. Ownership and control of firms are still largely linked. The incompleteness of the 'managerial revolution' in France is a major distinguishing trait of French capitalism. Family ownership limits opportunities for outsiders. Firms in which outstanding managers can rise to the very top solely by dint of their professional competence are few in number.

The patron as company founder

Setting up a company is undoubtedly the fastest route to becoming a *patron*. Bauer and Bertin-Mourot (1991) analysed the numbers of company founders in various categories of firms. They found that in French companies with less than ten employees, 59 per cent were set up by their current managers. The proportion declined as the size of firm increased. Interestingly, they also found that of France's 200 largest firms, 21 were run by their founders.

In France, the company founder has not always enjoyed social prestige. In the post-war period, company founders were associated with the backward mentality that Landes (1951) criticised so harshly. His view was widely shared. Bucaille and Costa de Beauregard (1987) indicated that it was commonly believed in the post-war years that the small- and medium-firm sector was incompetent and doomed to decline.

In the 1970s, it became clear that big was not always beautiful, that large firms were often unable to adapt, leading to mass unemployment. In the aftermath, the popular image of the entrepreneur and company founder has vastly improved.

As Le Van-Lemesle (1988) pointed out, such cyclical changes in attitude have historical precedents. At times of economic crisis, the status of entrepreneurs improves since they are frequently considered to hold the solution to economic recovery. With the about-turn in attitudes, the entrepreneur has been promoted to near-hero status as innovator, job creator and embodiment of tomorrow's economy.

While there are examples of both extremes to be found in real life, polarised views of the entrepreneur are rife with half-truths. In the majority of successful business start-ups, company founders already have experience in their sector and activity. They develop their skills and their business in an evolutionary, not revolutionary, manner. Incremental and limited innovations are the norm. Radically new products and processes are the exception. Further, employment growth is limited, slow and frequently insecure. Small firms are generally vulnerable and unstable, often with high risks taken by those involved. Business start-ups are frequent occurrences but so too are closures. In France, 19,063 small industrial firms were formed in 1980. This fell to 16,612 in 1983 and rose to 21,312 in 1986. In the same years, there were 3,231, 4,639 and 5,107 closures (Ministère de l'Industrie, 1989). The new-found public recognition of the entrepreneur has only partially been accompanied by an understanding of the fragility of the small firm sector.

Entrepreneurs and company founders do represent an important source of renewal of the business community. But a lasting change in the composition of the *patronat* depends on a buoyant economic environment for company founders and on greater opportunities for professional managers.

CHARACTERISTICS OF THE *GRAND PATRONAT*

The *grand patronat* provides the focus of this section because it sets the tone in business life by the preponderance of power and influence it enjoys within the French business community. Three aspects of the *grand patronat* will be successively considered: its social stability over time, its ability to harness the French educational system to its own ends and the interpenetration of business and administrative elites.

The social stability of the grand patronat

Sociological studies of the *grand patronat* reveal considerable long-term stability in its social origins. This stability was most marked in the nineteenth century, but though in decline since, is an important contemporary feature and is likely to remain so.

In the early nineteenth century, astute family alliances through marriage allowed retention and enhancement of the family business. They also increased social cohesion by reinforcing the sense of identity of the *patronat*. Lévy-Leboyer (1976) indicates that in the second half of the nineteenth century, two developments helped to dilute, though not destroy, that cohesion. Technological progress in mechanical engineering and electrical equipment offered new opportunities. Low barriers to entry in new fields allowed the influx of entrepreneurs from other social groups. Advances in the provision and quality of education also allowed new talent entry into the ranks of the business bourgeoisie. But these trends have not accelerated markedly over the twentieth century. The most striking characteristic of the *grand patronat* remains its relative impermeability.

A number of studies have demonstrated this stability. Lévy-Leboyer (1979) analysed the social origins of top managers over the period between 1912 and 1973. He found that 88 per cent of his sample were *grande école* graduates (discussion of the French educational system is held over until pp. 162-3). In addition, 45 per cent of the sample had social origins in the industrial and financial bourgeoisie. The families of a further 37 per cent were either top civil servants or leading professionals. This left 18 per cent whose family was not already part of the upper classes. His conclusion emphasised the narrowness of the social backgrounds from which top managers were recruited, though he also pointed to some inter-generational mobility.

A study undertaken by Deleforterie-Soubeyroux (1961) of the social origins of 2,000 top managers during the 1950s found that 41 per cent had fathers who had been top managers, 15 per cent had fathers who were top civil servants and 15 per cent came from the professional classes. The remaining 29 per cent were from other social groups.

Hall and Bettignies (1969) analysed a sample of 149 top French managers and produced similar results. Over 40 per cent of the sample had a father who was himself a *patron*. Just over 20 per cent had fathers from the professional classes and the fathers of another 15 per cent were middle managers. Civil servants did not figure prominently. Office and factory workers, farmers and artisans produced only approximately 12 per cent of the sample.

The study also analysed the professions of the grandfathers of managers in the sample. Some 50 per cent of grandfathers were not from the business classes, showing that there were some signs of social mobility across the generations. For a working class person to become a top manager was rare but occurrences of a two generation movement from the working classes to top management (usually via the professional classes) were more frequent.

Over the longer term, greater mobility occurred, indicating better opportunities for individuals from outside the business classes.

Monjardet (1972) looked at the bosses of France's largest 100 industrial firms in 1968. Of these, 76 were from the upper and middle classes; only 2 were from the lower classes. (The remainder did not indicate their social origin.) Those with a diploma from the *Ecole Polytechnique* numbered 33; a further 41 had a diploma from another *grande école*. Brizay (1975) indicated that of the managers of France's 500 largest firms, 76 per cent came from the upper and middle classes. In his sample, 51 per cent of patrons had a *grande école* diploma and a further 29 per cent had a university degree.

All the data have shown considerable stability over time within a core business class. This reading is confirmed by Marceau (1989) who examined the social origins of students of the prestigious business school, INSEAD whose graduates represent part of the next generation of top managers. Analysis by father's profession again revealed a preponderance of top businessmen (around 50 per cent) with some 25 per cent drawn from what she called the 'non-business upper middle class'. She concluded that 'in Europe in the 1990s and beyond, business will continue to be managed by people born and raised in the business world' (Marceau, 1989, p. 35). In an earlier article, Marceau (1981) had pointedly summarised this tendency by using the phrase *'plus ça change, plus c'est la même chose'*.

Clearly, the central questions raised by these data are why and how the business class can remain so stable. The most clear-cut case of self-perpetuation among the business classes is where the family business or shareholdings are passed on from parent to offspring. Discussion in the sections on the *patron* as inheritor and the *patron* as professional manager indicated the prevalence of family ownership and the incompleteness of the 'managerial revolution' and these factors help explain the high degree of closure that exists within the ranks of the *grand patronat*. However, inheritance of financial or industrial capital is only one mode of self-perpetuation by the business classes.

A major component of the heritage passed on within business families is cultural awareness and 'know-how'. 'Cultural' is used here not in the narrow sense of 'highbrow' arts but in the wide sense of a world-view, a body of explicit or implicit knowledge about the rules and patterns of social behaviour. (For fuller definitions of culture, the reader is referred to p. 221.) Parents from the managerial and professional classes pass on a rich world-view to their children. Without needing to train their children in business practices (though some do so), business knowledge, attitudes and behaviours pervade the business family. Marceau (1989) discovered that in her sample of INSEAD students, not only did a majority come from top managerial and professional classes but there was considerable family pressure on the offspring to be successful in business. In a number of cases, no other way of life was ever envisaged by parents or offspring.

Apart from the intangible part of the cultural heritage, there are operational components too. The business family has social and business links which allow the offspring to find a first job, gain work experience and develop a career. Such a family usually knows how careers are made and which are the slow and fast routes to success. An essential element of the legacy to the offspring of French business families is an understanding of the educational system.

The role of the grandes écoles

In principle, the French educational system is egalitarian and meritocratic. In practice, it is an extremely elitist system, characterised by biased modes of access and affording differential opportunities not only in secondary but also in higher education.

France has a binary higher education system, with a large university sector and a smaller sector known as the *grandes écoles*. A pass at the *baccalauréat* (broadly the equivalent of A levels) automatically confers the right to study at a *université*, paying nominal fees. There is considerable value and achievement in following this route. But the high road to success passes through the parallel but far more prestigious system of the *grandes écoles*.

There are a large number of these (perhaps 150 depending on definitions), each with its own specialisations. Even within the top-tier of the educational system, a hierarchy exists. The most prestigious establishments are the *Ecole Polytechnique, Ecole Nationale d'Administration (ENA), Ecole des Arts et Métiers, Ecole Normale Supérieure, Institut d'Etudes Politiques, Ecole centrale,* and *Hautes Etudes Commerciales*, all to be found in Paris. Most *grandes écoles* are in the provinces and as such are considered as playing in the second division.

Institutions such the *Ecole des Arts et Métiers*, the *Ecole Centrale*, the *Corps des Mines*, the *Corps des Ponts et Chaussées* and ENA were set up by the State to provide it with a supply of engineers and Civil Servants and complement older ex-military institutions such as the *Ecole Polytechnique*. Gradually, the graduates from all these establishments were drawn away from serving the State to the private sector. This osmosis occurred partly because of a short supply of jobs in the State sector, partly because of more attractive career prospects in the private sector. The transfer provided an early contribution to the professionalisation of French management.

The *grandes écoles* are based on republican and egalitarian principles. They recruit by merit, using a competitive entrance examination (*concours*). In principle, social origins are irrelevant in this meritocracy; class preferment is obsolete. As Vaughan (1981) pointed out, through the *grandes écoles* system inequalities of power in the republic would be justified by educational attainments, not by hereditary privilege or wealth.

The ideal is pure and bright, but the reality has always been mixed and muddy. Certainly, passage through the *grandes écoles* was one of the few routes to social promotion available to people from the lower classes. Indeed, for many years large numbers of X (recruits of the *Ecole Polytechnique*) were from underprivileged backgrounds: 39 per cent in 1872, 45 per cent in 1900 and 54 per cent in 1925 (Lévy-Leboyer, 1976, p. 106). But these proportions declined in subsequent years. A study of social origins of students at the *grandes écoles* in the 1960s revealed that around 10-20 per cent of students came from the lower classes (Marceau, 1977, p. 110).

The problem is that the entrance examinations to the *grandes écoles* simultaneously filter by academic achievement and by social class. Most students need two years of so-called preparatory classes to pass their entrance examination. The institutes turning out the greatest number of successful candidates at the *concours* are located in Paris. For the candidate, the difficulties of the process involve selection of an institute offering preparatory classes (preferably in Paris) and the ensuing costs of two years' study, which may or may not prove worthwhile. This process can only discourage and eliminate many candidates from less well-off backgrounds. The offspring of the business class, particularly the *grand patronat* are more cushioned: they have the know-how and the resources. Hence, though the *concours* is itself meritocratic, social bias is fostered by a prior self-selection process.

Yet this bias would be of little relevance to business careers were it not for the tight coupling between specific tiers of the French educational system and career opportunities in management. 'Fast-burn' openings are mostly given to the alumni of the major Parisian institutes. With rare exceptions, such as Paris-Dauphine, French universities are not well regarded by employers as sources of high-flying management trainees, though with the growing need for management trainees this is gradually changing (Alexandre, 1990). In addition, the fee-paying, mainly provincial business schools (the *écoles supérieures de commerce et d'administration des entreprises*) have expanded rapidly since the 1960s. They have a largely empirical approach to management skills and place the emphasis on producing graduates who can quickly become 'operational' in management roles (Bramley, 1991). In consequence, many French companies are keen to recruit and promote their graduates to management positions. Business school alumni are now a major source of renewal within the ranks of French management.

The interpenetration of business and administrative elites

There is yet another refinement of the steep hierarchy giving access to top careers, namely the fast lane of the elite *grands corps*.

There are a number of *grands corps*, all of which are organised by the State to serve its interests. In theory, their aim is to recruit the most talented minds to administer France. Purely civil service *corps* remain, such as the diplomatic *corps* and the prefectural *corps*. But the major engineering *corps* (*Corps des Mines, Corps des Ponts et Chaussées*), the financial *corps* (*Cours des Comptes, Inspection des Finances*) and the *Conseil d'Etat* have become springboards for would-be top managers. The members of a *corp* (called *corpsards*) represent a pool from which the major French corporations are eager to recruit what they consider to be the *crème de la crème*.

Why are *corpsards* so sought after and so successful in business careers? The first part of the answer lies in the rigorous selection process which favours both high intellect and high social status. The *grands corps* are at the pinnacle of France's elitist system. Admission to a *grands corps* is contingent on being among the *premiers de classement* in the finals of the top *grandes écoles*. In each year-group there is a *major de promotion* – the person with the highest marks – with the results of remaining students being set out in descending order of marks. The *grands corps* recruit from the top of these lists.

The second part of the answer lies in the advantages conferred by the *grands corps* themselves. Membership gives a seal of quality, a top-class training package and more besides. Each *grand corps* is an exclusive club of like-minded people. It is not for nothing that the expression *esprit de corps* has come into the English language. To the young entrant, the *corps* provides support structures. It offers the helping hand of highly-placed, older members. It provides a network of contacts and even an *annuaire* (phonebook) to get in touch with them. Telephoning a co-member out of the blue for help or advice is accepted practice. The community spirit is exemplified by the use of the informal *tu*, which tends to be preferred to the formal *vous*.

Masonic personal relationships are reinforced by institutional mechanisms. The *grands corps* provide the equivalents of careers officers, but with the all important distinction that they have connections at high levels within the State apparatus. Because the function of the *grands corps* is to serve the State and because the State has consistently acted as a major entrepreneur, the engineering *corps* have frequently been entrusted with implementation of industrial policy. In sectors such as the State-owned energy companies (both oil and nuclear), there are high concentrations of *corpsards* not just in research or technical functions but in top management positions. Likewise, members of the financial *corps* exercise a high-level supervisory function over the financial operations of the State, a function to which high status and influence are attached. In a phrase, *corpsards* monopolise the best State jobs. From the start of their career, *corpsards* are given challenging posts that foster leadership qualities. The exercise of real power from a relatively early age is the ideal preparation for a top management career.

Not only are *corpsards* employed on industrial projects but they have been integrated into French political power structures. The key example is the *corpsard* who is promoted to *directeur de cabinet*. The *directeur de cabinet* manages the business of a Minister. The *directeur de cabinet* has an operational role in the elaboration and implementation of ministerial policy. Given the size of ministerial budgets, this is a first-order responsibility. Especially in the *ministères techniques* (i.e. ministries such as industry, defence, telecommunications, transport), his desk is a veritable cross-roads of political, administrative and industrial concerns. He is very much at the 'sharp end' of policy making and policy implementation.

In later life, recruitment of an ex-*directeur de cabinet* to a top management function is a logical decision. The person concerned will have outstanding personal qualities, professional experience and an insider's knowledge of French politics and the Civil Service. Given the historical importance of the State in the French economy, these remain major considerations. Similar remarks apply to the other *corpsards*. Further, where the recruiter is himself a member of a *grand corps*, the 'old boy' network becomes self-perpetuating.

Leaving State service for the private sector is common practice and is known as *pantouflage*. The length of time during which *corpsards* serve the State varies between a minimal two or three years to the length of their careers, and anything in between. Thus the previous experience of ex-civil servants and their potential to learn new skills in a radically different environment also vary drastically. The value to the private sector of a recruit near the start of his career and that of a recruit near the end of his career are intrinsically different.

These features make evaluation of *pantouflage* difficult. A frequent criticism is that *pantouflage* results in the transfer of bureaucratic-minded civil servants, used to serving the public interest, into an environment of which they have no experience or understanding and which emphasises radically opposed values, namely entrepreneurship, the profit motive and private advantage.

Against this, the French State and its servants can point to *colbertisme* and its tradition of public entrepreneurship, while big business can have its own rigid bureaucracy. Further, talented young people with an understanding of French hierarchies have a clear interest in collecting the advantages of graduating from a *grande école* and gaining membership of a *grand corps* precisely in order to develop their career prospects. In addition, the process gives a quality assurance to future employers. As Barsoux and Lawrence (1990, 1991) have emphasised, top French managers do have outstanding intellectual qualities.

The sheer scale of *pantouflage* is its own endorsement. In their survey conducted in the mid-1980s, Bauer and Bertin-Mourot (1987) discovered that of the top 24 French industrial enterprises, 17 had former civil servants as CEOs; one in four of the *patrons* of the largest 200 firms was a member of a *grand corps*. If the interpenetration of administrative and business elites is stark at the top level of France's biggest companies, it also points to an extensive colonisation process of the *grands corps* at intermediate levels.

If we look down from the pinnacle of a *directeur de cabinet* turned *grand patron*, at the base of the pyramid is the entrance to a *grande école*. The route to the top has involved two types of filtering. One is selection on merit. As Cohen (1988) pointed out, the *corpsard* turned *grand patron* has gone through three stages of selection: the first by the educational system, the second by a *grand corps* and the third by company recruiters. But the other type of filtering has involved elimination on social grounds. Manifestly, the business classes are better placed to exploit the system than other social groups. Hence, if the successful individual is considered alone, a meritocracy is functioning. Yet if the composition of the business class is considered, a high degree of social stability and self-perpetuation occurs.

Bourdieu and Saint-Martin (1978, p. 11) have put this apparent paradox into a nutshell in their reference to an opposition between *'les intérêts de la classe que l'Ecole sert statistiquement et les intérêts des membres de la classe qu'elle sacrifie'* (between class interests which the educational system fulfils statistically and the interests of individual class members which the system sacrifices). Being born into a business family in France is not in itself a guarantee of a distinguished management career. Individuals must still prove their worth. On the route to the top, many fall by the wayside. But as a group, the interests of the business class are preserved. A heritage is passed on. Social capital proves almost as important as financial capital. Taken together, they are difficult to beat.

In consequence, the acquisition of educational credentials by the business class appears not only as worthwhile in itself or as a passport to a career but also as a way of justifying high social status. It legitimises transfer of high status to succeeding generations. Cohen (1988, p. 591) called this a 'transformation of an inheritance into merit'.

In summary, social stability among the *grand patronat*, educational hierarchies, career patterns in top management and the Civil Service, all intertwine in a self-perpetuating system. Critics have pointed to the dysfunctions of this system. Firstly, there is the narrow social base of the *grand patronat*. Secondly, much of the selection process takes place in late adolescence and in questionable fashion. The academic content of the preparatory classes with their emphasis on mathematics, and that of the prestigious *grandes écoles*, which often specialise in engineering, is relatively narrow and has little to do with the world of business.

Bauer and Bertin-Mourot (1987) suggested that a management recruitment system that uses selection criteria of early academic success and years of service in the Civil Service may be penalising the French economy. Using comparisons with the United States and Japan, they argued that longer in-company experience, particularly where managerial responsibilities are exercised outside of France, would better equip French managers to propel their companies toward success in increasingly competitive international markets. Further, the restrictions on recruitment to top positions caused by the tendency to 'import' *corpsards* with Civil Service experience demotivate individuals who have 'worked through the ranks' and whose talents only emerge in later professional life. One of the questions for the future will be the extent to which graduates of the specialised business schools displace the 'old guard' or whether they will present another variation on a familiar theme.

FRENCH EMPLOYERS' ORGANISATIONS

Although the *grand patronat* forms a distinctive and stable social layer, it does not follow that employers as a group automatically see eye to eye. Employers' organisations inevitably reflect the lines of force and patterns of conflict which characterise business communities operating in market economies. The distinctive feature of the French case is the ambivalent relationship between employers' organisations and the State which, depending on sectoral group and period, is variously viewed as interfering in unwarranted fashion in business affairs or as a legitimate and powerful ally. Accordingly, this section first addresses the functional questions of why and how French employers organise themselves while the section beginning on p. 170 will discuss changing relationships between the employers' organisations and the State.

Roles and objectives of employers' organisations

At first sight, the rationale for employers organising themselves is not entirely obvious. Unlike workers, employers can exercise considerable individual power.

In the case of workers, limited or non-existent individual power motivates collective organisation. Union organisation can overcome weakness, since there is strength in numbers. Although as Chapter 6 will illustrate considerable fragmentation exists in employee organisations, group solidarity comes about a little more easily among employees because the situation, outlook and prospects of individuals in particular occupations are often similar.

In the case of employers, one might expect that market relations based on competition translate into personal relationships based on arms-length dealings or outright rivalry due to incompatible interests. This certainly occurs but is not always the case. As indicated in Chapter 4, competition can be tempered by collusion. But apart from covert, usually illicit actions, employers have a need and a right to organise themselves openly in order to achieve a number of ends.

Firstly, employers prefer to organise themselves because they are not all-powerful. They are frequently faced by other social groups pressing divergent interests. Chapters 1 and 2 indicated that French governments have exercised a significant influence on the functioning and development of the business community through economic and industrial policies. The impact of legislation goes very wide, embracing areas as diverse as health and safety issues, industrial relations and, until recently, exchange controls. Taxation is a frequent source of contention between business leaders and politicians. In order to state their case to government, employers have felt the need to form collective organisations. This lobbying function is usually the primary *raison d'être* of employer organisations.

But a dialogue is necessary with other interlocutors too. Where trade union movements have been seen as a threat, employers have had a tendency to group together. At a later moment, collective bargaining calls for collective organisation on the parts of both employers and employees. In France, examples of collective agreements between employers' organisations, unions and the State include areas such as pensions and unemployment allowances (Mary, 1985; Oechslin, 1972). Further, consumer organisations have grown in strength and are often critical of producers. Employers have reacted by banding together to improve their image.

Secondly, power within the business community is not distributed evenly. Clearly, the *petit patronat* has considerably less power than the *grand patronat* in relation to both State and markets. Within the business community, many small- and medium-sized enterprises act as sub-contractors to large

firms. Often this engenders a situation of dependence. Rivalry between small
and large firm owners and managers frequently surfaces in the structures and
development of employers' organisations.

Thus, the major roles of the employers' organisations have been to
reconcile the *patronat* with the State, with other social groups such as the
unions and consumer groups and, perhaps as importantly, with themselves.
Wilson (1987, p. 98) summarised the role of France's major employers'
confederation as 'the defence of the broad, collective interests of the French
business community'. As Marin (1988) has argued, employers' organisations
go beyond economic actions. They play a role in political processes, in their
support of or opposition to parties and governments and in seeking to
influence legislation.

Employers' organisations also play a subsidiary but important role of
providing services. These include information collection and dissemination,
economic market and social analyses as well as publicity and general
representation activities.

Finally, employers' organisations often fulfil a social role as exclusive clubs
where like-minded people discuss common problems or projects. This in turn
reinforces the social identity of their members. Through these various means,
employers' organisations reinforce the visibility, prestige and authority of the
patronat.

The major employers' organisations in France

The peak employers' confederation in France is the *Conseil national du
patronat français* (CNPF). However, the *patronat* has not always presented
a united front. The CNPF has not managed to contain the divergent interests
of French employers.

The largest private sector firms have had their own groupings, namely, the
Association des entreprises françaises faisant appel à l'épargne (AGREF)
which became the *Association française des entreprises privées*, after a number
of the AGREF's members were nationalised in 1982. Their aim has been to
further the interests of the private sector, lobbying against the State and State
enterprises as they see fit. Members of this group of firms sometimes see the
CNPF as beholden to the State by the dues it receives from State-owned firms
and by the borrowed authority it draws from negotiations with the State.

On the other hand, small-firm owners have formed organisations specifically to lobby the cause of small business, sometimes against the cause of big
business. The major small-firms' federation has been the *Confédération
générale des petites et moyennes entreprises*, but it has had a vocal rival in the
Syndicat national de la petite et moyenne industrie.

Friction between the various wings of the *patronat* has been endemic since
the CNPF was founded in 1946 in a moment of historic weakness (see
pp.170-1 for further discussion). Though employers were agreed on the need
to organise, controversy raged over the type of organisation required. Two
currents of opinion confronted each other. One wished to combat the

increasing power of the Left in politics by constructing an organisation vested with authority and power. The other current preferred an organisation ensuring co-ordination but without giving coercive powers over its members to a strong central office. It was the second current which won the debate in 1946, hence the organisation became known as a *conseil*, an advisory body rather than an authoritative caucus.

Settling on this option resulted firstly from the considerable distrust between major industrial producers and smaller enterprises. The small-firm sector did not wish to be subordinated to the interests of large firms and the old, hide-bound dynasties that ruled many of them. Secondly, the interests of manufacturers and distributors were at variance. Thirdly, there was the usual rivalry between Paris and the provinces. Representatives from the provinces feared a centralisation of authority. Finally, a strong executive might spell a return to the *patronat de combat* mentality of the late 1930s when employers tried to take on government and workers. With the *patronat* seriously weakened by collaboration during the Occupation, such a reactionary policy would have been suicidal in the post-war reconstruction effort.

Despite the attempt to balance out competing interests within the new employers' confederation, small business owners still felt that CNPF policy was being framed by and for the industrial barons. In consequence, the leading representative of the small business community, Léon Gingembre, quit the CNPF in 1948. He headed up a rival organisation for small firms, the *Confédération générale des petites et moyennes entreprises*, which aimed to promote the interests of the small-firm sector, particularly to help protect its interests against both the State and large firms (Guillaume, 1987).

In reality, the CNPF in its early days was far from being a powerful, hegemonic organisation, as will be seen through an analysis of its structures and its relations with the State.

Structures of the CNPF

The CNPF has had repeated difficulties in articulating a coherent, collective policy. This is a direct result of the mixed composition of the CNPF, a confederation whose membership is drawn from a vast range of economic activities. Moreover, divergences of opinion are consecrated by the very structures of the confederation.

Friction arises between large- and small-firm managers and between firms competing with a similar product range. It arises *within* sectors and *between* sectors. A range of problems exist. Within any single industry, upstream producers sell to downstream buyers. It is in the interests of upstream producers to exercise upward pressure on prices while buyers seek to restrain their costs. Additionally, within a single nation, downstream producers and distributors may wish to diversify sourcing away from same-nation upstream producers. The latter may seek to prevent this by encouraging the State to take protectionist measures. There is also the case of rivalry between industries. Manufacturers of substitute materials (e.g. plastics for usages traditionally associated with metal, wood and glass, aluminium for steel) wish to see the enactment of building and safety regulations, packaging guidelines, etc. which favour their products at the expense of competitors' product lines.

The structure of the CNPF reflects these rivalries. Individual firms are not members of the CNPF itself. Firms affiliate to industrial associations, each representing a particular sector of industrial or commercial activity. It is these industrial associations which constitute the membership of the CNPF. Industrial associations do not necessarily see eye to eye with each other: they articulate the conflicts of interest noted in the previous paragraph. Because the CNPF federates a number of these lower-level associations, it has been referred to as a confederation in this chapter.

Apart from structures to ensure sectoral representation, the CNPF is also characterised by geographical structures. Up to 1978, it had regional committees. Though these have been abolished, local organisation still exists. Local and sectoral associations feed into national structures.

There are three tiers of national structures, the general assembly (i.e. the whole membership), the *Assemblée Permanente* (elected advisory representatives) and the *Conseil exécutif,* which has the last word in formulating and implementing policy previously discussed at lower levels.

After the events of 1968, the authority of the *Conseil exécutif* and of its president was reinforced and the over-complex structures of the confederation were somewhat simplified. However, these structures do display a genuine attempt to ensure representation of constituent members, albeit at the risk of an elaborate organisation chart. Because of the unwieldy nature of the structure of the CNPF, Brizay (1975, p. 250) argued that it was only after 1969 that central office could exercise any real authority over the confederation. Hence structural problems have weakened the CNPF as a pressure group. They limit its ability to exercise *collective* power in relationships with the State and in the formulation of policies towards business.

CONFLICT AND CO-OPERATION BETWEEN EMPLOYERS' ORGANISATIONS AND THE STATE

The French State and the *patronat* have not formed interlocking entities pursuing the same aims. In reality, relations between the French State and the *patronat* have gone through repeated cycles of conflict and co-operation. To demonstrate this thesis, the following paragraphs will review and analyse major turning-points in relationships between governments and employers' organisations over the post-war period.

The post-war compromise (1946-1974)

In 1946, the *patronat* was largely discredited in French popular opinion since a large number of employers had tacitly or overtly collaborated with the Nazis during the occupation of France in the Second World War. Given their lack of popularity, the *patronat* was on the defensive. To find strength in numbers, improve its public image and redress the balance of power became its main concerns.

Meanwhile, the State took the initiative in economic development through the planning process, through intervention in industry and through its influence in the finance sector. Hence it was well placed to impose its views of economic development on company owners and managers. In the short term, the CNPF tended to acquiesce rather than lead.

By 1950, the balance of power had evolved sufficiently for spokesmen of the iron and steel industry federation to challenge State policy. In 1950, the European Coal and Steel Community (ECSC) was formed to create a European marketplace for coal and steel products. French steel manufacturers complained to their government that they had not been consulted and that the *dirigiste* attitude of the government would harm the industry. They claimed that the weakened condition of French steel companies precluded successful competition against the Germans. The French government insisted on forming the ECSC, however, arguing that only international competition could increase national productivity. The steel companies found themselves isolated: the coal industry was largely nationalised, while employers in other sectors were indifferent. The government won the argument.

Although the affair prompted a temporary crisis in the CNPF, it is chiefly of interest in that it precipitated a wider debate on French protectionism. With the growing internationalisation of trade, more and more *patrons* were leaning toward a free trade stance within Europe. They were led by the president of the CNPF himself, Georges Villiers, who between 1955 and 1957 campaigned for the creation of a free-trade zone in Europe.

Yet a subtle rear-guard action was also fought by the traditionalists in the CNPF. While many patrons accepted the principle of free trade, in practice, they wanted tariff barriers between Member States in the newly formed EEC to be reduced as slowly as possible.

Confrontations between progressive and traditionalist elements of the CNPF continued in the 1960s. Progressive elements within the *Centre des Jeunes Patrons* (a sub-group of more youthful employers within the CNPF confederation) tabled a set of new proposals. They suggested that the definition of *patron* be extended from owners to top professional managers. To some extent, this would have counteracted the narrow view of management equating with ownership. They called for the authority of the confederation to be reinforced by a reorganisation of structures. They also wished to develop a policy on the development of industrial relations and on the implementation of new technology; areas in which the unions and the State technocrats had monopolised the initiative (Brizay, 1975, pp. 107-10; Belmont, 1964). Going down this road might have made the CNPF into a more proactive and influential body.

However, the response was a backlash from the traditionalists in the higher echelons of the organisation. They circulated the *Charte Libérale* (Liberal Charter) of 1964 which attacked State interventionism and called for greater respect for market forces and competition. The Charter emphasised the right of the *patron* to manage, claiming that authority within the firm could not be shared.

While these propositions had surface credibility, in reality they were written in code and the hidden agenda proved counter-productive. The attack on interventionism was unwelcome for the large French companies that had close ties with the State and benefited greatly from them. Beneath the rhetoric on management's right to manage was a reluctance to accept the changing face of industrial relations. Already by the 1960s, tripartite discussions between employers, unions and the State represented a potential solution for anticipating and defusing tense industrial relations. However, the opportunity to move to a more consensual style of industrial relations was missed. Eventually, in-depth tripartite negotiations were to develop, but only after the powder keg exploded with demonstrations and strikes in May 1968.

Paradoxically, the 1968 events reinforced the CNPF. Although some members criticised the leadership for making too many concessions to the unions in the form of wage rises and opportunities for union organisation within firms, the Grenelle agreements (which sought to defuse the industrial relations component of the 1968 crisis) consecrated the CNPF as a legitimate participant in three-way discussions on industrial relations between employers, employees and the State. Indeed, because the French State had actively sought a 'social partner' drawn from the *patronat* with the authority to make binding agreements, the State was prepared to reinforce the legitimacy of the CNPF's role.

In summary, during the early years of its existence, the CNPF was largely unable to exercise influence and leadership. Internal divisions meant that the CNPF tended to follow or be coerced, a quite inappropriate position for an organisation whose members prided themselves on being leaders. However, after 1968, the State was in need of a partner to achieve industrial harmony. In the late 1960s and early 1970s, the *patronat*, through the organisation of the CNPF, finally came to exercise *collective* influence, but only after first winning recognition as a legitimate actor from the State.

The vagaries of opposition politics (1974-1983)

Having had its legitimacy consecrated by the State, the CNPF had a vested interest in retaining political influence. However, the period of agreement between the CNPF and the government proved short-lived.

Developments in the 1970s demonstrated that a 'conspiracy theory' cannot explain the relations between the *patronat* and the State. On the contrary, the CNPF discovered that political positioning is a delicate art. Although the *patronat* has consistently preferred right-wing over left-wing politics, broad ideological tendencies did not in themselves solve policy issues. Further, in France's complex multi-party political system, ideological preference is too blunt a tool for the identification of the candidates and parties that are most likely to implement policies favourable to the business community.

Political complications became particularly acute once President Pompidou's sudden death in 1974 precipitated a leadership crisis in the French Right. In the presidential elections that followed, the two main candidates of the Right were Jacques Chaban-Delmas and Valéry Giscard d'Estaing. Many French employers remembered Giscard d'Estaing as the Finance Minister who in 1963 imposed a *dirigiste* austerity package. Chaban-Delmas had a reputation for a progressive approach in social policy and a belief in contractual relationships in industrial relations.

These were precisely the issues which divided progressives and traditionalists in the *patronat*. Thus neither politician was unanimously supported within the CNPF. In the run-up to the presidential election, the employers' confederation demonstrated considerable indecision and lack of tact in supporting first one candidate, then the other, then professing neutrality. The declaration of neutrality was supposed to prevent a candidate being marked down as a representative of big capital. However, relations were soured by the time of the election since each politician had seen support taken away from him, which pleased neither.

Giscard d'Estaing became President and as a mark of his displeasure, he had no direct contacts with the CNPF for a period of five months. In consequence, during the late 1970s, the CNPF found itself in a tight corner in terms of its political relationships. Clearly, it was not about to switch its alliance to the broad-left coalition. Yet a number of Giscard's policies – such as the need for administrative clearing to make major redundancies and increased social security payments by employers – did not agree with the CNPF. In consequence, the CNPF's hands were tied. Because of its political preferences, it did not wish to oppose a right-wing government too openly at a time when the left-wing parties were gaining popularity, yet it could not fully discharge its lobbying function. An uneasy stalemate continued through Giscard's presidency.

The victory of François Mitterrand in the presidential elections of 1981 received a hostile reception from most of the *patronat*. But with its hands no longer tied by implicit political allegiance, the CNPF threw its weight behind a campaign against the policies of the left-wing government, relishing its new-found freedom. The economic platform of the Left was based on reflation (see pp. 26-9) and on a major nationalisation programme (see pp. 60-3). The government also proposed increases in employers' *charges sociales*. New industrial relations legislation – the *lois Auroux* (see pp. 185-6) – was in the pipeline. The CNPF argued against all of these policies.

Antagonism from the *patronat* brought out a deep-seated left-wing distrust of capital, all the more so as the government included socialists and communists. The government overestimated the strength of the CNPF, swung onto the offensive and resolved to break the 'opposition' (Berger, 1985). Adopting a policy of divide and conquer, the government backed a rival employers' organisation, the *Syndicat national de la petite et moyenne industrie* (SNPMI) against the CNPF.

This was a misguided move for a number of reasons. Firstly, the SNPMI was an offshoot of the *Confédération générale des petites et moyennes entreprises* created in 1975 after an internal dispute (Martin, 1983). Being specifically for small firm owner/managers and being one of two rival organisations, the SNPMI had far less weight than the CNPF. Secondly, the SNPMI leadership was hostile to socialism even more than it was to big capital. Its reactionary tendencies are illustrated by the fact that its president, Gérard Deuil, still had a portrait of Marshal Pétain in his office (Bauer, 1985). After its new ally, the SNPMI, organised a series of violent demonstrations against its policies, the Socialist government recognised its error of judgement. It disassociated itself from the SNPMI and attempted to isolate it. To compensate, better relations were sought with the CNPF.

This change of heart opened a new chapter in relations between the CNPF and the State. From its opposition to governments under Giscard's presidency, the CNPF was to discover more common cause with left-wing governments under Mitterrand's presidency. This 'unnatural' development illustrates the unpredictability of relationships between business communities and political parties.

The ambiguities of consensus (1983-1991)

By 1983, reconciliation between the government and the CNPF made good sense.

In 1983, the Socialist government made a U-turn on its economic policy. Its new austerity package, though not liked by the *patronat*, nonetheless had their approval as being necessary. The attitude of the Socialists had changed from one of hostility to private enterprise to a new *'découverte de l'entreprise'* (discovery of the firm, of free enterprise). These developments brought them much closer to the business classes.

Over the same period, the CNPF had changed. In 1981, the CNPF had elected for the first time a president who was not the chief executive of a large corporation but an entrepreneur who had set up and developed his own firm. With both the new leader of the CNPF, Yvon Gattaz, and the government proclaiming the importance of entrepreneurship, the role of the market and the need for a balanced budget, the gap between government and *patronat* had diminished.

Further, some of the largest French companies had passed into State ownership. The managers of nationalised companies could not make hostility to the government a matter of company policy. A kind of equal and opposite reaction occurred among the largest private companies. Amboise Roux, together with 40 other *grands patrons*, formed the *Association française des entreprises privées* (French association of private sector firms). This group wished to reaffirm its independence from the State sector and the government's policies.

The latter development weakened the CNPF, making it more amenable to government overtures. CNPF lobbying continued, of course – for example, on flexibility in employment practices, on reductions of taxes and social security contributions – but debate focused on questions of detail, rather than on 180 degree differences of policy. Taxes on companies have indeed been gradually reduced (see p. 26-3- and 31-7).

A measure of consensus did not, of course, mean that employers and government had changed their respective spots. When the Right won the parliamentary elections in 1986, major sections of the *patronat* heaved a sigh of relief. Chirac, as the new right-wing Prime Minister, promised liberal reforms which the CNPF had campaigned for. These turned around deregulation, with measures on privatisation, greater flexibility in employment practices, in hours of working, in employers' rights of dismissal and further reductions in *charges sociales* and taxes. Price controls were abolished and exchange controls were progressively dismantled.

Despite the popularity of these reforms, the CNPF adopted a posture of neutrality in the 1988 presidential elections in which Chirac, Barre and Mitterrand were the front-runners. Jones (1989) indicated that the policy proposals of the main candidates were similar in that each promised further tax cuts to business. This was sure to please the *patronat* but did not differentiate between candidates. Some policy differences between candidates did exist, particularly as regards the future of State-owned firms, but privatisation was a hot potato for the CNPF when nationalised firms were among its major members. Most importantly, the CNPF appears anxious to have avoided a repeat of its bungling during the 1974 presidential campaigns. It knew it would have to work with whoever won the presidency and that Mitterrand's victory was highly likely. A carefully judged distance to the political contest was the preferred policy of the CNPF.

In consequence, after the elections in 1988, Chirac's exit from the post of Prime Minister and his replacement by Michel Rocard (with convictions slightly left of centre) was met with neither joy nor alarm by the *patronat*. Bérégovoy, a man with whom the *patronat* was used to doing business, returned as Finance Minister.

Paradoxically, by the late 1980s, the fruits of successful consensus had undermined the CNPF. With government intervention much reduced by abolition of price and exchange controls, with greater flexibility in hiring and firing a reality and with unions in accelerating decline, the major battles of the *patronat* had been fought and largely won. Further as Berger (1987) argued, the French business world had become more heterogeneous, with a greater diversity of interests. Beyond the call for further cuts in taxes and employer social security contributions, the CNPF has not been able to formulate a policy to rally the business community.

Disunity within its own ranks has increased. Even the current president and vice-president find it hard to agree. Although Gattaz was criticised as being too compliant with the Socialist government, François Périgot, the president of the CNPF since 1986 and a former top Unilever manager, has also favoured consensual policies. He eschews ideological debates, such as the question of the future of the nationalised firms. On the other hand, his vice-president, Ernest-Antoine Seillière, a descendant of the de Wendel dynasty (see p. 155), is an outspoken free-marketeer who wishes to have clear lines of demarcation between public and private sectors, and between government policies and CNPF views (Piquard, 1989; Routhier, 1989).

The scope for initiative at the level of the CNPF has in any case been reduced. The tripartite discussions that had brought together the CNPF, the unions and State in joint negotiations have declined in currency. Thureau-Dangin (1991) has indicated that at the start of the 1990s, firms are better prepared to negotiate and defend their individual interests while, where sectoral interests are concerned, industry associations play a bigger role and are recovering the authority that they lost in the 1970s to the CNPF.

In seeking to represent the diverse expectations and interests of its industry association members, the CNPF seems to have lost its direction and perhaps its identity. Further, it is faced by a government that has greater experience and better judgement than the one it faced in the early 1980s. In the absence of a clearly defined enemy, split by internal divisions and lacking a common set of goals around which to rally, the influence of the major employers' organisation in France has declined.

CONCLUSIONS

Since the 1940s, the *patronat* has demonstrated considerable heterogeneity in outlook but has been relatively homogeneous in social composition, particularly as regards the *grand patronat*. In terms of collective organisation, employers' federations have experienced a rise and fall in their authority.

Although there is still a rear-guard that prefers protectionism, State subsidies and, paradoxically, a low level of State intervention, it has declined in numbers; the majority of *patrons* are vociferously in favour of liberal trends in general (Bauer and Bertin-Mourot, 1985). Other divergences of opinion exist, but relate less to macro-issues then to sectoral concerns and the well-being of individual firms. This is a natural development in a market economy and a sign that competitive pressures are working.

The social composition of the *grand patronat* depends on long-term factors and so will probably remain stable. Even in areas where short-term change is possible, such as the appointment of chief executives of nationalised companies, accepted practices have remained unchanged, even under Socialist governments. New appointees continue to be drawn almost exclusively from the same *grandes écoles* and *grands corps* (Bauer, 1985; Cohen, 1985; Mangolte, 1986). Stability at the top may, however, impede the evolution of management culture, a theme that will be developed in Chapter 7.

As regards management education, the current elitist system favours recruitment from a narrow social base, so reducing opportunities for talented but less privileged individuals. But regardless of origins, most top French managers have outstanding intellectual qualities. Further, the *écoles supérieures de commerce*, together with a few university institutions, have risen in prominence and are producing a new generation of middle and senior managers. It is from their ranks and from France's new entrepreneurs that a change in the composition and attitudes of the *patronat* as a whole will probably occur.

Employers' organisations have gradually lost their influence and are dissolving back into their constituent elements. With the decline of the two great 'threats' to the *patronat*, namely State *dirigisme* (see Chapter 1) and trade unionism (see Chapter 6), the CNPF can no longer bolster employer solidarity by shouting wolf. Bar calls for tax reform, an internal consensus on policy eludes the CNPF.

Paradoxically, whereas the *patronat* has a stable and well-defined social identity, the voice of its collective organisations has grown less distinctive, if not indeed indistinct.

References

Alexandre, R. (1990) 'Grandes facs contre grandes écoles', *L'Expansion* (31 octobre-21 novembre), pp. 56-66

Anastassopoulos, J.-P. (1981) 'The French experience: conflicts with government' in Vernon, R. & Aharoni, Y. (eds.) *State-owned Enterprise in the Western Economies*, pp. 99-116, London: Croom Helm

Barsoux, J.-C. & Lawrence, P. (1990) *Management in France*, London: Cassell

Barsoux, J.-C. & Lawrence, P. (1991) 'The making of a French manager', *Harvard Business Review* (July-August), pp. 58-67

Bauer, M. (1985) 'La gauche au pouvoir et le grand patronat: sous les pavés ... des mouvements de classe dirigeante' in Birnbaum, P. (ed.) *Les Elites socialistes au pouvoir (1981-1985)*, pp. 263-306, Paris: PUF

Bauer, M. (1990) 'Pas de sociologie de l'entreprise sans sociologie des dirigeants' in Sainsaulieu, R. (ed.) *L'Entreprise: une affaire de société*, pp. 148-74, Paris: Presses de la Fondation Nationale des Sciences Politiques

Bauer, M. & Bertin-Mourot, B (1985) 'Grands patrons: oui, mais... au libéralisme', *Nouvel Economiste*, 482 (22 mars), pp. 60-5

Bauer, M. & Bertin-Mourot, B. (1987) *Les 200. Comment devient-on un grand patron?* Paris: L'Epreuve des Faits/Editions du Seuil

Bauer, M. & Bertin-Mourot, B. (1991) 'Les dirigeants: managers ou propriétaires?', *Problèmes économiques*, 2,223 (30 avril), pp. 1-3

Belmont, P (1964) 'CNPF et avenir du patronat français', *Economie et humanisme* 156 (sept), pp. 74-9

Berger, S. (1985) 'The Socialists and the *patronat*: the dilemmas of coexistence in a mixed economy' in Machin, H. & Wright, V. (eds.) *Economic Policy and Policy Making under the Mitterrand Presidency*, pp. 225-44, London: Frances Pinter

Berger, S. (1987) 'French business from transition to transition' in Ross, G. *et al. The Mitterrand Experiment. Continuity and Change in Modern France*, pp.187-98, London: Polity Press

Berle, A. A. & Means, G. C. (1932) *The Modern Corporation and Private Property*, New York: Macmillan

Bourdieu, P. & Saint-Martin, M. de (1978) 'Le Patronat', *Actes de la Recherche en Sciences Sociales*, 20-21 (mars-avril), pp. 3-82

Bourdois, J.-H. (1983) 'Trente ans d'essor industriel (1945-1974)', *Les cahiers français*, 211 (mai-juin), pp. 4-11.

Bramley, J. (1991) 'Management education and management styles in France: still culture specific?', *Modern and Contemporary France Review*, 44 (January), pp. 62-8

Brizay, B. (1975) *Le Patronat. Histoire, structure, stratégie du CNPF*, Paris: Editions du Seuil

Bucaille, A. & Costa de Beauregard, B. (1987) *PMI: Enjeux régionaux et internationaux*, Paris: Librairie du Commerce International

Clairvois, M. (1988) 'Les métamorphoses du patron', *L'Expansion* (21 oct-3 nov), pp. 161-4

Cohen, E. (1985) 'L'Etat socialiste en industrie' in Birnbaum, P. (ed.) *Les Elites socialistes au pouvoir. 1981-1985*, pp. 219-61, Paris: PUF

Cohen, E. (1988) 'Formation, modèles d'action et performance de l'élite industrielle: l'exemple des dirigeants issus du corps des Mines', *Sociologie du travail*, 4, pp. 587-614

Deleforterie-Soubeyroux, N. (1961) *Les Dirigeants de l'industrie française*, Paris: Colin

Guillaume, S. (1987) *Confédération générale des petites et moyennes entreprises. Son histoire, son combat, un autre syndicalisme patronal 1944-1978*, Bordeaux: Presses Universitaires de Bordeaux

Hall, D. & Bettignies, M.-Cl. de (1969) 'L'Elite française des dirigeants d'entreprise', *Hommes et techniques* (janvier), pp. 19-27

INSEE (1987) *Tableaux de l'économie française*, Paris: INSEE

Jones, G. (1989) 'Business as usual: the employers' in Gaffney, J. (ed.) *The French Presidential Elections of 1988 : Ideology and Leadership in contemporary France*, pp. 186-209, Aldershot: Dartmouth

Landes, D. S. (1951) 'French business and the businessman: a social and cultural analysis' in Earle, E.M. (ed.) *Modern France: Problems of the Third and Fourth Republics*, pp. 334-53, Princeton: Princeton UP

Le Van-Lemesle, L. (1988) 'L'éternel retour du nouvel entrepreneur', *Revue française de gestion* (septembre-octobre), pp. 134-40

Lévy-Leboyer, M. (1976) 'Innovation and business strategies in nineteenth and twentieth-century France' in Carter, E.C. *et al.* (eds.) *Enterprises and entrepreneurs in Nineteenth and Twentieth Century France*, pp. 87-135, Baltimore: John Hopkins University Press

Lévy-Leboyer, M. (1979) 'Le patronat français, 1912-1973' in Lévy-Leboyer, M (ed.) *Le Patronat de la seconde industrialisation*, pp. 137-88, Paris: Les Editions Ouvrières

Lévy-Leboyer, M. (1980) 'The Large Corporation in Modern France' in Chandler, A. & Daems, H. (eds.) *Managerial Hierarchies*, pp. 117-60, Cambridge, MA: Harvard UP

Mangolte, P.-A. (1986) *La Vie privée des entreprises publiques*, Paris: Editions ouvrières

Marceau, J. (1977) *Class and Status in France. Economic Change and Social Immobility 1945-1975*, Oxford: Clarendon Press

Marceau, J. (1981) *'Plus ça change, plus c'est la même chose*: access to elite careers in French business' in Howorth, J. & Cerny, P. G. (eds.) *Elites in France: Origins, Reproduction and Power*, pp. 104-33, London: Frances Pinter

Marceau, J. (1989) *A Family Business? The Making of an International Business Elite*, Cambridge: CUP

Marin, B. (1988) 'Qu'est-ce que le patronat? Enjeux théoriques et résultats empiriques', *Sociologie du travail*, 4, pp. 515-43

Martin, J.-M. (1983) *Le CNPF*, Paris: PUF

Mary, J.-F. (1985) 'Le patronat a-t-il encore besoin du CNPF?', *Revue politique et parlementaire*, 920, pp. 48-53

Ministère de l'Industrie (1989) *Les Chiffres-clés de l'industrie*, Paris: Dunod

Monjardet, D. (1972) 'Carrière des dirigeants et contrôle de l'entreprise', *Sociologie du Travail*, 14:2 (avril-juin), pp. 131-44

Morin, F. (1988) 'A qui appartient le capital des 200 premières entreprises privées?', *Science et Vie: Economie*, 41 (juillet-août), pp. 45-64

Morin, F. (1989) 'Qui possède les 200 premières entreprises françaises?', *Science et Vie: Economie*, 52 (août), pp. 43-60

Morin, F. (1990) 'Qui possède les 200 premières entreprises françaises?' *Science et Vie: Economie*, 63, (juillet-août), pp. 51-74

Oechslin, J-J (1972) 'The Role of Employers' Organisations in France', *International Labour Review*, 431 (Nov), pp. 391-413

Piquard, P. (1989) 'Patronat: le narcissisme a failli tuer le CNPF', *L'Evénement du jeudi* (4-10 mai), p. 18

Routhier, A. (1989) 'Les patrons sans boussole', *L'Expansion* (8 - 21 juin), pp. 144-52

Saglio, J. (1977) 'Qui sont les patrons?', *Economie et humanisme*, 236 (août), pp. 6-11

Thureau-Dangin, P. (1991) 'Le vrai pouvoir du CNPF', *Dynasteurs*, 57 (mars), pp. 36-51

Vaughan, M. (1981) 'The *grandes écoles*: selection, legitimation, perpetuation' in Howorth, J. & Cerny, P. G. (eds.) *Elites in France: Origins, Reproduction and Power*, pp. 93-103, London: Frances Pinter

Weber, H. (1988) 'Cultures patronales et types d'entreprises: esquisse d'une typologie du patronat', *Sociologie du travail*, 4, pp. 545-66

Wilson, F. L. (1987) *Interest Group Politics in France*, Cambridge: CUP

6

Industrial relations and trade unions

INTRODUCTION

Industrial relations in France have developed out of a complex series of interactions between employers, employees and the State.

The French State has played an important role in industrial relations. The legislative framework is highly developed. A number of institutions relating to industrial relations have devolved from it. Indeed, the French trade union movement has been extensively shaped by the regulatory framework. But wider patterns of social and industrial development have also played a crucial role.

Because of the high degree of interrelatedness of different components, the study of French industrial relations is rather like fitting together the pieces of a jigsaw puzzle. Only once a number of pieces have been brought together does the larger picture emerge. This chapter sets out to provide those pieces, with the interrelationships between them emerging gradually.

The next section sets out the most important elements of legislation regarding employee representation and the institutions that derive from them. The second section presents the major French trade unions. It discusses their influence as independent organisations and in relation to the institutions for employee representation presented in the first section. (For discussion of employer organisations, the reader is referred to pp. 166-76.) The third section on pp. 200-7 deals with the development in France of core industrial relations practices, including collective bargaining. The final section charts the processes of change in French industrial relations in the post-war period. By its chronological development, this section seeks to capture some of the diversity of French industrial relations and to demonstrate how the different parts of the jigsaw relate to each other.

Throughout, the aim will be to delineate the French industrial relations model and to evaluate the extent to which it has been modernised in recent years. That model is deceptive in a number of ways. The regulatory framework assuring employee rights is far less constricting for employers than appears on first sight. Systems for employee representation are highly elaborate yet finding a single voice has been a major difficulty, particularly for the divided French trade union movement. Traditionally, the French industrial relations model has been characterised by conflict between employers and employees. This is less the case today. Yet if the old model has lost much of its relevance, the construction of a new model continues to pose difficulties.

THE INSTITUTIONAL FRAMEWORK FOR EMPLOYEE REPRESENTATION

Industrial relations are often referred to in French as *relations sociales* while the major parties involved are termed the *partenaires sociaux* (social partners). These elements of terminology are revealing. Firstly, the French approach to industrial relations takes as its point of departure not so much workplace practices as wider social issues. Secondly, social aims tend to be achieved by political means. This becomes clear once the content of the term *partenaires sociaux* is 'unpacked'; along with employers and trade unions, the phrase also includes the State, government and parliament. Further, because relations between French employers and unions have been charac-terised by conflict (see pp. 187-8 for discussion), solutions to industrial relations problems have often been implemented by legislative means. A tripartite approach (State, employers, unions) has been an important charac-teristic of French industrial relations in the post-war years.

Labour law is central to any study of French industrial relations. The legislative framework is mostly contained in the *Code du Travail* (Work Code). The *Code du Travail* regulates the *minimum* standards (on safety, hours worked, employee representation, etc.) which apply at the workplace. Enforcement of the Code is entrusted to the *Inspection du Travail* (Labour Inspectorate), attached to the Labour Ministry. Labour inspectors have powers of entry and search in industrial and commercial establishments and can bring prosecutions for unacceptable practices.

The legislative framework is elaborate and has been influential in the development of French industrial relations. Major changes in industrial relations patterns have sometimes simply been confirmed by new legislation but there have been examples too of changes in the legislation being the catalyst for change in industrial relations. Historical instances include the repressive 1791 *loi Chapelier* which outlawed professional and worker organisations. At that time, the notion of an individual contract of employment between employee and employer precluded a collective dimension to industrial relations. This legislation was reversed gradually by the 1864 Act legalising strikes and the 1880 Act allowing freedom of association and the right to form trade unions. Discussion in the section on French trade unions will show how the legislative framework came to shape the French trade unions.

Major reforms of industrial relations legislation in the twentieth century have accompanied moments of social and political upheaval. The key dates were 1936 (when the left-wing Popular Front came to power), 1945 (the ending of the Second World War and of the Occupation – bringing a coalition government to power), 1968 (the May demonstrations and strikes) and 1981 (the first Socialist government during the Fifth Republic). In each of these periods, political will to improve industrial relations was demonstrated by setting up new institutions for employee representation. Motivations for modernisation have varied between the desire for greater social justice (by the recognition of workers' rights, by the reduction of exploitation) to the need for greater economic efficiency (harmonious industrial relations leading to higher productivity).

Most of these reforms have currency today. The institutions they created continue to play an industrial relations role. They will be presented in turn, starting with the oldest.

Conseils de Prud'hommes

The *Conseils de Prud'hommes* (industrial tribunals or labour courts) date back to the Napoleonic period but have evolved considerably since. Their role is to settle disputes between employee and employer related to the employment contract of particular individuals. (Collective disputes do not fall within the jurisdiction of the *Conseil de Prud'hommes*.)

Most cases before the courts are from workers seeking compensation from employers *after* quitting or being sacked. Lack of protection from suffering disciplinary action, even dismissal by the employer, prevent employees presenting their cases earlier. However, access to the tribunals is relatively easy and procedures swift. Conciliated agreements are sought, but where negotiation breaks down, the tribunals can impose settlements.

In order to achieve fairness, the *Conseils de Prud'hommes* are lay courts each composed of two employer representatives and two employee representatives. Some 90 per cent of decisions are unanimous. Most of the cases before the courts (78 per cent) concern small firms, as large firms take greater precautions with the law (Lévy, 1989).

The lay judges are elected and have a five-year mandate. Elections are by proportional representation by employers and employees for their respective representatives. All employees have the right to vote during working hours without loss of pay. As from the *loi Boulin* of 1979, there must be at least one Labour Court per *département* but there are some 279 in total (Delamotte, 1984). In consequence, the *Conseils de Prud'hommes* is the institution having the widest suffrage of any of France's systems of employee representation.

There has been an increase in the level of activity of the *Conseils de Prud'hommes* of late, apparently due to an erosion of employment protection.

Délégués du personnel

In 1936 the Popular Front government, which brought together Socialists and Communists, sought to improve the lot of working people. The reforms included a 40-hour week and two weeks paid holiday. By the same Matignon agreements, the government became a major partner to collective bargaining since it acquired the right to convene employers and unions. With the aim of giving greater involvement to employees, it also instituted the election of *délégués du personnel* (employee representatives). Employers were hostile to all these innovations on the grounds of their cost. They also feared an erosion of their authority.

The election of *délégués du personnel* is compulsory by law in firms having ten or more employees. All employees are entitled to vote under a proportional representation system. Unions have a monopoly in putting forward candidates at the first round of elections. If less than 50 per cent of electors vote at the first round, a second round is held when anyone can stand. Numbers of representatives vary with size of firm. Representatives have a one-year mandate, are allocated 15 hours of paid time per month to undertake their duties and enjoy protection from arbitrary dismissal.

The employer must convene the *délégués du personnel* at least once a month. Within their purview are issues related to individuals' grievances on wages and working conditions. The *délégués* transmit grievances to management and inform employees of the outcome. In cases of non-observance of the *Code du Travail*, they also have right of recourse to the *Inspection du Travail*. Although the institution of *délégués du personnel* survives as an attempt to fill a 'gap' in worker representation in small firms, in establishments employing between 11 and 49 employees, less than 40 per cent actually have *délégués du personnel* (Ministère du Travail, 1990).

In brief, the role of the *délégués du personnel* is to act as a communication channel between employees and management.

Comités d'entreprise

At the end of the Second World War, the euphoria of liberation allowed a temporary softening of ideological disputes between the Left and the Right, and a reduction in conflict between workers and management. It was in this atmosphere of reconciliation and national solidarity that the legislation on *comités d'entreprise* (works councils) was passed.

Just as the coalition government of the time sought to transcend doctrinal differences for the greater good of the French nation, so the institution of the *comité d'entreprise* sought to produce harmony at the workplace by bringing together employer and employees in a common structure in order to co-operate towards a common purpose. Co-operation quickly proved a Utopian ideal with little practical content. The requirement to co-operate was formally abandoned in 1982.

In practice, the *comité d'entreprise* has a number of more limited roles. It has the right to be informed and consulted on company accounts and on major policy decisions, such as mergers and redundancies (from 1975) and new technology initiatives (from 1982). Legislation in 1982 widened the range of information to be supplied to the *comité d'entreprise*. It gave powers of investigation into company accounts as well as of recourse to specialists in accountancy, technology, etc.

The *comité d'entreprise* has no real authority but does have limited prerogatives. The agreement of the *comité d'entreprise* is required for changes in working hours and on profit-sharing schemes. Moreover the *comité d'entreprise* has its own funds. From 1982, firms were obliged by law to allocate monies equivalent to at least 0.2 per cent of their wages bill to the *comité d'entreprise*. This income is used to finance *oeuvres sociales* (social activities) which include sports, holiday and education facilities.

Legislation stipulates that all firms having 50 or more employees shall organise a *comité d'entreprise*. From 1982, provision was made for a group *comité d'entreprise* in the case of multi-establishment corporations. Employee representatives are elected for two years following the same electoral mechanisms as for the *délégués du personnel* (see pp. 182-3). Each of the major unions has the right to nominate a delegate to the *comité d'entreprise*. Representatives have 20 paid hours per month to do their duties and are protected against arbitrary dismissal. Meetings are convened monthly by employers and chaired by them or their representatives. In 1982, a *comité d'entreprise* existed in 84 per cent of firms with over 50 employees, but this percentage dropped slightly by the end of the decade (Sellier, 1985; Dirn, 1991).

It is difficult to generalise on the value of the institution of the *comité d'entreprise*. In some small firms, it typically does little more than organise the traditional Christmas tree and presents. In some large companies, its financial resources make it a 'firm within the firm'.

In addition, parallel committees exist which increase the range of representation of employee interests, particularly the *comité d'hygiène, de sécurité et des conditions de travail* (committee for health, safety and working conditions) while firms with over 300 employees must have an employment training committee.

In brief, the *comité d'entreprise* is a consultative body whose influence varies considerably with firm size and employer policy.

Sections syndicales d'entreprise

After the massive May 1968 strikes, the 'Grenelle protocol' *or accords de Grenelle* made a number of concessions to employees (see also p. 208). Of primary interest here is the accordance of legal recognition *to sections syndicales d'entreprise* (union sections within the workplace) and to union representatives at plant level. From 1968, unions could organise a local section in firms employing more than 50 people as a matter of right.

As background, it should be added that unions had been free to organise since 1884, but only at sector and national levels. Organisation *within* firms was not a legal right, though by the 1960s workplace sections existed openly in some companies. The lack of provision for workplace representation was a glaring gap in the institutional framework which helps explain weaknesses within French unions (a theme to be developed on pp. 191-5).

The explanation lies mainly with the hostility of the *patronat* who had successfully resisted *sections syndicales*. After May 1968, employers were reluctantly forced to concede. But management reluctance had its pendant in the unfavourable attitude of top union officials towards giving authority to shopfloor delegates. Some of the higher union echelons had feared that the granting of opportunities for negotiation at local level would dilute the authority of the union hierarchy or even splinter the trade union movement. Certainly, the 'gap' at local level is part of the explanation for the slow development of plant level bargaining. However, in the medium term, the 1968 recognition of *sections syndicales* reinforced union authority in collective bargaining at all levels.

Union sections are entitled to an office and other facilities. They appoint their own shop stewards who can engage in activities such as collecting dues and distributing materials during working hours. Union meetings take place outside working hours. Union officials have the right to circulate freely around company property. They are protected from dismissal.

In brief, the main roles of union representatives are to defend employee interests, to transmit employee demands and, most importantly, to negotiate on pay and conditions with employers. In reality, the ability of the unions to fulfil these roles has been limited, as the section on French trade unions will illustrate.

Les lois Auroux

In 1981, a left-wing government with an ambitious economic and social programme arrived in office. Perceiving French industrial relations to be in need of modernisation, the new Socialist Labour Minister, Jean Auroux, introduced legislation which he said would produce *'une transformation profonde et durable des relations industrielles'* – 'a deep and lasting transformation of industrial relations' – (*Droit social*, 1984). Again, it was the State which took an industrial relations initiative. The results were a series of four acts, commonly called the *lois Auroux*. In summary, their contents were as follows.

The first Act (4 August 1982) introduced a new *droit d'expression des salariés*. In companies having a staff greater than 200, employees were given the right to a direct say regarding the content and organisation of work and the improvement of working conditions.

The second Act (28 October 1982) reinforced the three institutions assuring employee representation, namely the *délégués du personnel*, the *comité d'entreprise* and the *sections syndicales*. Union sections can now be formed in any firm regardless of size.

The third Act (13 November 1982) reinforced collective bargaining. Agreements at firm level became valid. Yearly negotiations on pay and conditions at company level were made compulsory within firms having over 200 employees, as were yearly negotiations on pay at sector level. Industry-wide negotiations on salary scales and job classifications were to be conducted every five years.

The obligation was simply to *negotiate*, not to come to an *agreement*. Although this may seem odd, French law distinguishes between an *obligation de moyen* and an *obligation de résultat*. In the first case, merely the means to be implemented are specified while in the second case, a precise outcome must be reached. Clearly, the obligation to negotiate falls within the first category.

An agreement is considered valid even if only a minority of unions sign it. In every instance, the employer retains the final word. These features curtail the obligation to negotiate but legislation does now make a dialogue compulsory, whereas previously it had been non-existent in many firms.

The fourth Act reinforced measures on health and safety at the workplace.

An underlying aim of the *lois Auroux* was to reinvigorate collective bargaining processes. The Auroux report had indicated that many employees (some 11 per cent in firms employing more than ten people) were not covered by collective agreements at all while plant-level agreements covered about a quarter of employees. Moreover, a new balance was sought between the *partenaires sociaux*. The extent of State involvement was to decline as industrial relations strategies were directed back to companies, with bargaining being made compulsory. At the same time, the involvement of employees in company matters was to increase, with greater powers for employee representatives and more encouragement to unions to deal with the concrete problems of wages and conditions at the workplace.

In brief, the agenda was to provide for a more equitable distribution of rewards from work by better systems of collective bargaining. In contrast to these high ideals, reactions and results have varied, as detailed discussion on pp. 211-13 will show. At this stage of the exposition, stress is placed on the delicate balancing act displayed in the *lois Auroux* between the interests of employers, of employees and of unions.

Overview

Perhaps the inevitable question at this point is whether the four sub-systems for employee representation allow for a genuine specialisation of functions or merely represent a confused patchwork of overlapping attributions. In reply, it can be said that some 'division of labour' does exist but it is far from clear-cut.

The major distinctive elements are as follows. Firstly, the *conseils de Prud'hommes*, being courts of law, are clearly in a special category. Secondly, the nitty-gritty of collective bargaining, namely the *negotiation* of pay and conditions, devolves by right to the unions. Thirdly, only one institution, the *comité d'entreprise* has a right to company funding. Consequently, it can undertake practical tasks within the firm, albeit of a limited kind. Fourthly, the institution of *délégués du personnel* can exist in all but the smallest firms (over ten employees) whereas a *comité d'entreprise* and a *section syndicale* involve heavier structures which usually only larger firms can support.

Over and against these elements of specialisation are problems of principle and practice. The *droit d'expression* contained in the *lois Auroux* is a right that every individual can exercise. The right to have a say invites a reply: without the reply, self-expression becomes futile. However, the mechanisms for this dialogue are omitted from the 1982 legislation. Further, there are overlaps with other institutions. The *délégués du personnel* are essentially just such a communication channel while the consultative role of the *comité d'entreprise* is another variation on the theme of dialogue. Hence the different channels appear to fulfil the same role, although they do so by different means.

Further, the three institutions of employee representation function by the relaying of individual opinions through the good offices of elected representatives. The granting of an individual *droit d'expression* may suggest that such delegation is somehow inadequate, that the electoral process sets up barriers between workers and management. This ambiguity relating to principles remains unresolved.

Problems of practice are also acute. Distinctions between the different institutions can be blurred. In the company having *délégués du personnel*, a *comité d'entreprise* and a *section syndicale*, it is possible, frequent even, for the same individual to hold more than one mandate. Can such an individual consistently draw a distinction between different roles? Do his management interlocutors perceive a difference?

On the other hand, smaller firms may lack one or other of *délégués du personnel*, *comité d'entreprise* or *section syndicale*. In such cases, the 1982 legislation allowed for some transfer of attributions. Where there is no *comité d'entreprise*, *délégués du personnel* may take on some of the roles of the work council. This practical solution confuses the 'division of labour'. Finally, when a *section syndicale* does not exist or when employers are hostile to unions, negotiations on pay and conditions are undertaken with the *comité d'entreprise*, regardless of the formal definition of roles.

Problems do exist. In appearance, the legislative framework imposes a strait-jacket on employers. In reality, the proliferation of modes of employee representation and expression can be a damnation in disguise. It dilutes worker protection. Individually, each of these institutions is weak. The multidimensional approach tries to cover the full range of company circumstances, but can result in disunity, confusion or plain apathy. Reform proposals to simplify the system have not been implemented. A unified and coherent system of employee representation would speak to management in a more authoritative manner.

As will be seen below, finding a single voice has also been the difficulty of the French trade union movement.

FRENCH TRADE UNIONS

The politics of the French trade union movement have played a major role in the development of industrial relations. The importance of ideological debates receded over the 1980s, but their earlier influence was enormous. Enough of that influence remains for discussion of political questions to be essential.

The history of the French trade union movement is rooted in the Marxist notion of a class struggle. The desire of sections of the working class to wrest power from the capitalist managers of the economy is the backcloth on which most French unions have embroidered variations on the theme of a class uprising. The fervour of the class struggle translated into the ideology of 'revolutionary syndicalism' – meaning workers organising themselves into unions in order to overthrow capitalism. In its most extreme form, this late-nineteenth century ideology rejected all participation in political systems under capitalism, considering them to be the instruments of the ruling classes. Class collaboration was pointless if the aim was to hasten the revolution and the downfall of capitalism. The major instrument in the struggle was taken to be the general strike, which would eventually bring capitalism to its knees.

Strong elements of class consciousness and of class conflict have undoubtedly figured in broad sections of the industrial proletariat (Bouzonnie, 1989). But as Meyers (1981) has suggested, it is doubtful that the majority of the working classes ever agreed with this outlook, nor did French unions subscribe to it fully in practice over the course of the twentieth century. The important consequence is that within French trade unions the ideology of revolutionary syndicalism was diluted into a low-key, but widespread distrust of employers and of the State.

This distrust fashioned attitudes within the industrial relations system. Workers distrusted employers. Employers distrusted workers and feared the unions, preferring to have as little to do with unionism as possible. Because the logic of the revolutionary struggle coloured day-to-day union tactics, the practical consequence of this mutual suspicion was the late development of collective bargaining in France. Conflict, especially in industry and in the public sector, between employers, employees and their respective representatives has been a central feature of industrial relations in France.

In order to bring together the largest number of workers possible for a general strike, French union activists wished to federate workers as a class. As Goetschy and Martin (1981, p. 180) indicated, the strength of this sense of class consciousness constituted a 'marked contrast' between France and her neighbours. Since unions based on trade or craft can splinter and weaken the working classes, 'trade' unions have not figured as strongly in France as in Britain . (Indeed, English terminology with its emphasis on 'trade' union is misleading and represents a cultural blind spot, but no valid alternative term exists.) The mainspring for the French workers' movement was not so much a sense of personal identity based on sharing common work skills (though this existed) but a sense of social belonging based on sharing common political goals. Worker association by trade or profession (*un syndicat*) does exist in France but usually within a larger grouping, called the *centrale syndicale* or union confederation. It is the French *centrales syndicales*, which are differentiated as much by political tendencies as by industrial relations strategies, which correspond to British trade unions.

A full inventory of French unions would include the FEN (a teachers' union), possibly the FNSEA (though this is more of a farmers' lobby), as well as company unions such as at Peugeot-Citroën and so on. But for current purposes, discussion is limited to the *centrales syndicales* that are most relevant to French business. These are the five trade unions which were assigned 'representativeness' under French law in 1966. (Having 'representativeness' confers the right to negotiate collective agreements, the right to be represented on consultative bodies and participate in the administration of systems related to social security, pensions and unemployment insurance.) The five unions are the CGT, the CFDT, the CFTC, FO and the CGC. In the past, the first two were considered as 'revolutionary' unions and the last three 'reformist' unions, but over time many of their characteristics have changed as the following descriptions will briefly illustrate.

The CGT

The *Confédération générale du travail* (General Confederation of Labour) was formed in 1895 and is the oldest surviving French union. It is the confederation whose history most closely resembles the prototype of revolutionary syndicalism set out above. Over the twentieth century, the revolutionary idealism of the CGT pushed it closer to the theses of Communist ideology, which likewise preached an overthrow of capitalism. In the post-war period, top CGT officials have also held office within the *Parti Communiste Français* (PCF). This does not mean that the entire rank and file of the CGT have been Communists, but it does explain the identification that is commonly made between the objectives of the CGT and those of the PCF.

In line with its wider political aspirations, the CGT favours *gestion démocratique* (democratic management) at the workplace. The practical meaning of this phrase is unclear but it translates an aspiration towards a radical break with traditional industrial relations.

Although its membership is in freefall decline (see Table 6.1), the CGT remains the largest French union. It is organised into 40 industry federations and into 94 *unions départementales* or regional unions (Goetschy and Rojot 1987). The largest federations affiliated to the CGT are in the metal, building and chemical industries and in municipal and health services.

FO

Force ouvrière (Workers' Strength) was a splinter movement from the CGT formed in 1947. The reason for the split was hostility to the Communist ideology of the CGT. FO has since tried to be politically neutral.

In terms of workplace policies, it does not advocate worker control because it believes that unions should not be involved in taking managerial decisions. In espousing this policy, FO displays an 'us and them' mentality. This characteristic has marked FO from its creation right through to the 1990s and is another variation on the theme of class consciousness. But whereas for the radical CGT and CFDT (at least in the 1960s and 1970s), class consciousness led directly to class war, for the 'reformist' FO, class consciousness seems to lead to an acceptance of the class *status quo*. FO has not found a way of extricating itself from this *impasse.*

FO was the earliest and consistently strongest advocate of collective bargaining. Therein lies its most important contribution to the French trade union movement. It is often seen as a public sector union, with a strong white-collar following, but by 1979, FO was claiming that over half its members worked in the private sector (Goetschy and Rojot, 1987, p. 144).

The CFTC

The *Confédération française des travailleurs chrétiens* (French Confederation of Christian Workers) was formed in 1919. Drawing on Christian thinking, it sought 'peaceful collaboration' (Goetschy and Rojot, 1987, p. 144) between labour and capital and formerly had a reputation for being a company union. Despite the split which produced the CFDT (see below) it retains fairly extensive representation being composed of 45 federations and 94 *unions départementales.* It is strongest among miners, health workers and Christian school teachers. The CFTC is an advocate of collective bargaining and of social and family policy.

The CFDT

In the early 1960s, a large majority within the CFTC wished to distance the union from social Christianity. It subsequently formed the *Confédération française démocratique du travail* (French Democratic Confederation of Labour) in 1964.

The CFDT quickly moved leftwards towards socialism. In the late 1960s and early 1970s, its ideas were close to those of the *Parti Socialiste Unifié* (which Michel Rocard then headed) and in the 1980s was probably the union closest to the Socialists. However, it has never given public support to any political party.

In 1970, the CFDT espoused the radical theme of workers' management of production (*autogestion*). Perhaps the closest this idea came to reality was the Lip affair of 1972. Lip, a watch manufacturer that had gone into receivership, was occupied by its workers who continued to make and sell watches until they were evicted.

The CFDT enjoyed rapid growth in the 1960s and 1970s and proved a potent rival to the CGT since it combined radical ideology with a willingness to bargain at local and national levels. Between 1966 and 1980, it formed a pact for 'unity of action' with the CGT, but continual political disagreements limited its effectiveness. The announcement in 1978 of the policy of *recentrage* put the CFDT at odds with the CGT since that policy emphasised concentrating on industrial issues rather than on wider political action, which the CGT continued to favour. In the 1980s, the ideas of *autogestion* and a break with capitalism were quietly dropped. Hence 'reformist' or 'modern' tendencies have gradually ousted radical ideology.

These changes in emphasis have sometimes backfired on the CFDT. Rather than acquiring a reputation for flexibility, a common view of the CFDT has been one of 'instability' (Mouriaux, 1981; Nousbaum, 1985). The CFDT has had repeated problems reconciling its discourse and conduct in the field and has suffered a large decline in membership from 1978 onwards. Though for most of its life the CFDT has been the second largest union, during the 1980s it was comparable in size to FO (see Table 6.1 below).

The CFDT is particularly strong in the metal, oil and chemical industries and in health, banking and insurance.

The CGC

The *Confédération générale des cadres* (CGC), established in 1946, draws its membership from a wide range of occupations including technicians, engineers and sales personnel as well as supervisory and managerial staff. Other confederations also have *cadre* sections but the CGC is the only union to represent solely the interests of this group.

It presents itself as politically 'neutral', though this is perhaps best read as an opposition to the heavy left-wing politicisation of the CGT and formerly of the CFDT. It is a workplace-orientated union which seeks to enhance the status of its members. The CGC guards against encroachment on middle management prerogatives due to advances in workers' rights while trying to persuade top management to devolve greater authority and power to middle managers. The CGC is a strong supporter of collective bargaining at all levels.

Union membership

France has the lowest levels of unionisation of any European country and they have been falling (Noblecourt, 1991). This sub-section analyses the causes behind these phenomena.

Turning first to data on union membership, certain caveats are in order. Calculations of the membership of French trade unions are notoriously unreliable and no independent system of verification exists. However, available data do present sufficient concordance to disembed broad tendencies over the long term. In order to mitigate discrepancies between modes of calculation, Table 6.1 gives high and low estimates of union membership .

As revealed in Table 6.1, periods of high union membership have been the exception in France. The peak years were 1919-20, 1935-8, 1945-7 and, to a lesser extent, 1968-75. They correspond to major political upheavals, rather than industrial relations developments *per se*. But the peaks were short-lived and were followed by falls in membership. Hence a cyclical pattern of union membership exists for the twentieth century as a whole.

The most striking development is that union membership has been in decline since the 1970s and the speed of decline has been accelerating. In this

Table 6.1 Membership of major French trade unions: 1912–1990

Year	CGT High estimate	CGT Low estimate	FO High estimate	FO Low estimate	CFTC High estimate	CFTC Low estimate	CFDT High estimate	CFDT Low estimate	CGC High estimate	CGC Low estimate
1912	400,000									
1920	2,400,000	1,053,532			150,000					
1935	1,000,000									
1936	5,000,000	1,000,000			500,000	230,000				
1939	2,854,900									
1948	4,428,022		340,000		563,755				100,000	
1951	3,615,440									
1958-59	1,624,322				600,000	415,000				
1961-62	1,993,120		400,000		700,000	455,000				
1967	2,000,000	1,500,000	600,000	500,000	80,000		711,628	500,000	200,000	
1968	2,301,543		700,000	636,392	100,000	60,000	816,261		250,000	
1975	2,377,551	1,808,388	900,000	700,000	200,000	180,000	1,066,637		300,000	
1982-83	1,721,463	980,090	1,150,000		260,000		958,990		306,000	150,000
1985		989,786	1,108,000						254,640	
1990	1,030,000	515,000	850,000	270,000	120,000	100,000	900,000	335,000	110,000	80,000

Sources: 1912–1983   Bouzonnie, H. (1987) 'L'évolution des effectifs syndicaux depuis 1912: essai d'interprétation', *Revue française des affaires sociales*, 4 (octobre - décembre), p.60

1985   Bridgford, J. (1990) 'French trade unions: crisis in the 1980's, *Industrial Relations Journal*, 21:2 (Summer), p. 128

1990   Cours-Salies, P. (1990) 'Syndicats: état des lieux', *L'Homme et la société*, 98:4, p.41
     Gibier, H. (1990) 'Des syndicats en réanimation', *Le Nouvel Economiste*, 755 (20 juillet), p. 32

regard, French trade unions are not alone. Union membership was in decline in most developed countries over the period. What aggravates the scale of decline is that French union membership has traditionally been lower than in neighbouring countries. When Bamber and Lansbury (1987, p. 257) calculated density of union membership (the relationship between actual and potential union membership) in a range of developed countries, France consistently had the lowest density. Further, between 1955 to 1984, density of union membership in France fell from 23 per cent to 18 per cent, while in the UK, Germany, Italy and Australia density ran at roughly twice the French level for any particular year. An OECD study for 1988 showed that France continued to have the lowest density – but the figure had dropped to 12 per cent against an average of 28 per cent in other OECD countries, with Scandinavian countries at over 70 per cent (Noblecourt, 1991). Although low levels of membership have been the norm over the century, the current membership crisis is of exceptional gravity.

The distribution of membership between the different unions calls for commentary. The CGT has suffered the largest haemorrhage; its membership being divided by a factor of four since 1948 and by two since the mid-1970s. It is tempting to explain this decline in terms of the political extremism of the CGT. Yet in reality, the so-called 'revolutionary' unions have had the largest membership. The CGT has consistently been the largest of all, the CFDT usually the second largest. The reformist union, FO, was unable to develop strong growth until the late 1960s. Further, after the 'old' Christian CFTC split into a radical CFDT and a reformist 'new' CFTC, it was the CFDT that rapidly developed a mass following. The CFDT had outstripped both the CFTC and FO by the 1970s. An interim conclusion might be that radicalism brought in relatively more members than reformism, though in absolute terms member-ship levels have usually been low. The French trade union movement has been all the weaker for this.

That weakness raises two major questions. Firstly, why has France consistently had the lowest levels of unionisation in developed countries? Secondly, why have even those levels fallen drastically? Replies to the first question will focus on structures; replies to the second on patterns of social and economic change.

Turning to the first question, a cross-national survey of differences in trade unionism cannot be attempted here. Rather stress will be placed on features endemic to the French situation. These include: the prohibition of closed shops in France (though some exist, in printing for example), the lack of specific benefits and services provided by unions to members, employer hostility to unions, a paternalist management style that preferred direct contacts with the workforce to mediated contact and the consequently late legalisation of plant-level union sections (Goetschy and Rojot, 1987; Amadieu, 1990).

Added to these factors is the deep-seated rivalry among French unions that is the result of their history and their ideology. Quarrels between factions have been common within the *centrales syndicales* (Reynaud, 1975). French unions have expended considerable energy attacking each other's 'errors' while devoting less attention to their common cause. Differentiation between unions has not occurred on the basis of specialisation but largely on doctrinal disputes.

Ideological preconceptions led to limited recruitment efforts. Attracting large numbers of 'ordinary' members was considered less important than recruiting and training activists who would foster strikes and political action (Reynaud, 1975). Further, as Sellier (1985, p. 203) noted, there were significant transfers of members from the CGT to the CFDT between 1973 and 1976 and from the CFDT to FO from 1976 to 1982. Apart from the peak years, French unions have generally competed within the same pool of potential members, rather than throwing their nets wider.

In-built rivalry between the unions was magnified by legislation. In a magisterial discussion, Lyon-Caen (1984) showed that the French trade union movement has been extensively shaped by labour legislation. One of those shaping forces has been the sharpening of competition between unions. Not only do unions compete for members but elections for employee representatives pits union against union (a theme to be developed in the next subsection). Union pluralism has been caught in a vicious circle of rivalry among unions, leading to further division.

Yet the underlying aim of the trade union movement was to achieve worker solidarity. The desire to maintain solidarity led to the perverse effect that some workers preferred not to favour one union over another with their membership, since overt affiliation reinforced partisanship. Many workers opted to 'sympathise' and take part in sporadic industrial action, but without taking out membership cards or paying dues. This helps explain how in France weak union membership can be accompanied by wider union support.

The granting of 'representativeness' by law to the five major unions compounded that perverse effect. Unions were considered representative regardless of numbers of members or extent of industrial coverage. This added to the disincentives to join. It also reduced the need for unions to campaign more actively for increased membership. The combined effects of these factors depressed unionisation in France to its lowest levels in Europe.

As regards the issue of a recent rapid decline in membership, a whole range of explanatory factors can be cited. Firstly, rising unemployment, especially after the oil crises, reduced numbers at work and depleted union membership.

Secondly, industrial decline was concentrated in traditional sectors and in the industrial 'heartlands'. Examples include steel in Lorraine and coal in the north of France. In those industries and regions unions had enjoyed their highest levels of support in the private sector. Attrition of membership subsequent to recession was proportionally high.

Thirdly, public sector unionisation has traditionally been higher in France than in the private sector. Though long-protected, public sector employment has been slowly dropping since the mid-1980s (Amadieu, 1990).

Fourthly, as Baglioni (1990) pointed out, increased segmentation of the labour force made the unions' task of defending workers more complex.

Traditional union appeals had been to the 'unity of the working class' but social developments gradually emptied this phrase of meaning. The archetypal worker could no longer be assumed to be the metal worker or the railwayman. Unions found it difficult to identify the outlook and needs of new categories of employees. Selecting appropriate modes of collective action became problematic. In any case, economic instability since the 1970s has pushed individuals into protecting their livelihood rather than fighting for change.

Fifthly, unions were not recruiting sufficiently in high-growth occupations, for example, insurance and banking. They were underrepresented in expanding social groups, such as the young and immigrants. Their appeal to women, of whom increasing numbers were going out to work, was limited (Jenson, 1984).

Practical difficulties explain most of these shortcomings. It is easier to recruit new employees in industries and firms where unions are already present. Recruitment in firms to which a union is new is a costly and slow process.

Further, employment in the small firm sector has increased. In 1978, 45 per cent of salaried employees worked in firms with fewer than 50 staff; by 1988 that percentage had increased to 52 per cent (Ministère de l'Industrie, 1990). The increase put unions at a disadvantage. Traditionally, small firm employees have been reluctant and difficult to unionise. One out of every two new small firms disappears within four years. By definition, numbers of potential recruits in small firms are low (Amadieu, 1990; Warcholak, 1991).

Sixthly, the French labour movement saw itself as an opposition force seeking radical reform of the economic and political system. Its opposition stance was relatively convincing against right-wing governments in affluent times. But the strong suits of the labour movement were neutralised by economic recession in the 1970s and by the presence of left-wing governments in France since 1981. Rather than just being an opposition movement, unions were called upon to produce constructive policies. This undermined their traditional ethos and led to a loss of direction.

Finally, the unions did not gain substantial advantage from government support or legislative measures under Socialist governments. Since 1981, the decline in unionisation has been more rapid in France than in most of her neighbours. This was despite the tacit acceptance by unions of government policies. At its inception, industrial relations legislation, notably the *lois Auroux*, seemed to favour the unions. However, over the decade, it appears that union influence in collective bargaining has declined (see p.204).

Considered solely in terms of membership, the position of unions in France is currently bleak. However, the French case is distinctive in that definitive conclusions on union strength are not possible on membership trends alone. Membership is but one measure of union influence as the following subsection will illustrate.

Union influence

The overall impact of trade union activities on industrial relations goes beyond total membership levels for three reasons.

Firstly, individual unions having a high concentration of members in particular firms or sectors can have substantial influence on employers within them.

Secondly, the French case reveals a series of institutions within which the unions can hold influential positions. These include the three institutions discussed earlier in this chapter, namely the *conseils de Prud'hommes*, the *délégués du personnel,* and the *comités d'entreprise.* Representatives are nominated by elections and unions compete for votes. Voting is not limited to union members but all employees, hence this larger electorate is referred to as the 'audience' of the labour movement. Their popularity (or unpopularity) with wider sections of French society is an important measure of their influence.

Thirdly, the nature and value of the relationship between the French trade union movement and the State is not dependent, at least in the short term, on overall membership figures. Unions are represented on certain official bodies by right.

The first point relating to union practices will be discussed in later paragraphs while these paragraphs will concentrate on the audience of the unions and on key relationships with the State.

Aujard and Volkoff (1986) argued that elections for the *conseils de Prud'hommes* are the most reliable indicator of the wider audience enjoyed by unions. All employees in the industrial and commercial sectors (some 13.6 million people in 1982) are eligible to vote. This category of employees is well placed to judge the ability of the unions to deliver technical services. However, only unions can field candidates, which limits the contest. As the *conseils de Prud'hommes* were reformed in 1979, only the results of the most recent elections are contained in Table 6.2.

Table 6.2 Results of elections for the *conseils de Prud'hommes* (1979-1987)
(% of votes cast)

	CGT	CFDT	FO	CFTC	CGC	Others
1979	42.3	23.2	17.3	7.2	5.2	4.8
1982	37.0	23.5	17.7	8.5	9.6	3.7
1987	36.5	23.0	20.4	8.3	7.4	4.4

Sources: Aujard, J.-P., and Volkoff, S. (1986) 'Une analyse chiffrée des audiences syndicales', *Travail et emploi,* 30 (décembre), p.48

Cours-Salies, P. (1990) 'Syndicats: état des lieux', *L'Homme et la société,* 98:4, p.42

Results of these elections closely correlated to the trends in union membership outlined above. The CGT, the CFDT, FO come first, second and third in order of popularity. The CGT has gradually lost part of its 'audience'. The FO and the smaller unions seem to have consolidated theirs. However, abstention rates were high: 26.8 per cent in 1979 and 54 per cent in 1987 (Bouzonnie, 1989, p. 158).

Elections for *comités d'entreprise* (CEs) reveal a similar distribution of votes between unions. Selected results from the past 40 years are presented in Table 6.3. A caveat on reliability of findings must apply to early data but after 1966 statistics were gathered systematically by the French Labour Ministry and can be considered accurate. Further, given the numbers of voters – some five million in the 1980s – the results are of considerable interest.

Table 6.3 Results of elections for *comités d'entreprise*: 1949-1989 (% of votes cast)

Year	CGT	CFDT	FO	CFTC	CGC	Other unions	Non- union lists
1949	59.5	—	12.0	12.9	2.7	2.0	10.9
1958	53.0	—	10.7	15.6	4.1	3.1	13.5
1966	50.8	19.1	8.0	2.4	4.2	3.5	12.0
1970	46.0	19.6	7.3	2.7	5.5	7.0	11.9
1975	38.1	19.4	8.4	2.6	5.7	6.1	19.0
1980	36.5	21.3	11.0	2.9	6.0	5.0	16.8
1984	29.3	21.0	13.9	3.8	7.1	4.8	19.7
1989	25.1	21.0	11.2	4.6	5.5	6.3	26.4

Sources: 1949-1966: Bouzonnie, H. (1989) 'L'audience des syndicats depuis les années cinquante', *Revue française des affaires sociales*, 3 (juillet-septembre), p.154

1970-1980: Aujard, J.-P., and Volkoff, S. (1986) 'Une analyse chiffrée des audiences syndicales', *Travail et emploi*, 30 (décembre), p.49

1980-1989: INSEE (1990) *Annuare statistique de la France*, Paris: INSEE, p.128

In terms of seats on *comités d'entreprise*, the CGT was in decline from as early as the 1950s, when it also registered a fall in members. Support for the CFDT has been surprisingly stable. The FO appears to have marked time for 30 years before making small gains. The largest gains have been made by non-unionists who, for the first time in 1989, drew a larger poll than the CGT which had consistently gained most seats in the past. The gains of non-unionists have apparently been made at the expense of the unions.

However, these readings need to be qualified. The decline in the CGT's audience is related both to lower levels of popularity among potential sympathisers and to an attrition of its strongholds in traditional industries where employment losses have been high. The position of the FO is somewhat different. The FO's major suit was the public sector. Results of voting in CEs, an institution existing largely in the private sector, do not give a faithful reflection of FO's 'audience'.

Two explanations exist for the rise in the numbers of non-unionists on CEs. Firstly, it probably indicates some decline in the popularity of the unions.

Secondly, employment in small firms has increased while it has decreased in large firms. Unions are better represented in large firms and are often absent from, or poorly organised in, small- and medium-sized ones. In consequence, they field few or no representatives in the latter and independent candidates win uncontested seats. As a change in firm demography has been an important factor in the increasing numbers of CE seats won by independents, the correlated decline in union representation cannot be read *solely* in terms of a loss of popularity.

The third elected institution is the *délégués du personnel*. Data on election results have not been systematically collected. However, Table 6.4 shows results of a survey for a single year, 1985.

Table 6.4 Results of the 1985 survey on elections for *délégués du personnel* (% of votes cast)

CGT	CFDT	FO	CFTC	CGC	Other unions	Non-union lists
24.8	15.5	10.1	2.5	5.1	3.4	38.5

Source: Aujard, J.-P., and Volkoff, S. (1986) 'Une analyse chiffrée des audiences syndicales', *Travail et emploi,* 30 (décembre), p. 54

As elections for *délégués du personnel* are held in firms with ten or more employees, the proportion of voters working in very small firms is automatically higher than in CE elections which are held in firms with 50 or more employees. The higher proportion of votes to independents reflects the union weaknesses in small firms indicated in the commentary on CE elections. Otherwise, the distribution of votes to the unions is similar to CE elections, confirming employee preferences across different modes of representation.

Yet, commentaries on in-company elections which stress transfers of allegiance *between* unions distract attention from the key issues. One is the effectiveness of the institutions for employer representation themselves. The other is that the trade union movement has largely maintained its 'audience' in all types of election. When given the opportunity, large sections of the French workforce and French society *do* vote for unions and union representatives. Taken together the unions easily poll a large majority over non-unionists in all elections referred to and derive a massive mandate from them. By inference, literally millions of French people see trade unions as providing a useful channel for their views. Taken as a whole, the French trade union movement exercises considerable influence.

The danger for French unions has been that competition in workplace elections, along with their own ideological bent, has encouraged them to act like political parties. As such, they have often been more concerned with competing for votes than for members.

Workplace elections have widened union influence. But they have also weakened the labour movement by institutionalising its divisions and reinforcing the illusion of catering to a captive audience of employees. Thus, unlike genuine political parties, French trade unions have rarely been concerned with generating broad appeal, with recognising and satisfying the aspirations of potential recruits and with increasing the range of specialised services on offer. The low rates of unionisation bear witness to the consequences of these shortcomings. As Bridgford (1990) indicated, the change from 'member-base unionism' to 'representative unionism' raises difficulties for trade unions in terms of their finances and ability to mobilise.

But French unions have a further card to play which is the support they draw from the State. Unions play a role in a number of national level institutions. These include the *caisses primaires d'assurance maladie* (steering committees of the French health insurance scheme), the *Conseil économique et social* which gives its views on draft legislation on economic and social issues, the *Commission supérieure de la négociation* (Higher Collective Bargaining Council) and the *Comité supérieur de l'emploi* (Higher Committee for Employment). Trade union representatives are elected to the *caisses primaires* but are nominated by government to the latter bodies. Trade unions are also involved in similar bodies at local and regional levels, so extending the sphere of influence of the trade union movement.

Keeler (1981, p. 185) referred to this type of influence as 'biased influence', which he defined as 'structured access to decision-making centres of the State and/or devolved authority for the administration of public policy'. In return for their 'services', the State gives various forms of subsidies to the unions (Bazex, 1973, pp. 145-51; Perrignon, 1985). Financial support together with 'biased influence' help overcome the problems of low membership and low receipts from union dues.

In conclusion, the relationships between membership, audience and influence are considerably more complex than appear at first sight. The French trade union movement *is* facing another membership crisis, its largest this century. It cannot go on indefinitely losing members without disappearing altogether. The scale of the French trade union movement has declined but, in the short term, a drop in membership has not led to a proportional drop in influence. Due to 'representative unionism' and 'biased influence', French unions have retained an important, though much diminished role. Accordingly, the next section looks at the place of the unions in specific industrial relations practices.

INDUSTRIAL RELATIONS PRACTICES

Three major types of industrial relations practices will be discussed below. They are employee participation, negotiation through collective bargaining and union coercion, especially by strikes.

Employee participation

In principle, employee participation can take a variety of forms. Participation methods range from share ownership and profit-sharing schemes to genuine involvement in decision making.

In France, a number of employee participation schemes have been tried out to improve industrial relations. However, the results have been limited. There has been a lack of real enthusiasm both from employers and unions. Employers have tended to stress their authority and right to manage, ruling out schemes involving shared decision making. Unions, particularly FO, have been suspicious of sharing responsibilities between management and employees. This has reduced the scope for the development of participation schemes, with the impetus often coming from the State.

The major channels for participation are in fact the institutions for employee representation discussed earlier in this chapter, namely the *comités d'entreprise* and *délégués du personnel*. 'Co-determination' or employee participation in decision making hardly ever occurs in France. In consequence, discussion will mainly be limited here to modes of financial participation.

Various formulae for allowing employees to share in company success have been put into practice. In 1967, legislation made the creation of a 'participation reserve' compulsory for companies having more than 100 employees and making a profit. The calculation of the size of the reserve is based on after-tax profits. The reserve can be used for a variety of purposes including share issues to employees or debentures in investment funds. In fact, as Nousbaum (1985, p. 55) indicated, issues of company shares to employees is the least common practice. In the mid-1980s, three to four million workers benefited from such schemes. Financial benefits amounted on average to less than 3 per cent of wages.

In 1980, an Act was passed to encourage greater distribution of shares to employees. As a result, some 600,000 employees held shares by 1983 (Delamotte, 1984). By the end of the 1980s, profit-sharing schemes were gaining popularity, with increasing numbers of small firms participating (Roche, 1990). This was facilitated by the 1986 decree on profit sharing, which simplified the system and gave enhanced tax incentives. Employers have been keen to use profit sharing as a way of increasing motivation and productivity, avoiding increases in social security payments and tying employee remuneration to company performance (Milner, 1990).

Higher level schemes, such as employee representation on boards of directors, have been very rare. In a small number of private companies, representatives of the works council have a consultative status on boards of directors. They are entitled to receive the same documents as directors but do not participate in decision making.

Legislation of 26 July 1983, introduced a more thorough scheme in nationalised companies. The law provided for employee representation on boards of directors and on supervisory boards in all nationalised companies and in subsidiaries having more than 200 employees. Public sector firms are a special case. The shareholder, the State (under mainly Socialist governments in the 1980s), has been more favourable to unions than in many private firms. Further, unions have been largely positive to co-determination in nationalised firms, since the ties with private capital have been cut.

Though the principles were ambitious, the practice has led to few substantive changes in decision making. Employee representatives have the same rights but do not have the same responsibilities as other board members. As Cattenat (1990), an employee director (*administrateur salarié*) in Rhône-Poulenc has indicated, the board of directors (*conseil d'administration*) serves to transmit information, it allows for some employee influence to be exercised, but in France it is not the place where major decisions are taken.

In brief, participation schemes in France have an incomplete character, particularly in comparison to co-determination systems between employers and unions in Germany.

Collective bargaining

In principle, collective bargaining covers any kind of agreements reached by negotiation between employers and employees. In France, the practice of collective bargaining has been less developed than in the UK. It has tended to involve tripartite negotiations between State, employers and unions. This is because the State has intervened to counterbalance the long-standing aversion of French employers to unions and to collective bargaining.

The beginnings of collective bargaining can be traced back to 1935, though pre-war instances of it were fairly rare. Collective bargaining began in earnest after the 1950 Act called for industry agreements at national, regional and local levels, that is to say *above* plant or enterprise level.

As Saglio (1991) emphasised, for the following thirty or so years, French collective bargaining was characterised by agreements at sector level, principally on wages and conditions. The results of collective bargaining at sector level were binding on all firms and employees, regardless of whether they were or were not members of the employers' federations or employee unions that participated in the negotiations.

These collective agreements set minimum levels and standards, which can only be improved at plant level. This system involves a legal pyramid of texts. At the base is the *Code du Travail* (Labour Code). At the next tier come the *conventions collectives* (collective agreements). *Conventions collectives* fall into lower-level industry-wide agreements and higher-level, company-specific agreements. Finally, at the top of the pyramid are individual contracts of employment. Legally speaking, no higher-level agreement or contract should compromise a lower-level text.

Although better rewards could be granted at plant or company level than were stipulated at sector level, there were disincentives to doing so. Individual firm agreements could be used by employees and unions in subsequent sector level discussions as leverage to gain an improved industry-wide agreement. For example, the 1955 agreement within Renault for a third week of paid holidays set wider precedents.

Further, once local advantages were incorporated into national or sectoral minima, they could no longer serve to attract or hold on to employees. This probably militated against giving them in the first place. Thus in a period of labour shortage, such as the 1950s, the value to employees of industry-wide agreements which ignored local circumstances can be doubted. Certainly, as will be seen in the next sub-section, strikes were frequent in the post-war years. These expressions of discontent raise questions about the effectiveness of collective bargaining.

To improve effectiveness, the State took a leading role in pushing collective bargaining forward. Tripartite negotiations played an important role in the development of institutions and systems that transcend particular sectors. These included the 1958 agreement on unemployment insurance, the 1968 agreement on *chômage partiel* ('partial unemployment') and the 1970 agreement on employment security. Subsequently, centralised tripartite bargaining figured less prominently but has nonetheless continued as in the 1982-4 partial agreement on the unemployment insurance system (UNIDIC). In addition, government macro-economic policy has an impact upon real salary levels. France has a minimum legal wage (the *SMIC*) whose level is set by the government in line with inflation and with its own analysis of need. As Saglio (1991) has pointed out, in sectors such as the cleaning industry, sector level negotiations have been extremely limited and salaries are largely set by the *SMIC*.

Patterns of collective bargaining also have sector-specific explanations. In a cross-sectoral comparison for the 1950-80 period, Lozier (1990) argued that the major determinants of the development of collective bargaining were the relative strengths of employers' federations and of employee unions. She illustrated the argument with a three-part typology. Firstly, in the steel and petrochemical industries, strong employers' federations succeeded in imposing their policy on divided unions. The level of co-operation between employers was extremely high and decision making was based on unanimity. Corporatism seems to have played its part here. Once an industry level agreement was concluded, renegotiation at another level was ruled out. Employers maintained a monopoly on the content of collective bargaining. Secondly, in the glass and cement industries, both employers and employees were well organised. They were also evenly matched, with the CGT being the dominant union on the employees' side. Agreements at both sector and company levels were common. In these industries, improved pay and conditions frequently started from company level agreements and worked upward and outward to sector level. A third case was constituted by sectors where employers were poorly organised, as in the construction and machine-tool industries. Fewer industry-wide agreements could therefore be signed, leaving more room for company negotiations. In addition, because of the lack of employer unity, company level agreements did not regularly translate into higher-level agreements at a later date. Far from forming a constraining monolith, French collective bargaining has formed a variegated system, involving numerous modes of adaptation at industry and plant levels by both employers and unions but also creating unevenness.

Developments in the 1970s and 1980s reinforced the dual nature of the French collective bargaining system (i.e. at both sector and company levels). Legislative amendments in 1971 extended the scope for plant level bargaining and for multi-industry discussions. The 1982 *lois Auroux*, which replaced the 1950 legislation, called for two-tier negotiations and imposed an obligation to negotiate yearly at company and sector levels.

The legislator's motivation for these changes has largely been the need to promote negotiation among a wider range of firms and across a wider number of employees. Given the gaps in sector level negotiations, many employees had not been covered by collective bargaining agreements. The employers' reaction has been to stress their freedom to manage and the need for 'flexibility' (see also pp. 214-15).

More negotiated agreements have been struck subsequent to the 1982 reforms, but the balance between industry-wide agreements and in-company solutions has been changing. The key point is that the importance of company level agreements has progressively increased while that of industry-level agreements has decreased. In 1982, 1,370 industry-wide agreements were signed (Segrestin, 1990a, p. 112) but the yearly number of agreements declined in subsequent years, falling to 840 in 1989 (Ministère du Travail, 1990). Conversely, in-firm agreements rose from 900 in 1983 to around 2,300 in 1989 (Fournier, 1990). By 1989, company agreements covered some 2,529,000 employees (Roche, 1990). Some 70 per cent of firms who were required to negotiate did so, involving some 80 per cent of the employees that the *lois Auroux* covered (*L'Entreprise*, 1988). There are then grounds for concluding that the contractual basis of French industrial relations has been strengthened.

On a negative note, the manner of reaching agreements and the contents of those agreements have their limitations. Faced with *centrales syndicales* whose authority has been undermined, employers have increasingly preferred to negotiate locally, with union representatives where they exist, or by going above the heads of union representatives and dealing directly with employees. Management has consequently found it easier to push through its policies on issues such as redundancies or changes in working conditions.

Most agreements relate to salaries. Agreements on wider issues, such as work organisation, hours worked, or new technology, have fallen substantially in number ((Ministère du Travail, 1990). Other criticisms against the trend toward company settlements include the danger of increased disparities in pay and conditions between large and small firms. Also, the absence of a need to agree at company level may transfer to national or sector level, blocking the whole collective bargaining process.

A frequent complaint relates to the individualisation of pay and conditions. There is a strong case for firms giving rewards commensurate to their ability to pay and some individuals do benefit from tailored bonus schemes. But the fear is that the pendulum has swung too far. In negotiations between employer and employees, the employee can be at a disadvantage, particularly where union representation is low or non-existent. As an antidote, unions have been seeking to revitalise industry-wide agreements by direct appeal to the French President (*Force ouvrière magazine*, 1991).

Decentralisation of bargaining to plant level led to increased difficulties for unions. A common interpretation is that unions have been weakened by Auroux's 1982 reforms. For example, Savatier (1989) contends that unions have been undermined by the employee's right to direct expression and by the fact that minority union agreements are enough for agreements, even at national levels – a collective agreement is valid even if a single union signs it. Both the need for unions and the influence of unions are reduced by these two factors.

However, the right of expression is not, in itself, an instrument for negotiation. As regards minority agreements, the consequences of the divisions between unions have to be brought into the equation. Some employers are faced with several unions. Given the divisions within the French trade union movement, collective bargaining could never be successful if agreements between unions were a prerequisite. Finally, allowing 'minority' agreements leaves more room for manoeuvre for the unions themselves.

In summary, collective bargaining in France developed unevenly in the post-war period but has gradually acquired importance. Its development has largely been driven by legislation. But industrial relations in the 1980s involved a measure of deregulation. More employees are covered by collective bargaining than in the past, but in the private sector their ability to negotiate improvements in pay and conditions has come to depend more on macro-economic developments and personal skills and less on trade union intervention.

Strikes

Traditionally, the strike was the major weapon in the union arsenal to gain economic or political advantage. The post-war period saw a rise and subsequent decline in its usage.

During the wartime totalitarian Vichy regime, strikes and unions had been banned. With the return to democracy, the right to strike was affirmed within the constitution of the Fourth Republic and maintained since as a fundamental human right. Five days' notice of strike action is required in the public sector, but in the private sector, the legal framework is more supple. Strikes can legally be launched without notification by any group of workers, whether unionised or not. In practice, approval from a union tends to follow the launching of 'spontaneous' strikes. However, because a strike is legally defined as a work stoppage, 'go-slows', 'work to rule' and secondary action are unlawful, as are sit-ins and lockouts.

Because of this 'spontaneous' element and because of the inadequacy of union strike funds, strikes in France have traditionally been short. One-day national stoppages, accompanied by large demonstrations, have been a frequent union tactic, particularly on the part of the CGT. Goetschy and Martin (1981) pointed out that the union strategy was typically to attract public support, rather than put economic pressure on employers.

These features mean that France has had one of the lowest levels of strike action in developed countries. Bamber and Lansbury (1987) used the criterion of numbers of working days lost per 1,000 employees to produce a cross-national comparison for the years 1974 to 1983. This showed that although Germany, Japan and Sweden were the most strike-free countries over the period, days lost in France were a third of those lost in the UK and a sixth of those lost in Italy. This tends to confirm that the ideology of French unions is often more militant than the actions of the workforce. On the other hand, it should be emphasised that industrial conflicts can take many forms other than strikes. Usually, a strike only occurs after an escalating series of measures – such as official and unofficial meetings, verbal confrontations, flouting of company rules and deliberate obstruction – have failed (Morel, 1981).

Table 6.5 gives details of days lost in France through strike action. The first observation that arises is that the 1950s were a time of considerable industrial conflict. Economic prosperity certainly increased (see pp. 2-3) but trickled through society slowly. In the interim, social conflicts ran high.

The 1960s saw a relative decline in strike intensity – until the 1968 outburst. High levels of conflicts continued in the mid-1970s as workers tried to protect their purchasing power against erosion by high inflation and retain their jobs in a climate of closures. A number of long strikes were caused by announcements of redundancies, for example in the steel industry in 1979 (Sellier, 1985).

In the early 1980s, economic problems were increasing while union membership was decreasing. In consequence, strikes fell in frequency and length, hitting new, low records. The CGT remained the most militant, being responsible for three-quarters of days lost in the early 1980s (Kergoat, 1986). Strikes rarely occurred in the private sector and tended to be defensive, last-ditch attempts to avoid closures or massive redundancies.

Strikes have been more frequent in the public sector where jobs are more 'protected'. The Chirac government faced major strikes by railwaymen and by electricity workers in the winter of 1986-7. In October 1988, under the Rocard government, nurses and the police organised demonstrations for better pay and conditions. In October 1991, there was renewed unrest and strikes in the public sector. Yet these have been the exceptions, rather than the rule. Yet if were there a resurgence of strike action in industry, the effects would be dramatic, given the popularity of the 'Just-in-Time' approach to inventory management.

Table 6.5 Numbers of days lost in France through
strike action: 1950-1989 (in thousands)

Year	Days
1950	11,710
1951	3,294
1952	1,732
1953	9,722
1954	1,440
1955	3,078
1956	1,422
1957	4,121
1958	1,137
1959	1,938
1960	1,070
1961	2,600
1962	1,901
1963	5,991
1964	2,496
1965	979
1966	2,523
1967	4,203
1968	150,000 approx
1969	2,223
1970	1,742
1971	4,387
1972	3,755
1973	3,914
1974	3,380
1975	3,868
1976	5,010
1977	3,665
1978	2,195
1979	3,636
1980	1,674
1981	1,169
1982	2,327
1985	727
1986	1,042
1987	500
1988	1,242
1989	904

Sources: Bernoux, P. (1981) 'Dossier: relations professionelles', *Economie et humanisme*, 259 (mai-juin), p. 18

Ministère des Affaires sociales published in Mermet, G. (1989, 1990) *Francoscopie*, Paris: Larousse

Overall, the massive fall in levels of strike action provides clear illustration of the significant change in the climate of industrial relations.

PROCESSES OF CHANGE IN FRENCH INDUSTRIAL RELATIONS

This section will review the processes of change in French industrial relations in the post-war period. It aims to analyse underlying trends and to make sense of the broader issues they reveal.

In the aftermath of the Second World War, the major development, as Segrestin (1990b) pointed out, was the 'rehabilitation' not of private sector firms, but of the trade union movement. The *patronat* had collaborated with the German Occupation under the Vichy regime whereas the unions had organised themselves in a common resistance front, the *Conseil national de la résistance*. After the war, unions were rewarded with enhanced status and membership swelled.

Barring a temporary experiment with 'co-operation' within the structures of *comités d'entreprise*, the French model for management-unions relations was based on negotiation, veering to conflict. The model grew from at least three different influences. The most immediate was the enforced corporatism of the Vichy period. Theoretically, Vichy corporatism brought workers and management into joint decision-making structures. In reality, worker organisation had little meaning – independent unions were banned. Additionally, in the wartime command economy, orders came from the top (see also pp. 126-7). The second influence was the long-standing ideology of the French trade union movement with its emphasis on class struggle. The third influence was the equally long-standing aversion, in some cases hostility, of French employers to unions. These three influences structured French industrial relations throughout most of the post-war period and made co-management unfeasible. However, each of them has gradually dwindled in strength and relevance. This section will show how and why the old model has lost its validity but will stress the current difficulty of constructing a new model.

Turbulence in the 1940s and 1950s

After the initial euphoria of the Liberation, harsh economic realities intruded. Production was low, goods scarce, inflation high. Purchasing power could not keep up. Worker discontent translated into major and violent strikes in 1947. Politicisation of unionism grew as the Cold War developed, leading to *Force ouvrière* breaking away from the CGT in protest at the latter's Communist, pro-Moscow leanings. In response to the need to develop a more consensual style of industrial relations, legislation in 1950 put collective bargaining on a firmer footing.

The 1950s were a confused period in which the threads of increasing negotiation, falling union membership and a high level of industrial disputes crossed and tangled. High inflation repeatedly lay close to the roots of discontent. In order to reduce inflation, economic policy utilised price and wages restraint. But the latter, along with working conditions, were perceived by workers as unjust, leading to high levels of strike action in the 1950s (see Table 6.5 on p. 206).

It is worth stressing the gap between perceptions at the time and those of more recent commentators. At the time, the working population had a close-up view of their long hours of toil – but no perspective on the long series of high annual growth rates which economists have since emphasised (see pp. 2-3). The cliché of *les trente glorieuses* (Fourastié, 1979) has stuck, but it bathes the turbulence of the period in a rosy and misleading nostalgia. The problem was one of lags and leads; improvements in living conditions trailed behind macro-economic expansion.

The calm and the storm of the 1960s

The industrial climate seemed to change at the start of the 1960s. As Parodi (1981) pointed out, the inauguration of the Fifth Republic and the Algerian War of Independence brought about a lull in industrial conflict.

The truce was temporary. In 1963, a major miner's strike enjoyed considerable popular support. In 1964, most of the old CFTC reformed into the CFDT and rapidly migrated towards the Left. In 1966, the new CFDT and the CGT agreed on a pact of common action. Yet these elements of continued 'class struggle' pale into insignificance compared to the events of 1968.

Because the May 1968 demonstrations and strikes have caused perhaps more ink to flow than any other single development in France this century, the present summary is deliberately brief. The scale and violence of the student and worker demonstrations caught government, political parties, employers and unions equally by surprise. Indeed, the conservatism with which the French Communist party and the CGT initially greeted the demonstrations made their 'revolutionary' rhetoric seem hollow. The agitation subsided as suddenly as it had begun. Yet as regards industrial relations, the demonstrations cannot be dismissed as a Parisian *soufflé*, lacking relevance for the rest of France.

After temporary panic at the highest levels of government, the tripartite agreement of 26 and 27 May (the *accords de Grenelle*) conceded major gains to the workforce. The minimum wage was increased by 35 per cent, general salaries were upped by 10 per cent as of October 1968, with no docking of pay for days lost on strike. Among other significant concessions was the legalising of workplace union organisations *(sections syndicales)*. This was a major turn-around. The interminable exclusion of unions from French firms was belatedly ended.

Yet these apparently positive outcomes for the workforce included elements of ambiguity. At face value, May 1968 seemed to confirm the model of French industrial relations outlined above. Workers and managers had remained true to typecasting. Worker aggression had extracted greater advantage from employers than years of negotiation.

Yet the May events placed a question mark over the role of the unions and the value of union membership. The unions had not initiated the demonstrations. They had experienced difficulties in clarifying their own reactions, let alone in channelling the discontent. Perhaps it is not surprising that 1968 did not lead to as large an increase in members as in 1936 or 1945 (see Table 6.1 on p. 192). Further, the hostility of sections of the *patronat* towards accepting unions within firms had not been overcome; employers had simply been forced to accept the change.

Economic crisis and labour gains during the 1970s

With the benefit of hindsight, it is clear that the old model of industrial relations started to crumble in the 1970s. Industrial relations based on arms-length agreements drawn over thinly veiled mutual hostility did not disappear, but were gradually overtaken by outside developments.

After 1968, the immediate problem for management was to find suitable union interlocutors. The outlook and objectives of management and of trade unions suffered from serious mismatch. The largest trade union, the CGT, with its French Communist Party links, was of an ideological persuasion alien to management. The CGT for long retained the myth of the general strike as the instrument for the overthrow of capitalism. The CFDT had veered further towards the Left at its 1970 conference where it had taken up the theme of *autogestion* (worker's management) and become active in worker take-overs as well as in other forms of industrial unrest. It too made a difficult interlocutor for employers. The remaining unions were smaller and unevenly represented. In large firms, negotiations with several unions having divergent views and objectives further complicated proceedings.

Yet a consistent policy of ignoring or attacking unions was rejected as non-viable by most employers. While taking care to protect their own authority, French employers developed a more supple range of policies towards union relationships. They developed proactive, rather than reactive, industrial relations strategies. They innovated in terms of work organisation and in levels of rewards (Rojot, 1986). Further, technological change, the 'micro-processor revolution' was to play a major role in changing job content and work organisation (Groux, 1984).

Improving work organisation was seen as a way of curing the causes, rather than the symptoms, of industrial unrest. This involved reducing the counterproductive aspects of 'Taylorism'. By 'Taylorism' is understood the piecemeal division of industrial work into tiny, highly specialised tasks. An assembly line where the role of each worker is limited to one operation is the traditional example of 'Taylorism' in practice. The definition of tasks is reserved to management representatives. Because the worker had no real part in defining methods and work speed, unions opposed 'Taylorism'. They contended that 'Taylorist' practice added to worker subservience. 'Taylorism' had stored up problems for management too. It speeds output, increases efficiency and boosts productivity but also correlates to low worker satisfaction, low motivation, high absenteeism and high staff turnover.

The way ahead was seen to be job 'enrichment'. Strategies include allocating more tasks – by job rotation or team work. 'Enrichment' involves developing higher skill levels and allowing greater independence and worker control in the accomplishment of tasks. The process of reforming work organisation continues today, but early changes went some way towards meeting union criticisms regarding unacceptable conditions, excessive work-speeds and alienation at the workplace.

However, as more differentiation appeared in job content and methods, the extent to which traditional worker identity had derived from and been conditioned by 'Taylorist' work modes became apparent. Towards the end of the decade, the relevance of union appeals to a united class front based on traditional worker identity progressively faded. Ironically, as Ruffier (1981) pointed out, the decline in 'Taylorism' eventually contributed to the decline in union membership.

Trends towards job enrichment and the post-May 1968 climate gave the labour movement significant gains in the early 1970s, just as the 'boom years' of post-war expansion were coming to an end. In consequence, once the mid-1970s recession occurred (see pp. 18-31), the enhancement of workers' rights afforded greater protection to individuals. The tendency towards a consultative style of industrial relations, involving bipartite or tripartite discussions proved advantageous to the workforce in the management of the economic crisis. Faced with social tensions and strikes, French governments preferred not to restrict the purchasing power of wages, despite the deterioration in the economic climate. Real wages continued to rise until 1980 (Sellier, 1985). Union strength contributed to this process (Mouriaux, 1981). But union success is less clear as regards unemployment. Union resistance may have *temporarily* slowed the rise in unemployment but unions were often drawn into simply 'managing' lay-offs by negotiating better redundancy deals.

As the recession bit deeper, the gains made by the labour movement were eroded. The effects of this process were felt differentially since economic crisis reinforced trends towards 'dualism' in labour markets. On the one hand, 'protected' workers in stable private companies and in the public sector enjoyed relative job security, decent salaries and conditions. On the other hand, the ranks of workers swelled in 'precarious' work, such as part-time, temporary or unregistered jobs. Young workers, women and immigrants found conditions particularly hard. They were often faced with the Hobson's choice of 'precarious' employment or none at all.

In this context, union membership spiralled downwards (for discussion see pp. 191-5) and union strategies modified. Levels of strike action fell (see Table 6.5 on p. 206). With the crisis years, unions entered a period of new realism, gradually abandoning ideological conflict and searching for practical solutions. The CFDT's emphasis on *recentrage*, on industrial solutions rather than on political leverage, provides one illustration.

By the start of the decade of the 1980s, the foundations of the French industrial relations model were subsiding. Employer hostility to unions had waned after three decades of collective bargaining and the more recent reduction in union militancy. Few unionists were still impressed by notions of class struggle and the strike as an instrument of economic and political change. Economic crisis and the sharpening of international competition had revealed that French firms were extremely vulnerable. The old diatribes against profiteering capitalists meant little when major firms were making losses or even folding (see pp. 59-62). Unions became more aware of the need for productivity and the costs of strike action on jobs. These factors pushed both sides together, reducing to some extent the conflict that had characterised industrial relations.

The surprises of the 1980s

The Socialist victory in the 1981 elections showed that hopes were still high of solving economic problems by political means. The new government, containing mainly Socialist, but some Communist ministers, offered rewards to its supporters in the labour movement by reducing the working week to 39 hours, giving a fifth week of paid holidays and reducing the retirement age to 60.

Hopes of a *dolce vita* quickly faded. The 1981 dash for growth failed and led directly to a period of austerity (see pp. 26-30). Prices and wages were frozen in 1982, with the 1950 law on free collective bargaining being suspended. Index-linking of wages was ended. Though there was some resistance to the latter measure, no widespread campaign was mounted against it (Goetschy, 1987, p. 184). As Sellier (1985, p. 182) indicated, this was the first time it had proved possible to adjust the purchasing power of wages to the higher costs imposed by the surges in oil prices. In their survey of French firms, Glais, Hardouin and Jolivet (1987, p. 173) found that the government wage freeze subsequently made it easier to restrain salary increases in the private sector during the mid-1980s. In later years, wage levels were no longer determined by union power achieving the index-linking of wages to inflation but by higher labour productivity and better business performance.

Clearly, the major event in industrial relations in the 1980s was the Auroux legislation. What is less clear is the extent to which the new legislation was a catalyst for change or simply consecrated processes already under way. In relation to the *lois Auroux*, this chapter has already set out the major elements of content, notably the individual's right of self-expression (see pp. 185-7) and the direction of change, namely the decentralisation of negotiations from industry level to firm level (see pp. 203-4). Accordingly, discussion here is limited to the context in which they were situated.

Industrial relations reform had long been called for both by unions and progressives within the administration. The Sudreau report (1975) had recommended a series of reforms including the granting of a greater role to *comités d'entreprise* and to unions as well as the extension of profit-sharing schemes. In 1976, Jacques Chirac proposed '*un véritable droit d'expression du travailleur*' (quoted by Bernoux, 1990, p. 100). The CFDT, in particular, favoured a genuine employee 'right of expression'.

Despite the incorporation within the *lois Auroux* of these features, early reactions were mixed. Of the unions, the CFDT was the most favourable, seeing the new legislation as promoting worker control and reducing employers' power over the workforce. The CGT was less enthusiastic but saw the new laws as a channel for intensifying criticism of management and for reaffirming its grip on the rank and file. The 'reformist' FO was the most hostile. It believed that direct expression would undermine union strength and that in-company negotiations would undermine industry level agreements. The CGC was unfavourable too. It feared that its middle management members would again be squeezed between the aspirations of the rank and file for greater autonomy and the desire of top management to retain authority. Management reactions were hostile. Spokesmen for the CNPF (the peak employers' federation) and the CGPME (the major small firms' federation) expressed worries about further politicisation within firms and the threat to management's authority (*Droit social*, 1984).

As the 1980s unfolded, some views modified, others remained unchanged. Union reactions are perhaps best judged by propensity to sign agreements stemming from the obligation to negotiate. In 1983 and in 1989, the CFDT signed some 49 per cent of agreements, revealing a broadly positive approach. The CFTC showed a similar profile: it signed 40 per cent of agreements in 1983, 39 per cent in 1989. Relevant figures for the FO are 14 per cent and 17.5 per cent, revealing its reticence. In these three cases, there was little change in attitude. The CGC, however, did change its attitude, signing 36 per cent of agreements in 1983, and 49 per cent in 1989. Apparently, the CGC discovered that its members gained from negotiations. On the other hand, the CGT attitude soured somewhat – relevant figures for the base years being 59 per cent and 48 per cent.

The change is even more stark in the case of leading protagonists. In a recent interview (Kocinski and Gless, 1991), Jean Auroux and Yvon Gattaz, ex-president of the CNPF, not only took views diametrically opposed to each other, but each did a U-turn on his position of a decade earlier. In 1982, Auroux had spoken of '*la révolution du bon sens*' – the common sense revolution (*Droit social*, 1984). But in 1991, he regarded his initiatives as having largely failed. He blamed the authoritarian tendencies of management. In his view, the main obstacles to change in industrial relations were the underlying characteristics of French management culture, an area to be developed in Chapter 7. On the other hand, Gattaz has abandoned the early hostility of CNPF positions and has taken a very positive view of the Auroux legislation.

Separating the turn-around in views is a decade of unforeseen change. Fairly quickly, it became clear that no revolution would take place, only incremental reform at best (Segrestin, 1986). Initially, employees were often inhibited or indifferent about expressing views; only gradually did they gain confidence (Le Goff, 1985). Conversely, employers discovered that the *lois Auroux* encouraged innovative personnel policies.

Foremost of these was the introduction of *cercles de qualité*. 'Quality circles' were based on Japanese practice. With Japan's international trade success, they enjoyed considerable prestige. In France, they were seen as a pragmatic implementation of the *droit d'expression* since criticism of work practices was to be accompanied by creative efforts to find solutions (Riley in Crozier, 1985, p. 34). Thus small groups of production workers, led by a manager or supervisor, would meet regularly in order to identify and solve problems stemming from their day-to-day work (Raveleau and Marinier, 1983). 'Quality circles' spread rapidly. By 1985, they involved 150,000 employees in some 2,000 firms (Segrestin, 1990a, p. 105).

'Quality circles', along with various '*groupes d'expression*', each bringing together representatives of workers, managers and other grades of employees, implied a radical change in the way work-activities are organised and accomplished. Their evolution suggests that a new spirit pervades the workplace. The new spirit involves working together towards a common goal, in distinction to a class struggle based on conflicting objectives.

The spread in co-operative practice was bound up with the *découverte de l'entreprise* – a new, strongly positive attitude towards private enterprise and its achievements. The fact that the 'discovery' was made jointly by large numbers of French people and by a left-wing government enhanced the legitimacy of workplace co-operation. Indeed, that 'discovery' was the logical recognition of fundamental changes within companies. Elements of more enlightened personnel policy together with the effects of accelerating technological change had gradually shifted many of the old barriers between groups of employees and modernised industrial relations. With fewer factors to divide former workplace antagonists – employees, unions, employers – it appears that little remains of the old model of French industrial relations.

Toward a new industrial relations model in the 1990s?

What then is the outlook for the future? There have been signs of greater recognition of a concordance of objectives between employers and employees. In time, these tendencies may cohere within a new approach to industrial relations, but it is still premature to speak of a 'new' model. A number of ambiguities and unanswered questions remain to be resolved. These turn around the role of State regulation, the place of the unions, developments in employer practices as well as the extent of popular enthusiasm towards recent industrial relations initiatives.

Changes in labour law have altered the balance between centralised collective bargaining and more 'deregulated' company level negotiations. Segrestin (1990a) argued that though centralised regulation has decreased, it is too early to claim that it has been replaced by a system of 'pluralist' deregulation since the regulatory framework remains strong. However, the direction of change is towards less, not more, regulation and towards more 'pluralism'.

In any event, legislation offers cold comfort to the labour movement. The *lois Auroux* were conceived as favouring the unions but in practice have partly 'short-circuited' them. The renovation of the French trade union movement requires something other than legislation. Increased support is essential for survival. Some encouraging signs exist. Popular views of the unions have changed. In surveys conducted in 1967, 1969 and 1982, numbers of French people considering that unions had too large a role rose steadily from 11 per cent to 24 per cent to 42 per cent (Duhamel and Parodi, 1983). By 1990, it had dropped back to 32 per cent (Boissard, 1990). Unions are no longer seen as a threat but they are in a cleft stick. They suffer from an image problem because for some they still represent aggressive militancy, while others consider that they have made concessions all along the line.

In 1990, a majority of survey respondents (54 per cent) also expressed a lack of confidence in the unions; it seems that unions do not accurately reflect their aspirations (Boissard, 1990). Interestingly, a survey of major employers showed support for *strong* unions, with 54 per cent of respondents considering the extent of union decline to be regrettable and with 97 per cent expressing the need for a responsible 'partner' in industrial relations (Moatti and Bentégeat, 1991). Thus the desire for a new unionism appears to exist.

On the union side, some renovation has occurred. The old distinction between 'revolutionary' and 'reformist' unions no longer holds. The CFDT, the CFTC and the CGC are considerably more progressive than the CGT and FO which have maintained a more traditional stance. Further renovation in terms of mergers between unions has been mooted. This makes sense given the inability, to date, to find a single voice. The CFDT has made overtures to the FO, the CFTC, the CGC and to the FEN, the teachers union (Gibier, 1990). To date, however, no progress has been made toward coalition with any of these. With no visible ground swell for a 'new' unionism, a question mark hangs over the labour movement.

Turning to employer strategies, workplace democracy has consistently been resisted by the *patronat*. However, the *style* of resistance has evolved – from outright opposition to unions, to insistence on the 'right to manage' and more recently, as Milner (1990) has indicated, by stressing the constraints imposed by market forces on in-firm decision taking. Although this latter tactic successfully downplays the discretionary power of managers and owners, it cannot altogether avoid the charge of a return to authoritarian personnel management. The major development in this regard has been so-called 'flexibility', a strategy having three main prongs.

The first is the matching of labour needs to demand fluctuations through redundancies and by recourse to temporary contracts of employment. Temporary contracts rose from around 2.3 million in 1980 to over 6.3 million in 1989 (INSEE, 1990). Redundancies were made easier in 1987 by the Chirac government with the repeal of the need for administrative authorisation for lay-offs. Mital and Rouge (1988) noted that although no major quantitative effects followed the repeal, the qualitative effects were significant. Employers could dangle the threat of redundancy over the workforce as a means of extracting concessions.

The second prong is the increase in sub-contracting, often to ex-company employees who have been obliged to become self-employed or create small firms by their former employer (Sicot, 1990). This reduces the costs and responsibilities of the former employer while increasing personal risks for the ex-employee.

The third prong is the increase in the individualisation of remuneration packages. A recent survey shows that it is precisely the occupational group most affected by the tailoring of salaries, namely *cadres*, who are the most disenchanted (Boissard, 1990). These strategies combine to create a climate of insecurity for employees. The lack of organised opposition to this 'bespoke' approach may give cause to the sceptical interpretation that far from there being a 'new' industrial relations model, the *patronat* has simply 'won the class war'.

Finally, popular enthusiasm for participative practices at the workplace and for elected institutions has been in decline. By the end of the 1980s, fewer employees were voting in work-related elections. Abstention rates in elections for the *conseils de Prud'hommes* were 36 per cent in 1979, 41 per cent in 1982 and 54 per cent in 1987. Abstention rates in elections for *comités d'entreprise* increased gradually from 29 per cent in 1976 to 33.5 per cent in 1989 (Bouzonnie, 1989, p. 158; Cours-Salies, 1990, p. 42). It is difficult to ascertain the causes of this electoral weariness. It may be another indicator of the loss of popularity of the unions. Or it may indicate dissatisfaction with the institutions themselves. Either way, the revival in the 1970s of 'electoral' participation in company affairs seems to have run its course.

At the same time, participative practices such as the *droit d'expression* and quality circles have also lost momentum (Chevalier, 1987; Jacquier, 1987). In practical terms, non-participation can amount to a recognition that power within firms lies with management. This raises the question of whether workforce resignation to employer authority will favour reactionary tendencies (of the 'macho-management' variety) or whether a new balance between hierarchical authority and employee participation can be struck.

CONCLUSIONS

This chapter's review of the four major variables in industrial relations, namely legislative reform, union strength, employer strategies and employee reactions, has shown that the sedimentation of cultural change has been slow but significant.

1945 saw the rehabilitation of unions at a time when firms were debilitated in both ideological and material terms. By around 1985, firms had been rehabilitated while unions were debilitated, again both ideologically and materially. This obviously constitutes a major turn-around.

Changes in their mutual positions have dissipated the violent antagonism between the *partenaires sociaux*. At the start of the 1990s, apparently little remains of the old, conflictual model of industrial relations. This evolution indicates a significant degree of modernisation in French industrial relations.

Paradoxically, though the cumulative weight of evidence suggests that the old model has been eroded, in a variegated landscape it has not proved possible to describe the contours of a new model with any confidence. Yet this is a familiar pattern in French history. From 1789 to 1968, instances abound of France's difficulty in recognising incremental social change and capitalising on its positive components. Sudden outbursts of violence have repeatedly been the force that shapes the 'old' into the 'new'. The decade of the 1990s will reveal whether a significantly new model of French industrial relations emerges by incremental change alone or whether reform occurs through social conflagration.

References

Amadieu, J.-F. (1990) 'Une interprétation de la crise du syndicalisme: les enseignements de la comparaison internationale', *Problèmes économiques*, 2182 (4 juillet), pp. 11-19

Aujard, J.-P. & Volkoff, S. (1986) 'Une analyse chiffrée des audiences syndicales', *Travail et emploi*, 30 (décembre), pp. 47-57

Baglioni, G. (1990) 'Industrial relations in Europe in the 1980s' in Baglioni, G. & Crouch, C. (eds.) *European Industrial Relations. The Challenge of Flexibility*, pp. 1-41, London: Sage

Bamber, G. J. & Lansbury, R. D. (eds.) (1987) *International and Comparative Industrial Relations. A Study of Developed Market Economies*, London: Allen and Unwin

Bazex, M. (1973) *L'Administration et les syndicats*, Paris: Editions Berger-Levrault

Bernoux, P. (1981) 'Dossier: relations professionnelles', *Economie et humanisme*, 259 (mai-juin), pp. 18-19

Bernoux, P. (1990) 'Les changements de la gestion sociale' in Sainsaulieu, R. (ed.) *L'Entreprise: une affaire de société*, pp. 89-116, Paris: Presses de la Fondation Nationale des Sciences Politiques

Boissard, D. (1990) 'Syndicats: la lente dégradation de leur image', *Liasons sociales mensuel*, 54 (décembre), pp. 22-5

Bouzonnie, H. (1987) 'L'évolution des effectifs syndicaux depuis 1912: essai d'interprétation', *Revue française des affaires sociales*, 4 (octobre-décembre), pp. 59-82

Bouzonnie, H. (1989) 'L'audience des syndicats depuis les années cinquante', *Revue française des affaires sociales*, 3 (juillet-septembre), pp. 153-83

Bridgford, J. (1990) 'French trade unions: crisis in the 1980s', *Industrial Relations Journal*, 21: 2 (Summer), pp. 126-35

Cattenat, R. (1990) 'Le rôle des administrateurs salariés', *Cadres CFDT*, 344 (décembre), pp. 30-1

Chevalier, F. (1987) 'Les cercles de qualité à bout de souffle?', *Gérer et comprendre*, 7 (juin), pp. 14-23

Cours-Salies, P. (1990) 'Syndicats: état des lieux', *L'Homme et la société*, 98:4, pp. 35-50

Crozier, M. (1985) *Les nouveaux modes d'organisation*, Paris: Institut de l'Entreprise

Delamotte, Y. (1984) *Le Droit du travail en pratique*, Paris: Editions d'Organisation

Dirn, L. (1991) 'Les instances de représentation du personnel n'assurent plus leur reproduction dans les entreprises privées', *Observations et diagnostics. Revue de l'OFCE*, 36 (avril), pp. 149-52

Droit social (1984) 'Le rapport Auroux' (various articles), 4 (avril)

Duhamel, O. & Parodi, J.-L. (1983) 'Images syndicales', *Pouvoirs*, 26, pp. 152-63

L'Entreprise (1988) 'Accords d'entreprise: les salaires d'abord', *L'Entreprise*, 38 (octobre), p. 123

Force ouvrière magazine (1991) 'Quarante années de négociation collective', *Force ouvrière magazine* (juillet-septembre), pp.20-1.

Fourastié, J. (1979) *Les Trente Glorieuses: ou la révolution invisible de 1946 à 1975*, Paris: Hachette

Fournier, G. (1990) 'La négociation de branche et d'entreprise en France', *Syndicalisme* (31 mai), pp. 9-10

Gibier, H. (1990) 'Des syndicats en réanimation', *Le Nouvel Economiste*, 755 (20 juillet), pp. 28-33

Glais, M., Hardouin, M. & Jolivet, E. (1987) *Analyse des politiques de contrôle des prix dans certains secteurs, sous l'angle de la concurrence et des échanges intra-communautaires*, Luxemburg: Office for the Official Publications of the European Communities

Goetschy, J. (1987) 'The neo-corporatist issue in France' in Scholten, I. (ed.), *Political Stability and Neo-Corporatism. Corporatist Integration and Societal Cleavages in Western Europe*, pp. 177-94, London: Sage

Goetschy, J. & Martin, D. (1981) 'The French industrial relations system' in IDE Research Group (eds.) *European Industrial Relations*, pp. 180-99, Oxford: Clarendon Press

Goetschy, J. & Rojot, J. (1987) 'France' in Bamber, G. J. & Lansbury, R. D. (eds.) *International and Comparative Industrial Relations. A Study of Developed Market Economies*, pp. 142-64, London: Allen and Unwin

Groux, G. (1984) 'Trade unionism and technology' in Kesselman, M. & Groux. G. (eds.) *The French Workers' Movement: Economic Crisis and Political Change*, pp. 132-45, London: Allen and Unwin

INSEE (1990) *Annuaire statistique de la France*, Paris: INSEE

Jacquier, J.-J. (1987) 'Que reste-t-il de la nuit du 4 août? Un syndicaliste face au droit d'expression', *Gérer et comprendre*, 7 (juin), pp. 45-50

Jenson, J. (1984) 'The "problem" of women' in Kesselman, M. & Groux. G. (eds.) *The French Workers' Movement: Economic Crisis and Political Change*, pp. 159-76, London: Allen and Unwin

Keeler, J. T. S. (1981) 'Corporatism and official union hegemony: the case of French agricultural syndicalism' in Berger, S. (ed.) *Organizing interests in Western Europe*, pp. 185-208, Cambridge: Cambridge University Press

Kergoat, J. (1986) 'La combativité à la baisse', *Le Monde*, 4 mars

Kocinski, A. & Gless, E. (1991) 'Que reste-t-il des lois Auroux?', *L'Entreprise*, 67 (avril), pp. 73-9

Le Goff, J. (1985) 'L'expression des salariés, deux ans après: propos d'étage', *Economie et humanisme*, 283 (mai-juin), pp. 51-61

Lévy, E. (1989) 'Prud'hommmes: morale d'une ambiguité', *Dynasteurs* (mai), pp. 126-30

Lozier, F. (1990) 'Une approche sectorielle des accords d'entreprise', *Sociologie du travail*, 1, pp. 1-22

Lyon-Caen, G. (1984) 'Droit syndical et mouvement syndical', *Droit social*, 1 (janvier), pp. 5-14

Mermet, G. (1989, 1990) *Francoscopie,* Paris: Larousse

Meyers, F. (1981) 'France' in Blum, A. A. (ed.) *International Handbook of Industrial Relations,* pp. 169-208, London: Aldwych Press

Milner, S. (1990) *Power within the French Firm,* Loughborough: European Research Centre, Loughborough University, Studies in European Culture and Society, paper 4

Ministère de l'Industrie (1990) *Les Chiffres clés de l'industrie,* Paris: Direction Générale de l'Industrie

Ministère du Travail (1990) *Bilan de la négociation collective 1989,* Paris: Ministère du Travail

Mital, C. & Rouge, J.-F. (1988) 'La France: paradis des patrons?', *L'Expansion* (3-16 juin), pp. 50-6

Moatti, G. & Bentégeat, H. (1991) 'Les patrons veulent des syndicats forts', *L'Expansion* (7-20 mars), pp. 57-64

Morel, C. (1981) 'Les conflits sociaux entre la grève et la paix', *Economie et humanisme,* 259 (mai-juin), pp. 8-17

Mouriaux, R. (1981) 'Le syndicalisme français à l'épreuve de sept années de crise (1974-1981)' in Armingeon, K. *et al., Les Syndicats européens et la crise,* pp. 171-207, Grenoble: Presses Universitaires de Grenoble

Noblecourt, M. (1991) 'La France a le plus faible taux de syndicalisation des pays de l'OCDE', *Le Monde* (23 juillet), p. 12

Nousbaum, J. (1985) 'France' in Roberts, B. C. (ed.) *Industrial Relations in Europe. The Imperatives of Change,* pp. 45-74, London: Croom Helm

Parodi, M. (1981) *L'Économie et la société française depuis 1945,* Paris: Armand Colin

Perrignon, C. (1985) 'Les syndicats grattent les fonds de tiroir', *Le Matin* (14 novembre), p. 18

Raveleau, G. & Marinier, F. (1983) *Les Cercles de qualité français,* Paris: Entreprise Moderne d'Edition

Reynaud, J.-D. (1975) *Les Syndicats en France,* Paris: Seuil

Roche, J. (1990) 'Le regain de la négociation d'entreprise', *Problèmes économiques,* 2198 (7 novembre), pp. 24-8

Rojot, J. (1986) 'L'évolution de la politique des employeurs français vis-à-vis des organisations syndicales', *Travail et société,* 11:1 (janvier), pp. 1-16

Ruffier, J. (1981) 'Mort du taylorisme et recul des syndicats', *Economie et humanisme,* 259 (mai-juin), pp. 50-7

Saglio, J. (1991) 'La régulation de branche dans le système français de relations professionnelles', *Travail et emploi,* 47:1, pp. 26-41

Savatier, J. (1989) 'Les transformations de la fonction représentative des syndicats' in G. Lyon-Caen *et al., Les transformations du droit du travail,* pp. 180-91, Paris: Dalloz

Segrestin, D. (1986) 'Deux années d'expression directe: attention, bilan' in Borzeix, A., Linhart, D. & Segrestin, D. *Sur les traces du droit d'expression,* Paris: Conservatoire National des Arts et Métiers

Segrestin, D. (1990a) 'Recent changes in France' in Baglioni, G. & Crouch, C. (eds.) *European Industrial Relations. The Challenge of Flexibility,* pp. 97-126, London: Sage

Segrestin, D. (1990b) 'Le syndicalisme français et l'entreprise (1968-1988)' in Sainsaulieu, R. (ed.) *L'Entreprise: une affaire de société*, pp. 46-68, Paris: Presses de la Fondation Nationale des Sciences Politiques

Sellier, F. (1985) 'Economic change and industrial relations in France' in Juris, H., Thompson, M. & Wilbur, D. (eds.) *Industrial Relations in a Decade of Economic Change*, pp. 177-210, Madison: Industrial Relations Research Association

Sicot, D. (1990) 'Les dérives de la flexibilité', *Science et vie économie*, 60 (avril), pp. 25-9

Sudreau, P. (1975) *La Réforme de l'entreprise*, Paris: La Documentation française

Warcholak, M. (1991) 'Première centrale syndicale: la CGT', *Le Peuple*, 1326 (28 mars), pp. 27-9

7

French management culture

INTRODUCTION

The need to succeed in international markets has brought new urgency to questions relating to national management culture. Over the last two decades, management practitioners and theorists have increasingly focused their attention on the relationship between culture and business performance. The premisses of this approach are that differences in management culture exist and that such differences matter.

Much of this increase in attention has been due to Japan's export success. Managers and researchers during the 1980s attempted to discover how national management culture has contributed to Japanese business success in order to see what lessons can be learnt. The interest in culture is not a fad linked solely to changing perceptions of Japan. In earlier decades, the USA had enjoyed the same veneration in Europe as exemplar of economic success and source of management models. But in both cases, disenchantment with imported 'recipes' eventually set in

In consequence, the emphasis is now placed on cultural relativity. Different regions and organisations are perceived as having their own styles and methods. Indigenous solutions have inherent strengths and weaknesses, but they have the merit of working.

The gradual construction of the European Community has reinforced this philosophy. The road to the 'open market' of 1993 has already involved a massive increase in contacts and trade between EC Member States. These will accelerate in the twenty-first century. For harmonious, productive relations there is a need for greater knowledge and awareness of our neighbours. This means acting on the similarities that bind Western European nations in a common project. It also means perceiving differences that can serve both as a source of misunderstanding and as a reservoir of variety, originality and human potential. This implies an understanding of one's own culture and of other people's. This chapter is aimed, therefore, at increasing awareness of the particularities of French management culture.

Because culture is a notoriously slippery term, it is essential to provide explanation about how the term is used in this chapter. Firstly, culture will *not* be used in the 'high art' sense of Western literary and artistic masterpieces, classical music and so forth. Rather it is used to refer to the broad foundation upon which a society is built. An anthropologist's definition of culture is useful here:

Culture consists in patterned ways of thinking, feeling and reacting, acquired and transmitted mainly by symbols, constituting the distinctive achievements of human groups, including their embodiment in artefacts. (Kluckhohn, 1951, p. 86)

The stress is on *patterns* of thought, expression and behaviour which are meaningful in themselves and are the sources of systematic differences between defined human societies. The anthropological view reveals that all human activities are conducted following manners and rituals which are rarely predetermined by material circumstance or necessity. This is true even of such essential functions as eating and drinking. Thus the behaviour of French executives at work, at meal times, in leisure time has its own specific characteristics, as Barsoux and Lawrence (1990, pp. 89-117) indicated.

Activity is the key. In an insightful phrase, Crozier (1964, p. 7) described culture as a 'design for living'. He insisted that cultural theories be related directly to 'problems of action', that is to problems of change and development within specific organisations and in societies at large.

This perspective raises the question of the sources of culture. Heller (1985, p. 17) cited a wide range, including child-rearing practices, educational systems, socio-structural factors (such as social class, religious practice, etc), as well as economic, legal and political systems. From this reading it follows that many earlier sections of this book also relate to French culture. But the reason for setting aside this chapter specifically to the topic is to look more closely at sources of management culture and to study their effects on management styles, organisational structures, patterns of relationships among managers and employees, as well as attitudes and values at the workplace.

The perspective adopted is a 'macro' one, dealing with characteristics of French management culture at a national level. This does not imply the assumption that French management culture forms a single, homogeneous block. Other levels of analysis are clearly possible. They include regional differences, differences between firms ('corporate culture'), between occupations and between social classes. However, lack of space precludes treatment of all these levels.

Cultural analysis at national level runs the risk of excessive generalisation. Hence the next section considers the knotty question of how to treat national stereotypes. It will emphasise that care and sensitivity are required in the handling and treatment of cultural models. The remainder of the chapter falls into four sections, each devoted to a major body of work dealing with particular facets of French management culture. By comparing and confronting these views, certain differences of emphasis regarding 'typical' French characteristics will emerge, but so too will much common ground. The conclusion will point to a common body of traits that make up a French management model, whose existence calls for recognition by practitioners working with the French.

NATIONAL STEREOTYPES REVISITED

National stereotypes are often based on superficial observations and emotional reactions. They are the result of drastic simplification, grotesque caricature or mere vilification of perceived differences. The root of the problem is that any reference point or means of measurement used to describe another culture will itself be culture-bound. There is little point in lending one's tailor-made suit to another person and laughing at its poor fit.

Yet to ignore popular national stereotypes is futile. Even when buried, they will not lie down. Accordingly the strategy proposed here is to confront a number of stereotypes and attempt to discover something of their real content.

Their history and culture have made the French known all around the world. Consequently, stereotypes of the French are numerous and pervasive. Every reader will be familiar with at least some. Gruère and Morel (1991, pp. 45-52) produced a wide-ranging compendium of popular views of the French taken from different nationalities. These range from derogatory dismissals – the French as chauvinistic, racist, pretentious, supercilious, etc.– to declarations of admiration at French *savoir-faire* and *art de vivre*. Curiously, though elements of overlap exist between different national perceptions of the French, it would be inappropriate to speak of consensus. The French provoke strong reactions, but often of diametrically opposed kinds.

Indeed, when the French give their own view of themselves, a similar spread of dichotomous judgements often emerges. The French can be simultaneously hospitable and xenophobic, preoccupied alternately with France itself or with France's world role. France sees itself as a *terre d'asile* (haven for refugees) yet it is the home of the racist *Front National*, the largest political party of its kind in Europe. The list could go on. But what is important is not just the contents of the list but the fact that an inventory of dichotomies can be drawn up at all. Indeed it *is* regularly drawn up and so will be omitted here (cf. Gruère and Morel, 1991; Nevers, 1985). The French are not blind to their contradictions. Perhaps the only point consistently made from both inside and outside France is that the French are paradoxical. Indeed, they sometimes make a virtue out of paradox itself.

A relevant example is found in a book by Soyer (1987). His aim was to show French firms how they might increase their exports by paying attention to France's image abroad. He indicated that the French are not well liked because, among other things, they are *arrogants, beaux parleurs, superficiels* (arrogant, prone to fine words and superficial). His suggestions for making France's image more positive include an emphasis on French prestige and *art de vivre*. But though going under a different name, these are the very characteristics that Soyer said gave France a bad name.

Paradox is also the key to the image of the *coq gaulois*, the French rooster. This symbol of the French is less well known by the British than by some other nationalities. The symbol pulls together a number of stereotypical features of the French. Put briefly, this image pictures a corner of a farmyard where a rooster crows and preens itself, perched atop a pile of manure. No unkindness is intended in reporting this unflattering image. Rather it is treated because it is frequently put about by the French themselves. (A French brand of sportswear is even called the *coq sportif*.)

The image evokes character traits of individualism, prestige and a sense of superiority. However, a rooster bestriding a pile of manure involves a comical touch. He is brought down to earth, literally. An additional anecdote reports the rooster's mistaken belief that the sun rises *because* he crows, not *when* he crows. The rooster's sense of self-importance is perhaps due to his faulty logic. This is a cruel twist for a nation which prides itself on its rationalism.

The image of the *coq gaulois* is not of course presented as a summary of the French character. As circulated by the French, it is a self-deprecating caricature. The interest of the image lies in its use of contradictions: the beauty of the bird and the lowliness of its surroundings, the apparent importance of its song and the real futility of its activity, the rooster's superiority when there is apparently nothing to be superior about. In being couched in paradoxes, the image suggests that French reality is less than straightforward.

If we turn from French culture in general to French management in particular, the image is extremely useful for highlighting a problem that exists within French organisations. The cock asserts its individualism. It seeks ascendency and seeks to come out 'top of the heap'. It sees itself as 'number 1'. However, if we assume for a moment that the *coq gaulois* represents (in however caricatural a form) some deep aspiration of large numbers of French people, it remains the case that few can be 'number 1'. A hierarchy needs many Indians and few chiefs. Personal aspirations to ascendency can only be satisfied at the expense of others.

How can these tensions be resolved? A simple image such as the *coq gaulois* cannot contain the solution, but it does state the problem. The symbol registers the French dilemma of reconciling individual aspirations with group organisation, creative anarchy with collective order. The major studies of management culture to be reviewed will show French solutions to this dilemma. The next section considers the logical consequence of the individual's desire to stand out and be qualitatively different; namely elitism.

ELITISM AND ITS CONSEQUENCES

If seeking to rise above the crowd has been an aspiration in all layers of French society, that desire has been most strongly manifested by the business classes. The sociological gap between the *grand patronat* and other social groups in France has already been indicated on pp. 159-66. France's *patrons* form a fairly small, often tightly-knit elite. When Antoni (1989, p. 38) described *le management à la française*, she found it natural to talk in terms of '*une logique des clans et des familles, des castes et des corps*'.

Clans and families are inevitably important, given the scale of family capitalism in France (see pp. 155-6). Caste belonging is evident in other ways.

Manière (1989) has described the closed world of the board rooms of France's major companies. A relatively small number of directors sit on a relatively large number of boards – this is the phenomenon of so-called 'interlocking directorates'.

However, the supervisory function of boards of directors is minimal. Directors often find it impossible to give enough time to their multiple duties. Board room absenteeism is high. Further, in the small world of the 'interlocking directorate', no-one wants to rock the other man's boat when making waves is liable to capsize your own. With little interference from the board of directors, with shareholder meetings very rarely using their power of sanctions and with take-overs rare, the French chief executive is often free to do as he will. These features point to the existence of a very particular management culture. This section will examine the historical reasons for that culture and set out some of the consequences.

The importance of historical factors in the evolution of French management culture has been extensively discussed by Weber (1986, 1988). He emphasised the relatively low social status of the industrial bourgeoisie during the nineteenth century. Despite the 1789 revolution, greater prestige was attached to the aristocracy than to the middle classes. The new breed of capitalists who made their fortunes in industry or finance still sought to be integrated into the aristocracy.

The means to integration included buying titles, acquiring land and arranging marriages between offspring and aristocrats. This process involved accepting aristocratic values, including the caste system itself. Not only was society divided into tightly-drawn groups with large social distances separating them, but there was little movement between them. The large social gap between high and low status groups meant that little consultation was required between the former and the latter.

Further, aristocrats had fixed ideas on which activities were 'noble' and which were not. The bourgeoisie modified those ideas of appropriateness somewhat, but did not reject them. Hence working for the State came to be regarded as 'noble', whereas servicing a mass market was not. Grand designs – such as the construction of the railways – were noble because of State patronage and because of engineering prowess. This particular conception of prestige has left a lasting imprint on management styles and culture. The study of French industrial policy (see Chapter 2) showed that the *grands projets* of the 1960s and 1970s – Concorde, the TGV, nuclear power – shared those features of a grand design implemented under State patronage in a high-tech field. Consequently a theme throughout this book has been the extent to which the State in France has been both patron and model for the business community.

Large social distances, together with the importance of 'family capitalism', have resulted in a tendency to 'top-down' management styles. The foundation for such styles is encapsulated in the ironical phrase *patron de droit divin* (boss by divine right). In pre-revolutionary times, the monarch was said to rule by divine right. As God had willed him to exercise absolute power, any questioning of the monarch's decisions was treason. The nineteenth century industrialists, in taking over aristocratic values, warmed to the idea that they held undisputed authority within their firms as of legitimate right. They considered that those rights set them apart from their employees.

The division of society into near-watertight compartments has left its traces in organisation at the workplace. Top management (*le patronat*) sees itself as qualitatively different from middle management, the *cadres*. Yet *cadre* status itself carries prestige. Moreover, it is a legally recognised rank, rather than an *ad hoc* title, like 'executive' in English. 'Executive' is a loose term covering many sins; *cadre* indicates a walk of life. Barsoux and Lawrence (1991) compared being named *cadre* to passing an intelligence test. French *cadres* see themselves as the brains of their firms – with considerable justification given their usually high qualifications.

Employees and workers have been considered as belonging to a different group again. Further, over the past century, the revolutionary ideology of sections of the working class had paradoxical similarities with the world-view of the *patronat*. Although left-wing worker groups sought to overthrow the capitalist class, they actually agreed with the proposition that workers and managers displayed intrinsic differences that created an insuperable gap between them. Thus, as discussed in Chapter 6, a move to more participative styles of industrial relations has been extremely difficult due to the entrenched attitudes of managers and employees.

The rejection, through much of this century, of compromise at the workplace was reinforced by the French predeliction for Cartesian rationality. The French often prefer to work from *a priori* principles, involving neat demarcations and dichotomies, rather than working with the muddy world of practice. From believing that logical arguments admitted only one conclusion, it is a short step to insisting that there is only 'one best way' to solve any problem. The *patron*, by virtue of his *grande école* education emphasising abstract and mathematical reasoning, has been inclined to think that only he could find the 'right' answers. For those holding this view, there is no room for negotiation. With tongue in cheek, Gruère and Morel (1991, p. 59) commented that '*négocier consitutue une faute contre la logique et l'esprit cartésien*' (the practice of negotiation offends logic and the Cartesian ethos). Faith in reason made negotiation superfluous. This contrasts to the British view where being 'reasonable' involves taking the other person's view on board. Gauthey and Ratiu (1989, p. 322) pointed out that these differences in cognitive strategies have been responsible for many misunderstandings between the British and the French.

French intellectual style reinforced the tendency to autocratic methods of management. Because of their assumed intellectual superiority and high social position, giving orders became second nature to business leaders. A command structure was part of their outlook. In the French tradition, the aristocracy had a duty to defend the realm and in copying the aristocracy, the *patronat* took on military values. This military component is easily overlooked but its currency can be quickly illustrated. The *Ecole Polytechnique* is probably

France's top *grande école*. Many of its graduates go on to key positions in the Civil Service and business. But it started life in 1794 as a military academy and has preserved its military ethos. *Polytechniciens* have a uniform and they take part in military parades. True to the traditions of a warrior caste, the *Ecole Polytechnique* was all-male until the start of the 1970s.

The aristocratic and military command ethos of French business often strikes both the French and foreign observers. The former Minister of Labour, Jean Auroux (in Kocinski & Gless, 1991), has described French management structures as '*un système hiérarchisé, hérité de l'armée napoléonienne*' (a hierarchical system inherited from Napoleon's armies). The current French Prime Minister, Edith Cresson (1989) has referred critically to '*le fonctionnement monarchique de l'entreprise*' (the regal style of running companies). She has claimed that '*les patrons français doivent faire leur révolution culturelle*' (French bosses must undertake their own cultural revolution).

Researchers have frequently pointed to the autocratic tendencies of French management. Gruère and Morel (1991, p. 95) indicated the culture problems encountered by French executives working in Japan. They are perplexed that when they 'give orders' to their Japanese subordinates, nothing happens. The French are then forced to approximate a Japanese approach, which usually involves a group discussion leading to a consensus on how every detail is to be implemented; frenetic activity then ensues. American commentators have made similar observations on the French. For example, Harris and Moran (1979, p. 223) stated that 'the very top French executives tend to be more autocratic in their managerial style'. Thus there is considerable agreement that a military style of command, resulting from a large social and organisational gap between the manager and his employees, is an important feature of French management culture.

Having recognised this feature, the danger is to stop the analysis and to see the 'steep pyramid' – created by elitism, centralisation of authority, autocratic power structures and hierarchical controls – as the only features of French management culture worth commenting on. This danger is illustrated by an early article by Graves (1972, p. 54) in which he claimed that 'the Frenchman tends to have a clear conception of role authority: he accepts authority absolutely or rejects it entirely'. It is not that Graves was wrong, but that his statement contains half-truths. His observation is applicable to times of crises when there are no half-way houses between steadfast solidarity or outright revolution. But on a day-to-day, routine basis, the French do not have such absolutist reactions to authority. Despite the 'steep pyramid', they rarely wish to be on the giving or the receiving end of absolute authority.

The problem with dwelling too fixedly on the apparently large concentration of power at the top of the pyramid is that phenomena lower down are ignored. An example of the Japanese reaction to top-down orders has been given, but how do the French react? How have the French reconciled individual autonomy with the dependence relations implicit in a command structure? The rest of the chapter looks more closely at how the reconciliation has been achieved.

ISOLATED BUREAUCRATS

One of the organisational forms taken by the 'steep pyramid' is the bureaucracy. In an influential work, Michel Crozier (1964) studied French bureaucracies as functioning organisations, as expressions of a culture and as a certain 'design for living'. His conclusions are central to the concerns of this chapter.

Crozier studied lines of command and personal relationships in two representative bureaucracies, a 'clerical agency' within the French Civil Service and a State-owned 'industrial monopoly'. In these bureaucracies, he identified four basic elements, namely: impersonal rules, centralisation of decisions, strata isolation and the development of parallel power relationships.

The analysis of the 'industrial monopoly' showed an organisation based almost entirely on written rules and procedures. On paper, authority within each production unit in the monopoly was centralised in the hands of the director. This seems to conform to the popular view of French management structure. But this centralisation of power was more apparent than real. The secure position of the monopoly meant that rules governed most major decisions such as hiring, promotion, workrates and so forth. The rules gave employees protection at every level – they had job tenure while work content and employment progression were predictable. Being unable to reward or punish, the director lacked personal power of a discretionary kind. His role was limited to the fair application of the rules. He was a judge, not a king.

Likewise in his study of the 'clerical agency', Crozier noted a tendency to centralisation of decision taking. However, the passing of decisions up the hierarchy was caused by a desire to reduce face-to-face tensions. Superiors who were remote from the problem, rather than those personally implicated, were asked to solve it. Because they were remote, they often lacked the necessary information to decide. To solve the predicament, the organisation resorted to impersonal rules. The impersonal rules were seen as a way of resolving conflict while protecting each side from abuse. Thus rules created hierarchical slots, circumscribed limits to individual authority and provided standardised procedures for problem solving.

The existence of a hierarchy, based on a series of strata, had positive and negative aspects for the individuals concerned. The positive aspect of strata formation was that individuals working in a particular tier of the bureaucratic pyramid had a strong group identity. The design of the pyramid was initially responsible for the creation of that identity. Individuals at any point on its slope perceived functional and status differences between themselves and higher and lower tiers. Group belonging provided protection for the individual, since the rules of the bureaucracy defined the limits of duties and responsibilities, so minimising arbitrary interference within a stratum. At the same time, rules produced a high degree of equality between group members.

But negative characteristics also emerged. Movements, even communications, between the ranks were difficult and rare. Relationships between members of hierarchically distinct groups were infrequent due to the difficulty in reconciling differences of status and because of the dangers of favouritism. This gap between groups produced the first type of isolation to which Crozier referred, namely the isolation of groups from each other. Further, because the strata were created by impersonal rules and because of the strong pressures for conformity within groups, strata were essentially rather cold, *formal* groups. As such, Crozier considered that they militated against the formation of informal friendships, of which he found very few between employees in the 'clerical agency'. This produced the second type of isolation, the isolation of the individual.

In summary, these social structures were formed of paradoxical components. Authority was centralised, yet the top managers lacked discretionary power. Employees formed sub-groups, affording themselves protection, yet were individualistic and even isolated within them.

Crozier perceived causal links between the isolation of the individual, the lack of collective spirit and the limited ability of the French to form bottom-up organisations. The direction of causality was not entirely clear, but as evidence of widespread links he cited a large range of studies of French culture.

The major explanation offered is that of the historical political process. In seventeenth century France, the monarchy had accumulated absolute power by systematically disempowering other social groups. The most dangerous threat was the aristocracy, but independent corporate bodies, such as municipal institutions or trade associations, were repressed. Collective action was discouraged by the reinforcement of divisive group particularities, stemming from social ranks. Such factionalism minimised co-ordinated action against central authority. Further, the only exit from the impasse of intractable inter-group hostilities was arbitration exercised by the monarchy, thus reinforcing the latter's authority.

Over time, centralisation of political authority has lessened. But it has been a gradual and hard-fought process. A single example must suffice here. At the start of the 1980s, the Socialist government set great store by *decentralisation* – a measured transfer of power from the centre and its representatives, the *préfets*, to democratically elected regional institutions. That they could still present this policy as the *grande affaire* (major project) of the decade illustrates the success of the policy of disempowerment of the *ancien régime*.

Crozier (1964, p. 218) summarised the consequences of those historical processes as 'individual isolation and lack of constructive co-operative activities on the one side, strata isolation and lack of communication between people of different rank on the other'. He terms the net result as 'negative solidarity': a group hostility to hierarchical superiors. So far this reading might refer to attitudes in some British hierarchies. It is at the next stage that a specifically French characteristic emerges. In France, the usual pattern is that group hostility is directed not towards a new collective order but to creating a space for individual autonomy, creativity or even caprice.

The French bureaucratic system has had to reconcile strong aspirations to individual freedom within a rule-governed system. It has done so not by a mobilising consensus nor even by autocratic fiat, as is sometimes supposed, but by a sophisticated pincer mechanism. There is scope for the individual to exercise independent powers at each stratum but his real authority is sandwiched between official rules and unofficial social pressures. At any rank, rules preserve the individual's prerogatives from arbitrary interference from above, thus ensuring a high degree of autonomy. At the same time, peer group pressure from below counters tendencies to abuse of power, for each rank is aware of its own rights and knows the extent of the prerogatives of other ranks. The inequalities of rank are accepted because the rule of reason has eliminated arbitrary power. Because the rights of the individual are respected and because servile subjugation is not exacted, contradictory pressures can be contained in one system.

In consequence, Crozier emphasised that though senior management ostensibly had great powers, their real power was limited by the resistance of lower strata. Only exceptional circumstances allowed them to use their theoretical powers. Crozier rejected the conventional thesis of militaristic command structures. In his view, they were undermined by the existence of competing power bases.

The latter usually arise in the major 'blind spot' of rule-based bureaucracies, namely the question of how to deal with the unforeseen. Established procedures are geared to routine but they cannot cope with uncertainty. Crozier's major example was the case of maintenance workers in the 'industrial monopoly'. Written rules could not legislate for a variable as unpredictable as machine breakdowns. Maintenance staff could exploit this random variable. They alone had the statutory power to correct breakdowns. Production workers came to depend on them. This gave maintenance an unofficial power base.

However, the inability to deal with uncertainty and the stand-off between strata members raised the fundamental problem of change in bureaucracies. The danger is of rigid social structures and methods of working. Crozier's statement (1964, p. 187) that 'a bureaucratic organisation is an organisation that cannot correct its behaviour by learning from its errors' showed an acute perception of the threat. He argued that in the routine-dominated world of bureaucracy, change comes from the outside. Lacking the ability to resolve dysfunctions internally, change in bureaucracy comes as the result of dramatic crisis.

The major limitations of Crozier's analysis relate to its field of investigation and its age. Both of the organisations he studied were in the public sector while the field research was conducted in the late 1950s. These features raise questions about the relevance of the analysis for French business today. Also, a State-owned 'industrial monopoly' is an extreme case. In most businesses, middle and top managers have far greater discretionary powers on matters such as hiring, lay-offs, promotion, investment, marketing, business strategy, etc. than was the case in either of Crozier's bureaucracies.

However, Crozier's study proved to have wider relevance for French society. He considered the bureaucratic stand-off to be a fundamental characteristic of French culture. He argued that the fossilised features of bureaucratic systems noted above were also present in the French education system and the business world. Because he saw France in general as a *société bloquée* ('stalemate society'), Crozier (1964, p. 301) suggested that French society was approaching 'a breaking point' or crisis. The violent events of May 1968 proved him right. Student demonstrations and worker strikes led to reforms in the industrial relations system and in the educational system. Change was forced on French social systems by crisis.

One of the strongest tests of theory is its ability to predict correctly. The 1968 events vindicated Crozier's analysis and raised its stature. But they also raised the question of whether change precipitated by crisis was a satisfactory mode of social development. In a later work, Crozier (1970, pp. 131-5) reflected that a major crisis per generation was an affordable solution, but that in a fast-changing world a crisis every five years was absurd. Gradual reform through self-adjustment processes in organisations was the only alternative. The question then is whether the bureaucratic culture Crozier saw at work has changed subsequently. The studies to which we turn next will reveal other sides to French managerial culture, but will also corroborate much of Crozier's analysis.

DEPENDENT INDIVIDUALISTS

Probably the largest cross-national survey of differences in management culture ever carried out was by Geert Hofstede (1980, 1983, 1987a, 1987b). Hofstede analysed a total of 116,000 written questionnaires, completed in 1968 and 1972 by respondents from over 50 countries, all working for the same American multinational which he code-named Hermes, from the Greek god of commerce.

Hofstede's aim was to trace 'culture's consequences' by throwing up contrasts between national populations. In order for meaningful contrasts to emerge, this necessitated comparing as large a number of nations as possible. Thus his work is not specifically about France but he does cover France in an illuminating manner. In this section, we look at what his publications reveal about French management culture, while emphasising that his insights make even better sense when replaced in the context of the broader pictures that he paints.

Hofstede (1980, p. 25) defined culture as 'the collective programming of the mind which distinguishes the members of one human group from another'. Although this seems a rather deterministic approach, which considers family, education and the workplace as the sources of conditioning processes, Hofstede stressed that he was concerned with societies as a whole, not with individuals and accepted that large degrees of freedom exist for the individual. His primary interest has been in national cultures, which he has traced along four dimensions. He called those dimensions power distance, uncertainty avoidance, individualism and masculinity. While acknowledging that other insightful dimensions may exist, he argued that these four have the merit of universal relevance to humanity's basic problems. They therefore had explanatory value in discussions of employee motivations and of structural differences within organisations.

With power distance, Hofstede constructed a scale measuring the continuum of styles of exercising authority in organisations. This continuum ran from the pole of centralised or autocratic procedures to the pole of consultative or participative management. On this scale, France was distinctive in having the highest power distance rating of any European nation. This indicated that authority tended to be centralised and that individuals who exercised it did so in an autocratic way. Conversely, subordinates did not expect or seek to be consulted on decision making, thereby demonstrating a dependency reaction toward their superiors.

By uncertainty avoidance Hofstede understood reactions to the unpredictability of the future and the risks it holds. Some populations are more relaxed, some more anxious about the open-endedness of the future. With the uncertainty avoidance index, populations that sought to minimise or avoid risk were placed at the high end of the scale. This was France's case.

Because Hofstede used individualism in its ordinary meaning, no special commentary of the term is required. But he added the clarification that his individualism index measured *non*-dependence on the organisation. On this index, the score of French respondents was again relatively high.

The masculinity scale derived from the tendency noted across a range of human communities to socialise males toward assertiveness, self-reliance and achievement while females were socialised toward nurturing and caring for others. The scale measured the relative importance of 'achievement' in terms of recognition, promotion, challenge and pay. Conversely, it measured the relative (un)importance of personal relations at work, co-operative behaviour and security. The French had a medium to low score on this scale, indicating a tendency to a 'feminine' outlook.

Having set the scene, it is essential to see what these readings mean. Firstly, we turn to the connotations of each of the four dimensions as set out by Hofstede. To these connotations will be added examples drawn from French life to illustrate the relevance and usefulness, but also some of the limits, of Hofstede's approach. Secondly, the discussion will move on to the ways in which the four dimensions interrelate to produce a distinctive national profile.

Turning first to the connotations of uncertainty avoidance, these include conservatism, the existence of written codes, a search for security and for absolute truths and an appeal to higher authorities. An aggravated perception of risk induces higher anxiety, greater stress, more emotional behaviour and a tendency to intolerance. Competitive values tend not to be espoused, since competitions involve unpredictable outcomes.

In the past, French politics and society have provided ample evidence of these tendencies. Between 1946 and 1981, France almost continuously had right-wing, conservative governments. The search for security is evident in interminable evocations of *la France profonde*, of an idyllic rural calm, gently ruffled only by *le changement dans la continuité* (a slogan in a recent French presidential campaign). In the same vein, Crozier (1964, p. 226) described the French as disliking 'everything that may bring uncontrolled relationships: they cannot move in ambiguous, potentially disruptive situations'.

It is consistent then that French law is based on general and absolute principles. Whereas English common law prefers to deal with specifics in a somewhat *ad hoc* manner, much of French law is collected in a series of codes which seek to approximate a universally valid system. At this juncture, it is worth noting that on Hofstede's readings British culture is characterised by a very low uncertainty avoidance index.

The archetypal French philosophers are Descartes and Sartre. Descartes, being racked by doubt, sought certainty on the bedrock of the *cogito*: '*je pense donc je suis*'. It has taken three centuries and an Irish Francophile, Samuel Beckett, to draw out in his plays and novels the humour and pathos of seeing an absolute truth in the demonstration of one's own existence. Sartre's works were based on the notion of personal autonomy, a philosophical vantage point that sits easily with French individualism. But he also stressed the severe anxiety that the sense of freedom induces: the exercise of choice opens a gateway to the unknown. The reduction or elimination of that anxiety was stigmatised by Sartre, but the desire for the calm of certainty remains a recurrent feature in French culture. Observers of the French scene will have noted the systematic recourse at any difficult juncture to *les experts* and even *les sages*. The latter term has no equivalent in English, so to convey its flavour a literal translation of 'the wise ones' may for once be acceptable. The search for father figures illustrates how uncertainty avoidance and great power distance are closely linked.

The French have frequently accused themselves of 'Malthusianism'. In the context of demographic trends, this term refers to a (supposedly) voluntary restriction of the birth-rate, a sure sign of anxiety before the future. In the business context, the term refers to 'play safe' policies that stifle entrepreneurial flair by seeking business stability rather than company expansion. A famous article by Landes (1951) had put forward this thesis. Lévy-Leboyer (1974) argued that 'Malthusianism' was an inadequate explanation for French business performance in the past. But even if 'Malthusianism' does not amount to a global, scientific explanation, the frequency of the self-accusation gives an insight into the psychology of a part of the *patronat*.

Finally, as shown in Chapter 4, the French were late in overcoming an aversion to free market competition. Protectionism as a defence against foreign competitors, corporatism and collusion on home markets were traditionally the favoured means to avoid uncertainty in business dealings. The recourse to economic planning (reviewed on pp. 9-16) and the scale of French industrial policy (reviewed in Chapter 2) illustrate the tendency to reduce economic uncertainty by transferring risk to the State.

Against these features must be set the different mood of the 1980s. In 1981, left-wing parties won their first victory in national elections since the start of the Fifth Republic. Moreover, the Socialists held on to power during most of the decade. By the mid-1980s a new consensus favouring entrepreneurship and competition gripped the French nation (see Chapter 4). By the end of the 1980s, the French business community was vociferously in favour of the 1993 'Single European Market'. It favoured open frontiers, in contra-distinction to the old style preference for protectionism (see Chapter 3). Industrial policy and State interventionism have declined in scale (as indicated in Chapter 2). On these readings, a cultural shift seems to be occurring.

In France, high uncertainty avoidance occurs simultaneously with great power distance. France shares this characteristic with other Latin countries and, interestingly, Japan. Although hierarchical structures are a basic fact of most societies – as are inequalities in the distribution of strength, power and wealth – Hofstede pointed out that their connotations vary markedly. In cultures characterised by high power distance, superiors are considered to be intrinsically or existentially different to subordinates. This contrasts with low power distance countries – such as the US – where superiors are considered to be intrinsically the same as their subordinates and with whom they may even trade places.

In France, the possibility of trading places is much reduced by caste structures (see pp. 223-5) and by the education system. Discussion on pp. 162-3 showed that French higher education is eminently elitist. It is elitist as a result of the major divide between low-status universities and high prestige *grandes écoles*, the hierarchies pertaining among the *grandes écoles* themselves and the ranking of students by descending order of marks. Through these mechanisms, the education system both conditions perceptions and puts up real barriers. The French tend to view society in the image of the *grandes écoles*; namely as a pyramid with steep sides and a sharp point. Those with the best 'pedigree' – social and/or educational – rise the highest. These features create the unconscious assumptions that:

(a) individuals toward the top of the pyramid are somehow 'intrinsically' different; and

(b) the distance between ranks is insuperable.

'Pyramid' culture is reflected in management styles. High power distance nations are characterised by a high degree of centralised, autocratic or paternalistic decision making. According to Hofstede and Bollinger (1987b, p. 203), the French tended to prefer an enlightened despot (*autocrate éclairé*) or kindly father as the ideal manager. The 'traditional' tendency in French management towards autocracy and paternalism has already been indicated in the section on elitism and its consequences. Chapter 6 registered the severe limitations on experiments with 'participative' management in France. Sicot (1990) provided some recent evidence that paternalistic management styles are on the way back, rather than on the way out. In this area of management culture, it is difficult to see major change.

The tendency to creating hierarchies is illustrated by the fact that French plants have often had five hierarchical levels compared to Germany's three (Hofstede, 1980, p. 134). These hierarchical differences are accompanied not only by greater status but also by large salary differentials. The larger number of hierarchical levels, the greater structuring of activities and the greater power distance all help to explain many of the industrial relations difficulties discussed in Chapter 6. Industrial 'democracy' is an alien concept for many French employers and even some trade unionists.

Inequalities produce latent conflicts between the powerful and the disempowered, but the choice of road to reform varies with culture. In high power distance countries, the road to change is usually taken to be the dethroning of powerful persons and their replacement with another set of powerful persons, whereas in low power distance countries, change can be effected by a redistribution of power or a change of system.

Hofstede's picture of the consequences of high power distance accords well with the French polity and with certain French business practices. French history provides the archetype of an absolute monarch: Louis XIV. It is striking also that in France bloody revolutions and palace coups alike frequently produced changes of ruler rather than changes of system. Over the past two centuries, autocratic emperors have replaced autocratic monarchs, only to be dethroned in turn. Traditionally, the key feature of the French polity has been the *centralisation* of power, in the hands of a restricted elite operating from Paris.

Certainly today's Fifth Republic, being based on a stable and representative system of democracy, demonstrates the results of considerable political evolution. However, a criticism of its constitution has repeatedly been the scale of the powers accorded to the French President. For some, he is an 'elected monarch'. Indeed, the architect of the constitution of the Fifth Republic and the instigator of the French system of presidential elections was Charles de Gaulle, a military general who was suspected of megalomania by the British during the Second World War, and whose political style was characterised by a tendency to autocracy.

In analogous manner, in French companies, the *Président-Directeur Général* can exercise autocratic power, sometimes for life since he needs no real mandate from shareholders or board members. Personalised power is a feature of family-owned businesses (see pp. 153-9). The practice of incoming governments to replace heads of nationalised firms by more amenable candidates, indeed the whole system of *pantouflage* (discussed on p. 165), are further examples of a French tendency to rotate people, not overhaul structures.

For the French mind, authority resides in the person, not in the role, as the following quotation from a French CEO tellingly illustrates:

Un système fonctionne tant que le chef le voudra, mais le jour où le chef s'en va, cela va tomber en désuétude. (Schramm-Neilsen, 1991, p. 65)

A system will work as long as the top man wants it to, but once he leaves, the system becomes obsolete.

In this view, systems have no life of their own; they draw their vitality from specific, usually outstanding, individuals.

This brings us back to the individualism of the French, a trait that Hofstede's findings corroborated. Connotations of individualism include seeking autonomy, variety, status and pleasure for self. Making one's own decisions is important, which usually involves retaining a critical distance from organisations and institutions, both emotionally and intellectually. Thus the relationship of individualists with organisations does not involve a moral commitment, but is primarily calculative. The individual accepts the goals of the group only so far as they coincide with his own agenda. Two further consequences follow. The individual's sense of distance from organisations results in a sharp division between the workplace and private life. The other is an emphasis on personal initiative and on the leadership ideal. Clearly these observations hold true in France where *le système D* or *la débrouillardise* (solving problems by hook or by crook) is elevated to the status of national virtue and where authority figures are so important. In fairness, it must be added that all of the developed nations had high individualism readings, with the UK, the USA and Australia having the highest.

However, the combination of a high individualism rating with great power distance is distinctive and highlights a paradoxical trait of the French. In Hofstede's insightful phrase (1980, p. 221), the French were frequently 'dependent individualists'. He also found this characteristic in other Latin European countries, namely Spain, Italy and Belgium. It had two components. Firstly, the French preferred clear lines of authority. This preference emerged from Hofstede's surveys and was corroborated by Laurent's work (1981) on 'matrix' organisations. In a 'matrix' system, an executive reports to two bosses. Laurent showed that French managers consistently rejected 'matrix' reporting and opted for a traditional hierarchical chain. Secondly, because of the preference for a single 'boss', they become dependent on their hierarchical superior's judgement, goodwill and favour.

The paradox is compounded by the fact that dependence can leave room for individual autonomy. Firstly, in delegating decision making upwards, the individual shrugs off personal responsibility and unloads the uncertainties inherent in making choices. Political manoeuvres leave the subordinate free to distance himself from his superior's decisions, unlike consultative modes of policy making which implicate all concerned. Thus, a large power distance does not necessarily arise from the superior taking two steps back from the subordinate. In some contexts, the power distance grows from each party taking a step back from the other.

For Hofstede, the combination of large power distance and high uncertainty avoidance meant that the French were among those nations who looked to powerful people to resolve uncertainties. In terms of organisational structures, this combination produced what he called a 'full bureaucracy', one based on pyramid structures and strong centralisation. Such structures also helped reduce uncertainties. Thus a number of elements of Hofstede's analysis concurred with Crozier's.

However, as Lane pointed out (1989, p. 30), Hofstede's surveys were not so much on the structures of organisations *per se* as on perceptions of structures at different hierarchical levels. The origins and composition of 'ranks' in the business world remained unclear, as did elements of the day-to-day relationships between ranks. The next section will throw some light into those corners.

HONOUR'S LOGIC

In a series of publications on management styles, Philippe d'Iribarne (1985, 1986, 1987, 1989, 1990a, 1990b) has attempted to find a specifically French model of work relations. Iribarne's field research, like Hofstede's, was limited to a single, multinational company. Iribarne dealt with three countries – France, Holland, the USA – and his methodology was based on transcriptions and analyses of face-to-face interviews. His research was thus more qualitative and less quantitative than Hofstede's. He has provided an insider's view of French management culture, whereas Hofstede's 40 nation study is inevitably an outsider's view.

Iribarne discerned a French model of management culture which is characterised by quasi-aristocratic notions of professional 'honour'. He observed that through tradition and custom members of an occupation acquired an implicit, but clear view of their work roles and objectives. They were aware of the responsibilities and duties incumbent on them and considered that they had certain prerogatives in the accomplishment of their work. Occupational roles conditioned the outlook of the individual and formed a body of professional principles. This code of practice was not necessarily formulated in written form. Rather it was internalised by the individual and became part of his or her world-view. The articulated ensemble of rights, responsibilities and values constituted a professional identity. The integrity of their professional identity was zealously guarded by members of an occupation as the principal means of differentiating themselves from other occupations.

Like Crozier (1964) and Weber (1988), Iribarne traced these conceptions of social organisation back to pre-revolutionary France. Under the *ancien régime*, social classes were loosely defined in terms of three 'estates': the clergy, the aristocracy and the rest. Each social order lived by its own conception of 'honour'. Hence Iribarne (1989) entitled his analysis *'la logique de l'honneur'* ('honour's logic'), by which he understood a code of professional conduct.

He argued that despite the passing of time, the underlying social structures found at the workplace still functioned according to the same principles of a division into social orders, each governed by its own code of honour. Perhaps the major consequence of such codes was that individuals exact more stringent standards of themselves than they would find acceptable from an outside authority. In this schema, the rule of law was relegated to a second-order obligation. Rules and regulations were followed or not, depending on how they squared with the individual's code of ethics. This is an interesting explanation for the frequently observed tendency of the French to *contourner la loi* (roughly, 'bend the law'). Iribarne called this selective behaviour *obéir dans l'honneur* (to obey within the code of honour). These features have a number of important consequences for hierarchical relations.

Iribarne discerned three main social strata in the French factory where he conducted his research. These were *ingénieurs* (by which he understood managers with a qualification from an engineering *grande école*), *maîtrise* (shop-floor supervisors) and *ouvriers* (workers). Rigid frontiers separated the ranks, making movement between them very difficult. Long experience and training – tantamount to an initiation – were required for the rare individuals who moved up. Clearly the hierarchical system of *grandes écoles*, which confer high status for life, was part and parcel of this highly stratified approach. But moves down were rare too. The employee who failed to give satisfaction after promotion was usually moved sideways or to a backwater. This saved face but preserved efficiency. Because of the near-permanence of rank and status, social structures at the workplace resembled a caste system.

Each stratum had its own tasks and objectives, its own code of behaviour, its sphere of influence within which it has discretionary power. Relations between the strata and incursions into each other's spheres of influence, were governed by implicit but strict rules. The caste system involved what Iribarne called degrees of 'nobility'. Legitimate authority devolved from 'nobility'. The *ingénieur* had a particular 'pedigree' which conferred legitimacy. But so too did the supervisor with several decades of experience and craft skills, albeit at a lower level.

This issue of legitimate authority was further illustrated by research done by Jean-Pierre Segal, a collaborator of Iribarne. Segal (1987) studied the recruitment and training of production supervisors in France and the USA. He noted that in France, potential supervisors were recruited from within the firm but were sent off on long, residential courses to learn supervisory skills. In comparable American firms, new supervisors were frequently recruited outside of the factory, almost regardless of previous experience, but were trained 'on-the-job'. Segal concluded that in the USA rank is enough to ensure authority, even in the short term, but that in France 'hierarchical legitimacy' correlated with social status and was acquired only over the long term.

In consequence, to benefit from the appropriate type of legitimacy, it was not enough for an individual placed higher up in the organisation chart to invoke his hierarchical position. To command respect, he had to display professional qualities of the same kind as his hierarchical inferior but at a higher level of achievement. Where the hierarchical superior displayed those qualities, his subordinate could continue to *obéir dans l'honneur*. However, where the person exercising authority is lower on the 'nobility' scale, the subordinate perceived it as dishonourable to obey orders which went against his internalised code. Where this happened, it led to conflict. The hierarchical superior in such a position had large theoretical powers yet could not exact obedience. Outside of crisis situations, he was forced to temper the recourse to authoritarianism. Social pressures of rank and 'honour' pushed him towards compromises which would save the face of both parties.

Iribarne stressed the general importance of moderation in the exercise of power at the French workplace. The arbitrary exercise of power was avoided partly because of the professional conscience of the superior, partly because of social checks and balances. In a phrase, the key to the whole affair was an 'unwritten constitution'.

In consequence, Iribarne has called into question two common stereotypes of French management style. One is the recourse to a bureaucracy characterised by abundant written rules. In the factories he observed, there were relatively few written regulations, unlike the organisations observed by Crozier (1964). Moreover, where regulations existed, there was a considerable gap between official, explicit rules and the unofficial, implicit rules which had developed through custom and precedent.

Iribarne has also cast doubts on the stereotype that French firms are highly centralised, with powerful, authoritarian bosses. He argued that no single uniform pattern existed, but that reactions depended on context. By way of clarification, he suggested that power is centralised when an individual at a lower hierarchical level has insufficient legitimate authority to master the situation. At that point, his superior is more or less forced to step in and command several lower echelons.

One of the merits of this model is its attempt to cover a range of real situations. Iribarne (1985) gave four scenarios to illustrate the variations in the functioning of his model.

(1) 'Normal relations'

There may be an apparent concentration of authority at particular levels but these are only the trappings of power. Real authority in the system is broken down into discrete spheres of influence. Little negotiation or consensus seeking goes on between the spheres, though some friction occurs due to demarcation difficulties. Each actor 'gets on with the job' with a minimum of interference or even supervision from higher echelons.

(2) A 'crisis scenario'

In times of crisis, the centre can legitimately regain power, arbitrate between spheres of influence, even override lower level authority, without encountering opposition, at least until the danger is past.

(3) 'Co-operative relations'

Where relationships between parties are good, authority can be delegated extensively. But this is very much a personal relationship. If the personnel change, so does the balance of power, usually reverting to its previous state.

(4) 'Confrontational relations'

Each party jealously guards their sphere of influence, refusing to budge an inch, even though this may disrupt productive efficiency.

An inherent feature of this system is that the individual assumes great prominence. Because implicit rules and demarcations lack the clarity of codified description, personal interpretations are central. This is in congruence with the conception of authority that *la logique de l'honneur* implies. In France, authority is vested in the person, not in the role as in the USA. Iribarne considered that in French firms, unlike American firms, the limits of a manager's authority were rarely defined clearly. This allowed greater freedom to take initiatives and decisions but put the individual directly in the line of fire when problems or conflicts arose.

In a cross-national analysis of manager behaviours that usefully corroborates this perspective, Laurent (1985, p. 46) noted that French, Italian and Belgian managers held a personal and social concept of authority, considering authority to be a property of the individual. On the other hand, American, Swiss and German managers held a rational or instrumental view, considering authority to be an attribute of the role or function.

Further, Laurent indicated that French and Italian respondents perceived organisational structures as having fuzzy outlines which allowed power games and a greater tendency to 'political' behaviour. On the other hand, British and Danish respondents had a clearer vision of company organisations as defined structures, seemed more ready to work within their confines and exhibited less 'political' behaviour.

The French tendency to political behaviour is connected both to individualistic conceptions of power and to social pluralism, namely the social ranks and professional groups described by Iribarne. Power resides in the individual, but is exercised through allegiances within peer groups and by shifting coalitions with 'outside' groups. Political processes render French organisations systems subtle but flexible.

Iribarne has developed other consequences of this model. As tradition fixes roles and aims, American style 'management by objectives', which is based on contracts between managers and employees, has not found great favour in France. Further, as professional conscience is highly developed, excessive checking up on subordinates is considered to show a lack of respect for their professional integrity.

Turning to evaluation of the model, the emphasis on aristocratic motivations is provocative. Iribarne noted that, as a result of the striving for 'nobility', the French seemed to prefer complex, prestigious projects such as Concorde, Ariane, the TGV or the Channel Tunnel to mundane, household products. This may be considered as much a weakness as a strength. As indicated on pp. 96-7, France displays weaknesses in market-driven, consumer sectors ranging from clothes to home electronics.

In addition, it may be asked whether Iribarne has overstated his case by exaggerating the specificity of the model. A highly developed professional conscience, which is based on an implicit value system emphasising high standards and which guides the individual at work without the need for outside supervision, is not a uniquely French phenomenon. It is one way of defining the professional in many parts of the world.

Yet if similar causes of behaviour exist in different national groups, the intensity of their effects can vary. This is particularly true when the mix of cultural influences itself varies. These comments will be illustrated by a case-study published by Iribarne's collaborator, Segal.

Segal (1991) analysed the development of a 'turnkey' factory project involving technology transfer from a French firm to a French Canadian firm. The French firm, specialising in high-tech electrical engineering, was commissioned to build a new factory in Quebec and to provide necessary training for the French Canadian personnel who would take over all management and operational functions after the initial 'running in' period. Top management on both sides was aware that major differences of national and corporate culture existed between the two firms, regardless of their 'common' French heritage. Considerable attention was paid to questions of intercultural communication. But this did not prevent the development of friction and conflict between French ex-patriots and French Canadians during the 'running in' period. It transpired that the policy aimed at eliminating cultural misunderstanding had emphasised overcoming *communication* barriers but had neglected differences in work *organisation*.

The core of the problem was that, at both the commissioning and training stages, the French engineers and managers acted out roles which to them were only 'normal'. Typical features of the French approach were a strong hierarchical element and line of command. But precisely because divisions between ranks created 'spheres of influence', the French model allowed a high degree of individual independence in decision making within each rank.

On the other hand, current French Canadian conceptions on the delegation of authority are distant from French conceptions but close to US models. North American views of the devolution of decision-making power emphasise the hierarchy of roles and tasks, rather than a pecking order of persons, which tends to be the French view. Further, the French Canadian managers believed that structural problems – whether relating to the hierarchy of roles and tasks, to the relationships between departments such as production and maintenance, or to work organisation in general – should be solved by discussion and consensus. However, the French managers and engineers simply failed to turn up for meetings. No consensus was evolved, leading to a deterioration of relations between the two national groups.

The reasons for the French 'oversight' were related to management culture. Whereas a consultative style was well-rooted and meaningful in the French Canadian context, Chapter 6 has indicated that 'participative' management is underdeveloped in France. In the hothouse context of commissioning a new plant, these cultural differences were exacerbated. The French ex-patriots, being concerned mainly with quickly and efficiently accomplishing the technical part of their mission and returning home, had a short-term view. On the other hand, the French Canadian management, who needed a satisfactory technology transfer but also wanted to set industrial relations on a solid foundation, took a long-term view. This produced a culture clash, conflicting styles of action and mutual incomprehension.

At the general level, Segal's case study is fascinating because it offers the spectacle of two different systems of work organisation and two different styles of industrial relations, evolving within a single technological context. In the process, it demonstrates that the same technology can be harnessed differently within different social orders. The study reinforces the view that management cultures are contingent and that they have a practical impact.

The work of Iribarne and Segal both clarifies French management culture and raises questions about it. What is extremely interesting about their model is the stress it places on multiple social structures, on spheres of influence, on the conflicts between them and on a style of political accommodation between rival factions. Hence the model moves away from viewing French management culture as a homogeneous block to seeing it as a complex and composite entity.

However, the reality that the model describes clearly presents difficulties for practising managers. Iribarne noted that conceptions of 'honour' varied among employee groups. He indicated that it required considerable skill to perceive the boundaries of group loyalties and advised the use of considerable subtlety to manoeuvre within and around them. But to follow this advice requires long years of experience in a particular French industry.

The problems this raises for foreign nationals loom large. The implication is that there are major cultural barriers to bringing foreigners into the dynamics of French groups. Certainly, it is quite usual to find that the chief executive of an overseas subsidiary of an American multinational company is a foreign national, whereas in an equivalent French company an overseas chief executive is usually French. The cultural problems faced by the foreign manager have been indicated by Ferran (1990, p. 112), an executive of the French aluminium giant, Pechiney, who stated:

le groupe Pechiney était un tel maquis en France que jamais un Japonais ne s'y retrouverait.

In France, the Pechiney corporation was such a jungle that a Japanese national would be permanently lost.

Cultural problems can, of course, arise between nationals of any group of countries, but the 'political' behaviour of French managers referred to by Laurent (1985) probably complicates the French scene. In today's international economy, it has become increasingly necessary for multinational firms to deal productively with different cultures and to have an equitable distribution of high-rank jobs between employees of different nationalities. Achieving this constitutes a major challenge.

A specific challenge for French firms is the evolution of the French model itself. Iribarne has stressed the role of tradition as the mainspring of professional values and motivation. He viewed custom as the arbiter of job definition and as the origin of spheres of influence. However, where implicit assumptions and conventions hold sway, adaptation to change is slow and uncertain. The analysis of French industrial relations in Chapter 6 indicated the uncertain progress to date of gradual, incremental reform. Just as with Crozier's analysis of bureaucracies, the barriers erected by custom raise the thorny issue of how changes of management culture can best be achieved within the French model.

CONCLUSIONS

A key commonality in the studies reviewed has been the delineation of social structures which reconcile a marked French aspiration to individual autonomy with an equally strong need for order. In France's case, this is frequently achieved by hierarchical systems with large distances between the ranks. This often creates elitism based on differences in social or educational 'pedigree'. In appearance, this produces a high degree of centralisation and a strong concentration of power at the peak of a 'steep pyramid'. This mode of functioning constitutes the most frequent conception of the 'French model'. This mode does exist, but in reality other styles of interrelationship are also to be found.

The tiers of the pyramid are constituted by groups with a distinctive social or occupational identity. Most of the studies referred to have made this point. Peer groups allow some satisfaction of the contradictory aspirations of the archetypal French slogan, handed down from the 1789 revolution: *liberté, égalité, fraternité*. Crozier's analysis of bureaucratic organisations and Iribarne's work on professional ranks have both pointed to egalitarian ideals and pressures (*égalité*) as constituents of group identity and hallmarks of group belonging (*fraternité*).

Further, each rank has its 'sphere of influence'; an area in which it can exercise discretionary decision making. The size of the 'sphere of influence' is no doubt proportional to the holder's proximity to the peak of the pyramid, but is no less real for that. Under 'normal' circumstances, discretionary decision making can be exercised with relatively little interference from above. The expectation is that, within boundaries set by convention, individuals can be left to *se débrouiller* – to find their own salvation. With the ends understood, individuals use personal initiative to find the means – indeed it is here that they appear to have most latitude *(liberté)*.

Up to a point, the conundrum posed by the *coq gaulois* earlier in this chapter, namely the reconciliation of desires for independence, initiative and creativity with social order, is solved. Multiplying the number of groups and ranks, each with its own prerogatives, preserves autonomy while high but sometimes flexible barriers between groups produce order. By the tokens of group identity, the individual emerges from the undifferentiated crowd with his or her own rights.

The paradox of 'dependent individualism', of the individual's dependence on a group or father figure, sums up a number of tensions in France. On the one hand, there is the drive to conformity, the acceptance of long-standing traditions, of elitist and hierarchical institutions. On the other, are tendencies to individual self-expression, to rebellion against authority, to revolutionary idealism, to radical egalitarianism. Major social and political crises have been the result of the conflict between these contradictory tendencies. But as Crozier (1964, 1970) indicated, France cannot now afford the luxury of change through internal crisis. Other solutions to social and cultural dysfunctions must be found.

Renewal via political behaviour may present one viable option. In their various ways, the studies by Crozier, Iribarne and Laurent have illustrated the peer pressures and inter-group conflict that are resolved by the political means of compromise, subtle adjustments and skilful regrouping. These processes go on within companies; they also feature in the wider landscape of relations between private enterprise and the State discussed in earlier chapters. Being well-versed in the political art of manoeuvre in a narrow place, the French are likely to resort to it in order to develop their businesses, economy and society. Supple political accommodations serve to humanise the 'steep pyramids' of business in France.

References

Antoni, M.-L. (1989) 'Le management à la française', *Le Nouvel Economiste*, 713 (29 septembre), pp. 38-43

Barsoux, J.-C. & Lawrence, P. (1990) *Management in France*, London: Cassell

Barsoux, J.-C. & Lawrence, P. (1991) 'The making of a French manager', *Harvard Business Review* (July-August), pp. 58-67

Cresson, E. (1989) 'Les patrons doivent faire leur révolution culturelle', *Nouvel Economiste*, 699 (16 juin), p. 42

Crozier, M. (1964) *The Bureaucratic Phenomenon*, Chicago: University of Chicago Press

Crozier, M. (1970) *La Société bloquée*, Paris: Seuil

Ferran, R. *et al.* (1990) 'Exemples de fonctionnement d'entreprises japonaises au Japon' in Gauthey, F. & Xardel, D. (eds.) *Management interculturel. Mythes et réalités*, pp. 111-21, Paris: Economica

Gauthey, F. & Ratiu, I. (1989) 'Impact des différences culturelles sur l'organisation et le management' in Camilleri, C. & Cohen-Emerique, M. (eds.) *Chocs des cultures. Concepts et enjeux pratiques de l'interculturel*, pp. 311-34, Paris: Editions L'Harmattan

Graves, D. (1972) 'The impact of culture upon managerial attitudes, beliefs and behaviour in England and France', *Journal of Management Studies*, 9:1, pp. 40-56

Gruère, J.-P. & Morel, P. (1991) *Cadres français et communications interculturelles*, Paris: Eyrolles

Harris, R. P. & Moran, R. T. (1979) *Managing Cultural Differences*, Houston: Gulf Publishing Company

Heller, F. (1985) 'Some theoretical and practical problems in multi-national and cross-cultural research on organisations' in Joynt, P. & Warner, M. (eds.) *Managing in Different Cultures*, pp. 11-22, Oslo: Universitetsforlaget

Hofstede, G. (1980) *Culture's Consequences. International Differences in Work-related Values*, London: Sage

Hofstede, G. (1983) 'National cultures in four dimensions. A research-based theory of cultural differences among nations', *International studies of management and organisation*, XIII: 1-2, pp. 46-74

Hofstede, G. (1987a) 'Relativité culturelle des pratiques et théories de l'organisation', *Revue française de gestion*, 64 (septembre-octobre), pp. 10-21

Hofstede, G. & Bollinger, D. (1987b) *Les Différences culturelles dans le management*, Paris: Editions d'organisation

Iribarne, P. d' (1985) 'La gestion à la française', *Revue française de gestion*, 50 (janvier-février), pp. 5-13

Iribarne, P. d' (1986) 'Vers une gestion "culturelle" des entreprises', *Gérer et comprendre*, 4 (septembre), pp. 77-85

Iribarne, P. d' (1987) 'Ce qui est universel et ce qui ne l'est pas', *Revue française de gestion*, 64 (septembre-octobre), pp. 6-9

Iribarne, P. d' (1989) *La Logique de l'honneur. Gestion des entreprises et traditions nationales*, Paris: Seuil

Iribarne, P. d' (1990a) 'Misère et grandeur d'un modèle français d'entreprise' in Sainsaulieu, R. (ed.) *L'Entreprise: une affaire de société*, pp. 254-66, Paris: Presses de la Fondation Nationale des Sciences Politiques

Iribarne, P. d' (1990b) 'L'importance des spécificités culturelles nationales dans la gestion des ressources humaines', *Problèmes économiques*, 2,171 (19 avril), pp. 27-32

Kluckhohn, C. (1951) 'The study of culture' in Lerner, D. & Lasswell, H. D. (eds.) *The Policy Sciences*, pp. 86-101, Stanford, California: Stanford UP

Kocinski, A. & Gless, E. (1991) 'Que reste-t-il des lois Auroux?', *L'Entreprise*, 67 (avril), pp. 73-9

Landes, D. S. (1951) 'French business and the businessman: a social and cultural analysis' in Earle, E.M. (ed.) *Modern France: Problems of the Third and Fourth Republics*, pp. 334-53, Princeton: Princeton UP

Lane, C. (1989) *Management and Labour in Europe. The Industrial Enterprise in Germany, Britain and France*, Aldershot: Edward Elgar

Laurent, A. (1981) 'Matrix organisations and Latin cultures. A note on the use of comparative-research data in management education', *International studies of management and organisation*, X: 4, pp. 101-14

Laurent, A. (1985) 'The cultural diversity of Western conceptions of management' in Joynt, P. & Warner, M. (eds.) *Managing in Different Cultures*, pp. 41-56, Oslo: Universitetsforlaget

Lévy-Leboyer, M. (1974) 'Le patronat français a-t-il été malthusien?', *Le mouvement social*, pp. 3-49

Manière, P. (1989) 'Les copains d'abord', *Le Nouvel Economiste*, 700 (23 juin), pp. 38-44

Nevers, G. (1985) *Les Français vus par les Français*, Paris: Barrault

Schramm-Nielsen, I. (1991) 'Relations de travail entre Danois et Français dans les entreprises privées' in Gauthey, F. & Xardel, D. (eds.) *Management interculturel. Modes et modèles*, pp. 53-71, Paris: Economica

Segal, J.-P. (1987) 'Le prix de la légitimité hiérarchique. Une comparaison franco-américaine', *Gérer et comprendre*, 7 (juin), pp. 66-75

Segal, J.-P. (1991) 'Le management interculturel peut-il plaire à tout le monde? Une étude de cas au Québec' in Gauthey, F. & Xardel, D. (eds.) *Management interculturel. Modes et modèles*, pp. 151-77, Paris: Economica

Sicot, D. (1990) 'Le retour du paternalisme', *Science et vie économie*, 64 (septembre), pp. 18-25

Soyer, M. (1987) *Label France, mode d'emploi: clés pour l'exportation*, Paris: Le Hameau

Weber, H. (1986) *Le parti des patrons. Le CNPF (1946-1986)*, Paris: Seuil

Weber, H. (1988) 'Cultures patronales et types d'entreprises: esquisse d'une typologie du patronat', *Sociologie du travail*, 4, pp. 545-66

Postword

Over the post-war period, the essential development in French business has been the increase in convergence between France and her partners in the developed world.

Distinctively French features do remain. They include the importance of family ownership (even in very large firms), the social composition of the *patronat*, the characteristics of French management culture and, to an extent, of French industrial relations. In addition, the pace of change in these areas has been less rapid.

Yet in terms of her economic, industrial and international trade policies, France has grown increasingly similar to her European neighbours. The formerly tight bonds between the State and the French economy have loosened. Whereas French business life was once characterised by *dirigisme*, *colbertisme*, interventionism and protectionism, liberal policies directed towards increased market competition and free trade now have greater currency in France than ever before. The 'old style' of doing business has not entirely disappeared, but after several decades of rapid change, it has far less relevance today.

The probability that the clock will be turned back is low. France has fervently embraced the European cause. The 'Single Market' of 1993 has acquired almost magical attraction for the French business community. Over and against these positive attitudes, it is true that the problem of market distortions caused by State aids to public sector firms must be addressed. But this is a failing that other European Community members must also overcome. The reactionary hostility of the French farming community to certain agricultural imports and to reform of the CAP also raises concern. However vocal, even violent, the French farming lobby may be, the likelihood is that its minority status will eventually lead to its marginalisation.

In any event, a challenge as large as the construction of European unity inevitably throws up obstacles *en route*. For France, it has involved a gradual renouncement of the Gaullist ideology of national independence. Acceptance of interdependence in the European, but also world, context has at times been begrudging, at others enthusiastic. Nonetheless, the internationalisation of French business has become an irreversible reality.

Although the French are sometimes suspected of leanings to 'Euro-protectionism', the will and the ability to maintain high barriers to the outside world are likely to lessen. Already in 1991, EFTA and EC countries have reached new agreements on trade. Closer links between West and East Europe are being developed. Further Europe, the USA, Japan and the developing nations are gradually recognising the reality of global interdependency. In these contexts, the prospects are that French society in general and French business in particular will maintain its course and grow increasingly open.

Index

Advertising, 143
Aeronautical and aerospace industries, 4, 50, 51, 52, 58, 60, 65, 69, 73, 83, 92, 94, 96, 107, 155
Aérospatiale, 52, 65, 94, 96, 107
Africa, 5, 78, 82, 101-2, 111-4
Agriculture, 3, 5, 11, 49, 69, 83, 87, 93-4, 96, 98, 104-5
Airbus, 50, 73, 94, 107
Air France, 60, 68, 96, 101
Air transport, 5, 60, 68, 96, 101, 138, 149
Algeria, 5, 8, 16, 102, 112, 208
Aluminium industry, 58, 59, 60, 62, 63, 65, 68, 96, 110, 139-40, 170, 241
Ancien régime, 153, 228, 236
Ariane, 50, 52, 73, 107, 239
Armaments, 46, 47, 52, 58, 60, 83, 95-6, 97, 115
Auroux, Jean, 185, 212, 226
Austria, 104
Autogestion, 190, 209
Aviation – *see* aeronautical and aerospace industries

Balance of payments, 25, 29, 81, 98, 100, 109, 117
Balladur, Edouard, 36, 65, 67
Banking and financial sector, 13, 28, 49, 60, 66, 84, 86, 113, 116, 117, 149, 155, 191
Banque de France, 117, 155
Banque Française pour le Commerce Extérieur, 86, 116
Banque Indosuez, 60, 66, 84
Barre, Raymond, 25-9, 31, 36, 60, 132, 149, 175
Belgium, 77, 103, 105, 138, 140, 235, 239
Bérégovoy, Pierre, 36, 175
Bic, 155
Bio-technology, 46, 107, 116
Bourse – *see* Stock exchange
Bouygues, 58, 155
Bretton Woods Agreement, 20
BSN, 59, 94, 131, 146
Bull, 51, 60, 63, 65, 68, 96, 106

Cadres, 17-18, 157-8, 191, 215, 225
Calvet, Jacques, 94, 158
Capital, 4-6, 21, 33, 58, 63, 81, 83, 87, 88, 103, 113
Capital goods, 5-6, 24, 58, 80, 88, 92, 109, 111

Careers. 162-5

Car industry, 14, 34, 36, 46, 58-63, 65, 68, 92, 94, 96, 107, 110, 155, 158, 189, 202

Cartesianism, 225

Centrales d'achat, 142, 146, 148

Centralisation, 1, 19, 69, 103, 126-7, 153, 169, 202, 223-8, 238-42

Cereals, 92

CGE, 51, 54, 55, 58, 60, 61, 62, 63, 65, 66, 86, 106, 131

Channel Tunnel, 73, 107, 239

Charges sociales, 29, 30, 37, 50, 53, 56, 87, 173, 175

Chemical industry, 57-60, 62, 63, 65, 68, 84, 92, 93, 106, 109, 189, 191, 202

Chévènement, Jean-Pierre, 54

Chirac, Jacques, 24-5, 26, 30, 32-4, 35, 36, 54, 55, 56, 64, 67, 108, 115, 134, 149, 175, 205, 212, 214

Civil Service, 9, 15, 18, 24, 27, 29-30, 34, 35, 37, 117, 126, 128, 160, 162, 163-6, 226-7

Clothing industry - *see* textiles and clothing

Club Méditerranée, 155

Coal industry, 11, 46, 49, 53, 58, 69, 71, 140, 171, 194

Code pénal, 128

Code du Travail, 181, 183, 201

COFACE, 86, 116

Colbert, Jean-Baptiste, 13

Colbertisme, 13-14, 39, 48, 165, 245

Cold War, 95, 108, 207

Collective bargaining, 181-2, 185-6, 188-91, 195, 199, 201-4, 207, 211, 213

Collusion, 15, 19, 50, 123, 128-40, 146, 167, 232

Comités d'entreprise, 183-4, 185-7, 196-8, 200, 207, 211, 215

Comités d'hygiène, de sécurité et des conditions de travail, 184

Comités d'organisation, 126-7

Commission de la Concurrence, 132-4

Commission Technique des Ententes, 128-32

Common Agricultural Policy, 104-5, 117, 245

Computer industry – *see* information technology

Concentration (industrial), 13, 50, 54, 56-9, 69, 123, 132-3, 157

Concorde, 47, 50, 224, 239

CFDT, 189, 190-1, 192, 193, 194, 196, 197, 198, 208-10, 212, 214

CFTC, 189, 190, 192, 193, 196, 197, 198, 208, 212, 214

CGC, 189, 191, 192, 196, 197, 198, 212, 214

CGPME, 168, 169, 174, 212

CGT, 14, 189, 190, 191, 192, 193, 194, 196, 197, 198, 202, 205, 207, 208, 209, 212, 214

CNPF, 127, 168-77, 212

Conseil de la Concurrence, 134-7, 147

Conseil économique et social, 199

Conseil d'Etat, 163

Conseils de Prud'hommes, 182, 186, 196, 215

Construction industry, 5, 11, 52, 58, 60, 86, 95, 100, 111, 155, 156, 203

Consumer goods, 58, 73, 86, 92, 97, 109, 111, 116, 156-7, 239

Consumer protection, 123, 132, 135, 141, 143-4, 167

Conventions collectives – *see* collective bargaining

Corporate culture, 221

Corporation tax, 29, 30, 33, 37, 58
Corporatism, 124-30, 143, 145, 148, 207, 232
Corps des Mines, 162-3
Corps des Ponts et Chaussées, 162-3
Cour des Comptes, 163
Cresson, Edith, 39, 68, 72, 74, 108, 137, 147, 226

Dairy products, 92-3
Dassault, 51, 52, 54, 58, 60, 65, 96, 155
DATAR, 15, 70-1
Decentralisation, 70, 204, 211, 213, 228
Defence, 43, 47, 51, 52, 164
Délégués du personnel, 182-3, 185-7, 196, 198, 200
Delors, Jacques, 29, 61
Descartes, René, 232
Devaluation, 28, 30, 32, 87-8, 90-1, 113
DGCC, 135-6, 143
Direction générale des prix, 128, 135
Dirigisme, 1, 10-12, 17, 27, 32, 38, 78, 103, 109, 127-9, 134-6, 171, 173, 177, 245
Distribution sector, 140-8

Eastern Europe, 9, 45, 102, 108-10, 116
Ecole des Arts et Métiers, 162
Ecole centrale, 162
Ecole Nationale d'Administration, 162
Ecole Normale Supérieure, 162
Ecole Polytechnique, 161, 162, 225-6
Ecoles supérieures de commerce, 163, 176
Education and training, 5-6, 11, 29, 33, 37, 42, 74, 157, 160-1, 164, 166, 184, 237
Educational system, 162-3
EFTA, 108, 245
Electrical industry, 4, 11, 22, 23-4, 25, 38, 49, 57-8, 69, 92, 96, 131, 136, 139-40, 160, 205, 240
Electricité de France, 139-40
Electronics industry, 4, 46, 47, 54, 58, 60, 62-3, 68-9, 137
    consumer electronics, 53, 73, 84, 92, 93, 97, 111
    professional electronics, 51, 83, 92, 111, 239
Elf Aquitaine, 58, 62
Elites, 17-18, 38, 163-6, 223-7, 242
Employee participation, 200-1
Employee representation, 181-7
Employers' organisations, 166-77
Employment, 3-5, 7, 9, 16, 19, 21, 23-30, 32-5, 37, 46, 50, 58, 60, 63, 70, 72, 80, 106, 123, 126, 131, 144, 159, 174, 194-5, 198-9, 202, 210, 214
Energy, 11, 19-21, 23-6, 28, 32, 38, 42, 49, 50-3, 58, 62, 72, 78, 80-2, 85-6, 90-3, 95, 98, 111-12, 115, 138-40, 164
Engineering, 47, 53, 57, 58, 69-70, 73, 84, 96, 98, 160
Engineers, 157, 162-4, 166, 237
Ententes - see collusion
European Coal and Steel Community, 171

European Community (EC), 8-9, 33, 37-8, 42-3, 50, 56, 77-8, 80, 84, 90, 93-4, 101, 102, 103-8, 109, 112, 113, 116-17, 130-1, 137-40, 171, 220, 245
Exports, 8, 16, 23-5, 28, 36, 43, 46, 48, 50, 52, 60, 61, 77-121, 139-40, 220, 222

Family firms, 152-61, 223-41, 245
Finance, Ministry of, 13, 28, 130-3, 135-6
Financial sector – *see* banking and financial sector
Food industry, 83, 92-4, 98, 104-5, 109
Force ouvrière, 189-90, 191, 192, 193, 194, 196, 197-8, 200, 212, 214
Ford, Henry, 6
Fordism, 6-7, 17, 18, 21
Foreign trade, 8-9, 24, 28, 35, 42, 49, 61, 77-121, 122, 232
Free trade, 8, 18, 50, 77-80, 82, 103-4, 117, 171, 245

Gas industry, 25, 58, 136, 139-40
GATT, 50, 80
Gaulle, Charles de, 13, 16, 38, 45, 49, 50, 53, 141, 234
Gaullism, 50, 51, 54, 61, 245
Gaz de France, 140
Germany, 2, 3, 10, 13, 17, 20, 26, 29, 35, 43, 47, 51, 64, 77, 79-84, 87, 88, 93, 100, 103-5, 107, 109-10, 114, 126, 133, 138, 140, 146, 171, 193, 201, 205, 207, 234, 239
Gervais-Danone, 146
Giscard d'Estaing, Valéry, 15, 17, 23-4, 26-7, 49, 51, 53-4, 173-4
Glass industry, 58, 59, 60, 92, 106, 111, 131, 156, 170, 202
Grandes écoles, 160-6, 176, 225-6, 233, 237
Grands contrats, 86-7, 98, 100, 115
Grands corps, 162-4, 176
Grands projets, 50, 72-3, 86, 224
Greece, 105
Grenelle agreements, 172, 184, 208
Gross domestic product, 2, 8, 11, 19, 25, 27, 28, 31, 35, 36, 37, 43, 110
Gulf War, 91, 96, 115

Hautes Etudes Commerciales, 162
Havas, 66
Hierarchies, 162-3, 165-6, 223, 226-8, 233-8, 240, 242
Holland, 77, 87, 105, 138
Housing, 5, 24

Immigration, 3, 5, 30
Imports, 7-8, 16, 20, 23-5, 28, 49, 77-121, 140
Individualism, 223, 226-36, 239-40, 242
Indo-China, 8, 78
Inflation, 5, 15-17, 19-21, 23-30, 32, 35-7, 58, 85, 89, 113, 129, 132, 134, 144-5, 149, 205, 207-8, 211
Information technology, 22, 46, 47, 49, 50, 51, 57, 58, 59, 60, 63, 68-9, 73, 83, 86, 93, 96-7, 110, 116
Infrastructure, 5, 11, 26, 42, 71, 98, 104, 115, 136
Inheritance, 154-6, 158, 161, 166
Innovation, 6, 21-2, 37, 58, 71, 73, 88, 101, 122, 152, 159

INSEE, 14
Inspection des Finances, 163
Inspection du Travail, 24, 33, 181, 183
Institut d'Etudes Politiques, 162
Insurance sector, 13, 60, 68, 86, 98, 100, 136, 149, 158
Intermediate goods, 58, 80, 86
Internationalisation, 7-9, 13, 16, 18, 31, 38, 50, 55, 57, 61, 68, 77-121, 137-40, 171, 211, 220, 241
Interventionism, 11, 13-14, 18, 29, 37-9, 42-3, 45-49, 54-6, 61, 72-4, 84-5, 96-7, 103, 105, 108, 129, 136, 141, 148-9, 157, 171-2, 176, 201, 233, 245
Investment, 5-7, 10-11, 14, 19, 21, 23-4, 26, 28, 30, 32, 35, 37, 42, 49-50, 52-5, 60-1, 63-4, 67-8, 71, 88, 90, 95, 106, 110, 113-16, 147, 149, 158, 200
Iran, 19, 95
Iraq, 19, 52, 91, 95, 115
Ireland, 105
Italy, 3, 5, 13, 20, 36, 43, 64, 79, 80, 84, 99, 103, 105, 193, 205, 235

Japan, 3, 20, 38, 43, 47, 51, 53, 64, 73-4, 78-84, 87-8, 93-4, 100, 106-7, 111, 114, 117, 166, 205, 213, 220, 226, 233, 241, 245

Kuwait, 91, 95, 115

Labour costs, 27, 30
Labour force, 4-6, 63, 194
Labour relations, 180-219
Leclerc, Edouard, 134, 145-6
Les trente glorieuses, 2-18, 20, 21, 23, 38, 129, 208
Liberalism, 10, 13, 25, 32-3, 39, 44, 53, 55, 64-9, 77, 127, 138, 148-9, 171, 175-6, 245
Liberation, 183, 207
Lobbying, 94, 134, 141-2, 145, 167-8, 173-4, 189, 245
Loi Boulin, 182
Loi Chapelier, 181
Loi Royer, 142-5
Lois Auroux, 185-6, 187, 195, 203-4, 211-14
Lomé convention, 112
Luxury goods, 92, 96

Machine tools, 55, 84, 88, 109
Maghreb countries, 5, 111
Malthusianism, 232
Management skills, 163
Marketing, 73, 96-7, 106, 109, 116, 145, 152, 157
Marshall Plan, 10-11
Matra, 60, 65, 66
Mauroy, Pierre, 27-9, 149
May 1968, 15, 19, 22, 170, 172, 182, 184-5, 191, 202, 208-10, 216, 230
Michelin, 58, 61, 155
Middle East, 19, 49, 52, 78, 82, 90, 91, 95-6, 98, 102, 111-12, 115
Mitterrand, François, 26-7, 34, 45, 49, 55, 61, 67-8, 107, 173-5
Multinational firms, 85-6, 110, 157, 241

Napolean, 226
Nationalisation, 10, 13, 34, 49, 54-5, 59-63, 72, 96, 108, 157, 174-6, 201, 234
Nicoud, Gérard, 141-2, 145
Nobility, 224-6, 237, 239
Nuclear industry, 22-4, 26, 38, 47, 49-52, 72-3, 83, 90, 115, 139, 164, 224

Occupation (German), 2, 10, 17, 26, 169-70, 181, 207
OECD, 24, 26, 30, 35, 82, 87, 101-3, 110, 193
Oil crises, 11, 18-21, 23-6, 28, 35, 51-2, 53, 58, 78, 80-1, 85-6, 90, 95, 115, 132, 149, 194, 211
Oil industry, 19, 58, 62, 164, 115
OPEC, 19, 115
Output – *see* production

Pantouflage, 52, 164-5, 234
Paribas, 60, 64, 66
Parti communiste français, 189
Patents, 98, 101
Paternalism, 153, 155, 193, 233
Patronat, 17, 127, 152-79, 184, 207, 209, 214-15
Pechiney, 58, 59, 60, 62, 63, 65, 68, 96, 110, 139-40
Personnel policies, 213-14
Peugeot, 34, 58, 59, 61, 92, 94, 155, 158, 189
Pharmaceutical industry, 57, 60, 62, 83, 96, 111, 125, 136, 145
Planning (economic), 9-18, 26-7, 171, 232
Pompidou, Georges, 50, 51, 53, 173
Portugal, 5, 99, 105
Poujade, Pierre, 141-2, 145
Power distance, 231-5
Préfets, 228
Président Directeur-Général, 64
Press, 81
Privatisation, 32-4, 54-5, 64-9, 139, 157, 175
Production, 3-4, 6-9, 19-22, 24, 27, 29, 32, 34-5, 51, 54, 56-8, 60, 68, 70, 83, 85, 87-8, 94-5, 101, 104-7, 123, 125, 127-31, 138-40, 207, 209,
Productivity, 3, 6, 11, 21-2, 25, 27, 35, 87, 104, 122, 139, 171, 182, 200, 209, 211
Profitability, 6, 19, 21-3, 29-30, 32, 35, 51, 53, 56-7, 59, 61-5, 68, 73, 74, 83, 87-8, 94-7, 112, 123, 129, 145, 147, 157
Protectionism, 7-8, 11, 15-16, 43, 49-50, 53, 77-82, 90, 96-7, 103-5, 107, 110, 112, 116-17, 122, 129, 131, 136, 140, 169, 171, 176, 232-3, 245
  Euro-protectionism, 117, 245
  Neo-protectionism, 117, 137

Qualifications, 5, 70, 225, 237
Quality circles, 213, 215

Railways, 5, 26, 33, 38, 42, 50-1, 73, 100-1, 107, 115, 136, 138, 205, 224, 239
Raw materials, 20, 51, 80, 83, 87, 93, 111, 114, 127
Recruitment, 24, 33, 152, 160, 162-6, 176, 237
Regionalism, 69-72

Renault, 14, 36, 46, 58, 60, 62-3, 65, 68, 94, 96, 107, 110, 202
Renault, Louis, 10
Research and development, 6-8, 11, 14-16, 42-3, 47, 49-50, 52-3, 57, 63, 73-4, 77-82, 90, 96-7, 101, 103-5, 107, 110, 112, 116-17, 122, 129, 131, 136, 140, 164, 169, 171, 176, 232-3, 245
Retailing - *see* distribution sector
Revenu minimum d'insertion, 34
Rhône-Poulenc, 59-60, 62, 65, 68, 106
Rocard, Michel, 15, 34-8, 55-6, 61, 68, 108, 149, 175, 190, 205
Rossignol, 155
Rueff, Jacques, 13, 16
Rural exodus, 3

Sacilor, 48, 58-9, 60-3, 65, 68, 94-6, 155
Saint-Gobain, 58, 59, 60-2, 64-6, 86, 106, 131
Salamon, 155
Salaries, 2, 6-7, 20, 22-3, 25-30, 33-5, 50, 70, 185-7, 201-4, 208, 210-11, 215, 234
Sartre, Jean-Paul, 232
Savings, 17, 67
Scandinavia, 108
Sections syndicales d'entreprise, 184-5, 193, 208
Selection, 152, 155, 163, 165-6
Services balance, 81, 97-101
Shareholders, 33, 61, 65-71, 156-8, 200, 224, 234
Ship-building, 50, 71
Single European Market, 37, 45, 91, 105-7, 111, 117, 137-40, 233, 245
Small firms, 43, 53, 57-8, 69-73, 86, 107, 116-17, 123, 129, 133, 141-7, 152, 154, 156, 159, 167-9, 174, 182-4, 195, 198, 200, 204, 212, 215
SMIC, 27, 202
SNPMI, 168, 173
Social security, 11, 22, 25, 26, 29, 37, 107, 173-5, 189, 200
Société Générale, 66
Soviet Union, 9, 10, 45, 47, 95, 109
Spain, 5, 35, 64, 99, 105, 235
Steel industry, 11, 46, 48-50, 53, 55, 57-63, 63, 65, 68-9, 71-2, 83, 92, 94-6, 111, 130, 155-6, 170-1, 194, 202, 205
Stock exchange, 33, 64, 67, 68, 157
Strikes, 33-4, 141, 172, 181-2, 184, 188, 194, 204-11, 230
Suppliers, 28, 70, 128, 139, 142, 145-7
Switzerland, 104, 108

Taxation, 25, 27, 29-30, 32-4, 36-7, 42, 55, 64, 72, 74, 87, 100, 105, 107-8, 139, 141-2, 167, 174-5, 177, 200
Taxe professionnelle, 37
Taylor, F.W., 7
Taylorism, 22, 209-10
Telecommunications, 24, 34, 38, 42, 51-2, 55, 57, 60, 62, 72-3, 100, 138, 164
Telephone, 24, 26, 38, 52
Television, 3, 7, 20, 21, 53, 65, 73
Textiles and clothing, 2, 4, 46, 53, 55, 57-8, 60, 69, 72-3, 92, 97, 111

TF1, 65, 66
TGV, 26, 38, 50, 73, 107, 224, 239
Third World, 8, 20, 51, 80, 98, 111-15
Thomson, 51, 54, 58-60, 62, 65-8, 96-7, 137
Tourism, 98-100
Trade balances, 19, 25, 26, 28, 36, 81, 85-6, 88-97, 103, 105, 110
Training - *see* education and training
Transport, 5, 11, 34, 49, 60, 68, 71, 96, 98, 100-1, 111, 138, 149

Unemployment – *see* employment
Unions, 180-219
United Kingdom, 2, 3, 6, 8, 13, 16, 17, 20, 26, 29, 35, 43, 46, 55, 64-6, 78, 80-4, 91, 93, 97, 100, 105-9, 114, 126, 128, 133, 143, 139, 143, 157-8, 188, 193, 201, 205, 222, 225, 232, 234-5, 239,
United States of America, 2, 3, 6, 9, 10, 20, 31, 43, 46-7, 49-51, 53, 57, 64, 68, 71, 73-4, 78-82, 84, 87-8, 91, 93-7, 99, 100, 104-6, 107, 110-11, 114-15, 117, 123, 126, 128, 129, 133, 156, 166, 220, 226, 233, 235-7, 239-41, 245
Universities, 162-3, 176
Usinor, 55, 58-60, 62-3, 65, 68, 94-6

Values, 18, 22, 124, 145, 154, 165, 221, 224-5, 231, 236, 241
VAT, 37, 107
Vichy government, 17, 126-8, 204, 207
Volontarisme, 39, 45

Wages – *see* salaries
Wendel, François de, 155-6
Wines and spirits, 92-6
Works committees - *see* *Comités d'entreprise*
World War Two, 2, 6, 9, 47, 126, 170, 181, 183, 207, 234

Yaoundé convention, 112

Zone franc, 9, 112-14